Quantum Machine Learning with Python

Using Cirq from Google Research and IBM Qiskit

Santanu Pattanayak

Apress®

Quantum Machine Learning with Python

Santanu Pattanayak
Bangalore, Karnataka, India

ISBN-13 (pbk): 978-1-4842-6521-5   ISBN-13 (electronic): 978-1-4842-6522-2
https://doi.org/10.1007/978-1-4842-6522-2

Managing Director, Apress Media LLC: Welmoed Spahr
Acquisitions Editor: Celestin Suresh John
Development Editor: James Markham
Coordinating Editor: Aditee Mirashi

Cover designed by eStudioCalamar

Cover image designed by Freepik (www.freepik.com)

Distributed to the book trade worldwide by Springer Science+Business Media New York, 1 New York Plaza, Suite 4600, New York, NY 10004-1562, USA. Phone 1-800-SPRINGER, fax (201) 348-4505, e-mail orders-ny@springer-sbm.com, or visit www.springeronline.com. Apress Media, LLC is a California LLC and the sole member (owner) is Springer Science + Business Media Finance Inc (SSBM Finance Inc). SSBM Finance Inc is a **Delaware** corporation.

For information on translations, please e-mail booktranslations@springernature.com; for reprint, paperback, or audio rights, please e-mail bookpermissions@springernature.com.

Apress titles may be purchased in bulk for academic, corporate, or promotional use. eBook versions and licenses are also available for most titles. For more information, reference our Print and eBook Bulk Sales web page at www.apress.com/bulk-sales.

Any source code or other supplementary material referenced by the author in this book is available to readers on GitHub via the book's product page, located at www.apress.com/978-1-4842-6521-5. For more detailed information, please visit www.apress.com/source-code.

Printed on acid-free paper

To my wife, Sonia

Table of Contents

About the Author

Santanu Pattanayak currently works as a staff machine learning researcher at Qualcomm Corp R&D and is the author of the deep learning book *Pro Deep Learning with TensorFlow: A Mathematical Approach to Advanced Artificial Intelligence in Python*. He has about 12 years of work experience, with 8 of those years in the data analytics/data science field. Prior to joining Qualcomm, Santanu worked at GE, RBS, Capgemini, and IBM. He graduated with a degree in electrical engineering from Jadavpur University, Kolkata, and has a master's degree in data science from Indian Institute of Technology (IIT), Hyderabad. Santanu is an avid math enthusiast and enjoys participating in Kaggle competitions where he ranks within the top 500 across the world. Santanu was born and raised in West Bengal, India, and currently resides in Bangalore, India, with his wife.

About the Technical Reviewer

 **Santanu Ganguly** has been working in the fields of quantum technologies, cloud computing, data networking, and security covering research and customer delivery for more than 20 years in Switzerland and the United Kingdom (UK) for various Silicon Valley vendors. He has two postgraduate degrees, one in mathematics and the other in observational astrophysics; has researched and published articles on quantum optics; and is currently leading global projects out of the UK related to quantum computing and quantum machine learning.

Acknowledgments

I am grateful to my wife, Sonia, for encouraging me at every step while writing this book. I would like to thank my mom for her unconditional love and my dad for instilling in me a love for mathematics. I would also like to thank my brother, Atanu, and my friend, Partha, for their constant support. Thanks to Santanu Ganguly for his technical input while reviewing this book. I would like to express my gratitude to my mentors, colleagues, and friends from current and previous organizations for their input, inspiration, and support. Sincere thanks to the Apress team, especially Aditee and Celestin, for their constant support and help.

Introduction

Alan Turing laid the mathematical foundations of computing around 80 years ago, followed by John von Neumann, who made computing practical a decade later. Since then there has been rapid development in information technology fueled by core technological advancements. This rapid development in computing can be described by Moore's law. In 1965 Moore predicted that the number of transistors we can squeeze into a microchip would double every 24 months. However, 40 years after the publication of Moore's law, Moore observed that this law of exponentials cannot continue forever since the size of the transistors we would have in 20 years from now would be as small as the size of an atom, which provides a fundamental barrier to the reduction of transistor size.

Hence, after 50 years of extraordinary growth, we now find ourselves at the twilight of Moore's law where we need to reinvent the core technologies to sustain the computational needs of the world. As data continues to double every two years, we need new computing platforms and an inversion in computing ideologies to process such a massive amount of data. Breakthroughs such as specialized chips for machine learning and distributed computing as opposed to server farms are already making headways in the computing arena. The next big advancement in computing is supposed to come from our ability to build infrastructure that can probe the quantum nature of fundamental particles as opposed to the classical paradigm of computing that we rely on currently.

In this book, we are going to explore quantum computing and quantum machine learning with an emphasis on the latter. Quantum computing, which leverages the quantum mechanical properties of subatomic particles such as electrons and photons, can be efficiently used to provide an exponential boost in compute over its traditional classical counterpart. Quantum machine learning is an upcoming research area at the intersection of quantum mechanics, machine learning, and computer science that has the potential to change the way we do compute today and help us solve some of the most challenging problems in forecasting, financial modeling, genomics, cybersecurity, supply chain logistics, and cryptography, among others. With quantum computing already in the proof-of-concept phase in organizations such as Microsoft, Google, IBM, and others, the enterprise-level quantum-based deployment is not too far away. This book will help readers to quickly scale up to quantum computing and quantum machine learning foundations and related mathematics and expose them to different problems that can be solved through quantum-based algorithms.

The initial part of the book introduces readers to the fundamental concepts of quantum mechanics such as superposition, entanglement, and interference followed by postulates and the mathematical foundations of quantum computing. In this regard, we touch upon all the important topics of linear algebra required to understand quantum states and their transformation under the influence of various quantum gates. Note that the transformation of the gates on the quantum states is linear and unitary in nature.

Once the foundational base is set, we delve deep into quantum-based algorithms such as quantum teleportation, Deutsch–Jozsa, the Bernstein–Vazirani algorithm, Simon's algorithm, and Grover's search algorithm, among others. We follow this up with more advanced algorithms pertaining to quantum Fourier transforms such as quantum phase estimation, quantum period finding, and Shor's algorithm. Quantum Fourier transform algorithms are the building blocks for several quantum machine learning algorithms, and hence we dedicate an entire chapter to them.

Finally, the book introduces quantum machine learning and quantum deep learning–based algorithms and ends with the advanced topics of quantum adiabatic processes and quantum-based optimization, which are critical aspects for advancements in machine learning and data sciences. When discussing machine learning, we initially start with the matrix inversion routine of Harrow, Hassidim, and Lloyd, popularly known as the HHL algorithm, since it is a key component of several machine learning optimization routines relying on matrix inversion for its parametric solution. We follow this topic with quantum algorithms for regression, support vector machines, quantum principal component analysis, and quantum-based clustering. In this regard, we discuss and implement quantum algorithms such as the swap test for computing dot product and Euclidean distance between quantum state vectors. After working through the quantum implementation of the traditional machine learning algorithms, we look at quantum deep learning and some of the subtleties associated with it such as backpropagation through the quantum layers.

The final chapter of the book exposes readers to advanced optimization techniques such as a variational quantum eigensolver and adiabatic optimization-based routines such as the quantum approximate optimization algorithm (QAOA). These algorithms can be used to optimize complex objective functions expressed in terms of the Hamiltonian of a quantum system. In this regard, we discuss in detail the Isling model for Hamiltonian objectives and solve algorithms such as maximum cut graph clustering problems using these advanced techniques.

Throughout the book there are Python implementations of different quantum machine learning and quantum computing algorithms using Cirq from Google Research and the Qiskit toolkit from IBM.

This book will bring readers up to speed on the latest research developments in quantum computing and quantum machine learning around the world. All the practical aspects of quantum machine learning that are currently relevant are presented in this book so that readers can easily relate to this evolving field and at the same time use these prototypes to build new quantum machine learning solutions with ease. Also, the mathematical and technical rigor of quantum computing and quantum machine learning presented in the book will enable readers to engage in research and optimization of quantum-based algorithms and help them transition to this emerging field. I wish readers all the best.

CHAPTER 1

Introduction to Quantum Computing

I think I can safely say that nobody understands quantum physics.

—Richard Feynman

Present-day computers work on the principles of classical mechanics. Imagine a coin in the classical regime. When we toss the coin, it can take up either of these two states: "head" (H) or "tail" (T). However, in a quantum world, a coin, or rather a quantum one, can exist in both the states "head" and "tail" simultaneously. This property of quantum mechanical objects—existing in multiple states simultaneously—is known as *superposition*. Similarly, quantum mechanical objects can exhibit a much stronger correlation than their classical counterparts through the phenomenon of *entanglement.* Using entanglement, two or more quantum particles can be linked in perfect unison, even when they are placed at opposite ends of the universe. Quantum computing harnesses and exploits the laws of quantum mechanics, especially superposition, entanglement, and interference, to process information. An important idea in quantum computing is to collapse a probability distribution toward specific measurement states. *Quantum interference* is a by-product of quantum superposition, and it helps bias quantum measurement toward specific quantum states.

Returning to our quantum coin, when we *observe* the state of the quantum coin in superposition, it will mysteriously reveal only the classical information of either "head" or "tail." The process of observing the state of a quantum mechanical object is called *quantum measurement*. Quantum measurement interacts with the state of the quantum object and collapses the superposition state.

If a classical coin represents a bit in the classical computing paradigm, then the quantum coin represents a *qubit* in the quantum computing. Qubit stands for a *quantum bit*—the smallest unit of computation in quantum computing.

© Santanu Pattanayak 2021
S. Pattanayak, *Quantum Machine Learning with Python*, https://doi.org/10.1007/978-1-4842-6522-2_1

In classical computing, n bits can represent only one of the 2^n possibilities. A quantum system of n qubits, on the other hand, can be in a superposition of all the 2^n possibilities. This quantum behavior opens up the possibility of exponential speedups in many computation tasks that would take ages for classical algorithms to compute.

All fundamental particles such as electrons and photons in this universe are quantum objects. The states and the properties of these fundamental quantum particles are leveraged to build quantum mechanical systems. These quantum mechanical systems, in theory, are much more powerful than their classical counterparts for several complex and compute-intensive tasks, as we will see in a while.

Quantum computing deals with the information processing tasks that can be accomplished using quantum mechanical systems. Quantum mechanics is a mathematical framework that helps explain physical processes at a microscopic level. When we try to observe the macroscopic properties of a system, classical mechanics turns out to be enough. These macroscopic systems, however, when viewed at a microscopic level, still behave as per the rules of quantum mechanics.

With this little preface, we will get started with the key concepts of quantum computing.

Quantum Bit

A bit is the fundamental unit of information in classical computing. A bit at a given instance of time can be in one of these two states: "on"(1) or "off" (0).

The quantum counterpart of a bit is called a *quantum bit* (or *qubit*) as we briefly discussed earlier. A qubit can also take up two fundamental states: 0 and 1. However, a qubit can exist as the superposition of these two fundamental states, while a classical bit cannot. In the realm of quantum mechanics, the states corresponding to 0 and 1 are represented by the two-dimensional vectors $\vec{0}$ and $\vec{1}$ where

$$\vec{0} = \begin{bmatrix} 1 \\ 0 \end{bmatrix}$$

$$\vec{1} = \begin{bmatrix} 0 \\ 1 \end{bmatrix} \tag{1-1}$$

Before we go any further, we will discuss *Dirac notation*, where we represent a vector $\vec{v}$ as $|v\rangle$. The Dirac notations for linear algebra concepts are convenient for quantum mechanics, and we will follow them throughout this book.

So, a qubit that exists as a superposition of the states 0 and 1 assumes a state $|\psi\rangle$. The state $|\psi\rangle$ can be expressed as a linear combination of the basis states $|0\rangle$ and $|1\rangle$, as shown here:

$$|\psi\rangle = \alpha|0\rangle + \beta|1\rangle \tag{1-2}$$

The linear coefficients α and β are complex numbers, i.e., $\alpha, \beta \in \mathbb{C}$. Hence, the state $|\psi\rangle$ belongs to a two-dimensional complex plane where the states $|0\rangle$ and $|1\rangle$ form an orthonormal basis often referred to as *computational basis states*. In this computation basis, $|\psi\rangle$ can be expressed as follows:

$$|\psi\rangle = \begin{bmatrix} \alpha \\ \beta \end{bmatrix} \tag{1-3}$$

Let's now try to interpret what the complex numbers α, β represent. When we probe a classical bit, we get either a 0 or an 1 based on the exact state it is in. However, if we try to fetch the state of a qubit, we would not be able to retrieve the values of α, β. A qubit on measurement would reveal either of the computational basis states of $|0\rangle$ or $|1\rangle$. Quantum mechanics cannot predict which of the computational basis states would appear when making a measurement on the qubit. It tells us that the qubit in state $|\psi\rangle = \alpha|0\rangle + \beta|1\rangle$ has a probability of $|\alpha|^2$ of appearing in state $|0\rangle$ and a probability of $|\beta|^2$ of appearing in state $|1\rangle$. Hence, for a qubit,

$$|\alpha|^2 + |\beta|^2 = 1 \tag{1-4}$$

The sum of the probabilities of appearing in either one of the computational basis states should sum to 1 since the states are mutually exclusive and exhaustive.

Just to brush up on elementary probability theory, n events are mutually exclusive if the occurrence of one event prohibits the other $(n - 1)$ events from happening. Similarly, n events are exhaustive if at least one of them will occur. So, for n mutually exclusive and exhaustive events $A_1, A_2. \ldots A_n$, we have the following:

$$P\left(\bigcup_{i=1}^{n} A_i\right) = \sum_{i=1}^{n} P(A_i) = 1 \tag{1-5}$$

3

The linear coefficients α, β are called *probability amplitudes*. These probability amplitudes being complex numbers can take up even negative values unlike probabilities, which are strictly non-negative. A qubit, which is in an equal superposition of $|0\rangle$ and $|1\rangle$, can be represented by the following state:

$$|+\rangle = \frac{1}{\sqrt{2}}|0\rangle + \frac{1}{\sqrt{2}}|1\rangle \qquad (1\text{-}6)$$

The $|+\rangle$ state, also known as the Hadamard state, plays an important role in quantum computing, as we will see later.

The contrast between the unobservable state of the qubit and the observations we make using measurement lies at the heart of quantum computing and quantum information. Since we are so much tuned to the classical world where an abstract model correlates directly with the physical world, we find the collapse of an unobservable state on measurement counterintuitive. However, the qubit states can be manipulated in ways using superposition, entanglement, and interference so as the measurement outcomes correlate uniquely to the unobservable state. This property of the quantum states renders power to quantum computation, as we will see in various quantum algorithms.

Realization of a Quantum Bit

There are several ways we can realize a qubit. We can use an electron as a qubit (see Figure 1-1). As per the atomic model, the electron can exist either in the *ground state*, which is the lowest energy state, or in the one of the remaining energy states, which we collectively call the *excited state*. The ground state of the electron is denoted by the state $|0\rangle$, while the excited state is denoted by the state $|1\rangle$. By projecting light on an atom for an appropriate duration of time, an electron in the ground state $|0\rangle$ can be moved to the state $|1\rangle$, and vice versa. An electron can be moved to a superposition state of $|0\rangle$ and $|1\rangle$ by reducing the duration of time that light is projected on an atom.

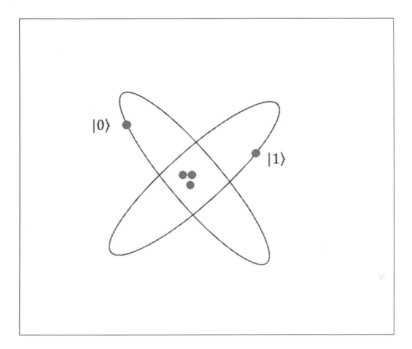

Figure 1-1. *Qubit realization using electron energy states*

One can also use the two different polarizations of a photon or the nuclear spin alignment in the presence of a uniform magnetic field for realizing a qubit.

Bloch Sphere Representation of a Qubit

We have already established the fact that unlike a classical bit a quantum bit or qubit can exist in an infinite continuum of states from $|0\rangle$ to $|1\rangle$. It is useful to look at a geometric representation of a qubit in terms of what is called a Bloch sphere representation of a qubit (see Figure 1-2).

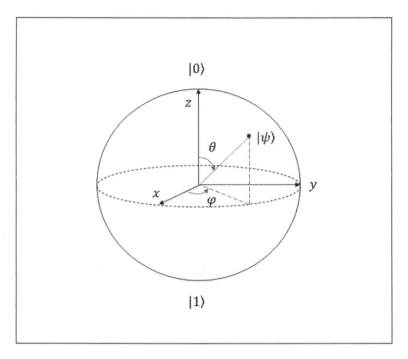

Figure 1-2. *Bloch sphere representation of qubit*

Any point on the surface of the Bloch sphere represents a qubit state. Hence, any generalized state $|\psi\rangle$ of the qubit can be represented by the three parameters γ, θ, and φ, as shown here:

$$|\psi\rangle = e^{i\gamma}\left(\cos\frac{\theta}{2}|0\rangle + \sin\frac{\theta}{2}e^{i\varphi}|1\rangle\right) \qquad (1\text{-}7)$$

Because α and β both are complex numbers, they have two degrees of freedom each. The constraint that the sum of their amplitudes should be 1 (i.e., $|\alpha|^2 + |\beta|^2 = 1$) takes away one degree of freedom, and hence the number of parameters required to represent a qubit turns out to be $2 \times 2 - 1 = 3$.

Let's try to get to the Bloch sphere representation of qubit state mathematically.

The state of the qubit as we have seen can be expressed as $|\psi\rangle = \alpha|0\rangle + \beta|1\rangle$ where α and β are complex numbers.

We can express any complex number α in the Cartesian coordinates as $\alpha = a + ib$ (see Figure 1-3). Alternatively, we can choose to express any complex number α in polar coordinates as $\alpha = re^{i\phi}$ where $r = \sqrt{a^2 + b^2}$.

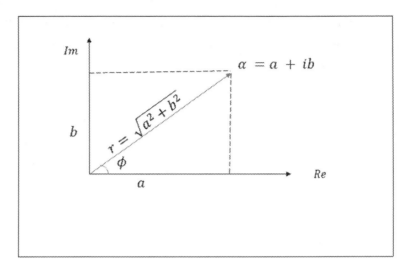

Figure 1-3. *Complex number representation*

If we take $\alpha = r_\alpha e^{i\phi_\alpha}$ and $\beta = r_\beta e^{i\phi_\beta}$, then we have the following:

$$|\psi\rangle = r_\alpha e^{i\phi_\alpha}|0\rangle + r_\beta e^{i\phi_\beta}|1\rangle \tag{1-8}$$

$$= e^{i\phi_\alpha}\left(r_\alpha|0\rangle + r_\beta e^{i(\phi_\beta - \phi_\alpha)}|1\rangle\right) \tag{1-9}$$

Since r_α and r_β are the magnitude of the complex numbers α and β, we have $r_\alpha = |\alpha|$ and $r_\beta = |\beta|$, and hence $r_\alpha^2 + r_\beta^2 = 1$.

We can take $r_\alpha = \cos\dfrac{\theta}{2}$ and $r_\beta = \sin\dfrac{\theta}{2}$ and the expression for $|\psi\rangle$ would simplify to the following:

$$|\psi\rangle = e^{i\phi_\alpha}\left(\cos\frac{\theta}{2}|0\rangle + \sin\frac{\theta}{2}e^{i(\phi_\beta - \phi_\alpha)}|1\rangle\right) \tag{1-10}$$

Replacing ϕ_α with γ and $(\phi_\beta - \phi_\alpha)$ with φ in the previous expression, we get the required Bloch sphere representation of a qubit state, as shown here:

$$|\psi\rangle = e^{i\gamma}\left(\cos\frac{\theta}{2}|0\rangle + \sin\frac{\theta}{2}e^{i\varphi}|1\rangle\right) \tag{1-11}$$

The component $e^{i\gamma}$ is a global phase factor that does not get detected in any experiment. For this reason, we can treat all state vectors of the form $|\psi_k\rangle = e^{i\gamma_k}|\psi\rangle$ as the state vector $|\psi\rangle$. We will discuss in more detail why the global phase factor has no observable effect when we come to measurement and expectations of the observable states. If we ignore the global phase factor, the Bloch sphere representation of the state can be expressed as follows:

$$|\psi\rangle = \cos\frac{\theta}{2}|0\rangle + \sin\frac{\theta}{2}e^{i\varphi}|1\rangle \tag{1-12}$$

The expression in Equation 1-12 lets us represent the state of a qubit in terms of two parameters, θ and φ.

If we think about it, the Bloch sphere lets us project the state of a qubit in the two-dimensional complex plane onto the surface of a three-dimensional sphere of unit radius. Let's get a feel for the qubit states and what each of the axes x, y, and z stand for in the Bloch sphere (see Table 1-1). All we need to do is substitute the relevant values of θ and φ in the qubit state representation in Equation 1-12.

***Table 1-1.** Qubit States on the Bloch Sphere*

Axis	Value of θ and φ	Qubit State
$\|z\rangle$	$\theta = 0;\ \varphi = 0$	$\|0\rangle$
$\|-z\rangle$	$\theta = \pi;\ \varphi = 0$	$\|1\rangle$
$\|x\rangle$	$\theta = \dfrac{\pi}{2};\ \varphi = 0$	$\dfrac{1}{\sqrt{2}}\|0\rangle + \dfrac{1}{\sqrt{2}}\|1\rangle$
$\|-x\rangle$	$\theta = \dfrac{\pi}{2};\ \varphi = \pi$	$\dfrac{1}{\sqrt{2}}\|0\rangle - \dfrac{1}{\sqrt{2}}\|1\rangle$
$\|y\rangle$	$\theta = \dfrac{\pi}{2};\ \varphi = \dfrac{\pi}{2}$	$\dfrac{1}{\sqrt{2}}\|0\rangle + \dfrac{i}{\sqrt{2}}\|1\rangle$
$\|-y\rangle$	$\theta = \dfrac{\pi}{2};\ \varphi = -\dfrac{\pi}{2}$	$\dfrac{1}{\sqrt{2}}\|0\rangle - \dfrac{i}{\sqrt{2}}\|1\rangle$

There are an infinite number of points on the Bloch sphere, each of which corresponds to a qubit state. On measurement of the qubit, however, we observe only one of the two states $|0\rangle$ or $|1\rangle$ if the measurement is done in the standard $0 - 1$ basis. Subsequent post measurements on the qubit continue to reveal the measured state.

Hence, if we measure the qubit state to be $|0\rangle$, successive post-measurements will continue to reveal the state $|0\rangle$. So, measurement changes the state of the qubit.

As discussed earlier, the collapse of the qubit state into one of the computational basis states is one of the mysteries of quantum mechanics to which no one has a definite answer. There are, of course, several interpretations of this quantum phenomenon; the most popular one is the Copenhagen interpretation. According to the Copenhagen interpretation, developed mainly by eminent physicists Niels Bohr and Werner Heisenberg, physical systems do not have definite properties prior to being measured, and quantum mechanics can only predict the probability distribution of the possible states prior to measurement. The act of measurement collapses the set of probabilities into one of the possible states after the measurement. If we were to think about the moon, as per the Copenhagen interpretation, it is as if the moon does not exist until we look at it.

One question that might come up at this point is whether it is possible to know the state of the quantum state before the qubit state collapses on measurement. The answer to this would be "yes" provided we know the initial state of the quantum mechanical system and the transformations the quantum system has been subjected to thereafter. In fact, quantum computing algorithms are all about designing suitable quantum transformations on suitable initial states to bias the probability distribution of the transformed state toward favorable outcomes. The second important thing to answer is how does one estimate the probability of different states in superposition since measurement collapses the state into one of the constituent states? If we take a qubit, for instance, one way we can get an estimate for the magnitudes of α and β is by measuring multiple identically prepared qubits and noting the frequency of the observed states. For example, if we have 1,000 identically prepared qubits and we measure them to get 501 0s and 499 1s, we would know that the probabilities of $|\alpha|^2$ and $|\beta|^2$ are roughly $\frac{1}{2}$ each. One of the key points to understand is that nature evolves the quantum system and keeps track of the information in its states. Furthermore, when we deal with a quantum system with multiple qubits, the information hidden in the state grows exponentially large. The key to harnessing the extreme power of quantum computing lies in our ability to decipher the hidden information in the state of the quantum systems.

Stern–Gerlach Experiment

The Stern–Gerlach experiment is one of the earliest experiments conducted to understand the properties of qubits. This experiment was conceived by Stern in 1921, and he collaborated with Gerlach to conduct the experiment in 1922. In the experimental setup, hot silver atoms emitted in all directions are passed through a collimator to align the beam of silver atoms in the horizontal direction. In the next stage, the beam of silver atoms is made to pass through two pole pieces of a magnet, as illustrated in Figure 1-4.

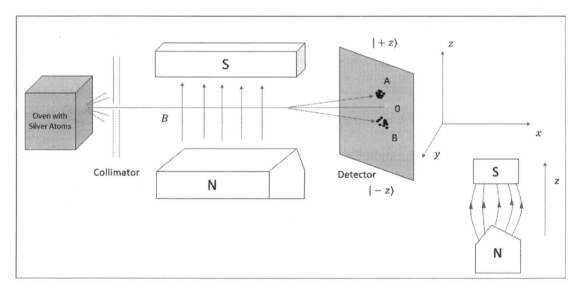

Figure 1-4. *Stern–Gerlach experimental setup*

The magnet has a special setup where the south pole is flat and the north pole has sharp edges. This causes the silver atoms coming out of the collimator to undergo a deflection because of the inhomogeneous magnetic field in the region. Subsequently, the deflected silver atoms are collected in the detector screen. The inhomogeneous magnetic field B would have the three components B_x, B_y, and B_z along the x, y, and z directions, respectively, and hence $B = B_x \hat{i} + B_y \hat{j} + B_z \hat{k}$. The design of the magnet is such that the field along z, i.e., B_z, is significant, and hence $B \approx B_z \hat{k}$. The inhomogeneous magnetic field B in general should detect the atoms in a way that they should hit any location in the detector between the two extremes, but they impinge on two distinct locations, A and B.

Silver atoms, while passing through the magnetic field, experience a force F given by the negative of the gradient of the potential energy U, as shown here:

$$F = -\nabla U \tag{1-13}$$

The potential energy is nothing but the negative of the dot product of the magnetic moment μ of the silver atom and the inhomogeneous magnetic field B of the Stern Gerlach setup. Hence, the potential energy U can be written as follows:

$$U = -\mu.B \tag{1-14}$$

Substituting U from Equation 1-14 into Equation 1-13, we simplify the expression for the force on the silver atoms as follows:

$$F = -\nabla U = -\nabla(-\mu.B) = \mu.\nabla B \tag{1-15}$$

If u_z is the magnetic moment component of the silver atom along the z direction, then the expression for force reduces to the following:

$$F = -\nabla U = -\nabla(-\mu.B) = \mu_z \frac{dB}{dz} \tag{1-16}$$

The gradient of the inhomogeneous field $\frac{dB}{dz}$ is negative. Hence, we see that when the magnetic moment of the atom along the z direction u_z is negative, the force exerted on an atom is positive. Positive force will push the atom possibly above point O in the deflector screen, while negative force will push the atom to any point below point O in the deflector screen. Again, classically the magnetic moment along the z direction μ_z can be expressed in terms of magnetic moment of the atom as follows:

$$\mu_z = |\mu|\cos\theta \tag{1-17}$$

The parameter θ is the angle μ makes with the z-axis. Based on Equation 1-17, μ_z should take a continuum of values between $+|\mu|$ and $-|\mu|$. Hence, all the atoms should have been distributed between these two values. However, as discussed earlier, this does not happen, and the atoms show up at two discrete points. To put things into perspective, let's try to explain this phenomena and its connection to the quantization of the angular momentum.

A silver atom has 47 electrons where for 46 electrons the total angular momentum is zero. The total angular momentum of an atom consists of the orbital angular momentum and the spin angular momentum. Furthermore, the orbital angular momentum of the 47th electron is zero. Hence, the only angular momentum associated with the silver atom is the spin angular momentum from the 47th electron. We should get a signature of the spin angular momentum of the 47th electron on the deflector screen. The nucleus of the atom has insignificant contribution to the angular momentum of the atom and so can be ignored. So, the magnetic moment of the silver atoms is effectively due to the spin angular momentum of the 47th electron. The two discrete zones that all the atoms impinge on should correspond to the intrinsic spin angular momentum that can take two discrete values of $\frac{\hbar}{2}$ corresponding to the discrete region around O and $-\frac{\hbar}{2}$ corresponding to the discrete region below O. Conventionally, the state corresponding to $\frac{\hbar}{2}$ is represented as the $|0\rangle$ state, while $-\frac{\hbar}{2}$ is represented as the $|1\rangle$ state. Hence, the Stern–Gerlach experiment established the fact that angular momentum is quantized. The Stern–Gerlach up and down states match perfectly with the Bloch sphere representation, and hence $|+z\rangle = |0\rangle$ and $|-z\rangle = |1\rangle$. In fact, that atoms have spin angular momentum along with orbital angular momentum was first conceived in this experiment. In this Stern Gerlach setup, if the atoms only had orbital angular momentum, then since for silver atoms the orbital angular momentum is zero, one would have expected the beam of atoms not to have deflected under the influence of the magnetic field. The fact that it did led physicists to believe in the existence of spin angular momentum in addition to the orbital angular momentum.

In the schematic diagram of the Stern–Gerlach experiment in Figure 1-5A, the model has been greatly simplified wherein the input beam from the oven outputs two beams of atoms $|+Z\rangle$ and $|-Z\rangle$.

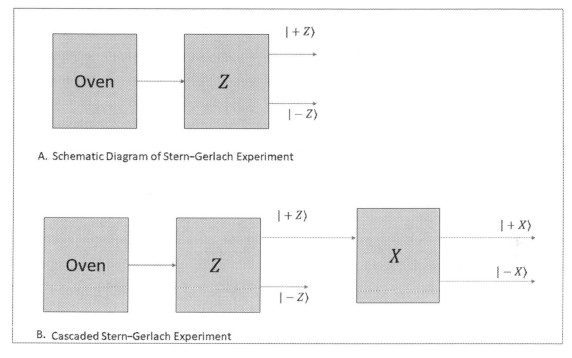

A. Schematic Diagram of Stern–Gerlach Experiment

B. Cascaded Stern–Gerlach Experiment

Figure 1-5. *Stern–Gerlach experimental setup*

In Figure 1-5B, we cascade two Stern–Gerlach apparatus together. The first apparatus deflects the atoms along the z direction, which the second apparatus defects the atoms along the x direction. The atoms corresponding to the $|+Z\rangle$ state detected after the first apparatus is only sent through the second apparatus oriented along the x-axis. Contrary to what one would anticipate, it was seen that there were two beam of atoms in the x direction that we can conveniently refer to as states $|+X\rangle$ and $|-X\rangle$. The state $|+X\rangle$ corresponds to $\frac{1}{\sqrt{2}}(|0\rangle+|1\rangle)$, while $|-X\rangle$ corresponds to $\frac{1}{\sqrt{2}}(|0\rangle-|1\rangle)$. Just to be clear, although the $x,\ y,\ $ and z axes are orthogonal to each other, the state vectors $|+Z\rangle$ is not perpendicular to either of $|-X\rangle$ or $|+X\rangle$.

Multiple Qubits

With two classical bits, we can have four states: 00, 01, 10, and 11. A quantum system with 2 qubits A and B can be in the superposition of the 4 states corresponding to the computational basis states 00, 01, 10, and 11. We can represent the state of a two-qubit system as follows:

$$|\psi\rangle_{AB} = \alpha_{00}|00\rangle + \alpha_{01}|01\rangle + \alpha_{10}|10\rangle + \alpha_{11}|11\rangle \tag{1-18}$$

In the computational basis state of the form $|ij\rangle$, i stands for the basis state of the first qubit, and j stands for the basis state for the second qubit. Hence, the probability amplitude a_{ij} stands for the joint state $|ij\rangle$. These probability amplitudes belong to the complex plane, and the square of these amplitude magnitudes should sum to 1.

$$|\alpha_{00}|^2 + |\alpha_{01}|^2 + |\alpha_{10}|^2 + |\alpha_{11}|^2 = 1 \tag{1-19}$$

Now let's see what will happen to the state $|\psi\rangle_{AB}$ if we happen to measure one of the qubits, say qubit A, and we observe the state $|0\rangle$. Since we have observed qubit A to be in the $|0\rangle$ state, the computational basis states corresponding to qubit A in $|1\rangle$ state would vanish. The new combined state $|\psi'\rangle_{AB}$ of the qubits A and B would be as follows:

$$|\psi'\rangle_{AB} = \alpha_{00}|00\rangle + \alpha_{01}|01\rangle \tag{1-20}$$

Of course, for ensuring that the probabilities in the new state sum to 1, we need to normalize the new state with respect to its constituent amplitudes (see Equation 1-21).

$$|\psi'\rangle_{AB} = \frac{\alpha_{00}|00\rangle + \alpha_{01}|01\rangle}{\sqrt{|\alpha_{00}|^2 + |\alpha_{01}|^2}} \tag{1-21}$$

Bell State

One of the most interesting two-qubit states is the state represented by the following:

$$|\psi\rangle_{AB} = \frac{1}{\sqrt{2}}|00\rangle + \frac{1}{\sqrt{2}}|11\rangle \tag{1-22}$$

The state is the superposition of the states $|00\rangle$ and $|11\rangle$ in equal proportion. If we observe qubit A and measure its state to be $|0\rangle$, then the two-qubit state collapses to the state $|00\rangle$. If we now measure the state of qubit B, then there is only one state we can find for qubit B, the state $|0\rangle$. Similarly, if we measure qubit A to be in state $|1\rangle$, the two-qubit state collapses to $|11\rangle$. In this state, if we make a measurement of qubit B, we will find it in state $|1\rangle$ with 100 percent certainty. The superposition state of two entangled qubits in Equation 1-22 is also known as the Bell state. In this Bell state, as we can observe, the states of the two qubits are perfectly correlated, and this quantum phenomenon is known as *quantum entanglement*. Imagine we create this Bell state using quantum entanglement between two electrons and then we separate these two electrons by a large distance. Now if we measure one electron and observe it to be in state $|0\rangle$, then the other electron if measured would also be in state $|0\rangle$ even though they are separated by a large distance. This Bell state has been of great interest to researchers including Einstein.

Multiple-Qubit State

In general, an n-qubit system would have 2^n computational basis states of the following form:

$$\left| x_1, x_2, \ldots\ldots, x_n \right\rangle \tag{1-23}$$

where x_i denotes the computational state of the ith qubit of the n-qubit system. There are 2^n probability amplitudes corresponding to the 2^n computational basis states. Each of the qubit's basis state variables $x_1, x_2 \ldots x_n$ can take up either of the two values 0,1, and hence each computational basis state can be thought of as a binary representation of a number, as shown here:

$$\left| x_1, x_2, \ldots\ldots, x_n \right\rangle = \left| k \right\rangle \tag{1-24}$$

where

$$k = \sum_{i=0}^{n-1} x_i 2^i \tag{1-25}$$

So, the superposition state of an n-qubit system can be expressed using the computational basis representation from Equation 1-24, as shown here:

$$\left| \psi \right\rangle = \sum_{k=0}^{2^n-1} \alpha_k \left| k \right\rangle \tag{1-26}$$

One of the things to observe here is that with an increase in the number of qubits, we can get an exponential increase in the number of states. For $n=500$, the number of computational basis states 2^{500} exceeds the number of atoms in the universe.

Dirac Notation

"Mathematicians tend to despise Dirac notation, because it can prevent them from making important distinctions, but physicists love it, because they are always forgetting such distinctions exist and the notation liberates them from having to remember."

—David Mermin

In quantum mechanics, the states of the quantum systems lie in complex Hilbert spaces. A Hilbert space is a vector space equipped with the inner product norm. It is also a complete vector space where the convergence of sequences of quantum states will not be a problem. We will not dwell much here on defining complete vector spaces. Readers not familiar with complete vector spaces can think of them as spaces where all the possible states that a quantum system can pick up are available.

Let's motivate the idea of a complete vector space with a counter example. Say we have a qubit whose probability amplitudes are restricted to be rational numbers. In this case, the qubit state $|\psi\rangle$ belongs to the two-dimensional rational space $\mathbb{Q}^2$ instead of belonging to the standard two-dimensional complex plane given by $\mathbb{C}^2$. Now let's say the quantum system changes the state of the qubit in a finite Δt from duration the $|0\rangle$ state to an equal superposition state given by $\frac{1}{\sqrt{2}}|0\rangle + \frac{1}{\sqrt{2}}|1\rangle$. One can think of the state update trajectory as a sequence, as shown here:

$$|\psi_o\rangle = |0\rangle, |\psi_1\rangle, |\psi_2\rangle, \ldots, |\psi_m\rangle, \ldots, |\psi_n\rangle \qquad (1\text{-}27)$$

such that

$$\lim_{n\to\infty}|\psi_n\rangle = \frac{1}{\sqrt{2}}|0\rangle + \frac{1}{\sqrt{2}}|1\rangle \qquad (1\text{-}28)$$

Now since the state of the qubit is restricted to be within the two-dimensional rational space $\mathbb{Q}^2$, it cannot converge to the limiting state in Equation 1-28. We would not have this convergence problem in $\mathbb{C}^2$ since you can think of any possible qubit state and that state would be available to the qubit to converge to. Although the explanation was not mathematically rigorous, it should provide you with an intuitive sense of a complete vector space.

Ket Vector

As per the Dirac vector notation, the column vector pertaining to a quantum state is represented as $|\psi\rangle$. This symbolic representation of a vector is called the Ket representation. For example, a qubit with complex probability amplitude can have the state $\frac{1}{\sqrt{2}}|0\rangle + i\frac{1}{\sqrt{2}}|1\rangle$. In the Dirac notation, the state $|\psi\rangle$ corresponds to the following column vector:

$$|\psi\rangle = \begin{bmatrix} \dfrac{1}{\sqrt{2}} \\ \dfrac{i}{\sqrt{2}} \end{bmatrix} \tag{1-29}$$

Bra Vector

The complex conjugate transpose of a Ket vector is called a Bra vector, and it is represented as $\langle\psi|$. For instance, the Bra vector corresponding to the Ket vector in Equation 1-29 is as follows:

$$\langle\psi| = \begin{bmatrix} \dfrac{1}{\sqrt{2}} & -\dfrac{i}{\sqrt{2}} \end{bmatrix} \tag{1-30}$$

Observe that the column vector has been transposed to a row vector, and the amplitudes have been transformed to their complex conjugates. For a complex number $(a + ib)$, its complex conjugate is given by $(a - ib)$. If a Ket vector has only real probability amplitudes, then the corresponding Bra vector is just its transpose.

Inner Product

The inner product between the two vectors $|\psi_1\rangle$ and $|\psi_2\rangle$ in Dirac notation is represented as follows:

$$\langle\psi_1|\psi_2\rangle \tag{1-31}$$

The inner product is symmetric and hence as follows:

$$\langle\psi_2|\psi_1\rangle = \langle\psi_1|\psi_2\rangle \tag{1-32}$$

Here's an example of an inner product:

$$|\psi_1\rangle = \begin{bmatrix} \dfrac{1}{\sqrt{2}} \\ \dfrac{i}{\sqrt{2}} \end{bmatrix} \quad |\psi_2\rangle = \begin{bmatrix} \dfrac{3}{5} \\ \dfrac{4i}{5} \end{bmatrix} \tag{1-33}$$

$$\langle\psi_2|\psi_1\rangle = \begin{bmatrix} \dfrac{3}{5} & -\dfrac{4i}{5} \end{bmatrix} \begin{bmatrix} \dfrac{1}{\sqrt{2}} \\ \dfrac{i}{\sqrt{2}} \end{bmatrix} = \dfrac{3}{5\sqrt{2}} - i^2\dfrac{4}{5\sqrt{2}} = \dfrac{7}{5\sqrt{2}} \tag{1-34}$$

Magnitude of a Vector

The magnitude of a vector in the Hilbert space is also called the l^2 norm of the vector and is defined to be the square root of the inner product of the vector with itself. In terms of the Ket and Bra notations, the norm of the vector $|\psi\rangle$ is given as follows:

$$\big\||\psi\rangle\big\| = \langle\psi|\psi\rangle^{\frac{1}{2}} \tag{1-35}$$

Let's say we have a vector $|\psi\rangle$ with complex components $c_i \in \mathbb{C}$ as follows:

$$|\psi\rangle = \begin{bmatrix} c_1 \\ c_2 \\ \vdots \\ c_n \end{bmatrix} \tag{1-36}$$

Its inner product with itself gives the square of the magnitude of the vector (see Equation 1-37).

$$\langle\psi|\psi\rangle = \big\||\psi\rangle\big\|^2 = \begin{bmatrix} c_1^* & c_2^* & \dots c_n^* \end{bmatrix} \begin{bmatrix} c_1 \\ c_2 \\ \vdots \\ c_n \end{bmatrix} \tag{1-37}$$

$$= \sum_{i=1}^{n} c_i^* c_i = \sum_{i=1}^{n} |c_i|^2 \tag{1-38}$$

The c_i^* is the complex conjugate of c_i, the ith component of the vector $|\psi\rangle \in \mathbb{C}^n$.

The inner product $\langle\psi|\psi\rangle$ of a quantum state $|\psi\rangle$ with itself is equal to 1. The square of the amplitude $|c_i|^2$ pertains to the probability of the state $|\psi\rangle$ collapsing to the state $|i\rangle$ on measurement. Since the computational basis is mutually exclusive and exhaustive, the probabilities corresponding to them should sum to 1, and hence from Equations 1-37 and 1-38, we can write this:

$$\langle\psi|\psi\rangle = \sum_{i=1}^{n} c_i^* c_i = \sum_{i=1}^{n} |c_i|^2 = 1 \tag{1-39}$$

Outer Product

The outer product of two vectors $|\psi_1\rangle$ and $|\psi_2\rangle$ is expressed as $|\psi_1\rangle\langle\psi_2|$ in the Dirac notation. It produces a matrix of dimension $m \times n$ where $|\psi_1\rangle \in \mathbb{R}^m$ and $|\psi_2\rangle \in \mathbb{R}^n$.

$$|\psi_1\rangle = \begin{bmatrix} c_1 \\ c_2 \\ \vdots \\ c_m \end{bmatrix} \quad |\psi_2\rangle = \begin{bmatrix} d_1 \\ d_2 \\ \vdots \\ d_n \end{bmatrix} \tag{1-40}$$

$$|\psi_1\rangle\langle\psi_2| = \begin{bmatrix} c_1 \\ c_2 \\ \vdots \\ c_m \end{bmatrix} \begin{bmatrix} d_1^* & d_2^* & \dots d_n^* \end{bmatrix} \tag{1-41}$$

$$= \begin{bmatrix} c_1 d_1^* & c_1 d_2^* & \cdots & c_1 d_n^* \\ \vdots & .. & \ddots & \vdots \\ c_m d_1^* & c_m d_2^* & \cdots & c_m d_n^* \end{bmatrix} \tag{1-42}$$

Tensor Product

The tensor product of two vectors $|\psi_1\rangle \in \mathbb{C}^m$ and $|\psi_2\rangle \in \mathbb{C}^n$ is another vector of dimension $m \times n$ and is denoted as $|\psi_1\rangle \otimes |\psi_2\rangle$. Here is an illustration of a tensor product with two-dimensional vectors:

$$|\psi_1\rangle \otimes |\psi_2\rangle = \begin{bmatrix} c_1 \\ c_2 \end{bmatrix} \otimes \begin{bmatrix} d_1 \\ d_2 \end{bmatrix} = \begin{bmatrix} c_1 d_1 \\ c_1 d_2 \\ c_2 d_1 \\ c_2 d_2 \end{bmatrix} \tag{1-43}$$

The tensor product gives us a convenient way of creating a larger vector space from two or more existing vector spaces. If we have a vector space $V \in \mathbb{R}^m$ with a basis of $\{|v_1\rangle, |v_2\rangle ... |v_m\rangle\}$ and another vector space $U \in \mathbb{R}^n$ with a basis of $\{|u_1\rangle, |u_2\rangle ... |u_n\rangle\}$, then by using a tensor product we can get a larger vector space $W \in \mathbb{R}^{m \times n}$ with $m \times n$ number of basis set elements of the form $|v_i\rangle \otimes |u_j\rangle$. For ease of convenience, we write the basis vectors $|v_i\rangle \otimes |u_j\rangle$ as $|v_i u_j\rangle$.

The tensor products are important in quantum computing since they allows us to create quantum states of several qubits from their individual states. For an easy illustration, let's consider the state of a qubit A given by $|\psi_1\rangle = \alpha_1|0\rangle + \beta_1|1\rangle$ and that of a qubit B given by $|\psi_2\rangle = \alpha_2|0\rangle + \beta_2|1\rangle$.

Their combined state can be expressed as the tensor product of the two states as follows:

$$\begin{aligned} |\psi\rangle_{AB} &= |\psi_1\rangle \otimes \psi_2\rangle = \left(\alpha_1|0\rangle + \beta_1|1\rangle\right) \otimes \left(\alpha_2|0\rangle + \beta_2|1\rangle\right) \\ &= \alpha_1\alpha_2|00\rangle + \alpha_1\beta_2|01\rangle + \beta_1\alpha_2|10\rangle + \beta_1\beta_2|11\rangle \end{aligned} \tag{1-44}$$

One thing to note is that not all multiple qubit states can be expressed as the tensor product of the individual qubit states. One classical example is the Bell state $\frac{1}{\sqrt{2}}|00\rangle + \frac{1}{\sqrt{2}}|11\rangle$, which cannot be factored as a tensor product of the individual qubit states. This happens when the qubits are in the entangled state.

Single-Qubit Gates

In quantum computing, one should be able to manipulate the state of the quantum systems. Just as in classical systems, we manipulate the state of the bits through different gates such as OR, AND, NOT, XOR, etc. In quantum computing, we use quantum gates to manipulate the states of the qubits. Let's first look at the quantum equivalent of the NOT gate.

Quantum NOT Gate

A classical NOT gate changes the state of the bit to 1 when the existing state is 0, and vice versa. A quantum gate does something similar but in terms of the amplitudes of the qubit computational basis states. It assigns the probability amplitude of the $|0\rangle$ state to the $|1\rangle$ state, and vice versa. The quantum NOT gate works as an operator X, as shown here:

$$X : \alpha|0\rangle + \beta|1\rangle \rightarrow \beta|0\rangle + \alpha|1\rangle \tag{1-45}$$

If we express the state of the qubit as a vector in the computational basis, then we have this:

$$X : \begin{bmatrix} \alpha \\ \beta \end{bmatrix} = \begin{bmatrix} \beta \\ \alpha \end{bmatrix} \tag{1-46}$$

Now let's try to decode what the representation of X as a matrix would look like. As we can see from Equation 1-46, X transforms a vector into another vector of the same dimension, and hence X can be represented as a square matrix. A square matrix that just reverses the components of a two-dimensional vector is nothing but the matrix X as shown below.

$$X = \begin{bmatrix} 0 & 1 \\ 1 & 0 \end{bmatrix} \tag{1-47}$$

The total probability should be conserved under the transformation of a quantum gate. For the NOT gate, we can see the probability is conserved. In general, to ensure that the probability is conserved, any quantum gate needs to obey only one property; they should be unitary matrices.

A matrix U with real entries is called *unitary* if and only if the following relation holds true:

$$UU^T = U^T U = I \qquad (1\text{-}48)$$

The matrix U^T is the transpose of the matrix U, and I is the identity matrix. In quantum mechanics, the unitary operators as well as the state space components can be complex numbers.

For a matrix U with complex entries to be unitary,

$$UU^{*T} = U^{*T} U = I \qquad (1\text{-}49)$$

where U^{*T} is the complex conjugate transpose of the matrix U.

Any invertible matrix U when multiplied by its inverse U^{-1} gives us the identity matrix and the matrix multiplication is commutative.

$$UU^{-1} = U^{-1}U = I \qquad (1\text{-}50)$$

Comparing Equations 1-49 and 1-50, we can see the inverse U^{-1} of any unitary matrix U is its complex conjugate transpose U^{*T}.

$$U^{-1} = U^{*T} \qquad (1\text{-}51)$$

The matrix U^{*T} is generally represented by $U^\dagger$, and hence one can write the following in general for a unitary matrix:

$$U^{-1} = U^\dagger \qquad (1\text{-}52)$$

Note   In Chapter 2 we cover linear algebra concepts related to quantum mechanics and quantum computing.

Now let's do some math and figure out whether the sum of probabilities is really conserved under a unitary transformation on the state of a quantum system.

Let the state $|u_1\rangle$ of the quantum system change to the state $|v_1\rangle$ when applying the unitary transform U (see Figure 1-6).

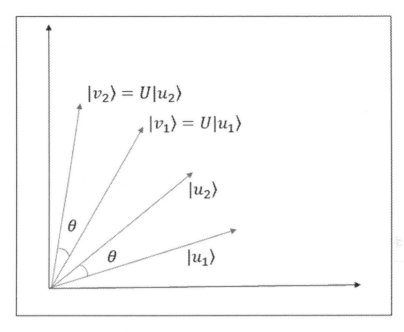

Figure 1-6. *Transformation by unitary matrices*

The probabilities corresponding to each of the computational basis states sum to 1, and hence we can write $\langle u_1|u_1 \rangle = 1$.

After applying the unitary transform U on the quantum state $|u_1\rangle$, the new state is $|v_1\rangle = U | u_1\rangle$. The bra vector representation for $|v_1\rangle$ is $\langle v_1 | = \langle u_1 | U^\dagger$.

Now the sum of the probabilities of each computational basis states in the state $|v_1\rangle$ is given as follows:

$$\langle v_1|v_1 \rangle = \langle u_1 |U^\dagger U|u_1 \rangle \tag{1-53}$$

Since for unitary matrices $U^\dagger U = I$, Equation 1-53 simplifies to the following:

$$\langle v_1|v_1 \rangle = \langle u_1|U^\dagger U |u_1 \rangle = \langle u_1|u_1 \rangle = 1 \tag{1-54}$$

Hence, we see that for the probability axiom to hold true, the transformation on the quantum states should be unitary.

In fact, not only the state norm but the dot product in general between two vectors is preserved under a unitary transform. Taking the two vectors $|u_1\rangle$ and $|u_2\rangle$ that are transformed to $|v_1\rangle$ and $|v_2\rangle$ by the unitary transform U (see Figure 1-6), we have the dot product between $|v_1\rangle$ and $|v_2\rangle$ as follows:

$$\langle v_1|v_2 \rangle = \langle u_1|U^\dagger U |u_2 \rangle = \langle u_1|u_2 \rangle \tag{1-55}$$

Since the dot product of two vectors is invariant under unitary transformation, the distance between two vectors is also preserved since the distance between two vectors is nothing but a linear sum of dot products.

Hadamard Gate

The Hadamard gate acts on a qubit in the state $|0\rangle$ and takes it to the equal superposition state of $\frac{1}{\sqrt{2}}|0\rangle + \frac{1}{\sqrt{2}}|1\rangle$. It also transforms the state $|1\rangle$ to the state $\frac{1}{\sqrt{2}}|0\rangle - \frac{1}{\sqrt{2}}|1\rangle$. The unitary matrix corresponding to the Hadamard Gate is as follows:

$$H = \frac{1}{\sqrt{2}}\begin{bmatrix} 1 & 1 \\ 1 & -1 \end{bmatrix} \tag{1-56}$$

In terms of the Bloch sphere representation, the Hadamard gate takes the state $|0\rangle$ aligned along the z-axis to the state $\frac{1}{\sqrt{2}}|0\rangle + \frac{1}{\sqrt{2}}|1\rangle$ aligned along the positive x-axis. (See Figure 1-7.)

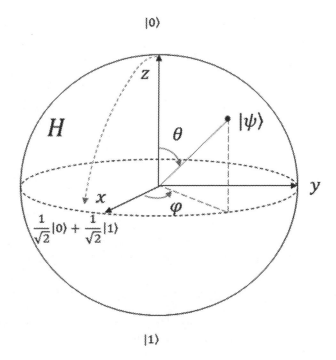

Hadamard transform on $|0\rangle$ state

Figure 1-7. Transformation by unitary matrices

One thing to notice is that if we apply the Hadamard gate twice in succession, the state of the qubit remains unchanged. This is because the square of the Hadamard matrix H^2 is equal to the identity.

Quantum *Z* Gate

The quantum Z gate leaves the state $|0\rangle$ unchanged while it changes the state $|1\rangle$ to $-|1\rangle$. The transformation of the quantum Z gate is represented as follows:

$$Z = \begin{bmatrix} 1 & 0 \\ 0 & -1 \end{bmatrix} \tag{1-57}$$

So, given any arbitrary state $|\psi\rangle = \alpha|0\rangle + \beta|1\rangle$, the Z gate changes and transforms it to $\alpha|0\rangle - \beta|1\rangle$. The quantum Z gate can be written down in terms of the outer products of the computational basis states as follows:

$$Z - \begin{bmatrix} 1 & 0 \\ 0 & -1 \end{bmatrix} = |0\rangle\langle0| - |1\rangle\langle1| \tag{1-58}$$

Multiple-Qubit Gates

We have gone through a few of the important single-qubit gates. Now we will shift our attention to a few of the important multiqubit gates.

When we think about 2-bit classical gates, we think about the AND, XOR, NAND, and NOR gates. In fact, the NAND gate in the classical computing paradigm is called the *universal gate* since any other gate on bits can be constructed by combining NAND gates.

One of the two qubit gates that has helped us construct universal quantum gates is the conditional NOT, or CNOT, gate illustrated in the next section.

CNOT Gate

The CNOT gate works on two qubits: qubit A, which is referred to as the control qubit, and qubit B, which is the target qubit. On application of a CNOT gate, the control qubit state remains unchanged. The target qubit state is flipped in case the control qubit is in state $|1\rangle$.

The computational basis state of two qubits is the tensor product of their corresponding basis states. For instance, the two-qubit state when both qubits are in zero state is given by $|0\rangle_A \otimes |0\rangle_B$. We simplify the notation and write the state $|0\rangle_A \otimes |0\rangle_B$ as $|00\rangle$. Table 1-2 shows how the qubit computation basis state changes on application of a CNOT gate.

Table 1-2. *CNOT on the Computational Basis States of Two Qubits*

Before State	After State
$|00\rangle$	$|00\rangle$
$|01\rangle$	$|01\rangle$
$|10\rangle$	$|11\rangle$
$|11\rangle$	$|10\rangle$

The idea of learning how a quantum gate transforms the computational basis state is useful since the quantum gates are linear operators. This allows us to linearly sum up the transformed states corresponding to the computational basis states to understand the transformation by a quantum gate on a superposition state. Hence, for a unitary operator U (works for any linear operator) that works on a qubit state $\alpha|0\rangle + \beta|1\rangle$, we can write this:

$$U\big(\alpha|0\rangle + \beta|1\rangle\big) = \alpha U|0\rangle + \beta\, U|1\rangle \qquad (1\text{-}59)$$

Now if we carefully look at Table 1-2, we see that the state of the target qubit after applying the CNOT gate is nothing, but the modulo 2 addition of the states of the two qubits before the CNOT gate is applied. Hence, the CNOT operation on the two qubits can be represented as follows (see Figure 1-8):

$$CNOT : |A, B\rangle = |A, B \oplus A\rangle \qquad (1\text{-}60)$$

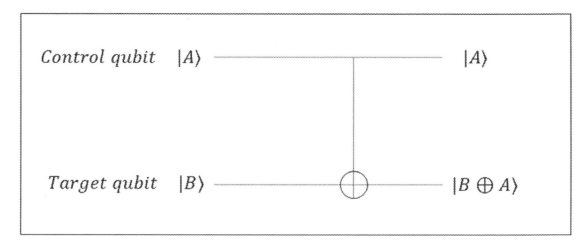

Figure 1-8. *CNOT gate logical circuit*

The matrix representation of the CNOT gate U_{CN} is a 4×4 square matrix.

$$U_{CN} = \begin{bmatrix} 1 & 0 & 0 & 0 \\ 0 & 1 & 0 & 0 \\ 0 & 0 & 0 & 1 \\ 0 & 0 & 1 & 0 \end{bmatrix} \tag{1-61}$$

Readers are advised to validate whether U is unitary by checking whether $U^{\dagger}U = I$.

The quantum state $|\psi\rangle = \alpha_{00}|00\rangle + \alpha_{01}|01\rangle + \alpha_{10}|10\rangle + \alpha_{11}|11\rangle$ where the first qubit is the control qubit and the second qubit is the target qubit to the CNOT gate is transformed to the state $|\psi_{new}\rangle = \alpha_{00}|00\rangle + \alpha_{01}|01\rangle + \alpha_{11}|10\rangle + \alpha_{10}|11\rangle$. See Equation 1-62.

$$|\psi_{new}\rangle = U_{CN}|\psi\rangle = \begin{bmatrix} 1 & 0 & 0 & 0 \\ 0 & 1 & 0 & 0 \\ 0 & 0 & 0 & 1 \\ 0 & 0 & 1 & 0 \end{bmatrix} \begin{bmatrix} \alpha_{00} \\ \alpha_{01} \\ \alpha_{10} \\ \alpha_{11} \end{bmatrix} = \begin{bmatrix} \alpha_{00} \\ \alpha_{01} \\ \alpha_{11} \\ \alpha_{10} \end{bmatrix} \tag{1-62}$$

The XOR gate can be in some sense thought of as the classical counterpart of the quantum CNOT gate if we just consider the output of the target qubit. The output of the XOR gate is nothing but the modulo 2 addition of its two input bits A and B. However, unlike the CNOT gate, the XOR gate is not reversible. Any quantum gate operation being unitary is reversible, and hence by applying the inverse transform of a unitary gate, we can recover the original state of the quantum system. It should be noted that the inverse of a unitary transform is also unitary. The classical XOR gate is not reversible since given the output of the XOR gate, we cannot determine its two inputs with certainty. We can, however, pass one of the bits, say bit A, as an additional output to make the XOR gate reversible. (See Figure 1-9.)

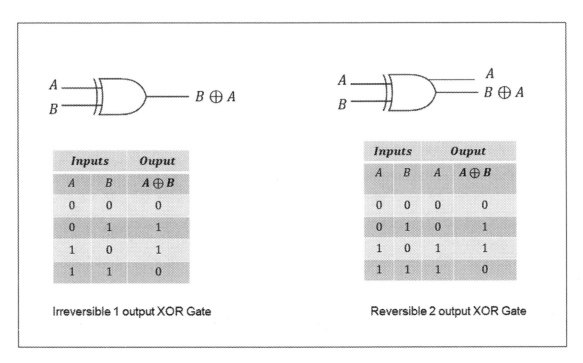

Irreversible 1 output XOR Gate

Reversible 2 output XOR Gate

Figure 1-9. *Irreversible and reversible XOR gates*

Of the several multiqubit gates, the CNOT gate is special because any quantum gate can be constructed using the CNOT gate and one or many single qubit gates. In other words, CNOT and single-qubit gates form a universal set of quantum gates using which we can construct any given quantum gate to an arbitrary level of accuracy.

Controlled-U Gate

Another multiqubit gate that deserves special mention is the controlled-U gate (see Figure 1-10). Suppose we have a unitary operator U that acts on a quantum system of n qubits. We can think of a controlled-U gate as one that applies the unitary operator U on the system of n target qubits based on the state of a control qubit. When the control qubit is in state $|1\rangle$, the unitary operator is applied on the system of n target qubits, while when the control qubit is in $|0\rangle$ state, no transformation is applied on the system of n target qubits. In fact, the CNOT gate is a special case of controlled-U gate, where the unitary operator is the single-qubit X gate.

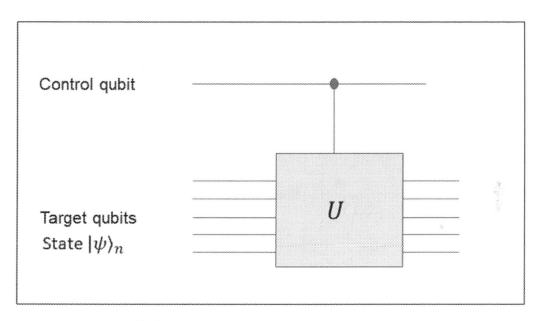

Figure 1-10. *Controlled-U gate*

The controlled-U gate is a key component of Fourier-based quantum implementations, as we will see in Chapter 4.

Copying a Qubit: No Cloning Theorem

In a classical computing paradigm, copying a bit of information is trivial. We can have a classical CNOT gate that takes the input bit to be copied as the control bit and a bit initialized to zero as the target bit to accomplish a bit copy mechanism. In other words, a classical CNOT gate is nothing but the XOR gate, as we established earlier. See Figure 1-11.

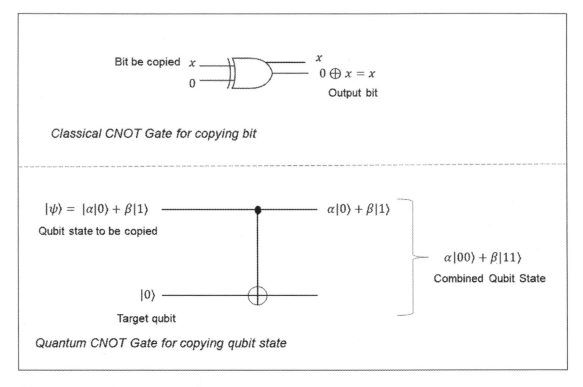

Figure 1-11. *Quantum qubit state copy*

Now let's see if we can copy the state of a qubit $|\psi\rangle$ using a CNOT gate. The input state of the two qubits can be written as follows:

$$|\psi\rangle|0\rangle = (\alpha|0\rangle + \beta|1\rangle)|0\rangle = \alpha|00\rangle + \beta|10\rangle \tag{1-63}$$

On applying the CNOT, the new state of the two-qubit system changes to $\alpha|00\rangle + \beta|11\rangle$. Now let's see if we have been able to copy the state $|\psi\rangle$ of the qubit. Had we copied the qubit successfully, then the two-qubit output state would have been

$$|\psi\rangle|\psi\rangle = (\alpha|0\rangle + \beta|1\rangle)(\alpha|0\rangle + \beta|1\rangle) = |\alpha|^2|00\rangle + \alpha\beta|01\rangle + \beta\alpha|10\rangle + |\beta|^2|11\rangle \tag{1-64}$$

Comparing the two-qubit output state of the CNOT $\alpha|00\rangle + \beta|11\rangle$ and Equation 1-64, we see that it is not possible for the CNOT to copy the state $|\psi\rangle$ unless $\alpha\beta = 0$. The condition $\alpha\beta = 0$ is satisfied only if either α or β is zero. The condition $\alpha = 0$ pertains to the state $|\psi\rangle = |1\rangle$, while the condition $\beta = 0$ pertains to the condition $|\psi\rangle = |0\rangle$. This tells us that we cannot copy the quantum state unless it is in one of the computational basis states. In fact, we can generalize this observation for one qubit to quantum system of any number of qubits. This property that the unknown superposition state of qubits cannot be copied is popularly known as the *no-cloning theorem*.

As discussed, if the qubit state is in one of the computation basis states, we can copy the qubit. Say the qubit is in state $|\psi\rangle = |1\rangle$. Then the output of the CNOT gate would be $|11\rangle$, which would be equal to the state $|\psi\rangle|\psi\rangle = |11\rangle$.

Measurements in Different Basis

So far, while discussing measurement of the state of a qubit, we have only looked at the canonical computational basis states $|0\rangle$ and $|1\rangle$. To be more precise, we have expressed the state of the qubit as $|\psi\rangle = \alpha|0\rangle + \beta|1\rangle$. When we make a measurement in the computation basis, either we get a 0 with probability $|\alpha|^2$, leaving the post measurement state of the qubit as $|0\rangle$, or we get a 1 with probability $|\beta|^2$, leaving the post measurement state of the qubit $|1\rangle$. We can express the qubit in other orthogonal basis states as well such as the $|+\rangle$ and $|-\rangle$ basis states where

$$|+\rangle = \frac{1}{\sqrt{2}}|0\rangle + \frac{1}{\sqrt{2}}|1\rangle; \quad |-\rangle = \frac{1}{\sqrt{2}}|0\rangle - \frac{1}{\sqrt{2}}|1\rangle \qquad (1\text{-}65)$$

Alternately, we can express the states $|0\rangle$ and $|1\rangle$ in terms of the $|+\rangle$ and $|-\rangle$ states as follows:

$$|0\rangle = \frac{1}{\sqrt{2}}|+\rangle + \frac{1}{\sqrt{2}}|-\rangle; \quad |1\rangle = \frac{1}{\sqrt{2}}|+\rangle - \frac{1}{\sqrt{2}}|-\rangle \qquad (1\text{-}66)$$

Using Equation 1-66, the state $|\psi\rangle = \alpha|0\rangle + \beta|1\rangle$ of the qubit in terms of the $|+\rangle$ and $|-\rangle$ states can be expressed as follows:

$$|\psi\rangle = \alpha|0\rangle + \beta|1\rangle = \alpha\left[\frac{1}{\sqrt{2}}|+\rangle + \frac{1}{\sqrt{2}}|-\rangle\right] + \beta\left[\frac{1}{\sqrt{2}}|+\rangle - \frac{1}{\sqrt{2}}|-\rangle\right]$$

$$= \frac{\alpha+\beta}{\sqrt{2}}|+\rangle + \frac{\alpha-\beta}{\sqrt{2}}|-\rangle \qquad (1\text{-}67)$$

Now if we measure the state of the qubit in the $|+\rangle$, $|-\rangle$ basis, either we will observe the + state with probability $|\alpha+\beta|^2$ leaving the post-measurement state as $|+\rangle$ or we will observe the – state with probability $|\alpha-\beta|^2$ leaving the post-measurement state as $|-\rangle$.

In general, we can write the state of the qubit in any linearly independent basis states $|\phi_1\rangle$, $|\phi_2\rangle$ such that $|\psi\rangle = \alpha_1|\phi_1\rangle + \alpha_2|\phi_2\rangle$. However, for the sake of the measurement with respect to the basis states, we chose an orthonormal basis such that we can observe $|\phi_1\rangle$ with probability $|\alpha_1|^2$ and $|\phi_2\rangle$ with probability $|\alpha_2|^2$. The orthonormality ensures that the basis states have no overlap, and we hence have $|\alpha_1|^2 + |\alpha_2|^2 = 1$.

In Figure 1-12 we illustrate a circuit representation for measuring the quantum state $|\psi\rangle$. On measurement, the quantum state would collapse to one of the computational basis states used for measurement. For instance, for a qubit state we may choose to measure in the $|0\rangle$, $|1\rangle$, and hence the measurement output would be either the 0 or 1 state. Similarly, if we chose to measure the qubit state in the $|+\rangle$, $|-1\rangle$, the output state would be either the + state or the – state.

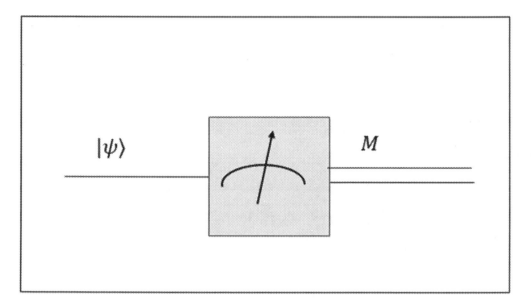

Figure 1-12. *Quantum circuit representation for measurement*

Bell States with Quantum Gates

We looked at the Bell state $\frac{1}{\sqrt{2}}|00\rangle + \frac{1}{\sqrt{2}}|11\rangle$ earlier in this chapter. When the two qubits A and B are entangled with each other as in the Bell state, it is not possible to separate the individual qubit states. In other words, we cannot express the Bell state as the tensor product of the individual qubit states, as illustrated here:

$$|\psi\rangle_{AB} = \frac{1}{\sqrt{2}}|00\rangle + \frac{1}{\sqrt{2}}|11\rangle \neq |\psi\rangle_A \otimes |\psi\rangle_B \tag{1-68}$$

In the Bell state, $\frac{1}{\sqrt{2}}|00\rangle + \frac{1}{\sqrt{2}}|11\rangle$, if we make a measurement on the qubit A, we get either a 0 with a 0.5 probability leaving the post-measurement state as $|00\rangle$ or we get a 1 with a 0.5 probability leaving the post-measurement state as $|11\rangle$. On subsequent measurement of the qubit B, we get a 0 with probability 1 if the qubit A is in state 0. Similarly, we get 1 state for the qubit B with probability 1 if the qubit A is in state 1. So, the states of the qubit in the Bell state are correlated with each other.

Now let's see how we can create the Bell state from the quantum gates we have looked at so far. We can create the Bell state $\frac{1}{\sqrt{2}}|00\rangle + \frac{1}{\sqrt{2}}|11\rangle$ by taking two qubits x and y initialized at the $|0\rangle$ state. We pass the first qubit through the Hadamard gate (see Figure 1-13), which transforms qubit x to the $|+\rangle$ state, i.e., $\frac{1}{\sqrt{2}}|0\rangle + \frac{1}{\sqrt{2}}|1\rangle$. Next we pass the output of the Hadamard gate $\frac{1}{\sqrt{2}}|0\rangle + \frac{1}{\sqrt{2}}|1\rangle$ as the control qubit and the qubit y initialized to the $|0\rangle$ state as the target qubit to the CNOT gate to get the final Bell state as follows:

$$CNOT: \left[\frac{1}{\sqrt{2}}|0\rangle + \frac{1}{\sqrt{2}}|1\rangle \right] \otimes |0\rangle \to \frac{1}{\sqrt{2}}|00\rangle + \frac{1}{\sqrt{2}}|11\rangle \qquad (1\text{-}69)$$

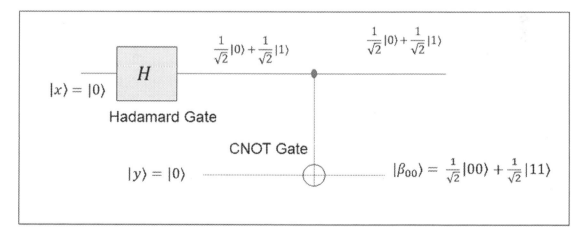

Figure 1-13. Bell state implementation with quantum gates

The Bell state $\frac{1}{\sqrt{2}}|00\rangle + \frac{1}{\sqrt{2}}|11\rangle$ is only one of the four possible equal superposition correlated states for a pair of qubits. We can use the quantum circuit in Figure 1-14 to create four different Bell states based on the states that the qubit x and y are initialized to.

The Hadamard gate transform (H) on the qubit states $|0\rangle$ and $|1\rangle$ can be generalized as follows:

$$H|x\rangle = \frac{1}{\sqrt{2}}|0\rangle + (-1)^x \frac{1}{\sqrt{2}}|1\rangle \qquad (1\text{-}70)$$

when $x = 0$, we get the Hadamard transformed state as $\frac{1}{\sqrt{2}}|0\rangle + \frac{1}{\sqrt{2}}|1\rangle$, while when $x = 1$, we get the Hadamard transformed state as $\frac{1}{\sqrt{2}}|0\rangle - \frac{1}{\sqrt{2}}|1\rangle$.

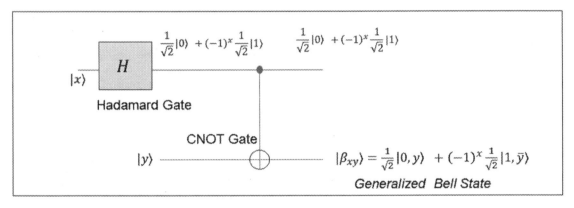

Figure 1-14. *Generalized Bell state implementation with quantum gates*

Now when the Hadamard transformed state $|\psi_{cntl}\rangle = \frac{1}{\sqrt{2}}|0\rangle + (-1)^x \frac{1}{\sqrt{2}}|1\rangle$ acts on the target qubit y in the CNOT gate, the state $|0\rangle$ of $|\psi_{cntl}\rangle$ doesn't change the state y, and we get the state $|0, y\rangle$, while the state $|1\rangle$ of $|\psi_{cntl}\rangle$ flips the state of y, and hence we get the state $|1, \bar{y}\rangle$. So, the final generalized Bell state we can get starting with two qubits initialized at $|x\rangle$ and $|y\rangle$ states can be written as follows:

$$\left|\beta_{xy}\right\rangle = \frac{1}{\sqrt{2}}|0, y\rangle + (-1)^x \frac{1}{\sqrt{2}}|1, \bar{y}\rangle \qquad (1\text{-}71)$$

Substituting different values of $x, y \in \{0, 1\}$ in Equation 1-71, we can get different Bell states, as illustrated in Table 1-3.

Table 1-3. *Truth Table for Different Bell States*

x	y	Bell State $\lvert \beta xy \rangle$
0	0	$\lvert \beta_{00} \rangle = \dfrac{1}{\sqrt{2}} \lvert 00 \rangle + \dfrac{1}{\sqrt{2}} \lvert 11 \rangle$
0	1	$\lvert \beta_{00} \rangle = \dfrac{1}{\sqrt{2}} \lvert 01 \rangle + \dfrac{1}{\sqrt{2}} \lvert 10 \rangle$
1	0	$\lvert \beta_{10} \rangle = \dfrac{1}{\sqrt{2}} \lvert 00 \rangle - \dfrac{1}{\sqrt{2}} \lvert 11 \rangle$
1	1	$\lvert \beta_{11} \rangle = \dfrac{1}{\sqrt{2}} \lvert 01 \rangle - \dfrac{1}{\sqrt{2}} \lvert 10 \rangle$

Quantum Teleportation

Quantum teleportation is an exciting quantum computing technique of transmitting quantum states between sender and receiver without using any communication channel.

To illustrate quantum teleportation, we will refer to the sender of the quantum state as Alice and the receiver of the quantum state as Bob. We will illustrate quantum teleportation with a story. Alice and Bob during their childhood shared a Bell state $\lvert \beta_{00} \rangle$, where the first qubit Q_2 belongs to Alice and qubit Q_3 belongs to Bob. Bob had to relocate to a different city because of work commitments. Now Alice wants to share some information: a third qubit Q_1 state $\lvert \psi \rangle$ to Bob.

Figure 1-15 shows the quantum teleportation circuit. One thing to note is that the single circuit lines are not physical wires. They merely depict the passage of time relative to which the different qubit gates operate. The double lines post the measurement are used to depict the classical information carried forward after measuring the qubit states.

Alice and Bob use their qubits Q_2 and Q_3 initially at state $|0\rangle$ to get to the Bell state $|\beta_{00}\rangle$ by using a quantum circuit of a Hadamard gate followed by a CNOT gate applied at time $t = t_0$. Now Alice wants to send the qubit Q_1 state $|\psi\rangle$ to Bob.

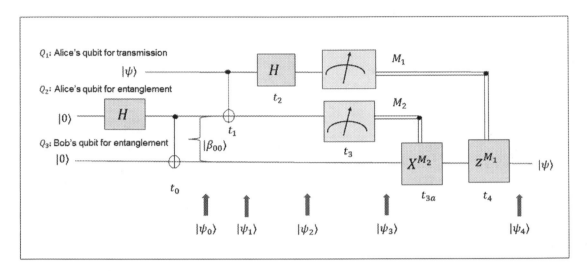

Figure 1-15. *Quantum teleportation circuit*

If we look at the three-qubit state $|\psi_0\rangle$ at any time t, where $t_0 < t < t_1$, it can be written as follows:

$$|\psi_0\rangle = |\psi\rangle \otimes |\beta_{00}\rangle = (\alpha|0\rangle + \beta|1\rangle) \otimes \frac{1}{\sqrt{2}}(|00\rangle + |11\rangle) \qquad (1\text{-}72)$$

$$= \alpha|0\rangle \frac{1}{\sqrt{2}}(|00\rangle + |11\rangle) + \beta|1\rangle \frac{1}{\sqrt{2}}(|00\rangle + |11\rangle) \qquad (1\text{-}73)$$

At time $t = t_1$, Alice's qubits Q_1 and Q_2 are control and target qubits, respectively, to the CNOT gate. The CNOT gate would change the different computational basis states in the superposition state $|\psi_0\rangle$, as shown here:

$$CNOT(Q_1, Q_2): \alpha|0\rangle \frac{1}{\sqrt{2}}(|00\rangle + |11\rangle) \rightarrow \alpha|0\rangle \frac{1}{\sqrt{2}}(|00\rangle + |11\rangle) \qquad (1\text{-}74)$$

$$CNOT(Q_1, Q_2): \beta|1\rangle \frac{1}{\sqrt{2}}(|00\rangle + |11\rangle) \rightarrow \beta|1\rangle \frac{1}{\sqrt{2}}(|10\rangle + |01\rangle) \qquad (1\text{-}75)$$

Hence, the state $|\psi_1\rangle$ at any time t, where $t_1 < t < t_2$, can be written as follows:

$$|\psi_1\rangle = \alpha|0\rangle\frac{1}{\sqrt{2}}(|00\rangle + |11\rangle) + \beta|1\rangle\frac{1}{\sqrt{2}}(|10\rangle + |01\rangle) \tag{1-76}$$

Now at time $t = t_2$, the Hadamard gate is applied on the first qubit and hence at any time t, where $t_2 < t < t_3$, the combined state $|\psi_2\rangle$ of the three qubits can be expressed as follows:

$$|\psi_2\rangle = \frac{\alpha}{\sqrt{2}}(|0\rangle + |1\rangle)\frac{1}{\sqrt{2}}(|00\rangle + |11\rangle) + \frac{\beta}{\sqrt{2}}(|0\rangle +$$

$$|1\rangle)\frac{1}{\sqrt{2}}(|10\rangle + |01\rangle) \tag{1-77}$$

$$= \frac{\alpha}{2}(|0\rangle + |1\rangle)(|00\rangle + |11\rangle) +$$

$$\frac{\beta}{2}(|0\rangle + |1\rangle)(|10\rangle + |01\rangle) \tag{1-78}$$

Expanding the terms in Equation 1-78, we get the state $|\psi_2\rangle$ as shown here:

$$|\psi_2\rangle = \frac{\alpha}{2}(|000\rangle + |011\rangle + |100\rangle + |111\rangle) +$$

$$\frac{\beta}{2}(|010\rangle + |001\rangle + |110\rangle + |101\rangle) \tag{1-79}$$

Since at time $t = t_3$ we are going to measure Alice's qubits, it makes sense to arrange the state $|\psi_2\rangle$ in terms of the computational basis states for Alice's qubits, i.e., $|00\rangle$, $|01\rangle$, $|10\rangle$, $|11\rangle$. On re-arranging the terms in Equation 1-79, we get this:

$$|\psi_2\rangle = \frac{1}{2}|00\rangle(\alpha|0\rangle + \beta|1\rangle) + \frac{1}{2}|01\rangle(\alpha|1\rangle + \beta|0\rangle) + \frac{1}{2}|10\rangle(\alpha|0\rangle -$$

$$\beta|1\rangle) + \frac{1}{2}|11\rangle(\alpha|1\rangle - \beta|0\rangle) \tag{1-80}$$

Now once we make measurements on Alice's qubit at time $t = t_3$, we will measure them to be in one of the four computational basis states, and the state of Bob's qubit would be the one entangled with it. For instance, if we measure both of Alice's qubits to be 0, i.e., $M_1 = 0$ and $M_2 = 0$, then the state of Bob's qubit is the one tied to the state $|00\rangle$, i.e., $(\alpha|0\rangle + \beta|1\rangle)$. This is the state that Alice desired to send to Bob.

Now, let's say we measure $M_1 = 1$ and $M_2 = 1$. Then Bob's state is the one tied to the state $|11\rangle$, i.e., $(\alpha|1\rangle - \beta|0\rangle)$. This is not quite the desired state. However, the transforms lined up on Bob's qubit; i.e., X^{M_2} and Z^{M_1} would take care of transforming $(\alpha|1\rangle - \beta|0\rangle)$ to the desired state $(\alpha|0\rangle + \beta|1\rangle)$.

In this case, $X^{M_2} = X$ is nothing but the quantum NOT gate having the following matrix representation:

$$X = \begin{bmatrix} 0 & 1 \\ 1 & 0 \end{bmatrix}$$

This flips the probability amplitudes, and hence the state $(\alpha|1\rangle - \beta|0\rangle)$ would be transformed to $(\alpha|0\rangle - \beta|1\rangle)$ on application of the X gate. Next, Bob's qubit will pass through the $Z^{M_1} = Z$ gate, which would just flip the phase associated with the state $|1\rangle$. This will transform the qubit state $(\alpha|0\rangle - \beta|\rangle)$ to the desired qubit state $(\alpha|0\rangle + \beta|1\rangle)$.

Table 1-4 lists all four possibilities corresponding to the measurements on Alice's qubits. Each of them produces the final state of Bob's qubit as $(\alpha|0\rangle + \beta|1\rangle)$.

Table 1-4. *Different Paths to Bob's Qubit State Post Measurement*

M_1	M_2	Bob's Qubit Post Measurement	X^{M_2} , Bvob's Qubit State Post X^{M_2}	Z^{M_1} , Bob's Qubit State Post Z^{M_1}
0	0	$\alpha\|0\rangle + \beta\|1\rangle$	$I, \alpha\|0\rangle + \beta\|1\rangle$	$I, \alpha\|0\rangle + \beta\|1\rangle$
0	1	$\alpha\|1\rangle + \beta\|0\rangle$	$X, \alpha\|0\rangle + \beta\|1\rangle$	$I, \alpha\|0\rangle + \beta\|1\rangle$
1	0	$\alpha\|0\rangle - \beta\|1\rangle$	$I, \alpha\|0\rangle - \beta\|1\rangle$	$Z, \alpha\|0\rangle + \beta\|1\rangle$
1	1	$\alpha\|1\rangle - \beta\|0\rangle$	$X, \alpha\|0\rangle - \beta\|1\rangle$	$Z, \alpha\|0\rangle + \beta\|1\rangle$

Quantum Parallelism Algorithms

Quantum parallelism allows one to evaluate a function for many different values of the inputs simultaneously. Suppose we have a function $f(x)$ where x takes in n number of distinct values. By developing an appropriate unitary transform, one can evaluate $f(x)$ for all possible values of x simultaneously using a quantum computer. Many quantum algorithms leverage quantum parallelism. See Figure 1-16.

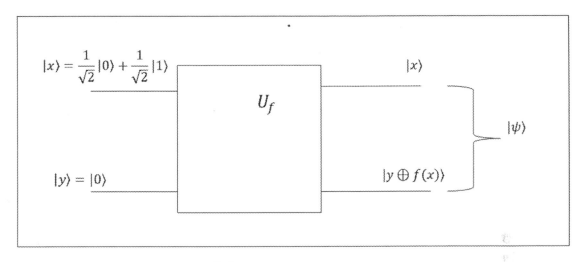

Figure 1-16. *Quantum parallelism*

Suppose we want to evaluate a function $f(x)$ that has a binary domain and range, i.e., $f: X \in \{0, 1\} \rightarrow \{0, 1\}$.

One convenient way to evaluate the function is to start with an equal superposition state $|x\rangle = \frac{1}{\sqrt{2}}|0\rangle + \frac{1}{\sqrt{2}}|1\rangle$ as the *data input* and a qubit initialized to the state $|y\rangle = |0\rangle$ as the *target*. With an appropriate unitary gate U_f, we transform this joint state $|x, y\rangle$ to $|x, y \oplus f(x)\rangle$ where $\oplus$ denotes modulo 2 addition.

The output state after applying the unitary gate U_f can be expanded as follows:

$$|\psi\rangle = |x, y \oplus f(x)\rangle = |x, f(x)\rangle = \frac{1}{\sqrt{2}}|0, f(0)\rangle + \frac{1}{\sqrt{2}}|1, f(1)\rangle \tag{1-81}$$

The state in Equation 1-81 is a useful state where we have as components both $f(0)$ and $f(1)$ entangled with their corresponding inputs. It is as if we have evaluated the function at once over its entire domain by creating a superposition state for all values in its domain. This quantum phenomenon is called *quantum parallelism*.

Now the question is, how can we get the function evaluations from this superposition state $|\psi\rangle$?

As we have already established, to be able to extract any information from a given state, we need to perform measurement. If we measure the data qubit to be 0, we collapse the state to $|0, f(0)\rangle$. Now if we make a measurement for the second qubit, we are sure to get the value of $f(0)$ as measurement with 100 percent certainty. Similarly, if we measure the first qubit to be 1 on the second qubit, we are sure to measure the value of $f(1)$.

We can generalize this approach to a function with multiple inputs values in its domain. Say we have a function with $N = 2^n$ values in its domain such that

$$f : X \in \{0, 1, 2, \ldots, 2^n - 1\} \to \{0, 1\} \tag{1-82}$$

We can create an equal superposition state of all the 2^n values as the computational basis states by using Hadamard gates on a system of n qubits.

To illustrate the idea, let's start with two qubits initially at the $|0\rangle$ state (see Figure 1-17). On applying Hadamard gate on each of them, we get the following:

$$H^{\otimes 2} : |00\rangle \to H|0\rangle \otimes H|0\rangle = \left(H|0\rangle \right)^{\otimes 2} = \left(\frac{1}{\sqrt{2}}|0\rangle + \frac{1}{\sqrt{2}}|1\rangle \right)^{\otimes 2} \tag{1-83}$$

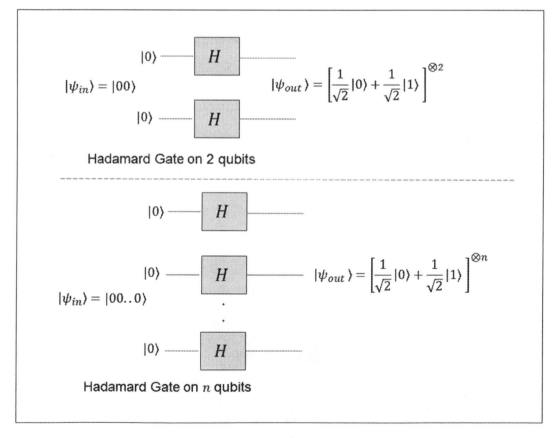

Figure 1-17. *Equal superposition states with Hadamard gates on multiple qubits*

We can expand the state in Equation 1-83 as follows:

$$\left(\frac{1}{\sqrt{2}}|0\rangle + \frac{1}{\sqrt{2}}|1\rangle\right)^{\otimes 2} = \left(\frac{1}{\sqrt{2}}|0\rangle + \frac{1}{\sqrt{2}}|1\rangle\right) \otimes \left(\frac{1}{\sqrt{2}}|0\rangle + \frac{1}{\sqrt{2}}|1\rangle\right)$$
$$= \frac{1}{2}\left(|00\rangle + |01\rangle + |10\rangle + |11\rangle\right) \tag{1-84}$$

So, we can see by using Hadamard gates on 2 qubits initialized at $|0\rangle$ state that we are able get an equal superposition of four computational basis states. We can denote a "binary string" representation of computational basis states in terms of its integer representation as follows:

$$\frac{1}{2}\left(|00\rangle + |01\rangle + |10\rangle + |11\rangle\right) = \frac{1}{2}\left(|0\rangle + |1\rangle + |2\rangle + |3\rangle\right) \tag{1-85}$$

Now instead of two qubits, if we start with n qubits initialized at $|0\rangle$ state, then by applying the Hadamard transform on each of the qubits, we get the following superposition state:

$$\left(\frac{1}{\sqrt{2}}|0\rangle + \frac{1}{\sqrt{2}}|1\rangle\right)^{\otimes n} = \frac{1}{2^{n/2}} \sum_{x_{n-1}=0}^{1} .. \sum_{x_1=0}^{1} \sum_{x_0=0}^{1} |x_{n-1},...,x_1,x_0\rangle \tag{1-86}$$

where $x_0, x_1... x_{n-1}$ represent the values of the qubits in an n dimensional computational basis state. We can simplify the expression in Equation 1-86 by treating the binary string as an integer number based on the following expansion: $x = x_{n-1}2^{n-1}... + x_1 2^1 + x_0 2^0$. This reduces the expression for the superposition of states.

$$\left(\frac{1}{\sqrt{2}}|0\rangle + \frac{1}{\sqrt{2}}|1\rangle\right)^{\otimes n} = \frac{1}{2^{n/2}} \sum_{x=0}^{2^n-1} |x\rangle \tag{1-87}$$

Now if we feed the state in Equation 1-87 as the input data through the unitary gate U_f for quantum parallelism, the output we end up with can be written as follows:

$$|\psi\rangle = \frac{1}{2^{n/2}} \sum_{x=0}^{2^n-1} |x, f(x)\rangle \tag{1-88}$$

So, we can see that by using n qubits, we can have a function evaluated for 2^n inputs in its domain at once. Of course, to get the function values, we would have to make measurements on the state $|\psi\rangle$, and each measurement would yield the input x and its corresponding function value $f(x)$.

Quantum Interference

As discussed earlier, in quantum computing algorithms, the aim is to bias the probability distribution given by the state of a quantum system to favor one or more outcomes. Let's discuss quantum interference with an example. The Hadamard gate H transforming the state $|\psi\rangle = \frac{1}{\sqrt{2}}|0\rangle - \frac{1}{\sqrt{2}}|1\rangle$ to the state $|1\rangle$ is a classic example of interference. The Hadamard transform works on each of the basis states in $|\psi\rangle$ and transforms the state $|0\rangle$ to the superposition state $\frac{1}{\sqrt{2}}|0\rangle + \frac{1}{\sqrt{2}}|1\rangle$ and the basis state $|1\rangle$ to $\frac{1}{\sqrt{2}}|0\rangle - \frac{1}{\sqrt{2}}|1\rangle$, as shown here:

$$H|\psi\rangle = \frac{1}{\sqrt{2}} H|0\rangle - \frac{1}{\sqrt{2}} H|1\rangle$$

$$= \frac{1}{\sqrt{2}} \frac{1}{\sqrt{2}} \big(|0\rangle + |1\rangle\big) - \frac{1}{\sqrt{2}} \frac{1}{\sqrt{2}} \big(|0\rangle - |1\rangle\big) \tag{1-89}$$

It is as if each basis state in $|\psi\rangle$ is transformed by H to a superposition of all its basis states. The superposition state pertaining to $\frac{1}{\sqrt{2}} H|0\rangle$ and $\frac{1}{\sqrt{2}} H|1\rangle$ interferes in such a way that the probability amplitudes of the $|0\rangle$ state undergo *destructive interference*, while that of $|1\rangle$ undergoes *constructive interference* to output state $|1\rangle$, as shown here:

$$H|\psi\rangle = \frac{1}{\sqrt{2}} \frac{1}{\sqrt{2}} \big(|0\rangle + |1\rangle\big) - \frac{1}{\sqrt{2}} \frac{1}{\sqrt{2}} \big(|0\rangle - |1\rangle\big)$$

$$= \frac{1}{2} \underbrace{(1-1)}_{\substack{Destructive \\ Interference}} |0\rangle + \frac{1}{2} \underbrace{(1+1)}_{\substack{Constructive \\ Interference}} |1\rangle$$

$$= \frac{1}{2} 0|0\rangle + \frac{1}{2} 2|1\rangle = |1\rangle \tag{1-90}$$

The qubit in state $|\psi\rangle = \frac{1}{\sqrt{2}}|0\rangle - \frac{1}{\sqrt{2}}|1\rangle$ has a 50-50 chance of showing up as either of the two computation basis states 0 or 1 on measurement. However, by applying the Hadamard transform, we take advantage of interference in such a way that it biases the new state $|\psi_{new}\rangle = H|\psi\rangle$ to output state 1 with 100 percent probability. Interested readers are advised to go through Young's double slit experiment to get more insights into quantum interference.

Summary

With this, we come to the end of Chapter 1. In this chapter, we covered a lot of ground on qubits, the fundamental unit in quantum computing. Also, we discussed the important quantum mechanical properties of entanglement and superposition. Further, we looked at several important single-qubit and multiqubit gates, which are important to manipulate the state of the qubits. Toward the end of the chapter we discussed Bell states, the concepts related to quantum teleportation, and quantum parallelism.

You will see in the chapters to follow that quantum parallelism is an important ingredient in several of the quantum computing and quantum machine learning applications. In the next chapter, we are going to touch upon important ideas from linear algebra that are required in the context of quantum computing and quantum machine learning, study the postulates of quantum mechanics, and then look in more detail at measurement in quantum systems. Finally, we will end the chapter with a few important quantum computing algorithms to gain further insight into the power of quantum computing and its related algorithms.

## CHAPTER 2

Mathematical Foundations and Postulates of Quantum Computing

We must know! We will know!

—David Hilbert

Quantum mechanics is more fundamental than classical mechanics, and it works at both the microscopic and macroscopic levels. However, the manifestation of quantum mechanics becomes more significant for particles and systems in the microscopic domain, which moves with high velocity. There are still questions about the interpretational aspects of quantum mechanics. However, at an operational level, it works over a wide range of phenomena with a high level of precision. The mathematics of quantum mechanics is much simpler than classical mechanics, and as a calculation device, quantum mechanics has been hugely successful. In this chapter, we will go through some of the topics in linear algebra and then move to the postulates of quantum mechanics.

Topics from Linear Algebra

Because the state of a quantum system exists in a Hilbert space and the operators on the state are linear, linear algebra becomes critical in the study of quantum mechanics. In Chapter 1, we touched upon a few topics in linear algebra to get a feel for quantum mechanics and quantum computing. However, a more rigorous knowledge of linear algebra is central to the understanding of quantum mechanics and quantum computing. In this chapter, we will look at specific ideas from linear algebra that are central to the idea of quantum states, quantum evolution, and quantum measurement.

© Santanu Pattanayak 2021
S. Pattanayak, *Quantum Machine Learning with Python*, https://doi.org/10.1007/978-1-4842-6522-2_2

Linear Independence of Vectors

The two vectors $|v_1\rangle$ and $|v_2\rangle$ are said to be linearly independent if one cannot be expressed as the linear scaling of the other. Mathematically speaking, $|v_1\rangle$ and $|v_2\rangle$ are linearly independent if $|v_1\rangle \neq k|v_2\rangle$ for some constant k. A set of n vectors $|v_1\rangle, |v_2\rangle....$ $|v_n\rangle \in \mathbb{R}^m$ is said to be linearly independent if none of them can be expressed as the linear combination of the others. To check whether a given set of n vectors is linearly independent, one must check that $c_1|v_1\rangle + c_2|v_2\rangle + ...c_n|v_n\rangle = 0$ only when each of the linear coefficients c_1 through c_n is zero. If we arrange the vectors $|v_1\rangle$ through $|v_n\rangle$ as vectors of a matrix A, we can express $c_1|v_1\rangle + c_2|v_2\rangle + ... + c_n|v_n\rangle = 0$ as follows:

$$
\begin{bmatrix} \uparrow & \uparrow & \uparrow \\ |v_1\rangle & .. & |v_n\rangle \\ \downarrow & \downarrow & \downarrow \end{bmatrix} \begin{bmatrix} c_1 \\ .. \\ c_n \end{bmatrix} = 0
\tag{2-1}
$$

Equation 2-1 should be zero only when the co-efficient vector $[c_1, c_2 .. c_n]^T$ is zero, and this is possible if the matrix formed by taking the column vectors $|v_1\rangle$ through $|v_n\rangle$ is of full rank. A matrix A of dimension $m \times n$ is said to be full rank if its rank is equal to the minimum of m and n. For the matrix in Equation 2-1 to be full rank, its rank has to be n, assuming $m > n$. If the matrix is a square $n \times n$ matrix, we can verify that the matrix is full rank by ensuring the determinant of the matrix is nonzero.

If a set of n vectors $|v_1\rangle, |v_2\rangle, .. |v_n\rangle \in \mathbb{R}^n$ is linearly independent, the vectors span the entire n-dimensional vector space. Spanning the n vectors means the different other vectors can be produced by taking a linear combination of the n vectors. Hence, using a set of n linearly independent vectors, one can produce all possible vectors in $\mathbb{R}^n$. If the vectors $|v_1\rangle, |v_2\rangle, .. |v_n\rangle$ are not linearly independent, then they would span a smaller subspace $\mathbb{R}^k$ within $\mathbb{R}^n$. Let's try to illustrate the concept of the span of vectors with an example.

Suppose we have a vector $|v_1\rangle = [1, 2, 3]^T$. Using this, we can span only one dimension in the three-dimensional space since all the vectors would be of the form $a|v_1\rangle$, where a is a scaler multiplier.

Now if we take another vector $|v_2\rangle = [5\ 9\ 7]^T$ that is not a scaler multiplier of $|v_1\rangle$, we can take linear combinations of the form $a|v_1\rangle + b|v_2\rangle$ to span a two-dimensional subspace in the three-dimensional vector space, as shown in Figure 2-1.

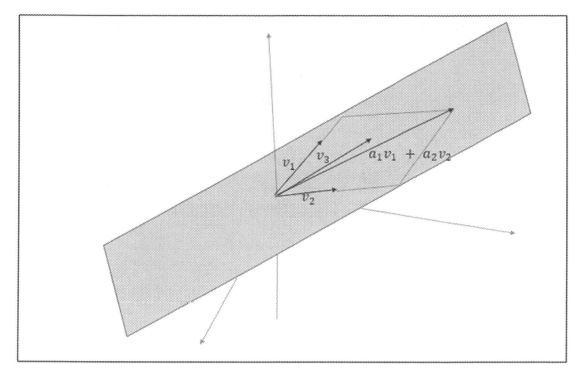

Figure 2-1. *A two-dimensional subspace within a three-dimensional vector space*

Now if we add another vector $|v_3\rangle = [4\ 8\ 1\ ]^T$ to our vector set, we can span the entire $\mathbb{R}^3$ vector space since $|v_1\rangle$, $|\ v_2\rangle$, and $|v_3\rangle$ are linearly independent.

Had we taken $|v_3\rangle$ to be a linear combination of $|v_1\rangle$ and $|v_2\rangle$, then it would not have been possible to span the whole three-dimensional space. We would have been confined to the two-dimensional subspace spanned by $|v_1\rangle$ and $|v_2\rangle$.

Basis Vectors

A set of n linearly independent vectors $|v_1\rangle$, $|v_2\rangle$, . . $|v_n\rangle$ forms the basis for representing any given vector in the n dimensional vector space. Using the linear combination of the n basis vectors once can create any vector in the n-dimensional vector space.

Orthonormal Basis

A vector space is said to have an orthonormal basis when the vector elements in the basis set are orthonormal to each other. A set of basis vectors $|\phi_1\rangle$, $|\phi_2\rangle$...... $|\phi_n\rangle$ are said to form an orthonormal basis if the following holds:

$$\langle\phi_i|\phi_j\rangle = \delta_{ij} \tag{2-2}$$

The term δ_{ij} is called the Kronecker delta, and its properties are as follows:

$$\delta_{ij} = \begin{cases} 0 & if \ \ i \neq j \\ 1 & if \ \ i = j \end{cases} \tag{2-3}$$

We do not need to explicitly cite the linear independence property as a condition for orthonormal basis since the orthonormality of vectors would always ensure the linear independence of the vectors.

In quantum mechanics, we always represent the quantum states in Hilbert spaces with the orthonormal basis.

Linear Operators

A quantum state resides in a complex Hilbert space. A quantum state evolves from one state to the other under the impact of a linear and unitary operator.

A linear operator A is a function that takes a vector $|v\rangle$ in vector space V to a vector $|w\rangle$ in the vector space W and is linear in its inputs. If $|v\rangle = \sum_i a_i|v_i\rangle$, then for a linear operator, we can write:

$$A\sum_i a_i|v_i\rangle = \sum_i a_i\,A|v_i\rangle \tag{2-4}$$

Since any vector can be expressed as a linear sum of its basis vectors, to understand how a linear operator transforms any given vector in a vector space, it is enough to know how the linear operator transforms its basis vectors. When the dimensions of the vector $|v\rangle$ and $|w\rangle$ match, we can think of A as the linear operator from V to V.

The two trivial operators on a vector space are the identity I operator that leaves the vector unchanged and the zero operator that transforms any vector to the zero vector.

If A is a linear operator from vector space V to vector space W and if B is a linear operator from vector space W to vector space Y, then one can define a linear operator BA through composition that maps a vector $|v\rangle \in V$ to a vector $|y\rangle \in Y$, as follows:

$$|y\rangle = BA|v\rangle \qquad (2\text{-}5)$$

Interpretation of a Linear Operator as a Matrix

A vector can be represented in terms of an underlying basis. For instance, when we represent the state of a qubit $|\psi\rangle = \alpha|0\rangle + \beta|1\rangle$ as $\begin{bmatrix} \alpha \\ \beta \end{bmatrix}$, this column vector representation of the qubit is with respect to the basis vectors $|0\rangle$ and $|1\rangle$. Similarly, a matrix represents a linear transformation with respect to two bases: one for the input vector space on which it operates and the other for the space of vectors it outputs on linear transformation. Unless specified, a given matrix denotes a transformation with respect to the usual bases. Suppose we have a linear operator $\hat{A}: V \in \mathbb{R}^n \to W \in \mathbb{R}^m$ and we use a matrix A of dimension $m \times n$ to implement the function of the linear operation. Also, suppose matrix A denotes the transformation with respect to the input and output bases B_1 and B_2, respectively, where B_1 consists of the basis vectors $|\phi_0\rangle, |\phi_1\rangle \ldots |\phi_{n-1}\rangle$ and B_2 consists of the basis vectors $|\omega_0\rangle, |\omega_1\rangle \ldots |\omega_{m-1}\rangle$. We now try to make a connection between each basis vector in B_1 to the basis vectors in B_2. Any basis vector $|\phi_k\rangle$ in its own basis B_1 would be represented as a column vector of all 0s but 1 in the kth row, as shown here:

$$|\phi_k\rangle_{B_1} = \begin{bmatrix} 0 \\ .. \\ 1 \\ .. \\ 0 \end{bmatrix} \leftarrow index\ k \qquad (2\text{-}6)$$

In Equation 2-6, $|\phi_k\rangle_{B_1}$ stands for the representation of $|\phi_k\rangle$ with respect to basis B_1.

So, the transformation of $|\phi_k\rangle$ with respect to basis B_1 would yield the vector $|w\rangle$ with respect to basis B_2 as shown here:

$$|w\rangle_{B_2} = \hat{A}|\phi_k\rangle = A|\phi_k\rangle_{B_1} = A\begin{bmatrix} 0 \\ .. \\ 1 \\ .. \\ 0 \end{bmatrix} = \begin{bmatrix} a_{0k} \\ a_{1k} \\ .. \\ a_{(m-1)k} \end{bmatrix} \qquad (2\text{-}7)$$

Now if we want to expand the vector to the usual basis representation $|w\rangle$, we can do so as shown here:

$$[|w_1\rangle|w_2\rangle \cdot |w_m\rangle]|w\rangle_{B_2} = [|w_1\rangle|w_2\rangle \cdot |w_m\rangle] \begin{bmatrix} a_{0k} \\ a_{1k} \\ .. \\ a_{(m-1)k} \end{bmatrix} = \sum_{i=0}^{m-1} a_{ik}|w_i\rangle \qquad (2\text{-}8)$$

If we combine Equations 2-7 and 2-8, we get the following:

$$\hat{A}|\phi_k\rangle = A|\phi_k\rangle_{B_1} = \sum_{i=0}^{m-1} a_{ik}|w_i\rangle \qquad (2\text{-}9)$$

So, Equation 2-9 captures the relation between the basis element in terms of the linear operator $\hat{A}$ or its corresponding matrix A with respect to the two bases. In general, the linear operator can also be thought of as a matrix with respect to the usual basis. In this book, we would not make any distinction between the linear operator and its corresponding matrix. Unless otherwise specified, the matrix transformation would be with respect to the usual basis. In quantum mechanics, the linear operators are square matrices, and hence a linear operator on vector space V can be thought of as a transformation from V to V. Furthermore, for linear operators of the form $A : V \rightarrow V$, we would assume the usual basis in case nothing is explicitly specified.

Since we have been particular about basis in defining linear operators and their corresponding matrices, let's spend some time learning about the usual basis for qubit states. For a single-qubit system, the usual basis vectors are $|0\rangle = [1\ 0]^T$ and $|1\rangle = [0\ 1]^T$.

Similarly, for a two-qubit system, the usual basis vectors would be the tensor product of the individual qubit usual basis states, i.e. , $|i\rangle \otimes |j\rangle$, where i denotes the usual basis state of qubit 1 and j represents the usual basis state for qubit 2. We can have four such combinations: $|0\rangle \otimes |0\rangle$, $|0\rangle \otimes |1\rangle$, $|1\rangle \otimes |0\rangle$, and $|1\rangle \otimes |1\rangle$. Their column vector representation can be derived by expanding the tensor product. Here's an example: $|1\rangle \otimes |0\rangle = [0\ 1]^T \otimes [1\ 0]^T = [0\ 0\ 1\ 0]^T$. In general, for a n-qubit system there would be 2^n basis state vectors of the form $|k_o\rangle \otimes |k_1\rangle \otimes |k_2\rangle ... \otimes |k_{n-1}\rangle$, where k_i stands for the basis vector of the i-th qubit.

To get the column vector representation of an n-qubit basis state $|k_o\rangle \otimes |k_1\rangle \otimes |k_2\rangle ... \otimes |k_n\rangle$, one can expand the binary string $k_o k_1 k_2 ... k_{n-1}$ into its corresponding decimal number $k = \sum_{i=0}^{n-1} k_{n-1-i} 2^i$ and set the entry corresponding to the k in the column vector of 2^n entries to 1.

Linear Operator in Terms of Outer Product

We can define a linear operator A from a vector space V to W as $|w\rangle\langle v|$ where $|v\rangle \in V$ and $|w\rangle \in W$. Let's see the action of the linear operator A on an arbitrary vector $|v_1\rangle \in V$.

$$A|v_1\rangle = |w\rangle\langle v|v_1\rangle = \langle v|v_1\rangle|w\rangle \qquad (2\text{-}10)$$

From Equation 2-10, the action of the linear operator can be interpreted as taking any vector in vector space V to the scaled version of the vector $|w\rangle \in W$. The scaling is based on how much overlap the arbitrary vector $|v_1\rangle \in V$ has with the vector $|v\rangle \in V$. If $v_1 \perp v$, i.e. , v_1 orthogonal to v_2, then the input vector would be mapped to the zero vector in W.

Another interesting thing to note in Equation 2-10 is that the linear operator A would only project the vectors in one dimension along the vector $|w\rangle$. This essentially means that the rank of the linear operator A is 1.

Suppose the dimension of vector space V is m and that of vector space W is n. Also suppose $m \geq n$. We can define a linear operator $B : V \to W$ to produce vectors that spans the entire W as shown here:

$$B = \sum_{i=0}^{n-1}|w_i\rangle \langle v_i| \qquad (2\text{-}11)$$

The vectors $|w_i\rangle \in W$ and the vectors $|v_i\rangle \in V$ are chosen to be linearly independent. Now if we take any arbitrary vector $|v_k\rangle \in V$, the action on it by the linear operator B can be written as follows:

$$B|v_k\rangle = \sum_{i=0}^{n-1}|w_i\rangle\langle v_i|v_k\rangle = \sum_{i=0}^{n-1}\langle v_i|v_k\rangle|w_i\rangle \qquad (2\text{-}12)$$

The term $\langle v_i|v_k\rangle$ denotes the overlap of the input vector $|v_k\rangle$ with each of the vectors $|v_i\rangle \in V$, and the final output vector representation is a linear sum of the vectors $|w_i\rangle$ that spans the entire vector space W.

If we have the orthonormal basis vector set, $|\phi_1\rangle, |\phi_2\rangle, ... |\phi_n\rangle$, the sum of their individual outer products will give the identity matrix shown here:

$$\sum_{i=0}^{n-1}|\phi_i\rangle\langle\phi_i| = I_{n\times n} \qquad (2\text{-}13)$$

Equation 2-13 is known as the *completeness relation.*

Pauli Operators and Their Outer Product Representation

We briefly touched upon the Pauli matrices in Chapter 1. The four Pauli matrices are linear operators with respect to the computational basis $|0\rangle$ and $|1\rangle$.

We can represent each of the Pauli matrices in terms of outer product representation. The four Pauli Matrices are as shown here:

$$\sigma_0 = I = \begin{bmatrix} 1 & 0 \\ 0 & 1 \end{bmatrix}$$

$$\sigma_x = X = \begin{bmatrix} 0 & 1 \\ 1 & 0 \end{bmatrix}$$

$$\sigma_y = Y = \begin{bmatrix} 0 & -i \\ i & 0 \end{bmatrix}$$

$$\sigma_z = Z = \begin{bmatrix} 1 & 0 \\ 0 & -1 \end{bmatrix} \tag{2-14}$$

The easiest way to represent the Pauli matrices as outer products is to determine the transformation of the computational basis state vectors when operated on by the Pauli matrices. For instance, if we take the Pauli matrix σ_z, it transforms the basis state $|0\rangle$ to $|0\rangle$ and the basis state $|1\rangle$ to $-|1\rangle$. So, as per Equation 2-11, we can write the following:

$$\sigma_z = |0\rangle\langle 0| - |1\rangle\langle 1| \tag{2-15}$$

Following the same procedure, we can express the other Pauli matrices in outer product form, as shown here:

$$\sigma_0 = I = |0\rangle\langle 0| + |1\rangle\langle 1|$$

$$\sigma_y = i|0\rangle\langle 1| - i|1\rangle\langle 0|$$

$$\sigma_x = |0\rangle\langle 1| + |1\rangle\langle 0| \tag{2-16}$$

Eigenvectors and Eigenvalues of a Linear Operator

The eigenvector of a linear operator A on a vector space V is a vector $|v\rangle$ such that $A|v\rangle = \lambda|v\rangle$. Here, λ is the eigenvalue, and $|v\rangle$ is the eigenvector corresponding to the eigenvalue λ. Figure 2-2 shows the transformation of an eigenvector.

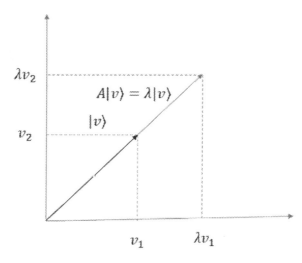

Figure 2-2. *Eigenvector and eigenvalue*

One can find the eigenvalues for a linear operator A by solving for its characteristic equation given by $\det|A - \lambda I| = 0$. The characteristic function corresponding to the characteristic equation of the linear operator A is defined as $c(\lambda) = \det|A - \lambda I|$. The characteristics equation comes in naturally from the eigenvector equation, as shown here:

$$A|v\rangle = \lambda|v\rangle \rightarrow (A - \lambda I)|v\rangle = 0 \qquad (2\text{-}17)$$

Equation 2-17 can have two solutions, with the trivial one being $|v\rangle = 0$. The more interesting solution, however, is when the column vectors of $(A - \lambda I)$ are not linearly independent. The matrix $(A - \lambda I)$ in such cases in not full rank, and hence its determinant $det(A - \lambda I)$ should be zero. This gives us the famous characteristics equation for the eigenvalue solution as follows:

$$det(A - \lambda I) = 0 \qquad (2\text{-}18)$$

The eigenvalues obtained by solving the characteristic equation are substituted in $A|v\rangle = \lambda|v\rangle$ to find the corresponding eigenvector.

Diagonal Representation of an Operator

If the eigenvectors of the operator A denoted by $|k\rangle$ are orthonormal and their corresponding eigenvalues are represented by λ_k, then the operator A can be expressed as follows:

$$A = \sum_k \lambda_k |k\rangle\langle k| \tag{2-19}$$

This representation is called a *diagonal representation* of an operator. The matrix corresponding to operator A would be diagonal if the operator is represented in a diagonal matrix form with respect to the eigenvectors as the basis. Not all matrices or operators have a diagonal representation. The linear operator A illustrated here has a diagonal representation with respect to the usual computation basis:

$$A = \begin{bmatrix} 3 & 0 \\ 0 & 4 \end{bmatrix} = 3 \times |0\rangle\langle 0| + 4|1\rangle\langle 1| \tag{2-20}$$

The eigenvectors in this case are $|0\rangle$ and $|1\rangle$ corresponding to the eigenvalues 3 and 4.

Let's take another operator whose representation with respect to the usual basis is given by the Pauli matrix σ_x.

$$\sigma_x = \begin{bmatrix} 0 & 1 \\ 1 & 0 \end{bmatrix} \tag{2-21}$$

The eigenvalues of the matrix on solving for $\det\left|\begin{bmatrix} 0 & 1 \\ 1 & 0 \end{bmatrix} - \lambda I\right| = 0,$ which gives us

eigenvalues $\lambda_1 = 1$ and $\lambda_2 = -1$. The eigenvector corresponding to $\lambda_1 = 1$ is $|\lambda_1\rangle = \begin{bmatrix} \frac{1}{\sqrt{2}} & \frac{1}{\sqrt{2}} \end{bmatrix}^T$

and that corresponding to $\lambda_2 = -1$ is $|\lambda_2\rangle = \begin{bmatrix} \frac{1}{\sqrt{2}} & -\frac{1}{\sqrt{2}} \end{bmatrix}^T$. Further, the eigenvectors are

orthonormal to each other. This Pauli matrix σ_x itself is not diagonal; however, it can be represented as the diagonal matrix with respect to the basis vectors $|\lambda_1\rangle$ and $|\lambda_2\rangle$. The corresponding matrix representation for the same is as follows:

$$\begin{bmatrix} \lambda_1 & 0 \\ 0 & \lambda_2 \end{bmatrix} = \begin{bmatrix} 1 & 0 \\ 0 & -1 \end{bmatrix} \tag{2-22}$$

The diagonal matrix essentially has the eigenvalues as its diagonal.

Adjoint of an Operator

The adjoint $A^\dagger$ of an operator A in a Hilbert space V is another operator such that for any two vectors $|v_1\rangle$, $|v_2\rangle \in V$, the following relation holds true:

$$\langle v_1,\ Av_2 \rangle = \langle A^\dagger v_1,\ v_2 \rangle \tag{2-23}$$

The adjoint operator also goes by the name *Hermitian conjugate operator*. In Chapter 1, we referred to an adjoint operator as the conjugate transpose of the operator since that is what it precisely is if we refer to the matrix notation of the operator. The conjugate transpose of a vector $|v\rangle$ that we denote as $\langle v|$ can also be expressed in the adjoint notation as $|v\rangle^\dagger$.

A few properties of the adjoint operator are outlined here:

- For two linear operators A and B, $(AB)^\dagger = B^\dagger A^\dagger$.

- The adjoint of an adjoint of an operator gives back the same operator. In other words, $(A^\dagger)^\dagger = A$.

- In general, the operator A and its adjoint $A^\dagger$ are not equal. Similarly, in general, the operator A and its adjoint do not commute; i.e., $AA^\dagger$ does not equal $A^\dagger A$ in general.

Self-Adjoint or Hermitian Operators

When an operator A equals its adjoint, i.e., $A = A^\dagger$, then the operator is said to be a *self-adjoint* or *Hermitian operator*. A few relevant properties of a Hermitian operator are as follows:

- A Hermitian operator always has real eigenvalues.

- For a Hermitian operator that is not a degenerate i.e. each eigenvalue corresponds to only one eigenvector, the eigenvectors of the Hermitian operator are orthogonal to each other.

The following matrix A is an example of Hermitian operator:

$$A = \begin{bmatrix} 1 & 3-4i \\ 3+4i & 2 \end{bmatrix} \tag{2-24}$$

Normal Operators

A linear operator A is said to be normal if it commutes with its adjoint $A^\dagger$. So, for a normal operator, $AA^\dagger = A^\dagger A$. A few important properties of a normal operator are outlined here:

- Hermitian operator A is naturally a normal operator since for Hermitian operators $A = A^\dagger$, and hence the relation $AA^\dagger = A^\dagger A$ would always be true. However, a normal operator need not be Hermitian.

- The normal operators admit a *spectral decomposition*. In the spectral decomposition form, one can represent a normal operator A as $\sum_{i=0}^{n-1} \lambda_k |k\rangle \langle k|$ where λ_k stands for the eigenvalue corresponding to the eigenvector $|k\rangle$. We will look at spectral decomposition in further detail in the subsequent sections.

Unitary Operators

We discussed unitary operators in detail in Chapter 1 since all transformations allowed on the state of a quantum system should be unitary in nature. For any unitary operator U, we know $UU^\dagger = U^\dagger U = I$, which automatically satisfied the condition for normal operators: $UU^\dagger - U^\dagger U = 0$. Hence, all unitary operators are normal operators.

So, the family of normal operators houses both Hermitian and unitary operators, as illustrated in Figure 2-1. Also, several unitary operators can be Hermitian, and vice versa. For instance, the Hadamard matrix is both unitary and Hermitian.

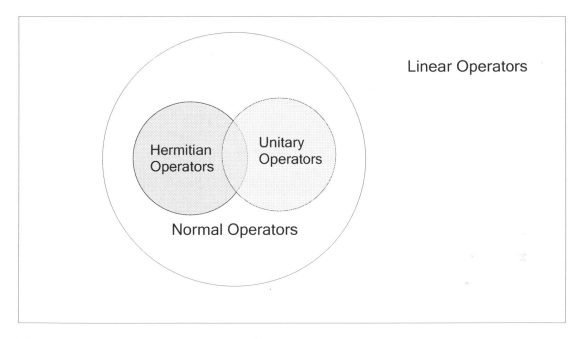

Figure 2-3. *Linear operator Venn diagram*

Spectral Decomposition of Linear Operators

Any normal matrix A can be written in the diagonal representation, as shown here:

$$A = \sum_k \lambda_k |\lambda_k\rangle\langle\lambda_k| \qquad (2\text{-}25)$$

This is called the *spectral decomposition* of a linear operator where the eigenvalues and the corresponding eigenvectors of the normal operator are by λ_k and $|k\rangle$, respectively. The Hadamard gate that we used extensively in Chapter 1 is a normal operator. Just to refresh your memory, the matrix representation of the Hadamard operator is given by $H = \dfrac{1}{\sqrt{2}}\begin{bmatrix} 1 & 1 \\ 1 & -1 \end{bmatrix}$.

The eigenvalues of H are $\lambda_1 = 1$ and $\lambda_2 = -1$. The corresponding eigen vectors are

$$|\lambda_1\rangle = \begin{bmatrix} \dfrac{1}{\sqrt{4-2\sqrt{2}}} \\ \dfrac{1}{\sqrt{2\sqrt{2}}} \end{bmatrix} \text{ and } |\lambda_2\rangle = \begin{bmatrix} \dfrac{1}{\sqrt{4+2\sqrt{2}}} \\ -\dfrac{1}{\sqrt{2\sqrt{2}}} \end{bmatrix}.$$

The eigenvectors are orthogonal to each other as can be verified by the fact that their inner product is zero (see below):

$$\langle \lambda_1 | \lambda \rangle_2 = \left[\frac{1}{\sqrt{4-2\sqrt{2}}} \quad \frac{1}{\sqrt{2\sqrt{2}}} \right]^T \left[\frac{1}{\sqrt{4+2\sqrt{2}}} \quad -\frac{1}{\sqrt{2\sqrt{2}}} \right] = 0 \qquad (2\text{-}26)$$

The spectral decomposition representation does give back the Hadamard operator, as illustrated here:

$$\lambda_1 | \lambda_1 \rangle \langle \lambda_1 | + \lambda_2 | \lambda_2 \rangle \langle \lambda_2 |$$

$$= \begin{bmatrix} \dfrac{1}{\sqrt{4-2\sqrt{2}}} \\[2ex] \dfrac{1}{\sqrt{2\sqrt{2}}} \end{bmatrix} \left[\frac{1}{\sqrt{4-2\sqrt{2}}} \quad \frac{1}{\sqrt{2\sqrt{2}}} \right] - \begin{bmatrix} \dfrac{1}{\sqrt{4+2\sqrt{2}}} \\[2ex] -\dfrac{1}{\sqrt{2\sqrt{2}}} \end{bmatrix} \left[\frac{1}{\sqrt{4+2\sqrt{2}}} \quad -\frac{1}{\sqrt{2\sqrt{2}}} \right]$$

$$= \frac{1}{\sqrt{2}} \begin{bmatrix} 1 & 1 \\ 1 & -1 \end{bmatrix} \qquad (2\text{-}27)$$

Trace of Linear Operators

The trace of a linear operator can be defined as the sum of its diagonal entries. A few properties of the trace of matrices are as follows:

- The sum of the eigenvalues of a linear operator equals the trace of an operator.

- If $|u\rangle$ and $|v\rangle$ are two vectors in vector space V and A is an operator on V, then we have this:

$$\langle v|A|u \rangle = trace(A|u\rangle\langle v|) \qquad (2\text{-}28)$$

The previous property for the trace of a linear operator would come in handy in quantum computing, as we will see throughout the book.

- For two linear operators A and B:

$$trace(AB) = trace(BA) \qquad (2\text{-}29)$$

- For two linear operators A and B:

$$trace(A+B) = trace(A) + trace(B) \tag{2-30}$$

- For a linear operator A and a constant $k \in \mathbb{C}$:

$$trace(cA) = c \times trace(A) \tag{2-31}$$

- The trace of a linear operator is invariant to a unitary similarity transform:

$$trace(UAU^{\dagger}) = trace(A) \tag{2-32}$$

Linear Operators on a Tensor Product of Vectors

If A and B are linear operators on vectors $|v\rangle$ and $|w\rangle$ in vector spaces V and W, respectively, then the linear operator on the vector $|v\rangle \otimes |w\rangle$ is given by $A \otimes B$.

The linear operator $A \otimes B$ works on $|v\rangle \otimes |w\rangle$ as follows:

$$A \otimes B|v\rangle \otimes |w\rangle = A|v\rangle \otimes B|w\rangle \tag{2-33}$$

So, $A \otimes B$ be can be thought of a linear operator on the tensor product of vector spaces V and W given by $V \otimes W$.

For any two vectors $|v\rangle \in \mathbb{R}^m$ and $|w\rangle \in \mathbb{R}^n$, as we have discussed, we compute their tensor product as follows:

$$|v\rangle \otimes |w\rangle = \begin{bmatrix} v_1 \\ v_2 \\ . \\ . \\ v_m \end{bmatrix} \otimes \begin{bmatrix} w_1 \\ w_2 \\ . \\ . \\ w_n \end{bmatrix} = \begin{bmatrix} v_1|w\rangle \\ v_2|w\rangle \\ \cdots \\ v_m|w\rangle \end{bmatrix} \tag{2-34}$$

For instance, for $|v\rangle = \begin{bmatrix} 1 \\ 2 \end{bmatrix}$ and $|w\rangle = \begin{bmatrix} 3 \\ 4 \\ 5 \end{bmatrix}$, their tensor product is given as follows:

$$|v\rangle \otimes |w\rangle = \begin{bmatrix} 1 \\ 2 \end{bmatrix} \otimes \begin{bmatrix} 3 \\ 4 \\ 5 \end{bmatrix} = \begin{bmatrix} 1 \begin{bmatrix} 3 \\ 4 \\ 5 \end{bmatrix} \\ 2 \begin{bmatrix} 3 \\ 4 \\ 5 \end{bmatrix} \end{bmatrix} = \begin{bmatrix} 3 \\ 4 \\ 5 \\ 6 \\ 8 \\ 10 \end{bmatrix} \tag{2-35}$$

Similarly, the tensor product of two matrices A of dimension $m \times n$ and B of dimension $p \times q$ can be written as follows:

$$A \otimes B = \begin{bmatrix} a_{11}B & \cdots & a_{1n}B \\ \vdots & \ddots & \vdots \\ a_{m1}B & \cdots & a_{mn}B \end{bmatrix} \tag{2-36}$$

To illustrate the tensor product of two matrices, let's take the Pauli matrices X and Y and work through their tensor product based on Equation 2-36.

$$X \otimes Y = \begin{bmatrix} 0 & 1 \\ 1 & 0 \end{bmatrix} \otimes \begin{bmatrix} 0 & -i \\ i & 0 \end{bmatrix}$$

$$= \begin{bmatrix} 0 \begin{bmatrix} 0 & -i \\ i & 0 \end{bmatrix} & 1 \begin{bmatrix} 0 & -i \\ i & 0 \end{bmatrix} \\ 1 \begin{bmatrix} 0 & -i \\ i & 0 \end{bmatrix} & 0 \begin{bmatrix} 0 & -i \\ i & 0 \end{bmatrix} \end{bmatrix}$$

$$= \begin{bmatrix} 0 & 0 & 0 & -i \\ 0 & 0 & i & 0 \\ 0 & -i & 0 & 0 \\ i & 0 & 0 & 0 \end{bmatrix} \tag{2-37}$$

A few properties of a tensor product of two linear operators A and B are as follows:

- The complex conjugation of $A \otimes B$ is given by $(A \otimes B)^* = A^* \otimes B^*$.

- The transpose of $A \otimes B$ is given by $(A \otimes B)^T = A^T \otimes B^T$.

- The complex conjugation or adjoint of $A \otimes B$ is given by $(A \otimes B)^\dagger = A^\dagger \otimes B^\dagger$.

Functions of Normal Operators

Any normal operator A can be represented in terms of its spectral decomposition as $A = \sum_i \lambda_i |\lambda_i\rangle \langle\lambda_i|$ where λ_i represents the eigenvalues and $|\lambda_i\rangle$ represents the corresponding eigen vectors. So, an arbitrary function f on A can be defined to be working on its eigenvalues, as shown here:

$$f(A) = \sum_i f(\lambda_i) |\lambda_i\rangle \langle\lambda_i| \tag{2-38}$$

The exponential function is of utmost importance in quantum mechanics, as we will see in the postulates of quantum mechanics later in this chapter. We can define the exponential function on a normal operator A as follows, where $c \in \mathbb{C}$ is any arbitrary constant. As per Equation 2-38, we can write $\exp(cA)$ as follows:

$$\exp(cA) = \sum_i e^{c\lambda_i} |\lambda_i\rangle \langle\lambda_i| \tag{2-39}$$

Another way to define an exponential function on a linear operator in general without any assumption for normal operators is to write down its exponential expansion as follows:

$$\exp(cA) = I + cA + \frac{(cA)^2}{2!} + \frac{(cA)^3}{3!} + \dots \tag{2-40}$$

Now if we take A to be a normal operator such that $A = \sum_i \lambda_i |\lambda_i\rangle \langle\lambda_i|$, we can write the following:

$$cA = \sum_i c\lambda_i |\lambda_i\rangle \langle\lambda_i| \tag{2-41}$$

Squaring cA from Equation 2-41, we get the following:

$$\left(cA\right)^2 = c^2 AA = \sum_i c\lambda_i |\lambda_i\rangle\langle\lambda_i| \sum_j c\lambda_j |\lambda_j\rangle\langle\lambda_j|$$

$$= \sum_i \sum_j c^2 \lambda_i \lambda_j |\lambda_i\rangle\langle\lambda_i|\lambda_j\rangle\langle\lambda_j| \tag{2-42}$$

Since the eigenvectors of a normal operator are orthogonal to each other for each outer index i, the dot product $\langle\lambda_i|\lambda_j\rangle$ would be nonzero only when j equals i. Assuming the eigenvectors are chosen to be orthonormal, Equation 2-42 simplifies to the following:

$$\left(cA\right)^2 = \sum_i \sum_j c^2 \lambda_i \lambda_j |\lambda_i\rangle\langle\lambda_i|\lambda_j\rangle\langle\lambda_j| = \sum_i c^2 \lambda_i^2 |\lambda_i\rangle\langle\lambda_i| \tag{2-43}$$

Expanding higher-order terms by using the same procedure one can see for any order k, we have this:

$$\left(cA\right)^k = \left(c\lambda_i\right)^k |\lambda_i\rangle\langle\lambda_i| \tag{2-44}$$

Using Equation 2-43, we can express Equation 2-40 as follows:

$$\exp\left(cA\right) = I + cA + \frac{\left(cA\right)^2}{2!} + \frac{\left(cA\right)^3}{3!} + \dots$$

$$\exp\left(cA\right) = I + \sum_i c\lambda_i |\lambda_i\rangle\langle\lambda_i| + \frac{c^2 \lambda_i^2 |\lambda_i\rangle\langle\lambda_i|}{2!} + .. + \frac{c^k \lambda_i^k |\lambda_i\rangle\langle\lambda_i|}{k!} + ..$$

$$= \sum_i \left(1 + c\lambda_i + \frac{c^2 \lambda_i^2}{2!} + .. + \frac{c^k \lambda_i^k}{k!} + ..\right) |\lambda_i\rangle\langle\lambda_i|$$

$$= \sum_i e^{c\lambda_i} |\lambda_i\rangle\langle\lambda_i| \tag{2-45}$$

Commutator and Anti-commutator Operators

The commutator operator of two linear operators M and N is as below:

$$[M,\, N] = MN - NM \tag{2-46}$$

For two operators that commute, the commutator operator is zero. If two operators commute, they can be simultaneously diagonalized.

The anti-commutator operator of two linear operators M and N looks like this:

$$\{M, N\} = MN + NM \tag{2-47}$$

The product of two matrices M and N can be expressed as a sum of the commutator and anti-commutator operators, as shown here:

$$MN = [M, N] + \{M, N\} \tag{2-48}$$

Postulates of Quantum Mechanics

In this section, we will go through the basic postulates of quantum mechanics. These postulates act as a bridge between the physical quantum world and the mathematical formulism of quantum mechanics.

Postulate 1: Quantum State

The state of a quantum system is represented by a vector $|\psi\rangle$ in the complex Hilbert space. A Hilbert space is complete vector space equipped with the norm induced by the inner product.

- The state vector $|\psi\rangle$ contains all the information about the quantum system at a given time.

- The state vector is a unit vector, and hence the norm of the state vector is 1; i.e., $\langle\psi|\psi\rangle^{\frac{1}{2}} = 1$.

- Based on the basis we chose, the states can represent different physical observables. For instance, we can look at the qubit state with respect to the $|0\rangle$ and $|1\rangle$ computational basis states and represent the qubit as $|\psi\rangle = \alpha|0\rangle + \beta|1\rangle$. Here α and β are the probability amplitudes corresponding to the states $|0\rangle$ and $|1\rangle$, and the qubit is in a superposition of the $|0\rangle$ and $|1\rangle$. For a spin electron qubit, the states 0 and 1 correspond to the $+\frac{1}{2}$ and $-\frac{1}{2}$ spin states. So, $|\alpha|^2$ denotes the probability of the electron in the $+\frac{1}{2}$ spin state, while $|\beta|^2$ denotes its probability of the electron in the $-\frac{1}{2}$ state. Similarly, we can express the qubit state $|\psi\rangle$ in the $|+\rangle$ and $|-\rangle$ basis as $|\psi\rangle = \gamma|+\rangle + \eta |-\rangle$, where $|\gamma|^2$ and $|\eta|^2$ denote the probability of the qubit in $|+\rangle$ and $|-\rangle$ state, respectively.

Postulate 2: Quantum Evolution

The state of a closed quantum system evolves under the influence of unitary operators. The state evolution of a quantum system from time t_0 to t_1 can be written as follows:

$$|\psi(t_1)\rangle = U(t_1, t_0)|\psi(t_0)\rangle \tag{2-49}$$

In Equation 2-49, $U(t_1, t_0)$ is the unitary operator that takes the quantum system from the state $|\psi(t_o)\rangle$ to $|\psi(t_1)\rangle$.

Schrodinger Equation for Time Evolution of Quantum State

Let's try to look at how the unitary operator $U(t_1, t_0)$ relates to one of the most important equations of quantum mechanics: the Schrodinger's equation.

As per Schrodinger's equation, the quantum state of a closed system evolves as per the following equation:

$$i\hbar\frac{d|\psi(t)\rangle}{dt} = H|\psi(t)\rangle \tag{2-50}$$

In the previous equation, $\hbar$ is the normalized Plank's constant and is equal to $\frac{h}{2\pi}$, where h is the Plank's constant. The term H here refers to the Hamiltonian of the closed quantum system and is not to be confused with the Hadamard transform. The Hamiltonian is a Hermitian operator and hence has a spectral decomposition as follows:

$$H = \sum_k E_k|E_k\rangle\langle E_k| \tag{2-51}$$

The eigenvalues are intentionally represented as E_k to denote energy. We denote the corresponding eigenstates by $|E_k\rangle$. A quantum system in the lowest energy state would be in the eigenstate $|E_{min}\rangle$ corresponding to the minimum energy eigenvalue E_{min}. Since the Hamiltonian is a Hermitian operator, we can only have real energy levels.

The solution to Schrodinger's equation is given by the following:

$$|\psi(t_1)\rangle = e^{\frac{-iH(t_1-t_0)}{\hbar}}|\psi(t_0)\rangle \qquad (2\text{-}52)$$

The expression $e^{\frac{-iH(t_1-t_0)}{\hbar}}$ is the unitary operator that takes a quantum system with the Hamiltonian H from state $|\psi(t_0)\rangle$ at time t_0 to $|\psi(t_1)\rangle$ at time t_1. It is precisely the unitary operator $U(t_1, t_0)$ in Equation 2-49, and hence we can say the following:

$$U(t_1, t_0) = e^{\frac{-iH(t_1-t_0)}{\hbar}} \qquad (2\text{-}53)$$

Some of the properties of the unitary evolution operator are as follows:

- If the spectral decomposition of the Hamiltonian operator is $H = \sum_i E_i |E_i\rangle \langle E_i|,$ then the spectral decomposition of $U(t_1, t_0)$ is as follows:

$$U(t_1, t_0) = \sum_k e^{\frac{-iE_k(t_1-t_0)}{\hbar}} |E_k\rangle\langle E_k| \qquad (2\text{-}54)$$

Basically, $U(t_1, t_0)$ has the same eigenvectors $|E_k\rangle$ as H with the eigenvalues $e^{\frac{-iE_k(t_1-t_0)}{\hbar}}$ being the exponentiated version of the Hamiltonian eigenvalues E_k.

Postulate 3: Quantum Measurement

We established earlier that we can express the state in terms of a suitable orthogonal basis that represents certain measurable physical quantities. The state $|\psi\rangle$ in general can be expressed as a superposition of these orthogonal basis states. If we try to measure the state of the qubit in the $|0\rangle$ and $|1\rangle$ basis state given the qubit is $|\psi\rangle = \alpha|0\rangle + \beta|1\rangle$, the measurement would yield one of the states 0 or 1.

- The probability that the measurement yields the state 0 is $|\alpha|^2$, while that of state 1 is $|\beta|^2$.

- The post-measurement state of the qubit is the basis state measured. For instance, if we measure the qubit state as $|0\rangle$ again, we will get the same state of $|0\rangle$.

When we make a measurement, the quantum system is no longer closed since it interacts with the measurement process. Hence, on measurement, the quantum state no longer evolves under the Schrodinger equation.

General Measurement Operators

Measurements of a quantum state $|\psi\rangle$ are defined in terms of the collection of measurement operators $\{M_k\} = M_0, M_1...M_{m-1}$. These measurement operators work on the state $|\psi\rangle$ of the system being measured. The measurement operators for the outcome k is defined by the operator M_k, and the probability of measuring the outcome as k is given by the following:

$$P(k) = \langle\psi|M_k^\dagger M_k|\psi\rangle \tag{2-55}$$

The state of the quantum system after the measurement of the outcome k is given by the following:

$$\frac{M_k|\psi\rangle}{\langle\psi|M_k^\dagger M_k|\psi\rangle^{\frac{1}{2}}} \tag{2-56}$$

The measurement operators $\{M_k\}$ should satisfy the completeness equation, as shown here:

$$\sum_k M_k^\dagger M_k = I \tag{2-57}$$

This completeness equation comes from the fact that the sum of the probabilities pertaining to the different measurement operators in the set $\{M_k\}$ should sum to 1. The same can be proved by summing over the probabilities of different outcomes illustrated in Equation 2-55.

$$\sum_k P(k) = 1$$

$$\rightarrow \sum_k \langle\psi|M_k^\dagger M_k|\psi\rangle = 1$$

$$\rightarrow \langle\psi|\sum_k M_k^\dagger M_k|\psi\rangle = 1 \tag{2-58}$$

The relation in Equation 2-58 will be satisfied only if $\sum_k M_k^\dagger M_k$ equals the identity matrix I.

So far, we have not made any assumption about the structure of these measurement operators $\{M_k\}$. As long as they satisfy the completeness equation and produce valid positive probability values, they would be valid measurement operators. Now let's look at how you can define these measurement operators when you plan to make measurements of the different computational basis states. If you work with the orthogonal computational basis state $\{|\phi_k\rangle\}$, then you can define the measurement operators as $M_k = |\phi_k\rangle\langle\phi_k|$. It is easy to verify that for a state $|\psi\rangle$ expressed in the computational basis $\{|\phi_k\rangle\}$ as $|\psi\rangle = \sum_k \alpha_k |\phi_k\rangle$ the measurement operators $M_k = |\phi_k\rangle\langle\phi_k|$ produce valid probability and satisfy the completeness equation, as shown in Equations 2-59 and 2-60.

$$\langle\psi|M_k^\dagger M_k|\psi\rangle = \sum_j \alpha_j^* \langle\phi_j|\phi_k\rangle \langle\phi_k|\phi_k\rangle \langle\phi_k|\sum_i \alpha_i|\phi_i\rangle$$

$$= \alpha_k^* \alpha_k \langle\phi_k|\phi_k\rangle\langle\phi_k|\phi_k\rangle = |\alpha_k|^2 \tag{2-59}$$

The measurement operators pertaining to a given orthogonal basis follow the completeness equation, as shown here:

$$\sum_k M_k^\dagger M_k = \sum_k |\phi_k\rangle\langle\phi_k|\phi_k\rangle\langle\phi_k| = \sum_k |\phi_k\rangle\langle\phi_k| = I \tag{2-60}$$

A few important properties of the measurement operators are as follows:

- The measurement operators are Hermitian.

- The measurement operators M_k are idempotent in nature, i.e., $M_k^2 = I$. In fact, for an idempotent matrix, $M_k^N = M_k$, where N is any integer greater than 1. The idempotent property is a desired property for a measurement operator M_k. This is because once the measurement k has been made, the state collapses to the state $|\phi_k\rangle$ pertaining to the outcome k, and hence no matter how many times we measure the system, we should always measure the state $|\phi_k\rangle$.

- Through measurement operators, we can reliably distinguish
  orthonormal states. If we have an orthonormal basis $|\phi_0\rangle, |\phi_1\rangle, \ldots |\phi_{n-1}\rangle$,
  we can define measurement operators of the form $M_k = |\phi_k\rangle\langle\phi_k|$ for
  each of the orthonormal basis vectors. For any given state $|\phi_k\rangle$, only the
  measurement operator state $M_k = |\phi_k\rangle\langle\phi_k|$ would be able to detect it
  with probability 1, as shown here:

$$\left\langle \phi_k \middle| M_k^\dagger M_k \middle| \phi_k \right\rangle = \left\langle \phi_k \middle| \phi_k \right\rangle \left\langle \phi_k \middle| \phi_k \right\rangle \left\langle \phi_k \middle| \phi_k \right\rangle = 1 \tag{2-61}$$

Now let's say the basis set $|\phi_0\rangle, |\phi_1\rangle, \ldots |\phi_{n-1}\rangle$ is nonorthogonal, and we, like before, define the measurement operator $M_k = |\phi_k\rangle\langle\phi_k|$ for detecting outcome k. Now since the states are nonorthogonal, even a basis state other than $|\phi_k\rangle$ denoted by $|\phi_{-k}\rangle$ can have a nonzero overlap with $|\phi_k\rangle$ (i.e., $\langle\phi_{-k}|\phi_k\rangle \neq 1$), and hence the probability of detecting a state other than k by the measurement operator M_k is nonzero.

$$\left\langle \phi_{-k} \middle| M_k^\dagger M_k \middle| \phi_{-k} \right\rangle = \left\langle \phi_{-k} \middle| \phi_k \right\rangle \left\langle \phi_k \middle| \phi_k \right\rangle \left\langle \phi_k \middle| \phi_{-k} \right\rangle \neq 1 \tag{2-62}$$

Projective Measurement Operators

Projective measurements are a way to combine the individual measurement operators $P_0, P_1, \ldots P_{N-1}$ corresponding to the orthogonal basis vectors $|\phi_0\rangle, |\phi_1\rangle, \ldots |\phi_{N-1}\rangle$. A projective measurement operator M is a Hermitian operator that has the representation given by the following:

$$M = \sum_k k P_k \tag{2-63}$$

Note that although the operators $P_0, P_1, \ldots P_{N-1}$ pertaining to the individual basis states are unitary, the projective measurement operator M is not a unitary operator.

Since $P_k = |\phi_k\rangle\langle\phi_k|$, we have $M = \sum_k k|\phi_k\rangle\langle\phi_k|$. The operators P_k can be thought of as projection operators onto the eigenspaces of the operator M with eigenvalues k.

The probability of measuring the outcome k upon measurement of the state $|\psi\rangle$ is given by the following:

$$P(k) = \langle\psi|P_k|\psi\rangle \tag{2-64}$$

The post-measurement state given the outcome m occurs is given by the following:

$$\frac{P_k|\psi\rangle}{\sqrt{P(k)}} \tag{2-65}$$

The individual projector operators P_m are idempotent, i.e., $P_k^2 = P_k$. The idempotent property ensures that if the outcome k occurs on measurement of the state $|\psi\rangle$, then on repeated measurements on the post-measurement state, the same outcome k would be observed. Also, the projector operators follow the completeness equation since the probabilities have to sum to 1, as shown here:

$$\sum_k P(k) = \sum_k \langle\psi|P_k|\psi\rangle = 1$$
$$\rightarrow \langle\psi|\sum_k P_k|\psi\rangle = 1 \tag{2-66}$$

Now for Equation 2-66 to hold true, $\sum_k P_k$ has to be equal to the identity matrix, which gives the completeness equation for projector operators as follows:

$$\sum_k P_k = I \tag{2-67}$$

The projector operators P_k, along with obeying completeness equation and producing valid probabilities, should follow this relation:

$$P_n P_m = \delta_{mn} P_m \tag{2-68}$$

Essentially, Equation 2-68 says the projection operations project the general state vector $|\psi\rangle$ into orthogonal subspaces. This can be easily validated since for $m \neq n$ from Equation 2-68 we have the following:

$$P_n P_m = |\phi_n\rangle\langle\phi_n|\phi_m\rangle\langle\phi_m| = |\phi_n\rangle 0\langle\phi_m| = 0_{N\times N} \tag{2-69}$$

The $0_{N\times N}$ in Equation 2-69 pertains to the $N \times N$ square matrix with all 0 entries. Similarly, when $P_n = P_m$, we have the following:

$$P_m P_m = |\phi_m\rangle\langle\phi_m|\phi_m\rangle\langle\phi_m| = |\phi_m\rangle\langle\phi_m| = P_m \tag{2-70}$$

Hence, from Equation 2-69 and Equation 2-70, we see that the relation in Equation 2-68 holds.

The projective measurement operators are useful in computing statistics properties of the outcomes that can be represented by an orthogonal basis. For instance, we can compute the mean outcome of a quantum system based on its state $|\phi\rangle$ as follows:

$$E[M] = \sum_k kp(k) \tag{2-71}$$

Let's express the quantum state in the measurement basis as $|\psi\rangle = \sum_i c_i |\phi_i\rangle$.

The probability of the outcome k can be expressed as $p(k) = \langle\psi| P_k |\psi\rangle$ since $\langle\psi| P_k |\psi\rangle = \langle\psi|\phi_k\rangle\langle\phi_k|\psi\rangle = c_k^* c_k = |c_k|^2$. Using this information, we can express the expectation of the measurement operator M as follows:

$$E[M] = \sum_k kp(k) = \sum_k k\langle\psi|P_k|\psi\rangle$$

$$= \langle\psi|\sum_k kP_k|\psi\rangle = \langle\psi|M|\psi\rangle \tag{2-72}$$

We generally denote the expectation of the outcome pertaining to a measurement operator M as $\langle M\rangle$.

The standard deviation ΔM can be expressed in terms of the measurement operator M as follows:

$$(\Delta M)^2 = E[M^2] - E[M]^2 = \langle M^2\rangle - \langle M^2\rangle \tag{2-73}$$

The standard deviation of the projective operator M is a measure of the spread of the outcomes if one were to make several identical copies of the quantum state $|\psi\rangle$ and make measurement with respect to the measurement operator M basis vectors. The standard deviation of the projective measurement operators leads to the famous Heisenberg uncertainty principle illustrated in the next section.

General Heisenberg Uncertainty Principle

The Heisenberg uncertainty principle gives a lower bound to the product of the standard deviation of two projective measurement operators, say M and N, given a quantum state $|\psi\rangle$.

Suppose we have two measurement operators M and N and we make multiple copies, say $2n$, of the quantum system in the exact state $|\psi\rangle$. Now if we make n measurements with respect to the operator M and n measurements with respect to the operator N, we will see that the standard deviation of the outcomes of M and N follows this relation:

$$\Delta M \Delta N \geq \frac{1}{2} \|\langle \psi |[M,N]| \psi \rangle\|$$

(2-74)

Equation 2-74 is called the general Heisenberg uncertainty principle.

To prove the Heisenberg uncertainty principle, we will take a mathematical interlude and look at Cauchy–Schwarz inequality. See Figure 2-4.

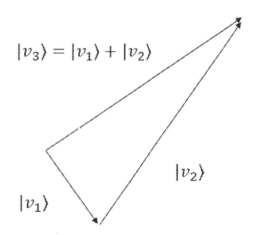

Figure 2-4. *Triangle inequality*

For any two vectors $|v_1\rangle$ and $|v_2\rangle$, the sum of their norms is greater than the norm of their sums. This is popularly referred to as the *triangle inequality*, which states the following:

$$\||v_1\rangle\| + \||v_2\rangle\| \geq \||v_1\rangle + |v_2\rangle\|$$

(2-75)

Now if we square the expression on both sides of the triangle inequality, we get the following:

$$\||v_1\rangle\|^2 + \||v_2\rangle\|^2 + 2\||v_1\rangle\| \||v_2\rangle\| \geq \||v_1\rangle\|^2 + \||v_2\rangle\|^2 + \langle v_1|v_2\rangle + \langle v_2|v_1\rangle$$

(2-76)

Note that the sign of the inequality does not change on squaring since the triangle inequality deals with the norms of vectors on either side and norms are non-negative. Removing the common terms from both sides of the inequality, we are left with the following expression:

$$2\||v_1\rangle\| \||v_2\rangle\| \geq \langle v_1|v_2\rangle + \langle v_2|v_1\rangle$$

(2-77)

Now for any two vectors $|v_1\rangle$ and $|v_2\rangle \in \mathbb{C}^n$ in the n-dimensional complex vector space, we have the following:

$$\langle v_1|v_2\rangle + \langle v_2|v_1\rangle = 2\,Real(\langle v_1|v_2\rangle)$$

$$\rightarrow \left\|\langle v_1|v_2\rangle + \langle v_2|v_1\rangle\right\| = 2\left\|Real(\langle v_1|v_2\rangle)\right\| \tag{2-78}$$

Now the norm of the real part of the complex number is always less than the norm of the complex number, and hence we have this:

$$\left\|\langle v_1|v_2\rangle + \langle v_2|v_1\rangle\right\| = 2\left\|Real(\langle v_1|v_2\rangle)\right\| \le 2\left\|\langle v_1|v_2\rangle\right\|$$

$$\rightarrow \left\|\langle v_1|v_2\rangle + \langle v_2|v_1\rangle\right\| \le 2\left\||v_1\rangle\right\|\,\left\||v_2\rangle\right\|$$

$$\rightarrow 2\left\||v_1\rangle\right\|\,\left\||v_2\rangle\right\| \ge \left\|\langle v_1|v_2\rangle + \langle v_2|v_1\rangle\right\| \tag{2-79}$$

This is the Cauchy–Schwarz inequality for vectors in a complex vector space, which we will work with to prove the Heisenberg uncertainty principle.

To begin with, M and N, being projective measurement operators, are Hermitian. Let's take the two states $|\phi_1\rangle$ and $|\phi_2\rangle$ that are outcomes of applying the projective measurement operators M and iN on the state of the system $|\psi\rangle$ as defined follows:

$$|\phi_1\rangle = M\,|\psi\rangle \tag{2-80}$$

$$|\phi_2\rangle = iN\,|\psi\rangle \tag{2-81}$$

Substituting $|v_1\rangle$ as $|\phi_1\rangle$ and $|v_2\rangle$ as $|\phi_2\rangle$, the left side of the Cauchy–Schwartz can be simplified to the following:

$$2\left\||v_1\rangle\right\|\,\left\||v_2\rangle\right\| = 2\left\||\phi_1\rangle\right\|\,\left\||\phi_2\rangle\right\|$$

$$= 2\langle \phi_1|\phi_1\rangle^{\frac{1}{2}}\langle \phi_2|\phi_2\rangle^{\frac{1}{2}}$$

$$= 2\langle \psi|M^\dagger M|\psi\rangle^{1/2}\langle \psi|-iN^\dagger iN|\psi\rangle$$

$$= 2\langle \psi|M^2|\psi\rangle^{\frac{1}{2}}\langle \psi|N^2|\psi\rangle^{\frac{1}{2}} \tag{2-82}$$

Now $\langle\psi|M^2|\psi\rangle$ and $\langle\psi|N^2|\psi\rangle$ are the expectations of the measurement operators M^2 and N^2 with respect to the state $|\psi\rangle$. Hence, we can write Equation 2-82 in terms of the expectation notation of the measurement operators as follows:

$$2\,\big|\big\||\phi_1\rangle\big\|\,\big\||\phi_2\rangle\big\|\big|=2\langle\psi|M^2|\psi\rangle^{\frac{1}{2}}\langle\psi|N^2|\psi\rangle^{\frac{1}{2}}$$

$$=2\langle M^2\rangle^{\frac{1}{2}}\langle N^2\rangle^{\frac{1}{2}} \tag{2-83}$$

We can substitute $|v_1\rangle$ with $|\phi_1\rangle$ and $|v_2\rangle$ with $|\phi_2\rangle$ on the right side of the Cauchy–Schwartz inequality and get

$$\big\|\langle v_1|v_2\rangle+\langle v_2|v_1\rangle\big\|=\big\|\langle\phi_1|\phi_2\rangle+\langle\phi_2|\phi_1\rangle\big\|$$

$$=\big\|\langle\psi|M^\dagger iN|\psi\rangle+-i\langle\psi|N^\dagger M|\psi\rangle\big\|$$

$$=\big\|i\langle\psi|MN-NM|\psi\rangle\big\|$$

$$=\big\|\langle\psi|MN-NM|\psi\rangle\big\| \tag{2-84}$$

Now $(MN-NM)$ is the commutator operator $[M, N]$, and hence Equation 2-84 can be expressed as follows:

$$\big\|\langle\phi_1|\phi_2\rangle+\langle\phi_2|\phi_1\rangle\big\|=\big\|\langle\psi|[M, N]|\psi\rangle\big\| \tag{2-85}$$

Using Equations 2-83 and 2-85 from Cauchy–Schwartz inequality, we have the following:

$$2\,\big\||\phi_1\rangle\big\|\,\big\||\phi_2\rangle\big\|\geq\big\|\langle\phi_1|\phi_2\rangle+\langle\phi_2|\phi_1\rangle\big\|$$

$$\rightarrow 2\langle M^2\rangle^{\frac{1}{2}}\langle N^2\rangle^{\frac{1}{2}}\geq\big\|\langle\psi|[M, N]|\psi\rangle\big\|$$

$$\rightarrow\langle M^2\rangle^{\frac{1}{2}}\langle N^2\rangle^{\frac{1}{2}}\geq\frac{1}{2}\big\|\langle\psi|[M,N]|\psi\rangle\big\| \tag{2-86}$$

We are close to proving the Heisenberg uncertainty principle at this point. $\langle M^2\rangle^{\frac{1}{2}}$ and $\langle N^2\rangle^{\frac{1}{2}}$ can be thought of as the standard deviation of the operators M and N had their expectation $\langle M\rangle$ and $\langle N\rangle$ been zero. We can replace M and N with $(M-\langle M\rangle)$ and $(N-\langle N\rangle)$, respectively, in Equation 2-86 to express the same thing in terms of the standard deviation of the operators M and N. Doing so, we can rewrite Equation 2-86 as follows:

$$\langle M^2 \rangle^{\frac{1}{2}} \langle N^2 \rangle^{\frac{1}{2}} \geq \frac{1}{2} \| \langle \psi | [M, N] | \psi \rangle \|$$

$$\rightarrow \left\langle \left(M - \langle M \rangle \right)^2 \right\rangle^{\frac{1}{2}} \left\langle \left(N - \langle N \rangle \right)^2 \right\rangle^{\frac{1}{2}} \geq \frac{1}{2} \left\| \left\langle \psi \left[M - \langle M \rangle, N - \langle N \rangle \right] \psi \right\rangle \right\| \qquad (2\text{-}87)$$

The commutator operator $[M - \langle M \rangle, N - \langle N \rangle]$ equals $[M, N]$. If we represent the standard deviation of M, i.e., $\left\langle (M - \langle M \rangle)^2 \right\rangle^{\frac{1}{2}}$, by ΔM and standard deviation of N, i.e., $\left\langle (N - \langle N \rangle)^2 \right\rangle^{\frac{1}{2}}$, by ΔN, then we have the following from Equation 2-87:

$$\Delta M \Delta N \geq \frac{1}{2} \| \langle \psi | [M, N] | \psi \rangle \| \qquad (2\text{-}88)$$

The inequality in Equation 2-88 is the most general version of the Heisenberg uncertainty principle for the two measurement operators M and N. If the operators M and N are chosen to be the position operator $\hat{x}$ and momentum operator $\hat{p}$, then the commutator operator $[\hat{x}, \hat{p}] = \hat{x}\hat{p} - \hat{p}\hat{x} = i\hbar$. Substituting this in Equation 2-88, one can get the Heisenberg uncertainty principle related to position and momentum as follows:

$$\Delta x \Delta p \geq \frac{1}{2} \| \langle \psi | i\hbar | \psi \rangle \|$$

$$\rightarrow \Delta x \Delta p \geq \frac{i\hbar}{2} \qquad (2\text{-}89)$$

Readers interested in learning about quantum mechanics in more detail beyond what is required for quantum computing are encouraged to deduce the relation $[\hat{x}, \hat{p}] = \hat{x}\hat{p} - \hat{p}\hat{x} = i\hbar$.

POVM Operators

The general measurement operators as well as the projective measurement operators not only give a rule for measuring the probability of various outcomes but also give a clear formulation of the post-measurement state. However, in various applications, the post-measurement state is not as important to an experiment; the capability to measure the probabilities of the various outcomes is the only thing that is important. In such cases, the POVM scheme of measurement turns out to be a convenient formulism. We can define a positive operators E_k such that the probability of the outcome of k when the state $|\psi\rangle$ is measured is as follows:

$$P(k) = \langle \psi | E_k | \psi \rangle \tag{2-90}$$

A positive operator A in a Hilbert space V is one that satisfies $\langle \psi | A | \psi \rangle \geq 0$ for every $|\psi\rangle \in V$. Hence, ensuring that the operators E_k are positive would ensure that we have the probabilities represented by $P(k) \geq 0$. If we have N outcomes of interest to us, we would have to build the positive operators E_k in such a way that the completeness equation is satisfied; i.e., $\sum_k E_k = I$. The operators E_k are known as the POVM elements, while the complete set $\{E_k\}$ is known as the POVM. Unlike the projective measurement operators $\{P_k\}$, the POVM operators $\{E_k\}$ do not need to satisfy the relation $E_n E_m = \delta_{mn} E_m$. Hence, the positive measurement operators $\{E_k\}$ are not constrained to only measure outcomes pertaining to an orthonormal set of basis states. Hence, in that sense, POVM is more general than projective measurement operators, and the latter is in fact a special case of the former. Instead of illustrating projective measurement to be a special case of POVM, let's look into the more interesting case where POVM differs from projective measurement. Suppose we want to detect two states that are not necessarily orthogonal. We can take the two states to be $|\psi_1\rangle = |0\rangle$ and $|\psi_2\rangle = \frac{1}{\sqrt{2}}(|0\rangle + |1\rangle)$. Needless to say, it would not be possible for us to measure these two states with full certainty because of the overlap between the states $|\psi_1\rangle$ and $|\psi_2\rangle$. Let's define three POVM elements as follows and see how best we can detect the two events:

$$E_1 = \frac{\sqrt{2}}{\left(1 + \sqrt{2}\right)} |1\rangle \langle 1|$$

$$E_2 = \frac{\sqrt{2}}{\left(1 + \sqrt{2}\right)} (|0\rangle - |1\rangle)(\langle 0| - \langle 1|)$$

$$E_3 = I - E_1 - E_2 \tag{2-91}$$

If the measured state is $|\psi_1\rangle = |0\rangle$, then E_1 would never be observed since it corresponds to the orthogonal state $|1\rangle$. However, if E_1 is detected, we can safely infer that the state being measured has to be the state $|\psi_2\rangle = \frac{1}{\sqrt{2}}(|0\rangle + |1\rangle)$. On similar lines, if E_2 is detected, then it has to be the state $|\psi_1\rangle = |0\rangle$. It cannot be the state

$|\psi_2\rangle = \dfrac{1}{\sqrt{2}}(|0\rangle + |1\rangle)$ since it is orthogonal to $(|0\rangle - |1\rangle)$. When E_3 is detected, we cannot

say anything with certainty about the state being measured. The central point here is that with POVM we never make a mistake of identifying the state we are being presented with to measure. It is just that at times we are not able to determine the actual state we are presented with.

Density Operator

So far we have been using the state vector $|\psi\rangle$ to represent a quantum system. A quantum system can be also expressed in terms of the density operator ρ. For a quantum system that is isolated from its surroundings and is in pure quantum state as we have been studying thus far, the density operator is nothing but the outer product of the state vector $|\psi\rangle$ with itself. Hence, we have this:

$$\rho = |\psi\rangle\langle\psi| \tag{2-92}$$

The trace of the density operator is 1, as illustrated here:

$$trace(\rho) = tr(\psi|\rangle\langle\psi|) = \langle\psi|\psi\rangle = 1 \tag{2-93}$$

Density Operator for Mixed Quantum States

Sometimes it is hard to determine the exact quantum state the quantum system is in. We can have a quantum state in either of the n pure quantum states $|\psi_i\rangle$ with classical probability p_i. In such cases, the density operator comes in handy, and we can define the density operator for such a mixed quantum state system as follows:

$$\rho = \sum_i p_i |\psi_i\rangle\langle\psi_i| \tag{2-94}$$

So, the density operator of the mixed quantum state is nothing but the mean value of the density operators for each of its constituent pure states.

The trace of a density operator for a mixed state is also 1. See the following:

$$tr(\rho) = tr\left(\sum_i p_i |\psi_i\rangle\langle\psi_i|\right) = \sum_i p_i tr(|\psi_i\rangle\langle\psi_i|) = \sum_i p_i tr(\langle\psi_i|\psi_i\rangle) = \sum_i p_i = 1 \tag{2-95}$$

Evolution of the Density Operator for a Mixed Quantum State

For a closed quantum system, the evolution of the state vector is given by $|\psi(t_2)\rangle = U(t_2, t_1)|\psi(t_1)\rangle$. Let's see how the density operator evolves when the system is in a mixed state. Note that in the mixed quantum state the n different possible states $|\psi_i\rangle$ evolve just like pure states. So, if the system were in the state $|\psi_i(t_1)\rangle$ with probability p_i after unitary evolution, it would be in the state $U(t_2, t_1) | \psi_i(t_1)\rangle$ with the same probability p_i. So, the density operator ρ_2 of the mixed state after the unitary evolution can be written as the mean of the density operators of the pure states after unitary evolution, as shown here:

$$\rho_2 = \sum_i p_i U(t_2, t_1)|\psi_i(t_1)\rangle \langle\psi_i(t_1)|U^\dagger(t_2, t_1)$$

$$= U(t_2, t_1)\left(\sum_i p_i|\psi_i(t_1)\rangle \langle\psi_i(t_1)|\right)U^\dagger(t_2, t_1)$$

$$= U(t_2, t_1)\rho_1 U^\dagger(t_2, t_1) \tag{2-96}$$

Measurements with the Density Operator

Suppose we have a measurement operator M_m corresponding to the outcome m. The measurement operator $M_m = | \phi_m\rangle\langle\phi_m|$ corresponds to the basis vector $| \phi_m\rangle$. Given that we know that the quantum system is in the pure state $|\psi_i\rangle$, the probability of the outcome m is given by the conditional probability $P(m/i)$.

$$P(m / i) = \langle\psi_i|M_m^\dagger M_m|\psi_i\rangle \tag{2-97}$$

The probability of the outcome m summed over all the different pure states is given by the following:

$$P(m) = \sum_i P(m/i)P(\psi_i) = \sum_i \langle\psi_i|M_m^\dagger M_m|\psi_i\rangle p_i \tag{2-98}$$

Using the trace trick, we can write $\langle\psi_i|M_m^\dagger M_m|\psi_i\rangle = tr\left(M_m^\dagger M_m|\psi_i\rangle\langle\psi_i|\right)$, which simplifies Equation 2-98 as follows:

$$P(m) = \sum_i tr(M_m^\dagger M_m|\psi_i\rangle\langle\psi_i|)p_i = tr\left(M_m^\dagger M_m \sum_i p_i|\psi_i\rangle\langle\psi_i|\right) = tr\left(M_m^\dagger M_m\rho\right) \tag{2-99}$$

Density Operator Post a Measurement

If we measure the outcome m, then the post-measurement state in each of the pure states indexed by i would be given by the following:

$$|\psi_i^{(m)}\rangle = \frac{M_m|\psi_i\rangle}{\sqrt{\langle\psi_i|M_m^\dagger M_m|\psi_i\rangle}} \qquad (2\text{-}100)$$

The corresponding density operator $\rho_i^{(m)}$ is given by the following:

$$\rho_i^{(m)} = \frac{M_m|\psi_i\rangle\langle\psi_i|M_m^\dagger}{\langle\psi_i|M_m^\dagger M_m|\psi_i\rangle} \qquad (2\text{-}101)$$

The density operator $\rho^{(m)}$ after the measurement of outcome m is the expectation of $\rho_i^{(m)}$ over the conditional distribution of the different pure states given the outcome m, i.e., $P(i/m)$.

$$\rho^{(m)} = \sum_i P(i/m)\rho_i^{(m)} \qquad (2\text{-}102)$$

Now $P(i/m)$ can be calculated as follows using Equations 2-97 and 2-99.

$$P(i/m) = \frac{P(m/i)P(i)}{P(m)} = \frac{\langle\psi_i|M_m^\dagger M_m|\psi_i\rangle p_i}{tr\left(M_m^\dagger M_m \rho\right)} \qquad (2\text{-}103)$$

Substituting $P(i/m)$ from Equation 2-103 and $\rho_i^{(m)}$ from Equation 2-101 in Equation 2-102, we have the following:

$$\rho^{(m)} = \sum_i \frac{\langle\psi_i|M_m^\dagger M_m|\psi_i\rangle p_i}{tr\left(M_m^\dagger M_m \rho\right)} \frac{M_m|\psi_i\rangle\langle\psi_i|M_m^\dagger}{\langle\psi_i|M_m^\dagger M_m|\psi_i\rangle} = \sum_i \frac{M_m p_i|\psi_i\rangle\langle\psi_i|M_m^\dagger}{tr\left(M_m^\dagger M_m \rho\right)}$$

$$= M_m \sum_i \frac{p_i|\psi_i\rangle\langle\psi_i|}{tr\left(M_m^\dagger M_m \rho\right)} M_m^\dagger = \frac{M_m \rho M_m^\dagger}{tr\left(M_m^\dagger M_m \rho\right)} \qquad (2\text{-}104)$$

Mixed State vs. Pure State from Density Operator

We saw in prior sections how mixed states differ from pure states in terms of their representation. However, given a density operator, we can check if it is a pure or mixed state by checking the trace of the square of the density operator. For a pure state, $tr(\rho^2) = 1$, while for a mixed state, $tr(\rho^2) < 1$. Readers are encouraged to do the math to validate this claim.

Joint Density Operator of Multiple Quantum Systems

The density operator ρ of n quantum systems with the density operators $\rho_1, \rho_2 ... \rho_n$ can be expressed as a tensor product, as shown here:

$$\rho = \rho_1 \otimes \rho_2 \otimes ... \otimes \rho_n \tag{2-105}$$

For instance, if we have two qubits with density operators ρ_1 and ρ_2, then the density operator of the system of the two qubit is given by $\rho = \rho_1 \otimes \rho_2$.

Reduced Density Operator

Let's suppose we have two quantum systems A and B and their combined density operator is given by ρ_{AB}. The density operator for system A can be obtained by taking the partial trace over B, as shown here:

$$\rho_A = tr_B \left(\rho_{AB} \right) \tag{2-106}$$

Given a state $\rho_{AB} = |\psi_{A1}\rangle\langle\psi_{A2}| \otimes |\psi_{B1}\rangle\langle\psi_{B2}|$ where $|\psi_{A1}\rangle$ and $|\psi_{A2}\rangle$ are states corresponding to the system A and $|\psi_{B1}\rangle$ and $|\psi_{B2}\rangle$ are states corresponding to system B, the partial trace over B is given by the following:

$$\rho_A = tr_B \left(\rho_{AB} \right) = |\psi_{A1}\rangle\langle\psi_{A2}| tr\left(|\psi_{B1}\rangle\langle\psi_{B2}| \right) \tag{2-107}$$

Partial Trace Over the Bell State

The density operator of the Bell state $|\psi\rangle = \frac{1}{\sqrt{2}}(|00\rangle + |11\rangle)$ is given by the following:

$$\rho_{AB} = \frac{1}{2}(|00\rangle + |11\rangle)(\langle00| + \langle11|) \tag{2-108}$$

On expanding the terms in Equation 2-107, we get the following:

$$\rho_{AB} = \frac{|00\rangle\langle00| + |00\rangle\langle11| + |11\rangle\langle00| + |11\rangle\langle11|}{2} \tag{2-109}$$

We can further simplify each of the four terms and express them as a tensor product of the qubit basic density operators.

$$\rho_{AB} = \frac{1}{2}(|0\rangle_A \langle 0|_A \otimes |0\rangle_B \langle 0|_B + |0\rangle_A \langle 1|_A \otimes |0\rangle_B \langle 1|_B + |1\rangle_A$$
$$\langle 0|_A \otimes |1\rangle_B \langle 0|_B + |1\rangle_A \langle 1|_A \otimes |1\rangle_B \langle 1|_B) \tag{2-110}$$

Now taking the partial trace over the qubit B, we get the following from Equation 2-110:

$$\rho_A = tr(\rho_{AB}) = \frac{1}{2}[|0\rangle_A \langle 0|_A \, tr(|0\rangle_B \langle 0|_B) + |0\rangle_A \langle 1|_A \, tr(|0\rangle_B \langle 1|_B) +$$
$$|1\rangle_A \langle 0|_A \, tr(|1\rangle_B \langle 0|_B) + |1\rangle_A \langle 1|_A \, tr(|1\rangle_B \langle 1|_B)]$$
$$= \frac{1}{2}[|0\rangle_A \langle 0|_A \langle 0|0\rangle_B + |0\rangle_A \langle 1|_A \langle 0|1\rangle_B + |1\rangle_A \langle 0|_A \langle 1|0\rangle_B + |1\rangle_A \langle 1|_A \langle 1|1\rangle_B] \tag{2-111}$$

In Equation 2-111, the second and third terms would vanish since the dot product involves orthogonal basis states of B, which gives us the density operator for A as follows:

$$\rho_A = \frac{1}{2}|0\rangle_A \langle 0|_A + \frac{1}{2}|1\rangle_A \langle 1|_A = \frac{I}{2} \tag{2-112}$$

If we carefully observe the trace of the square of the density operator of A, i.e., ρ_A^2, we see that it is not equal to 1.

$$tr(\rho_A^2) = tr\left(\frac{I}{4}\right) = \frac{1}{4} < 1 \tag{2-113}$$

This implies that the qubit A is in the mixed state. This is an interesting observation since the joint state of the two qubit is in a pure state, while the individual qubits are in a mixed state. This strange behavior is associated with the quantum entanglement phenomenon.

Principle of Deferred Measurement

In many quantum circuits, measurements are often made in the intermediate part of the circuit, and the results of measurement are used to conditionally control subsequent quantum gates. For instance, in Chapter 1, we observed in the quantum teleportation circuit the measurement on Alice's two qubits are used to control the unitary operators on Bob's qubit. Figure 2-5 shows the quantum teleportation circuit for reference, where the first two qubits, Q_1 and Q_2, belong to Alice, while the qubit Q_3 belongs to Bob.

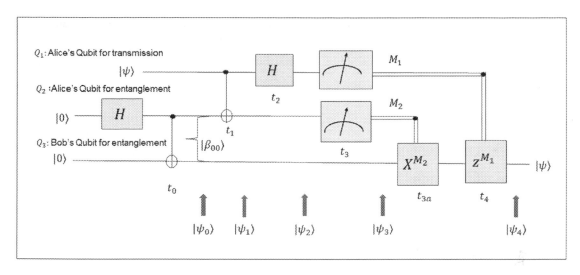

Figure 2-5. *Universal quantum gates set*

The measurement on Alice's qubits yields M_1 and M_2 as the measurement outcomes that control the unitary operations X^{M_2} and Z^{M_1} on Bob's qubits. Both the measurements on Alice's qubits can be moved to the end of the circuit without impacting the outcome, as illustrated in Figure 2-6.

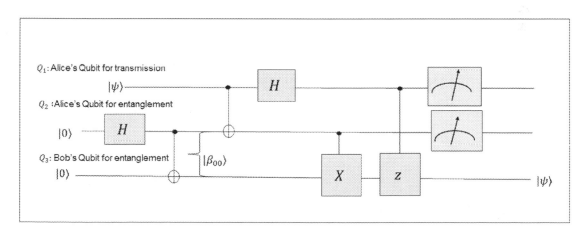

Figure 2-6. *Principle of deferred measurement using quantum teleportation circuit*

In effect, in the quantum teleportation circuit of Figure 2-5, on measurement of Alice's qubits, we get the classical information M_1 and M_2, which is used to conditionally control the unitary operators X and Z applied successively to Bob's qubit. What we have done differently in the quantum teleportation in Figure 2-6 is condition the X and Z operators on Bob's qubit on the quantum information (state) of Alice's qubits followed by the measurement of Alice's qubits to the end of the circuit.

One may say the quantum circuit in Figure 2-5 is much more intuitive and interpretable since it entails the passing of classical information from Alice to Bob; however, the central idea is that both the circuits in Figure 2-5 and Figure 2-6 are *equivalent*. This method of pushing the measurement to the end of the circuit is called the *principle of deferred measurement.*

To summarize the principle of deferred measurement states, the measurements in the intermediate part of the circuit can be moved to the end of the circuit. Also, if the measurements in the intermediate part of the circuit are used to classically control the unitary operations in the other part of the circuit, they can be replaced by conditional quantum operations. A result of the principle of deferred measurement is the fact that measurement commutes with a conditioning operation.

Approximating Unitary Operators

In the classical regime of computing, a small set of gates such as AND, OR, and NOT gates can be used to implement any classical function. Hence, such a set of gates is considered universal for classical computing. In the quantum computing paradigm, a set of gates is considered universal if any given unitary operator can be approximated to arbitrary precision by a quantum circuit consisting of these gates in the universal set. In Chapter 1, we have touched upon CNOT and Hadamard gates while implementing a few of the quantum algorithms. These two gates along with phase and $\frac{\pi}{8}$ gates are considered universal since any unitary gate can be approximated to arbitrary precision using these gates. Figure 2-7 shows the four gates along with their unitary transforms for reference.

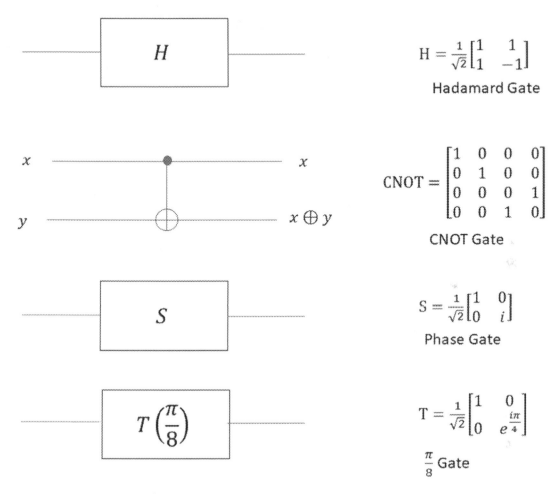

Figure 2-7. *Universal quantum gates set*

Now let's look at what approximating a unitary transform using a discrete set of quantum gates means. Let's take two unitary transforms U and V operating on the same state $|\psi\rangle$ where U is the unitary transform that we want to implement and V is the unitary transform that we are able to implement using the discrete set of gates. We can define the error in approximating U by V as follows:

$$E(U,V) = \max_{|\psi\rangle} \left\| (U-V)|\psi\rangle \right\| \tag{2-114}$$

The error $E(U, V)$, as we can see in Equation 2-114, is the maximum norm of the difference between the desired transformed state and the actual transformed state when V is used as the unitary operator instead of U. One must also pay attention to how the error in the transformation $E(U, V)$ relates to the error when the transformed state is measured. If we have a set of n measurement operators $M_1, M_2, \ldots, M_n$ pertaining to an orthogonal set $|\phi_1\rangle, |\phi_2\rangle, \ldots, |\phi_n\rangle$, then each of the measurement elements M_k gives the probability of measuring the state as $|\phi_k\rangle$. If the desired unitary operator U could have been simulated, then the measurement of the basis $|\phi_k\rangle$ following the transformation of the state $|\psi\rangle$ would have yielded probability $p_k(U)$ as follows:

$$p_k(U) = \langle\psi|U^\dagger M_k U|\psi\rangle \qquad (2\text{-}115)$$

Similarly, instead of U, had we used V as the unitary transform on $|\psi\rangle$ and followed that up with a measurement on the basis state $|\phi_k\rangle$ using the measurement operator M_k, then the probability of measuring the state $|\phi_k\rangle$ can be written as follows:

$$p_k(V) = \langle\psi|V^\dagger M_k V|\psi\rangle \qquad (2\text{-}116)$$

Combining Equations 2-115 and 2-116, the error in the probability of measuring the basis state $|\phi_k\rangle$ can be written as follows:

$$\left\| p_k(U) - p_k(V) \right\| = \left\| \langle\psi|U^\dagger M_k U|\psi\rangle - \langle\psi|V^\dagger M_k V|\psi\rangle \right\| \qquad (2\text{-}117)$$

If we represent the l^2 norm of the difference between the desired transformation $U|\psi\rangle$ and the actual transformation $V|\psi\rangle$ by $|\delta\rangle$, then we have this:

$$|\delta\rangle = (U - V)|\psi\rangle \qquad (2\text{-}118)$$

From Equation 2-118, we get $U|\psi\rangle = |\delta\rangle + V|\psi\rangle$ and $\langle\psi|V^\dagger = \langle\psi|U^\dagger + \langle\delta|$. Using these expressions for $U|\psi\rangle$ and $\langle\psi|V^\dagger$ in Equation 2-117, we have this:

$$\left\| p_k(U) - p_k(V) \right\|$$

$$= \left\| \langle\psi|U^\dagger M_k(|\delta\rangle + V|\psi\rangle) - (\langle\psi|U^\dagger + \langle\delta|)|V^\dagger M_k V|\psi\rangle \right\|$$

$$= \left\| \langle\psi|U^\dagger M_k|\delta\rangle + \langle\delta|M_k V|\psi\rangle \right\| \qquad (2\text{-}119)$$

Using Cauchy–Schwarz inequality on Equation 2-119, we have the following:

$$\|p_k(U) - p_k(V)\| = \|\langle\psi|U^\dagger M_k|\delta\rangle + \langle\delta|M_k V|\psi\rangle\|$$

$$\leq \|\langle\psi|U^\dagger M_k|\delta\rangle\| + \|\langle\delta|M_k V|\psi\rangle\|$$

$$\leq \||\delta\rangle\| + \||\delta\rangle\| \qquad (2\text{-}120)$$

Now the maximum norm of $|\delta\rangle$ is $E(U, V)$, as shown in Equation 2-114. This allows us to bound Equation 2-120 as follows:

$$\| p_k(U) - p_k(V) \| \leq \| |\delta\rangle \| + \| |\delta\rangle \|$$
$$\leq \| |\delta\rangle \| + \| |\delta\rangle \|$$
$$\leq 2E(U,V) \tag{2-121}$$

The inequality in Equation 2-121 tells us that if the error in approximating an operator U by V given by $E(U, V)$ is small, then the difference in measured probability and actual probability is also small. In fact, the norm of the error is upper bounded by the error in approximating U by V, i.e., $2E(U, V)$.

The inequality generalizes to a sequence of n unitary operators $U_1, U_2, ..., U_n$ approximated by a sequence of n unitary operators $V_1, V_2, ..., V_n$. It can be shown through induction that the error associated with the approximation with a sequence of n unitary operations follows this relation:

$$E\left(U_n U_{n-1} ... U_1, V_n, V_{n-1}, ... V_1\right) \leq \sum_{j=1}^{n} E\left(U_j, V_j\right) \tag{2-122}$$

To prove this, let's first prove the relation for a sequence of unitary operators U_1, U_2 approximated by V_1, V_2. The error $E(U_2 U_1, V_2 V_1)$ can be expressed as follows:

$$E\left(U_2 U_1, V_2, V_1\right) = \left\| \left(U_2 U_1 - V_2 V_1\right) |\psi\rangle \right\| \tag{2-123}$$

Adding and subtracting $V_2 U_1 |\psi\rangle$ inside the norm on the right-hand side of the equation and then applying triangle inequality, we have the following:

$$E\left(U_2 U_1, V_2, V_1\right) = \left\| \left(U_2 U_1 - V_2 U_1 + V_2 U_1 - V_2 V_1\right) |\psi\rangle \right\|$$

$$\leq \left\| \left(U_2 - V_2\right) U_1 |\psi\rangle \right\| + \left\| \left(U_1 - V_1\right) V_2 |\psi\rangle \right\| \tag{2-124}$$

Since U_1 and V_2 are unitary operators, their contribution to the norms is 1, and hence we can write Equation 2-124 as follows:

$$E\left(U_2 U_1, V_2, V_1\right) \leq \left\| \left(U_2 - V_2\right) |\psi\rangle \right\| + \left\| \left(U_1 - V_1\right) |\psi\rangle \right\|$$

$$\leq E\left(U_2, V_2\right) + E\left(U_1, V_1\right) \tag{2-125}$$

85

Hence, we see the relation is true for $n = 2$. By induction, we can extend this relation to any arbitrary sequence of unitary operator U_1, U_2..., U_n approximated by V_1, V_2.. V_n.

Solovay–Kitaev Theorem

Whenever we are looking at approximating elements in a space U, we look toward a smaller subset W of elements in that space, which is easy enough to implement. Using the elements from the smaller subset W through composition, we form a space V that is dense in U. In topology, a subset V is said to be a dense subset of U if the closure of V equals the set U. Informally, each element in a dense set V is arbitrarily close to an element in the set U. The best example of a dense set is the set of rational numbers denoted by $\mathbb{Q}$ as a subset of the real line denoted by $\mathbb{R}$. Each real number either is a rational number or is arbitrarily close to one. A dense subset V of U can be useful in representing the elements of U with arbitrary precision using the elements of V. For instance, classical computers can work only with rational numbers because of the binary representation of bits. However, since rational numbers form a dense subset of real line $\mathbb{R}$, we can approximate a real irrational number with high precision. Similarly, in the case of quantum computing, the set of possible gates form a continuum, and it is not always possible to construct a gate exactly with elements from $SU(d)$.

Let $SU(d)$ denote the group of unitary operators in the d-dimensional Hilbert state space.

The Solovay–Kitaev states that if $V \subseteq SU(d)$ is a universal family of gates closed under inverse (i.e., if $X \in V$, then $X^{-1} \in V$) and V generates a dense subset of $SU(d)$, then for all $U \in SU(d)$, $\epsilon > 0$, there exists elements v_1, $v_2...v_k \in V$ such that $\|U - U_{v_1} U_{v_2} ... U_{v_k}\| \leq \epsilon$ and $k = O\left(\log^2 \frac{1}{\epsilon}\right)$. Hence, the Solovay–Kitaev theorem gives an estimate for the approximate number of gates required from the universal set V (or which are the functions of the elements of the universal set V) based on the acceptable error ϵ. The lower the acceptable error in approximating a unitary operator, the larger the number of gates from the universal set required to build such a unitary gate.

ERP Paradox, Local Realism, and Bell's Inequality

In the classical world, whenever we think of any object, we assume that the physical properties of the object exist irrespective of whether we observe it or not. Any measurement on such an object merely reveals the physical properties. However, as per quantum mechanics, an object does not have any physical properties independent of its measurement. In fact, such physical properties come into existence only when the measurement is made on the system. This interpretation of objects possessing physical properties only on measurement is known as *Copenhagen interpretation*. For example, as per quantum mechanics, an electron does not possess any specific energy level such as ground state or excited state unless the specific energy level is measured. What quantum mechanics gives us is a set of postulates that tells us given the state of an electron what are the probabilities of the electron being in a specific state when measured.

Several physicists during the period from 1920 to 1930 including Einstein were not convinced about this new view that quantum mechanics had to offer. The famous paper "Can Quantum-Mechanical Description of Physical Reality Be Considered Complete?" by Einstein, Rosen, and Podolsky (collectively referred to as EPR) detailed a thought experiment to disprove Copenhagen interpretation. Their argument rested on the idea of quantum entanglement. Let's suppose we have a quantum system with zero angular momentum that emits two photons P_1 and P_2 simultaneously. Since photons have spin and angular momentum must be conserved, if one photon has spin-up state, the other photon must have spin-down state to ensure the system is in zero angular momentum. We denote the spin-up state as $|0\rangle$ and the spin-down state as $|1\rangle$. This phenomenon is known as *entanglement* in which the two photons are not independent. Given that each photon particle has equal inclination to be in the spin-up and down states, the joint state of the two particles is given by $|\psi\rangle = \frac{1}{\sqrt{2}}(|01\rangle + |01\rangle)$. If the spin of one of the photons is known, the spin of the other photon is known instantaneously. Let's say we separate the photons by a large astronomical distance of 1 light year, which is about 9.46×10^{12} kms. If we measure one of the photons P_1, we would have a 50 percent chance of measuring spins up and a 50 percent chance of measuring spin down. Now let's say we measure P_1 to be in a spin-up state $|0\rangle$, and thereafter we measure quickly, say within 1 second, the state of P_2. We see photon P_2 will always measure spin-up. Quantum mechanics states that the state of the particles is not predetermined and becomes available only after measurement. This means the measurement information of P_1 must travel much faster than light for it to reach P_2 within 1 second so that P_2 can adjust its state accordingly to the spin-down condition on measurement. EPR argued that since nothing can travel faster than light according to the rules of special relatively, this should invalidate the Copenhagen interpretation. This theorized violation of special relatively is called *ERP paradox*.

ERP instead proposed another likely theory to quantum entanglement, which states that the states of the two photons were predetermined from the beginning in a way that photon P_1 is a spin-up condition and photon P_2 is in a spin-down condition. This information is hidden within the photon particles locally so that when they are moved apart, no communication has to happen. This is called the *local hidden variable theory*. It is as if the two photon particles are a pair of gloves, and if one were a left-handed pair, the other would be a right-handed pair. Once we have found the left-handed pair, we know that the other pair wherever it is in the universe must be a right-handed pair. The local hidden variable theory was a valid interpretation of quantum mechanics for almost 30 years from 1935 to 1964 until Irish physicist John Bell appeared on the scene and proposed an experiment that would validate whether the local hidden variable theory was correct based on his famous Bell's equation.

To invalidate the claim made by ERP, we need to understand Bell's inequality. Bell inequality does not involve quantum mechanics. We perform a thought experiment to deduce Bell's inequality with similar sensibilities of how the common world works or how Einstein, Podolsky, and Rosen thought nature should obey. We follow up the common world analysis with a quantum mechanical analysis to show that it is inconsistent with the common world analysis.

We perform the experiment illustrated in Figure 2-8 where the referee Colin prepares two particles for Alice and Bob and sends them the particles for measurement.

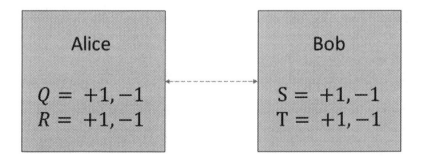

Q, R : Observables for Alice's particle   S, T : Observables for Bob's particle

Figure 2-8. *Experimental setup for Bell's inequality*

Once Alice receives her particle, she can choose to measure the physical property P_Q pertaining to the observable Q, or she can choose to measure the physical property P_R pertaining to the observable R. Alice on receipt of her particle tosses a fair coin to determine which property she wants to measure.

As shown in Figure 2-8, each physical property measurement can have two outcomes: +1 or −1. Similar to Alice, Bob on receiving his particle will measure one of the two physical properties P_S or P_T pertaining to the observables S and T. Bob does not choose up front which property he will measure until he has received the particle. Alice and Bob perform their measurement simultaneously so that the measurement results of one cannot change the measurement outcome of the other.

We now look at the simple quantity $(QS + RS + RT − QT)$ and try to compute its expectation. On simplifying the expression, we get the following:

$$QS + RS + RT - QT = S(Q+R) + T(R-Q) \tag{2-126}$$

From Equation 2-126, it is easy to see that at a time either of the $S(Q + R)$ or $T(R − Q)$ is nonzero and the nonzero value would be +2 or −2. Hence:

$$QS + RS + RT - QT \le 2 \tag{2-127}$$

For any generalized measurement state for Alice and Bob's particles given by $Q = q$, $R = r$, $S = s$, $T = t$, we have the expectation of $QS + RS + RT − QT$ as follows:

$$\mathbb{E}[QS + RS + RT - QT]$$

$$= \sum_{q,r,s,t} p(q, r, s, t)(qs + rs + rt - qt)$$

$$\le \sum_{q,r,s,t} p(q, r, s, t) \times 2 = 2 \tag{2-128}$$

Now since the expectation of the sum is equal to the sum of the expectation, we can rewrite Equation 2-128 as follows:

$$\mathbb{E}[QS] + \mathbb{E}[RS] + \mathbb{E}[RT] - \mathbb{E}[QT] \le 2 \tag{2-129}$$

Equation 2-129 is known as *Bell's inequality*. The result is also known as CHSH inequality after the initials of its four inventors.

Now let's try to analyze whether for quantum systems Bell's inequality holds true. Here Colin prepares an entangled quantum state of two qubits as follows:

$$|\psi\rangle = \frac{1}{\sqrt{2}}(|01\rangle - |10\rangle) \tag{2-130}$$

Colin passes the first qubit to Alice and the second one to Bob for measurement. Alice makes the measurements with respect to the observables Q and R, which we assign as follows:

$$Q = Z$$

$$R = X \tag{2-131}$$

Similarly, Bob makes the measurements with respect to the observables S and T, which we assign as follows:

$$S = \frac{-Z - X}{\sqrt{2}}$$

$$T = \frac{Z - X}{\sqrt{2}} \tag{2-132}$$

In Equations 2-131 and 2-132, Z and X are the Pauli matrices. Much like before, we compute the expectation $\mathbb{E}[QS] + \mathbb{E}[RS] + \mathbb{E}[RT] - \mathbb{E}[QT]$ in a quantum mechanical sense with respect to the entangled state $|\psi\rangle$. For instance, the $\mathbb{E}[QS]$ with respect to the state $|\psi\rangle$ can be expressed as follows:

$$\mathbb{E}[QS] = \langle Q \otimes S \rangle_\psi = \langle \psi | Q \otimes S | \psi \rangle$$

$$= \langle \psi | Z \otimes X | \psi \rangle$$

$$= \frac{1}{\sqrt{2}} (\langle 01| - \langle 10|) \begin{bmatrix} 1 & 0 \\ 0 & -1 \end{bmatrix} \otimes \begin{bmatrix} 0 & 1 \\ 1 & 0 \end{bmatrix} \frac{1}{\sqrt{2}} (|01\rangle - |10\rangle)$$

$$= \frac{1}{\sqrt{2}} \tag{2-133}$$

Computing the expectation for each term in $\mathbb{E}[QS] + \mathbb{E}[RS] + \mathbb{E}[RT] - \mathbb{E}[QT]$, we would see the following:

$$\mathbb{E}[QS] = \mathbb{E}[RS] = \mathbb{E}[RT] = \frac{1}{\sqrt{2}}$$

$$\mathbb{E}[QT] = -\frac{1}{\sqrt{2}} \tag{2-134}$$

Hence, the overall expectation of $\mathbb{E}[QS]+\mathbb{E}[RS]+\mathbb{E}[RT]-\mathbb{E}[QT]$ turns out to be as follows:

$$\mathbb{E}[QS]+\mathbb{E}[RS]+\mathbb{E}[RT]-\mathbb{E}[QT]=2\sqrt{2} \qquad (2\text{-}135)$$

In Equation 2-129 we can see that using the sensibilities of how the common world works or how ERP perceived the world to be gives us an upper bound expectation of $\mathbb{E}[QS]+\mathbb{E}[RS]+\mathbb{E}[RT]-\mathbb{E}[QT]$ as 2. However, we can see that quantum mechanics yields a value of $2\sqrt{2}$ for the expectation $\mathbb{E}[QS]+\mathbb{E}[RS]+\mathbb{E}[RT]-\mathbb{E}[QT]$, which violates Bell's inequality. This means that one or more assumptions that we made while deducing Bell's inequality must be wrong. The likely wrong assumptions made in Bell's inequality or by Einstein, Rosen, and Podolsky for that matter can be summarized as follows:

- *Assumption of realism*: The assumption that the physical properties have definite values independent of the observation or measurement

- *Assumption of locality*: The assumption that Alice performing her measurement does not influence the result of Bob's measurement

The two assumptions together are known as *local realism*, and the violation of Bell's inequality proves that at least one of them must be wrong. So, what we learn from the violation of Bell's inequality is that although local realism fits our day-to-day experience, it does not hold true for how the world works at the most fundamental level. As per recent experimental evidence, physicists conclude that either or both locality and realism should be dropped from our commonsense view of the world to get a deep intuitive understanding of quantum mechanics.

Hamiltonian Simulation and Trotterization

The evolution of a quantum system under a constant Hamiltonian H is given by the Schrodinger equation $i\hbar\dfrac{d|\psi(t)\rangle}{dt}=H|\psi(t)\rangle$. The solution to the Schrodinger's equation gives the unitary evolution of the state vector $|\psi\rangle$ between times t_0 and t as

$|\psi(t_1)\rangle = U(t_1,t_0)|\psi(t_0)\rangle$, where $U(t_1,t_0)=e^{-\frac{iH(t-t_o)}{\hbar}}$ and $t>t_o$.

In Hamiltonian simulation, given a Hamiltonian H and an evolution time t, we need to combine a sequence of gates to implement the unitary operator $U(t,0)=e^{-\frac{iHt}{\hbar}}$. Hamiltonian simulation is an important component of algorithms using adiabatic computation, such as the quantum approximate optimization algorithm (QAOA) that we are going to study in Chapter 7. The Hamiltonian in most physical systems can be expressed as a sum of local interactions of only a few particles. Thus, for a n body quantum system, we can write the Hamiltonian as follows:

$$H = \sum_k H_k \tag{2-136}$$

Each of the H_k Hamiltonians is often as simple as two body interactions. The point to emphasize here is that $e^{-iH_k t}$ is much easier to construct with quantum gates since it works on smaller subsystems on a local level than the unitary operator e^{-iHt}. If we were able to express $e^{-iHt} = \prod_k e^{-iH_k t}$, then the ability to construct $e^{-iH_k t}$ easily would have been useful. However, in general, $e^{-iHt} \neq \prod_k e^{-iH_k t}$ because in general the individual local Hamiltonians do not commute, i.e., $H_k H_l \neq H_l H_k$. It turns out even if two Hamiltonians H_1 and H_2 do not commute, one can take advantage of simulating individual Hamiltonians to simulate the overall Hamiltonian using Trotter's formula.

The Trotter's formula for two Hermitian matrices H_1 and H_2 is expressed as follows:

$$e^{-i(H_1+H_2)t} = \lim_{n\to\infty} \left(e^{\frac{-iH_1 t}{n}} e^{\frac{-iH_2 t}{n}} \right)^n \tag{2-137}$$

Let's try to deduce the proof of Trotter's formula. To begin with, $e^{\frac{-iH_1 t}{n}}$ can be expanded as follows:

$$e^{\frac{-iH_1 t}{n}} = I - \frac{1}{n} iH_1 t + O\left(\frac{1}{n^2}\right) \tag{2-138}$$

The $O(.)$ in the previous formula represents the Big O computational complexity. Combining expansions for both $e^{\frac{-iH_1 t}{n}}$ and $e^{\frac{-iH_2 t}{n}}$, we get the following:

$$e^{\frac{-iH_1 t}{n}} e^{\frac{-iH_2 t}{n}} = I - \frac{1}{n} i(H_1 + H_2)t + O\left(\frac{1}{n^2}\right) \tag{2-139}$$

Taking the nth power on both sides of equation 2-139, we have this:

$$\left(e^{\frac{-iH_1 t}{n}} e^{\frac{-iH_2 t}{n}} \right)^n$$

$$= I + \sum_{k=1}^{n} \binom{n}{k} \frac{(-1)^k}{n^k} [i(H_1 + H_2)t]^k + O\left(\frac{1}{n}\right) \tag{2-140}$$

With a little calculation, we can simplify $\binom{n}{k} \frac{1}{n^k}$ to the following:

$$\binom{n}{k} \frac{1}{n^k} = \frac{1 + O\left(\frac{1}{n}\right)}{k!} \tag{2-141}$$

Using equation 2-141, we can simplify 2-140 as follows:

$$\left(e^{\frac{-iH_1 t}{n}} e^{\frac{-iH_2 t}{n}} \right)^n = I + \sum_{k=1}^{n} \frac{[-i(H_1 + H_2)t]^k}{k!} + O\left(\frac{1}{n}\right) \tag{2-142}$$

Taking limit $n \to \infty$ on either side of 2-140, we get this:

$$\lim_{n \to \infty} \left(e^{\frac{-iH_1 t}{n}} e^{\frac{-iH_2 t}{n}} \right)^n$$

$$= \lim_{n \to \infty} I + \sum_{k=1}^{n} \frac{[-i(H_1 + H_2)t]^k}{k!} + O\left(\frac{1}{n}\right)$$

$$= \lim_{n \to \infty} \sum_{k=0}^{n} \frac{[-i(H_1 + H_2)t]^k}{k!} + O\left(\frac{1}{n}\right)$$

$$= e^{-i(H_1 + H_2)t} \tag{2-143}$$

Based on the Trotter formula, one can realize a unitary operator $e^{-i(H_1 + H_2)t}$ by a sequence of unitary operators achieved by alternating between H_1 and H_2 as follows:

$$e^{\frac{-iH_1 t}{n}}, e^{\frac{-iH_2 t}{n}}, e^{\frac{-iH_1 t}{n}}, e^{\frac{-iH_2 t}{n}}, \ldots \ldots \tag{2-144}$$

If the Hamiltonians H_1 and H_2 are much easier to simulate than $H = H_1 + H_2$, applying the sequence of unitary operator as in 2-142 turns out to be useful proposition.

The Trotter formula can be extended to a sum of more than two Hamiltonians. For instance, if we have $H = H_1 + H_2 + H_3$, we can Trotterize the unitary evolution of H by the sequence of unitary operators as follows:

$$e^{\frac{-iH_1t}{n}}, e^{\frac{-iH_2t}{n}}, e^{\frac{-iH_3t}{n}}, e^{\frac{-iH_1t}{n}}, e^{\frac{-iH_2t}{n}}, e^{\frac{-iH_3t}{n}} \ldots\ldots \quad (2\text{-}145)$$

Summary

With this, we come to the end of Chapter 2. In this chapter, we mostly covered the mathematics of quantum mechanics and its postulates to better equip us in understanding and implementing different quantum-based algorithms as well as quantum machine learning. We studied measurements and their different variants such as projective measurement and POVM in detail since measurement is an integral part of quantum-based algorithms. Furthermore, we covered specific important topics in linear algebra that are central to the quantum mechanical representation.

In the next chapter, we will take our learnings from the first two chapters and implement several quantum computing–based algorithms such as quantum teleportation, Deutsch–Jozsa, Grover's algorithm, and Bernstein–Vazirani, to name a few. We will implement these quantum algorithms in both `Cirq` from Google and `Qiskit` from IBM.

CHAPTER 3

Introduction to Quantum Algorithms

"If you think you understand quantum mechanics, you don't understand quantum mechanics."

—Richard Feynman

In 1981 Richard Feynman proposed the idea that a computer built of quantum mechanical elements obeying quantum mechanical laws can perform efficient simulations of quantum systems. Quantum computing works on the laws of quantum mechanical properties such as superposition, entanglement, and interference. Unlike in classical computing, in quantum computers a register can exist in all possible states at once due to its superposition properties. It is only when a quantum system is measured that we observe one of the possible states. Such a system is advantageous since, when measured, each state can appear with a certain probability encoded in the state prior to the measurement. Quantum computing works by increasing the probability of the desired state to a sufficiently high value so that the desired state can be obtained with high confidence with a minimal number of measurements. In this regard, quantum interference, which results from quantum superposition, plays a big role since it allows probability amplitudes corresponding to a given state to interfere and cancel each other. This property of quantum interference biases the measurement to a set of states that we desire as the outcome of quantum algorithms. Similarly, quantum entanglement allows one to create a strong correlation between quantum objects, especially qubits, to the advantage of quantum algorithms, as you will see throughout this chapter.

In this chapter, we will look at quantum algorithms with an aim to understanding the quantum supremacy of these algorithms over their classical counterparts. We have already looked at quantum teleportation algorithm and ways to formulate algorithms using quantum parallelism in Chapter 1. In this Chapter we will implement several

© Santanu Pattanayak 2021
S. Pattanayak, *Quantum Machine Learning with Python*, https://doi.org/10.1007/978-1-4842-6522-2_3

other quantum computing algorithms such as Deutsch Jozsa, Bell's inequality, the Bernstein–Vajirani algorithm, and Grover's algorithm to widen the range of quantum algorithms we understand. For these new algorithms, we will investigate their technical derivations first before going through the implementations. We will use `Cirq` from Google as the quantum computing framework of choice for implementing these algorithms. However, a few of these algorithms we will implement in `Qiskit` from IBM to gain experience with multiple quantum computing frameworks. Implementing these quantum computing algorithm in these quantum computing frameworks would give us a different perspective and help fill in any gaps that we may have while going through their technical details.

Cirq

`Cirq` is an open source quantum computing software library from Google Research that was released in 2018. Developers can build and run quantum algorithms comprising all of the relevant unary, binary, and ternary gates. Cirq does not provide access to Google's quantum computer currently. We will use `Cirq's` quantum computing simulator, called Simulator, to locally execute quantum algorithms.

Simulation in Cirq with a Hadamard Gate

Let's first get comfortable with the `Cirq` language with an easy quantum circuit simulation. Qubits in `Cirq` language are generally defined using a `LineQubit` or `GridQubit` option. `LineQubit` allows you to define qubits on a one-dimensional lattice, whereas `GridQubit` allows you to define qubits on a two-dimensional lattice.

Using `Cirq's` `GridQubit` functionality, we define a qubit initialized at the basis state $|0\rangle$ and apply the Hadamard transform $H = \frac{1}{\sqrt{2}}\begin{bmatrix} 1 & 1 \\ 1 & -1 \end{bmatrix}$ on it. The Hadamard transform in Cirq is defined as `H` itself. We then measure the new state in the computational basis using the measurement functionality `measure` in `Cirq`. Measurement does not require you to explicitly define a classical register for storing the results of measurement as required in many of the other quantum computing packages. All the operations on qubits are defined in the form of a quantum `circuit` in `Cirq`. Once the circuit is defined, you use the Cirq `Simulator` to run 100 simulations of the identical circuit and measure the outcomes. Cirq has `histogram` facilities to get the counts of each measurement outcome. Any measurement of state in the quantum circuit can be tied to a key. Once the simulator is run, the results can be accessed by the key, as you can see in the example in Listing 3-1.

Listing 3-1. Measurements After a Hadamard Transform on a Qubit Using Cirq

```
# Import the Package cirq
import cirq
# Define a Qubit
qubit = cirq.GridQubit(0,0)

# Create a Cirquit in cirq
circuit = cirq.Circuit([cirq.H(qubit),
                        cirq.measure(qubit,key='m')])
print("Circuit Follows")
print(circuit)
sim = cirq.Simulator()
output = sim.run(circuit,repetitions=100)
print("Measurement Output:")
print(output)
print("Histogram stats follow")
print(output.histogram(key='m')
```

Output:

```
Circuit Follows
(0, 0): ——H——M('m')——
Measurement Output:
m=10001111111111011110111001010001010110000100001101101010001011001110111010
0100100100000000010000001000
Counter({0: 54, 1: 46})
```

You can see from the output of Listing 3-1 that on measurement of the identical copies of the qubit in the equal superposition state $\frac{1}{\sqrt{2}}(|0\rangle + |1\rangle)$, we get 54 measurements in state 0 and 46 measurements in state 1, as illustrated in Figure 3-1.

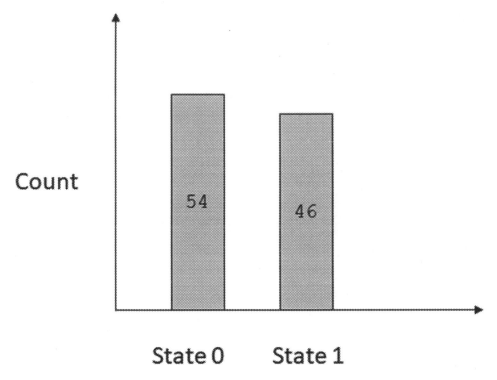

Figure 3-1. *Counts for states 0 and 1 on measurement*

The distribution is almost uniform over the two computational basis states 0 and 1, as expected. If we increase the number of copies on which we make measurements, the probabilities of each state would tend to $\frac{1}{2}$. If n is the number of copies of the quantum state on which we make a measurement and $P_n(0)$ and $P_n(1)$ are the probabilities determined from the measurements of these n copies, then the below holds true:

$$\lim_{n \to \infty} P_n(0) = \lim_{n \to \infty} P_n(1) = \frac{1}{2} \tag{3-1}$$

Now let's simulate the previous code for different values of n and see how the sequence of probabilities converge to their ideal values.

We create a function called `hadamard_state_measurement` to compute these probabilities for different values of n, as illustrated in Listing 3-2.

Listing 3-2. Measurement Convergence to Expected Probability of Outcomes

```python
# Import the Package cirq
import cirq
import matplotlib.pyplot as plt

def hadamard_state_measurement(copies):
    # Define a Qubit
    qubit = cirq.GridQubit(0, 0)
    # Create a Circuit in cirq
    circuit = cirq.Circuit([cirq.H(qubit)
            ,cirq.measure(qubit, key='m')])
    print("Circuit Follows")
    print(circuit)
    sim = cirq.Simulator()
    output = sim.run(circuit, repetitions=copies)
    res = output.histogram(key='m')
    prob_0 = dict(res)[0] / copies
    print(prob_0)
    return prob_0

def main(copies_low=10, copies_high=1000):
    probability_for_zero_state_trace = []
    copies_trace = []
    for n in range(copies_low, copies_high):
        copies_trace.append(n)
        prob_0 = hadamard_state_measurement(n)
        probability_for_zero_state_trace.append(prob_0)
    plt.plot(copies_trace, probability_for_zero_state_trace)
    plt.xlabel('No of Measurements')
    plt.ylabel("Probability of the State 0")
    plt.title("Convergence Sequence of Probability for State 0")
    plt.show()

if __name__ == '__main__':
    main()
```

In Listing 3-2, we compute the probability of the state $|0\rangle$ from different measurements of identical copies of the state $|\psi\rangle = \frac{1}{\sqrt{2}}(|0\rangle + |1\rangle)$. You can see from the graph in Figure 3-2 that with the increase in the number of copies from 100 to 500, the probability of the state $|0\rangle$ gradually converges toward the theoretical value of $\frac{1}{2}$ with diminishing oscillations.

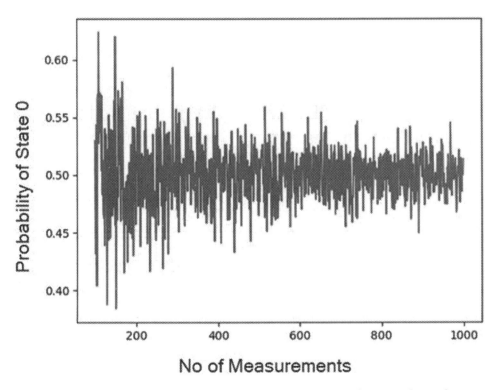

Figure 3-2. *Probability convergence with an increase in the number of measurements*

Qiskit

Qiskit is an open source quantum computing software library from IBM that was released in 2017. Qiskit stands for Quantum Information Science Kit and has four main components in its quantum computing stack, as listed here:

1. *Qiskit Terra*: This provides all the essential components for building quantum circuits.

2. *Qiskit Aer*: You can develop noise models for simulating realistic noisy simulations that can occur in real quantum computing devices using Aer tools. Aer also provides a C++ simulator framework.

3. *Qiskit Ignis*: This is a framework for analyzing and minimizing noise in quantum circuits.

4. *Qiskit Agua*: This contains cross-domain algorithms and logic to run these algorithms on a quantum real device or simulator.

You will use the Qiskit programming language from time to time in this book. To familiarize yourself with the basic coding syntax of Qiskit, you will implement the same program as illustrated earlier in Cirq: measuring a qubit after a Hadamard transform. See Listing 3-3.

Listing 3-3. Measurements After a Hadamard Transform on a Qubit Using Qiskit

```
"""
Measure a qubit after Hadamard Transform
"""
import numpy as np
from qiskit import QuantumCircuit, execute, Aer
from qiskit.visualization import plot_histogram

# Use Aer's qasm_simulator
simulator = Aer.get_backend('qasm_simulator')

# Create a Quantum Circuit with 1 Qubit
circuit = QuantumCircuit(1, 1)

# Add a H gate on Qubit 0
circuit.h(0)

# Map the quantum measurement to the classical register
circuit.measure([0], [0])

# Execute the circuit on the qasm simulator
job = execute(circuit, simulator, shots=100)
```

```
# Grab results from the job
result = job.result()

# Returns counts
counts = result.get_counts(circuit)
print("\nTotal count for 0 and 1 are:",counts)

# Draw the circuit
print(circuit.draw(output='text'))
```

output

```
Total count for 0 and 1 are: {'0': 51, '1': 49}

q_0: ┤ H ├┤ M ├
     └───┘└─╥─┘
c_0: ═══════╩══
```

In Qiskit, we define a quantum circuit using the QuantumCircuit option. Also, we define the qubits required while defining the circuit itself through the QuantumCircuit option. Other inputs to the QuantumCircuit option are the classical bits required to store the results of measurements. Since we are measuring the state of a qubit in equal superposition, we will require one classical bit for measurement. Unlike Cirq in Qiskit, we will have to explicitly define classical registers or bits to store the measurement outcomes. The Hadamard transform H in Qiskit is defined through the circuit created using QuantumCircuit. We define the Hadamard transform on the one and only qubit using circuit.h(0). One thing to note is that the classical bits for holding measurement outcomes are not implicitly tied to the qubits on Qiskit, and we will have to code this mapping while making measurements using the measure functionality of the circuit. The simulator that we are using is imported from the Aer framework in Qiskit. Much like the run command for simulating the quantum circuit in Cirq, we use the execute command in Qiskit.

Bell State Creation and Measurement

We discussed Bell's state in Chapter 1 while discussing quantum entanglement and in algorithms such as quantum teleportation. The Bell state for two qubits A and B is given by the following:

$$|\psi\rangle_{AB} = \frac{1}{\sqrt{2}}\left(|00\rangle + |11\rangle\right)$$

In Listing 3-4, we create the Bell state by first applying Hadamard transform H on the qubit A initialized at state $|\psi_A\rangle = |0\rangle$ to create a superposition state $|\psi\rangle_A = \frac{1}{\sqrt{2}}(|0\rangle + |1\rangle)$. We then apply the controlled NOT gate, popularly known as CNOT on qubit B initialized at state $|\psi\rangle_B = |0\rangle$ based on qubit A as the control bit.

Listing 3-4. Bell State Creation and Measurement Using Cirq

```
import cirq
# Define the two qubits using LineQubit
q_register = [cirq.LineQubit(i) for i in range(2)]
# Define the Cirquit with a Hadamard Gate on the qubit 0
# followed by CNOT operation
cirquit = cirq.Circuit([cirq.H(q_register[0]), cirq.CNOT(q_register[0],
q_register[1])])
# Measure both the qubits
cirquit.append(cirq.measure(*q_register,key='z'))
print("Circuit")
print(cirquit)
# Define the Simulator
sim = cirq.Simulator()
# Simulate the cirquit for 100 iterations
output = sim.run(cirquit, repetitions=100)
print("Measurement Output")
print(output.histogram(key='z'))
```

Output

```
Circuit
0: ——H——@——M('z')——
         |    |
1: ————————X——M————————
Measurement Output
Counter({0: 56, 3: 44})
```

In Listing 3-4, we use Cirq's LineQubit option to define the two qubits participating in the Bell state.

The output of Listing 3-4 shows the quantum circuit is cirq. On measurement of the Bell state, we get almost equal proportion of the integer outcome: 0 and 3. The integer outcome 0 stands for the state $|00\rangle$, while the outcome 3 stands for the state $|11\rangle$.

We now implement the Bell state creation and measurement in Qiskit, as illustrated in Listing 3-5.

Listing 3-5. Bell State Creation and Measurement Using Qiskit

```
"""
Quantum Entanglement Example with Qiskit
"""
import numpy as np
from qiskit import QuantumCircuit, execute, Aer
from qiskit.visualization import plot_histogram

# Use Aer's qasm_simulator
simulator = Aer.get_backend('qasm_simulator')

# Create a Quantum Circuit acting on the q register
circuit = QuantumCircuit(2, 2)

# Add a H gate on Qubit 0
circuit.h(0)

# Add a CX (CNOT) gate on control qubit 0 and target qubit 1
circuit.cx(0, 1)

# Map the quantum measurement to the classical bits
circuit.measure([0,1], [0,1])
```

```
# Execute the circuit on the qasm simulator
job = execute(circuit, simulator, shots=100)

# Grab results from the job
result = job.result()

# Returns counts
counts = result.get_counts(circuit)
print("\nTotal count for 00 and 11 are:",counts)

# Draw the circuit
print(circuit.draw(output='text'))
```

output

```
Total count for 00 and 11 are: {'00': 51, '11': 49}

q_0: ┤ H ├──────■──────┤ M ├──────────
                │        
q_1: ────────┤ X ├──────╫──┤ M ├──────
                        ║     
c_0: ═══════════════════╩═════╬═══════
                              ║
c_1: ═════════════════════════╩═══════
```

We can see from the output of Listing 3-5 that Qiskit has sampled the states $|00\rangle$ and $|11\rangle$ almost equally on measurement of the Bell state.

Quantum Teleportation

Quantum teleportation is the method of transmitting quantum states between a sender and a receiver without using any communication channel. Like in Chapter 1, we name the sender of the quantum state Alice and the receiver of the quantum state Bob to keep the references consistent. Figure 3-3 shows the high-level circuit for the quantum teleportation circuit.

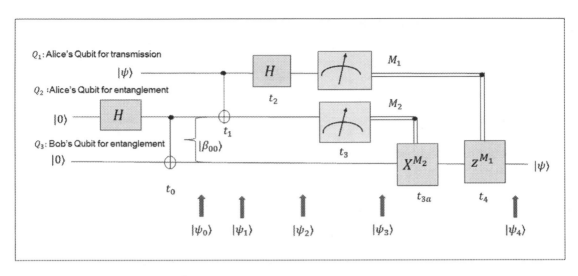

Figure 3-3. *Quantum teleportation circuit*

We pointed out at the beginning of the chapter that quantum algorithms benefit from quantum entanglement by creating meaningful correlation between qubits. The nature of these correlations is much stronger than what can be achieved by a classical system as quantum particles can exhibit high correlations even when separated by an infinitely large distance.

In quantum teleportation, Alice and Bob get their control qubits to share a Bell state through quantum entanglement. Alice wants to send Bob a qubit state, $|\psi\rangle$. We refer to this qubit for transmission as Q1 and the control qubits Alice and Bob use to share a Bell state as Q2 and Q3.

Here are the steps associated with the quantum teleportation algorithm:

1. Initialize the control qubits Q2 and Q3 to the state $|0\rangle$ and the qubit Q1 to the state $|\psi\rangle$ to be transmitted.

2. Create the Bell state $\frac{1}{\sqrt{2}}(|00\rangle + |11\rangle)$ between Q2 and Q3 by first applying Hadamard transform H on Q2 followed by the CNOT operation on Q3 where Q2 acts as the control qubit.

3. Once the Bell state is established between Alice's and Bob's control qubits Q2 and Q3, apply the CNOT operator on Alice's two-qubit Q1 and Q2 where Q1 acts as the control qubit and Q2 acts as the target qubit.

4.   Apply the Hadamard transform on qubit Q1 followed by measurement of Alice's qubits Q1 and Q2. We denote the measurement states of Q1 and Q2 as M1 and M2.

5.   Apply the CNOT Operator on Bob's qubit Q3 based on the measured state M2 as the control qubit. Finally, apply the conditional Z operator on Bob's qubit Q3 measured state M1.

6.   At this stage, Bob's qubit Q3 has the state $|\psi\rangle$ that Alice has transmitted.

We implement the quantum teleportation algorithm in Cirq and illustrate it by transmitting the equal superposition state $|\psi\rangle = \dfrac{1}{\sqrt{2}}(|0\rangle + |1\rangle)$. The state $|\psi\rangle$ to be transmitted in general can be specified through the circuit required to transform the $|0\rangle$ state to the required state $|\psi\rangle$. We use the qubit_to_send_op variable in the quantum_teleportation routine for this. For example, to transmit the equal superposition state variable $|\psi\rangle = \dfrac{1}{\sqrt{2}}(|0\rangle + |1\rangle)$, we send the cirq.H operator through the variable qubit_to_send_op to the quantum_teleportation routine. The Hadamard operator transforms the qubit Q1 initialized at state $|0\rangle$ to the equal superposition state. Readers are advised to experiment with different states to be transmitted using qubit_to_send_op. Once the qubit state has been transmitted, we measure Bob's qubit Q3 to see if the distribution of the measurements equals the probability distribution of the transmitted waveform. Listing 3-6 shows the detailed implementation of the quantum teleportation algorithm.

Listing 3-6. Simulating Quantum Teleportation

```
import cirq

def quantum_teleportation(qubit_to_send_op='H',
    num_copies=100):
    Q1, Q2, Q3 = [cirq.LineQubit(i) for i in range(3)]
    cirquit = cirq.Circuit()
    """
    Q1 : Alice State qubit to be sent to Bob
    Q2: Alices control qubit
    Q3: Bobs control qubit
```

```
    Set a state for Q1 based on qubit_to_send_op :
    Implemented operators H,X,Y,Z,I
    """

    if qubit_to_send_op == 'H':
        cirquit.append(cirq.H(Q1))
    elif qubit_to_send_op == 'X':
        cirquit.append(cirq.X(Q1))
    elif qubit_to_send_op == 'Y':
        cirquit.append(cirq.X(Q1))
    elif qubit_to_send_op == 'I':
        cirquit.append(cirq.I(Q1))
    else:
        raise NotImplementedError("Yet to be implemented")

    # Entangle Alice and Bob's control qubits : Q2 and Q3
    cirquit.append(cirq.H(Q2))
    cirquit.append(cirq.CNOT(Q2, Q3))
    # CNOT Alice's data Qubit Q1 with control Qubit Q2
    cirquit.append(cirq.CNOT(Q1, Q2))
    # Transform Alice's data Qubit Q1
    # on +/- basis using Hadamard Transform
    cirquit.append(cirq.H(Q1))
    # Measure Alice's qubit Q1 and Q2
    cirquit.append(cirq.measure(Q1, Q2))
    # Do a CNOT on Bob's qubit Q3 using Alice's
    # control qubit Q2 after measurement
    cirquit.append(cirq.CNOT(Q2, Q3))
    # Do a Conditioned Z Operation on Bob's qubit Q3
    # using Alice's control qubit Q1 after measurement
    cirquit.append(cirq.CZ(Q1, Q3))
    # Measure the final transmitted state to Bob in Q3
    cirquit.append(cirq.measure(Q3, key='Z'))
    print("Circuit")
    print(cirquit)
    sim = cirq.Simulator()
```

```
    output = sim.run(cirquit, repetitions=num_copies)
    print("Measurement Output")
    print(output.histogram(key='Z'))

if __name__ == '__main__':
    quantum_teleportation(qubit_to_send_op='H')
```

output

```
Circuit
0: ——H————————@——H——M————————@—————————
              |      |        |
1: ——H——@——X————————M——@——————|————————
        |              |      |
2: ————————X——————————————X——@——M('Z')——
```
Measurement Output
Counter({1: 51, 0: 49})

From the measurement outcome, we see that Alice has transmitted the equal superposition state to Bob.

Quantum Random Number Generator

Most of the random number generators in classical computers are not truly random since they are generated in a deterministic way through algorithms and hence obey the norms of reproducibility. To be precise, a classical random number generator starts with an initial seed state, and the sequence of random numbers generated using the seed state is always going to be the same. Hence, we see that the sequence of numbers these random number generators generate mimic the properties of a sequence of random numbers and at the same time are deterministic. These deterministic random number generator routines are called *pseduo-random generators*. Pseudo-random numbers have the advantage of reproducibility and speed but cannot be securely used for applications such as cryptography where random cryptographic keys are used to transmit the data securely.

The opposite of a pseduo-random generator is a hardware random number generator that generates random numbers, leveraging physical processes such as quantum processes, photolectric effect, etc. Since these physical processes are highly unpredictable, they serve as a good basis for true random number generators that can be used for secure applications such as crytography.

In this section, we will illustrate a random integer number generator routine using multiple qubits. The idea is simple, as illustrated here:

1. Determine the number of qubits required to represent the range of integer values to be sampled. For instance, if we have to sample from the eight integer numbers from 0 to 7, we would require $log_2(8) = 3$ qubits.

2. Create an equal superposition state by applying a Hadamard transform on each of the qubits initially in the $|0\rangle$ state. The equal superposition state is given by the following:

$$|\psi\rangle = H^{\otimes n}|0\rangle^{\otimes} = \frac{1}{2^{\frac{n}{2}}} \sum_{x=0}^{2^n-1} |x\rangle \tag{3-2}$$

Here $|x\rangle$ stands for the integer value for the computational basis state $|x_0 x_1 \ldots x_{n-1}\rangle$ where each $x_i \in \{0, 1\}$.

3. Map the computational basis states to the actual integers and store the mapping in a dictionary s2n_map. If the range of integral numbers to sample starts from zero, the dictionary from the computational basis state to actual integers can be just the binary to decimal transformation given by the following:

$$x_0 x_1 \ldots x_{n-1} = \sum_{i=0}^{n-1} x_i 2^{n-1-i} \tag{3-3}$$

If the range starts from an offset b, we can have the mapping from the computational basis states to integer values to sample as shown here:

$$x_0 x_1 \ldots x_{n-1} \rightarrow \sum_{i=0}^{n-1} x_i 2^{n-1-i} + b = 0 \tag{3-4}$$

4. Once we have defined the mapping, we can make measurements on the equal superposition state $|\psi\rangle$ and map the measured computational basis state to the integer value using the dictionary map s2n_map.

In Listing 3-7, we generate random numbers from 0 to 2^{10} using 10 qubits. Since we sample from 0, the offset b for our algorithm is 0.

Listing 3-7. Quantum Random Number Generator

```python
import cirq
import numpy as np

def random_number_generator(low=0,high=2**10,m=10):
    """

    :param low: lower bound of numbers to be generated
    :param high: Upper bound of numbers to be generated
    :param number m : Number of random numbers to output
    :return: string of random numbers
    """
    # Determine the number of Qubits required
    qubits_required = int(np.ceil(np.log2(high - low)))
    print(qubits_required)
    # Define the qubits
    Q_reg = [cirq.LineQubit(c) for c
                in range(qubits_required)]
    # Define the circuit
    circuit = cirq.Circuit()
    circuit.append(cirq.H(Q_reg[c]) for c
                    in range(qubits_required))
    circuit.append(cirq.measure(*Q_reg, key="z"))
    print(circuit)
    # Simulate the circuit
    sim = cirq.Simulator()

    num_gen = 0
    output = []
    while num_gen <= m :
        result = sim.run(circuit,repetitions=1)
        rand_number = result.data.get_values()[0][0] + low
```

```
        if rand_number < high :
            output.append(rand_number)
            num_gen += 1
    return output

if __name__ == '__main__':
    output = random_number_generator()
  print(output)
```

output

```
0: ———H———M('z')———

      |
1: ———H———M—————————

      |
2: ———H———M—————————

      |
3: ———H———M—————————

      |
4: ———H———M—————————

      |
5: ———H———M—————————

      |
6: ———H———M—————————

      |
7: ———H———M—————————

      |
8: ———H———M—————————

      |
9: ———H———M—————————
```

Sampled Random Numbers

[568, 377, 113, 1022, 775, 310, 696, 175, 568, 910, 445, 6, 504, 167, 29, 727, 660, 794, 864, 804, 216]

Mean of the Sampled Random Numbers 510.95

From the random number generator circuit, we can see that it consists of applying the Hadamard operator on each qubit followed by measurement. From the output of the quantum random number generator, we see that the sample mean of the 20 numbers it generated is 510.95. This is close to the mean of the numbers from which the random numbers are sampled, i.e., 0 through 2^{10} assuming uniform distribution.

Deutsch–Jozsa Algorithm Implementation

The Deutsch–Jozsa algorithm uses quantum parallelism that we have discussed briefly in Chapter 1. The Deutsch–Jozsa algorithm evaluates whether a binary function is balanced or constant. A function $f(x)$ is called *balanced* if half of the values in its domain evaluates to 0 and the other half evaluates to 1. A constant function always evaluates to the same binary values of either 0 or 1 for all values in its domain. For instance, if we work with a system of three qubits, we can have $2^3 = 8$ computational basis states of the form $|x_1 x_2 x_3\rangle$ where each $x_i \in \{0, 1\}$. If we define a function $f(x) = f(x_1, x_2, x_3)$ over these eight computational basis states and if half of them evaluate to 1 and the other half evaluate to 0, we say the function is balanced. Figure 3-4 shows the high-level diagram of the Deutsch–Jozsa algorithm.

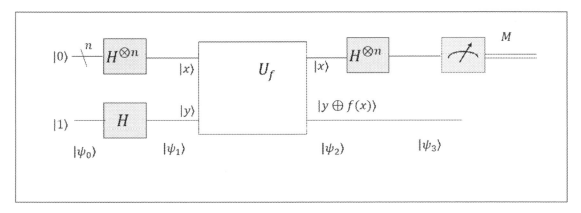

Figure 3-4. *Deutsch–Jozsa circuit*

The steps in Deutsch–Jozsa algorithm can be summarized as follows:

1. Based on the size of the domain of the function, we define the number of input qubits. For instance, if the domain for $f(x)$ has four values, then we need $log_2(4) = 2$ qubits. So in general, if we have 2^n values in the domain of the function, we need to work with n input qubits. Also, the algorithm requires a target qubit for holding the value of $f(x)$.

2. The input qubits initialized at state $|0\rangle^{\otimes n}$ are transformed to an equal superposition state by applying the Hadamard transform H on each input qubit.

$$|\psi_{in}\rangle = H^{\otimes n}|0\rangle^{\otimes n} = \frac{1}{2^{\frac{n}{2}}}\sum_{x=0}^{2^n-1}|x\rangle \tag{3-5}$$

3. The target qubit initialized at state $|0\rangle$ is transformed to the minus state $|-\rangle$ by successively applying the NOT transform X and the Hadamard transform H as shown here:

$$|\psi_t\rangle = HX|0\rangle = H|1\rangle = \frac{1}{\sqrt{2}}(|0\rangle - |1\rangle) \tag{3-6}$$

This gives us the combined state of the input and the target qubits as follows:

$$|\psi_1\rangle = |\psi_{in}\rangle \otimes |\psi_t\rangle = \frac{1}{2^{\frac{n}{2}+\frac{1}{2}}}\sum_{x=0}^{2^n-1}|x\rangle \otimes (|0\rangle - |1\rangle) \tag{3-7}$$

4. We have an oracle U_f that takes in each computational basis state binary string x as input and outputs $f(x)$ in the target qubit as shown here:

$$U_f|x\rangle \otimes |y\rangle = |x\rangle \otimes |f(x) \oplus y\rangle \tag{3-8}$$

So, for any computation basis state $|x\rangle$, the unitary transform U_f on $|x\rangle \otimes (|0\rangle - |1\rangle)$ can be expressed as follows:

$$U_f|x\rangle \otimes (|0\rangle - |1\rangle) = |x\rangle \otimes (|f(x) \oplus 0\rangle - |f(x) \oplus 1\rangle) \tag{3-9}$$

When $f(x) = 0$, we have the following:

$$U_f|x\rangle \otimes (|0\rangle-|1\rangle) = |x\rangle \otimes (|0 \oplus 0\rangle-|0 \oplus 1\rangle) = |x\rangle \otimes (|0\rangle-|1\rangle)$$

When $f(x) = 1$, we have the following:

$$U_f|x\rangle \otimes (|0\rangle-|1\rangle) = |x\rangle \otimes (|1 \oplus 0\rangle-|1 \oplus 1\rangle) = |x\rangle \otimes (|1\rangle-|0\rangle)$$

Generalizing for any binary value of $f(x)$, we have the following:

$$U_f|x\rangle \otimes (|0\rangle-|1\rangle) = (-1)^{f(x)}|x\rangle \otimes (|0\rangle - |1\rangle) \tag{3-10}$$

Based on this, we can say the application of the oracle transform U_f on the combined state $|\psi_1\rangle$ of all qubits can be expressed as follows:

$$|\psi_2\rangle = U_f|\psi_1\rangle = \frac{1}{2^{\frac{n}{2}}}\sum_{x=0}^{2^n-1}(-1)^{f(x)}|x\rangle \otimes \frac{1}{\sqrt{2}}(|0\rangle-|1\rangle) \tag{3-11}$$

An interesting observation to make here is that by applying the unitary transform on the target qubit in superposition, we can get the function value $f(x)$ to show up in the global phase. This is often referred to as the *phase kickback trick*.

5. Next we apply the Hamdard transform H on each input qubit, and this changes the computational basis for the input qubits. The new state $|\psi_3\rangle$ is as shown here:

$$|\psi_3\rangle = H^{\otimes n}|\psi_2\rangle = \frac{1}{2^n}\sum_{z=0}^{2^n-1}\sum_{x=0}^{2^n-1}(-1)^{f(x)+x \odot z}|z\rangle \otimes \frac{1}{\sqrt{2}}(|0\rangle-|1\rangle) \tag{3-12}$$

The new computational basis $|z\rangle$ is the integer representation of the binary sting $|z_0, z_1...z_{n-1}\rangle$ corresponding to the n input qubits. The term $x \odot z$ refers to the dot product between the binary strings of x and z modulo 2.

6. We make measurements on several identical copies of $|\psi_3\rangle$ and focus our attention on only the instances where all the input qubits measure as zero states, i.e., $z_0 = z_1 = \ldots = z_{n-1} = 0$. We can at this time disregard the target qubit since its state is not entangled with the input qubits. The amplitude for this input qubits state is as follows:

$$\frac{1}{2^n}\sum_{x=0}^{2^n-1}(-1)^{f(x)+x.0} = \frac{1}{2^n}\sum_{x=0}^{2^n-1}(-1)^{f(x)} \tag{3-13}$$

From Equation 3-13 we can see that if the function $f(x)$ is a balanced function, then the amplitude would be zero since the +1s corresponding to $f(x) = 0$ would cancel the −1s corresponding to $f(x) = 1$. This means for a balanced state we would not be able to observe the state $|z\rangle = |0\rangle$ corresponding to $z_0 = z_1 = \ldots = z_{n-1} = 0$. On the other hand, if we have a constant function, the probability amplitude would turn out to be 1, and we would end up observing the state $|z\rangle = |0\rangle$ in our measurement with 100 percent probability.

We implement the Deutsch–Jozsa algorithm for a domain size of 4 for the function $f(x)$, which means that we require two qubits for the input register and one qubit for the target register. Listing 3-6 shows the detailed code. The oracle transformation is implemented through the oracle function.

We define an oracle for a constant function by not applying any transformation to the state $|\psi_1\rangle$. Not applying any transformation on a state can be thought of as implementing the constant function $f(x) = 0$ through the oracle U_f as the identity transform. Hence, the output state $|\psi_2\rangle$ after the identity transform equals the input state $|\psi_1\rangle$.

$$|\psi_2\rangle = |\psi_1\rangle = \frac{1}{2^{\frac{n}{2}+1}}\sum_{x=0}^{2^n-1}|x\rangle \otimes (|0\rangle - |1\rangle) \tag{3-14}$$

We define the oracle for the balanced function $f(x)$ by applying the CNOT transformation on the target qubit based on the input qubit's states as control qubits. Through successive CNOT transformations, we implement the oracle for the balanced function with a truth table, as in Table 3-1.

Table 3-1. *Balanced Function Truth Table*

Input Qubit State $|x\rangle$	$f(x)$
00	0
01	1
01	1
11	0

Listing 3-8 shows the detailed implementation of the Deutsch–Jozsa algorithm.

Listing 3-8. Deutsch–Jozsa Implementation

```
import cirq
import numpy as np
```

The `oracle` function implements the oracle for the balanced function as well as for the constant function. For the constant function, we do not apply any transformation, and hence it ends up implementing the constant function $f(x) = 0$. Alternately, we implement the balanced function of four computational basis states using a CNOT transform on the target qubit based on the 2 input qubit states in succession. For the computation basis state given by $|x_1 x_2\rangle$ for the two-qubit input, the balanced function implemented can be written as $f(x) = f(x_0, x_1) = x_0 \oplus x_1$.

```
def oracle(data_reg, y_reg, circuit, is_balanced=True):
    if is_balanced:
        circuit.append([cirq.CNOT(data_reg[0], y_reg)
                      , cirq.CNOT(data_reg[1], y_reg)])

    return circuit

def deutsch_jozsa(domain_size: int,
            func_type_to_simulate: str = "balanced",
            copies: int = 1000):
    """

    :param domain_size: Number of inputs to the function
    :param oracle: Oracle simulating the function
    :return: whether the function is balanced or constant
```

117

```python
"""
#  Define the data register and the target qubit

reqd_num_qubits = int(np.ceil(np.log2(domain_size)))
#Define the input qubits
data_reg = [cirq.LineQubit(c) for c
                in range(reqd_num_qubits)]
# Define the Target qubits
y_reg = cirq.LineQubit(reqd_num_qubits)
# Define cirq Circuit
circuit = cirq.Circuit()
# Define equal superposition state for the input qubits
circuit.append(cirq.H(data_reg[c]) for c
                    in range(reqd_num_qubits))
# Define Minus superposition state
circuit.append(cirq.X(y_reg))
circuit.append(cirq.H(y_reg))

# Check for nature of function : balanced/constant
# to simulate and implement Oracle accordingly

if func_type_to_simulate == 'balanced':
    is_balanced = True
else:
    is_balanced = False

circuit = oracle(data_reg, y_reg,
circuit, is_balanced=is_balanced)
# Apply Hadamard transform on each of the input qubits
circuit.append(cirq.H(data_reg[c]) for
                    c in range(reqd_num_qubits))
# Measure the input qubits
circuit.append(cirq.measure(*data_reg, key='z'))
print("Circuit Diagram Follows")
print(circuit)
sim = cirq.Simulator()
result = sim.run(circuit, repetitions=copies)
print(result.histogram(key='z'))
```

```
if __name__ == '__main__':
    print("Execute Deutsch Jozsa for a Balanced Function of Domain size 4")
    deutsch_jozsa(domain_size=4, func_type_to_simulate='balanced',
    copies=1000)

    print("Execute Deutsch Jozsa for a Constant Function of Domain size 4")
    deutsch_jozsa(domain_size=4,
     func_type_to_simulate='',
     copies=1000)
```

output

Execute Deutsch Jozsa for a Balanced Function of Domain size 4

Circuit Diagram Follows

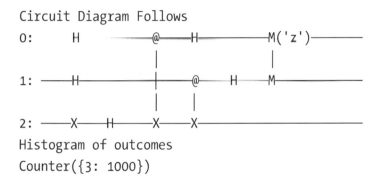

Histogram of outcomes
Counter({3: 1000})

Execute Deutsch Jozsa for a Constant Function of Domain size 4

Circuit Diagram Follows

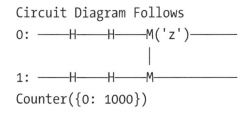

Counter({0: 1000})

From the output of the balanced function, we see all the states are 3 that correspond to the binary qubit state of $|11\rangle$. Since we do not have any state corresponding to $|00\rangle$ in our measurement, it confirms that the function is indeed balanced.

Similarly, for the constant function, we see that all the measurements are 0 corresponding to the binary qubit state $|00\rangle$ as anticipated.

Bernstein–Vajirani Algorithm

The Bernstein–Vajirani algorithm can be thought of as an extension of the Deutsch–Jozsa algorithm. Much like in the Deutsch–Jozsa algorithm, we are presented with an unknown function that takes as input a binary string of 0s and 1s and outputs a binary value of 0 or 1. Further, it is given that the function output can be written as follows:

$$f(x_0, x_1, \ldots, x_n) = s_0 x_0 + s_1 x_1 + \cdots . s_n x_n (mod\ 2)$$

$$= s.x\ (mod\ 2) = s \odot x \tag{3-15}$$

The objective of the Bernstein–Vajirani algorithm is to find out the secret binary string $s = s_0, s_1 \ldots, s_{n-1}$ that defines the function. Since the function is defined by its secret string s, we will refer to the black-box function as $f_s(x)$.

In the classical regime of computation, one can find out the secret string by querying the black-box function n times. In each of the n times, one can set only one input bit to 1 and the rest to 0s and then observe the outputs. For instance, by evaluating the function for the input pattern 10000..0, it would output the secret bit s_0 since the following is true:

$$f(x_0 = 1, x_1 = 1, \ldots, x_n = 1) = s_0 1 + s_1 0 + \ldots s_n 0 (mod\ 2) = s_0 \tag{3-16}$$

In the quantum computing paradigm, we can use quantum parallelism much like Deutsch–Jozsa to find out the secret string s with only one call to the oracle defining the black-box function. We will refer to Figure 3-4 from the Deutsch–Jozsa circuit while referring to the different intermediate states in the Bernstein–Vajirani algorithm since the high-level circuit diagram is the same for both.

The following are the detailed steps of the Bernstein–Vajirani algorithm:

1. Based on the domain of the function $f(x)$, define the number of input qubits required. For instance, if there are 2^n inputs to the function, then we would require n qubits. We initialize all the input qubits to the state $|0\rangle$. We define a target qubit initialized at the state $|0\rangle$ as well.

We apply the Hadamard transforms H on the input qubits to define the equal superposition state.

$$|\psi_{in}\rangle = H^{\otimes n}|0\rangle^n = \frac{1}{2^{\frac{n}{2}}}\sum_{x=0}^{2^n-1}|x\rangle \qquad (3\text{-}17)$$

The target qubit is transformed to the minus state by successively applying the NOT transform X and the Hadamard transform H.

$$|\psi_t\rangle = HX|0\rangle = H|1\rangle = \frac{1}{\sqrt{2}}\left(|0\rangle - |1\rangle\right) \qquad (3\text{-}18)$$

This gives us the combined state $|\psi_1\rangle$ (see Figure 3-4) of the input and the target qubits as follows:

$$|\psi_1\rangle = |\psi_{in}\rangle \otimes |\psi_t\rangle = \frac{1}{2^{\frac{n}{2}}}\sum_{x=0}^{2^n-1}|x\rangle \otimes \frac{1}{\sqrt{2}}\left(|0\rangle - |1\rangle\right) \qquad (3\text{-}19)$$

2. The oracle U_f for the unknown function $f_s(x)$ on the computational basis states $|x\rangle$ of the input qubits and the target qubit state $|y\rangle$ should work like this:

$$U_f|x\rangle \otimes |y\rangle = |x\rangle \otimes |f(x) \oplus y\rangle \qquad (3\text{-}20)$$

Using the same as Deutsch–Jozsa, we get the new state $|\psi_2\rangle$ (see Figure 3-4), as shown here:

$$|\psi_2\rangle = U_f|\psi_1\rangle = \frac{1}{2^{\frac{n}{2}}}\sum_{x=0}^{2^n-1}(-1)^{f_s(x)}|x\rangle \otimes \frac{1}{\sqrt{2}}\left(|0\rangle - |1\rangle\right) \qquad (3\text{-}21)$$

Please refer to the Deutsch–Jozsa algorithm to see how we get the $f(x)$ values to show up in the global phase by the phase kickback trick.

3. Like the Deutsch–Jozsa algorithm, we apply the Hadamard transform H on each of the input qubits in the combined state $|\psi_2\rangle$ to get to the state $|\psi_3\rangle$, as shown here:

$$|\psi_3\rangle = H^{\otimes n}|\psi_2\rangle = \frac{1}{2^n}\sum_{z=0}^{2^n-1}\sum_{x=0}^{2^n-1}(-1)^{f(x)+x\cdot z}|z\rangle \otimes \frac{1}{\sqrt{2}}\left(|0\rangle - |1\rangle\right) \qquad (3\text{-}22)$$

In Equation 3-22, $|z\rangle$ denotes the new computational basis for the n input qubits. The term $x \odot z$ denotes the dot product between the binary string representation of x and z modulo 2.

4. We know the function $f_s(x) = s \odot x$, and hence we can rewrite $|\psi_3\rangle$ as shown here:

$$|\psi_3\rangle = \frac{1}{2^n} \sum_{z=0}^{2^n-1} \sum_{x=0}^{2^n-1} (-1)^{s \odot x + x \odot z} |z\rangle \otimes \frac{1}{\sqrt{2}} (|0\rangle - |1\rangle) \tag{3-23}$$

If we ignore the target qubit and look at the amplitude of any input computational basis state $|z\rangle$, the amplitude is given by the following:

$$A(z) = \frac{1}{2^n} \sum_{x=0}^{2^n-1} (-1)^{s \odot x + x \odot z} \tag{3-24}$$

5. The amplitude of the input computational basis state z when it equals the secret string s is given by the following:

$$A(s) = \frac{1}{2^n} \sum_{x=0}^{2^n-1} (-1)^{s \odot x + x \odot s}$$

$$= \frac{1}{2^n} \sum_{x=0}^{2^n-1} (-1)^{2 \times s \odot x \bmod 2} \tag{3-25}$$

Since $2 \times s \odot x$ is divisible by 2, $2 \times s \odot x \bmod 2$ would always equal zero. This gives the amplitude of the computational basis state $|z\rangle = |s\rangle$ as follows:

$$A(s) = \frac{1}{2^n} \sum_{x=0}^{2^n-1} (-1)^0 = \frac{1}{2^n} \sum_{x=0}^{2^n-1} 1 = \frac{2^n}{2^n} = 1 \tag{3-26}$$

6. Since the amplitude of the computational basis state corresponding to the secret string s is 1, here if we measure the input qubits, we will get the state $|s\rangle$ with 100 percent probability.

We implement the Bernstein–Vajirani algorithm in a generalized way for any number of input qubits and execute it for six input qubits. The number of inputs in the domain of the function for six qubits is $2^6 = 64$. For each input qubit whose corresponding secret bit is set to 1, we apply the CNOT transformation on the target qubit with the input qubit as the control qubit. This transformation ensures that whenever the dot product between the secret string s and the computation basis state string x is even, then the resultant transformation on the target qubit is zero. On the other hand, when this dot product is odd, the target qubit undergoes a NOT operation. To summarize, this transformation implements the Oracle transformation:

$$U_f |x\rangle \otimes |y\rangle = |x\rangle \otimes |f_s(x) \oplus y\rangle \tag{3-27}$$

When the dot product between the secret string s and the computation basis state string x is even, then $f_s(x) = 0$, and hence $|f_s(x) \oplus y\rangle = |y\rangle$. As we can see in this condition, the state of the target qubit $|y\rangle$ is left unaltered. When this dot product is odd, $f_s(x) = 1$, and hence $|f_s(x) \oplus y\rangle = |1 \oplus y\rangle$. In this scenario, we can see a NOT operation is being applied to the state of the target qubit. Listing 3-9 shows the detailed implementation of the Bernstein–Vajirani algorithm.

Listing 3-9. Implementing the Bernstein–Vajirani Algorithm

```
import cirq
import numpy as np

def func_bit_pattern(num_qubits):
    """

    Create the Oracle function Parameters
    :param num_qubits:
    :return:
    """

    bit_pattern = []
    for i in range(num_qubits):
        bit_pattern.append(np.random.randint(0, 2))
    print(f"Function bit pattern: \
        {''.join([str(x) for x in bit_pattern]) }")
    return bit_pattern

def oracle(input_qubits,target_qubit,circuit,
          num_qubits,bit_pattern):
    """

    Define the oracle
```

```python
        :param input_qubits:
        :param target_qubit:
        :param circuit:
        :param num_qubits:
        :param bit_pattern:
        :return:
        """

        for i in range(num_qubits):
            if bit_pattern[i] == 1:
                    circuit.append(cirq.CNOT(input_qubits[i],
            target_qubit))
        return circuit

def BV_algorithm(num_qubits, bit_pattern):
        """

        :param num_qubits:
        :return:
        """

        input_qubits = [cirq.LineQubit(i) for
                        i in range(num_qubits)]
        target_qubit = cirq.LineQubit(num_qubits)
        circuit = cirq.Circuit()
        circuit.append([cirq.H(input_qubits[i]) for
                        i in range(num_qubits)])
        circuit.append([cirq.X(target_qubit)
                        , cirq.H(target_qubit)])
        circuit = oracle(input_qubits,target_qubit,
                        circuit,num_qubits,bit_pattern)
        circuit.append([cirq.H(input_qubits[i])
                          for i in range(num_qubits)])
        circuit.append(cirq.measure(*input_qubits,key='Z'))
        print("Bernstein Vajirani Circuit Diagram")
        print(circuit)
        sim = cirq.Simulator()
        results = sim.run(circuit, repetitions=1000)
```

```python
    results = dict(results.histogram(key='Z'))
    print(results)
    results_binary = {}
    for k in results.keys():
        results_binary["{0:b}".format(k)] = results[k]
    print("Distribution of bit pattern output
                from Bernstein Vajirani Algorithm")
    print(results_binary)

def main(num_qubits=6, bit_pattern=None):
    if bit_pattern is None:
        bit_pattern = func_bit_pattern(num_qubits)

    BV_algorithm(num_qubits, bit_pattern)


if __name__ == '__main__':
    main()
```

output

```
Function bit pattern: 111011
Bernstein Vajirani Circuit Diagram
0: ────H─────────@────H────────────────────────M('Z')─────

                 │
1: ────H─────────┼────@────H───────────────────M──────────

                 │    │
2: ────H─────────┼────┼────@────H──────────────M──────────

                 │    │    │
3: ────H────H────┼────┼────┼────────────────────M─────────

                 │    │    │
4: ────H─────────┼────┼────┼────@────H──────────M─────────

                 │    │    │    │
5: ────H─────────┼────┼────┼────┼────@────H─────M─────────

                 │    │    │    │    │
6: ────X────H────X────X────X────X────X─────────────────────

Distribution of bit pattern output from Bernstein Vajirani Algorithm
{'111011': 1000}
```

We can see from the output that the Bernstein–Vajirani algorithm has correctly identified the secret string 111011 on measurement of the input qubits with 100 percent probability. Readers are advised to execute the algorithm for larger domain sizes and see whether the algorithm is working as expected.

Bell's Inequality Test

Bell's inequality test illustrates the fact that by using quantum entanglement, one can achieve stronger correlation than that possible classically between two or more parties that cannot communicate with each other. Although entanglement can create strong correlation between two quantum objects, it alone is not useful in communication since a merely entangled state measurement on one quantum object makes the measurement of the other completely deterministic. For example, for the Bell state $|\psi_{00}\rangle = \frac{1}{\sqrt{2}}(|00\rangle + |11\rangle)$ shared between Alice and Bob, Alice's measurement of either $|0\rangle$ or $|1\rangle$ completely determines the state of Bob's qubit, and vice versa. However, if both Alice and Bob can perform measurement after entanglement and influence the final outcome of measurement, then a useful correlation between Alice and Bob can be created, which is not possible in a classical setting. We will motivate the Bell's inequality test through a cooperation game between Alice and Bob. However, before we move to the Bell's inequality test, let's deduce the probabilities of the different outcomes if Alice measures her qubit in the orthogonal basis $|\alpha\rangle$, $|\alpha_\perp\rangle$, while Bob measures his qubit in the orthogonal basis $|\beta\rangle$, $|\beta_\perp\rangle$ given that they share the Bell state $|\psi_{00}\rangle = \frac{1}{\sqrt{2}}(|00\rangle + |11\rangle)$. The knowledge of these probabilities would be required to come up with the winning strategy for the cooperation game.

We represent the general basis of measurement for Alice's basis as $|\alpha\rangle$ and $|\alpha_\perp\rangle$ where α is the angle the basis state $|\alpha\rangle$ makes with the $|0\rangle$ state. Hence, we can represent them as follows:

$$|\alpha\rangle = \cos\alpha|0\rangle + \sin\alpha|1\rangle$$

$$|\alpha_\perp\rangle = -\sin\alpha|0\rangle + \cos\alpha|1\rangle \qquad (3\text{-}28)$$

The projection of the computational basis state $|0\rangle$ on the basis state $|\alpha\rangle$ and $|\alpha_\perp\rangle$ are $\langle 0|\alpha\rangle = \cos\alpha$ and $\langle 0|\alpha_\perp\rangle = -\sin\alpha$. Similarly, the projection of the computational basis state $|1\rangle$ on $|\alpha\rangle$ is $\langle 1|\alpha\rangle = \sin\alpha$ and on $|\alpha_\perp\rangle$ is $\langle 1|\alpha_\perp\rangle = \cos\alpha$. Using this information, we can write $|0\rangle$ and $|1\rangle$ in the basis $\{|\alpha\rangle, |\alpha_\perp\rangle\}$ as follows:

$$|0\rangle = \cos\alpha|\alpha\rangle - \sin\alpha|\alpha_\perp\rangle$$

$$|1\rangle = \sin\alpha|\alpha\rangle + \cos\alpha|\alpha_\perp\rangle \tag{3-29}$$

Similarly, we can express $|0\rangle$ and $|1\rangle$ in another basis set $\{|\beta\rangle, |\beta_\perp\rangle\}$ where β is the angle the basis state $|\beta\rangle$ makes with the $|0\rangle$ state as follows:

$$|0\rangle = \cos\beta|\beta\rangle - \sin\beta|\beta_\perp\rangle$$

$$|1\rangle = \sin\beta|\beta\rangle + \cos\beta|\beta_\perp\rangle \tag{3-30}$$

Now if Alice were to measure her qubit in the $\{|\alpha\rangle, |\alpha_\perp\rangle\}$ basis and Bob his qubit in the $\{|\beta\rangle, |\beta_\perp\rangle\}$ basis, the entangled Bell state can be expressed in terms of the following:

$$|\psi_{00}\rangle = \frac{1}{\sqrt{2}}\left(|00\rangle + |11\rangle\right)$$

$$= \frac{1}{\sqrt{2}}\left(\cos\alpha|\alpha\rangle - \sin\alpha|\alpha_\perp\rangle\right) \otimes \left(\cos\beta|\beta\rangle - \sin\beta|\beta_\perp\rangle\right)$$

$$+ \frac{1}{\sqrt{2}}\left(\sin\alpha|\alpha\rangle + \cos\alpha|\alpha_\perp\rangle\right) \otimes \left(\sin\beta|\beta\rangle + \cos\beta|\beta_\perp\rangle\right)$$

$$= \frac{1}{\sqrt{2}}\cos(\alpha - \beta)|\alpha\beta\rangle + \frac{1}{\sqrt{2}}\sin(\alpha - \beta)|\alpha\beta_\perp\rangle$$

$$- \frac{1}{\sqrt{2}}\sin(\alpha - \beta)|\alpha_\perp\beta\rangle + \frac{1}{\sqrt{2}}\cos(\alpha - \beta)|\alpha_\perp\beta_\perp\rangle \tag{3-31}$$

Table 3-2 shows the probability of each of the outcomes with regard to Alice's basis states for measurement, i.e., $\{|\alpha\rangle, |\alpha_\perp\rangle\}$, and Bob's basis states for measurement, i.e., $\{|\beta\rangle, |\beta_\perp\rangle\}$.

Table 3-2. *Outcomes*

Computational Basis States	Probability
$\lvert\alpha\beta\rangle$	$\dfrac{1}{2}\cos(\alpha-\beta)^2$
$\lvert\alpha\beta_\perp\rangle$	$\dfrac{1}{2}\sin(\alpha-\beta)^2$
$\lvert\alpha_\perp\beta\rangle$	$\dfrac{1}{2}\sin(\alpha-\beta)^2$
$\lvert\alpha_\perp\beta_\perp\rangle$	$\dfrac{1}{2}\cos(\alpha-\beta)^2$

Let's now discuss the cooperation game between Alice and Bob to illustrate the Bell inequality test. The game consists of two players, Alice and Bob, and a referee. Alice and Bob are kept far apart, and they do not have any communication channel between them. In each round, the referee sends a bit x_1 to Alice and a bit x_2 to Bob. Based on the received bits, Alice and Bob are supposed to return bits $a(x_1)$ and $b(x_2)$, respectively. Alice and Bob win the round if the following condition is met:

$$a(x_1) \oplus b(x_2) = x_1 x_2 \tag{3-32}$$

Table 3-3 shows the truth table for winning the game for all pairs of x_1 and x_2.

Table 3-3. *Truth Table for Winning the Game*

$x_1 x_2$	$a(x_1) \oplus b(x_2)$
00	0
01	0
10	0
11	1

In a classical world, the best strategy Alice and Bob can come up with will win them the game at most 75 percent of the time. Here, the strategies are analogous to the decision functions $a(x_1)$ and $b(x_2)$ that Alice and Bob use to send back the bits. One can validate that the best strategy for Alice and Bob to play in a classical sense is to send back the same bits. Hence, the two best strategies that give the probability of success as 75 percent are as follows:

$$a(x_1) = b(x_2) = 0$$

$$a(x_1) = b(x_2) = 1 \tag{3-33}$$

Now let's see if Alice and Bob can do any better with a quantum strategy given that they share the Bell state $|\psi_{00}\rangle = \frac{1}{\sqrt{2}}(|00\rangle + |11\rangle)$. Well, here is one such strategy:

1. If Alice receives the bit $x_1 = 0$, she measures her qubit in the $\{|0\rangle, |\pi/2\rangle\}$ basis pertaining to $\alpha = 0$, which gives us the standard $\{|0\rangle, |1\rangle\}$ computational basis. If she receives bit $x_1 = 1$, she measures her qubit in the $\{|\pi/4\rangle, |3\pi/4\rangle\}$ basis.

2. Bob chooses a similar strategy wherein he measures the qubit either in $\{|\pi/8\rangle, |5\pi/8\rangle\}$ or $\{|-\pi/8\rangle, |3\pi/8\rangle\}$ based on whether he receives the bit $x_2 = 0$ or $x_2 = 1$.

For each of the measured basis $\{|k\rangle, |k_\perp\rangle\}$ Alice and Bob would send back 0 for $|k\rangle$ and 1 for $|k_\perp\rangle$. This is an important point since it will determine the value of the $a(x_1)$ and $b(x_2)$ returned by Alice and Bob.

When $x_1 = 0$, $x_2 = 0$

$$P(|\alpha = 0\rangle \otimes |\beta = \pi/8\rangle) = \frac{1}{2}\cos^2\left(0 - \frac{\pi}{8}\right) = \frac{1}{2}\cos^2\frac{\pi}{8} \tag{3-34}$$

Now $|\alpha = 0\rangle \otimes |\beta = \pi/8\rangle$ corresponds to $a(x_1) = 0$, $b(x_2) = 0$. Hence, we have $a(x_1) \oplus b(x_2) = 0 \oplus 0 = 0 = xy = 0 \times 0 = 0$ when $(x_1 = 0, x_2 = 0)$ with probability $\frac{1}{2}\cos^2\frac{\pi}{8}$. Similarly:

$$P(|\alpha_\perp, \alpha = 0\rangle \otimes |\beta_\perp, \beta = \pi/8\rangle) = \frac{1}{2}\cos^2\left(0 - \frac{\pi}{8}\right) = \frac{1}{2}\cos^2\frac{\pi}{8} \tag{3-35}$$

Also, $|\alpha_\perp, \alpha = 0\rangle \otimes |\beta_\perp, \beta = \pi/8\rangle$ corresponds to $a(x_1) = 1$, $b(x_2) = 1$. Hence, we have $a(x_1) \oplus b(x_2) = 1 \oplus 1 = 0 = xy = 0 \times 0 = 0$ when $(x_1 = 0, x_2 = 0)$ with probability $\frac{1}{2}\cos^2\frac{\pi}{8}$.

Combining Equation 3-34 and Equation 3-35, we can say when $(x_1 = 0, x_2 = 0)$, Alice and Bob have a $\left(2 * \frac{1}{2}\cos^2\frac{\pi}{8}\right) = \cos^2\frac{\pi}{8} = 0.85$ probability of winning.

When $x_1 = 0$, $x_2 = 1$:

$$P\left(|\alpha = 0\rangle \otimes |\beta = -\pi/8\rangle\right) = \frac{1}{2}\cos^2\left(0 + \frac{\pi}{8}\right) = \frac{1}{2}\cos^2\frac{\pi}{8} \tag{3-36}$$

Now $|\alpha = 0\rangle \otimes |\beta = -\pi/8\rangle$ corresponds to $a(x_1) = 0$, $b(x_2) = 0$. Hence, $a(x_1) \oplus b(x_2) = 0 \oplus 0 = 0 = xy = 0 \times 1 = 0$ when $(x_1 = 0, x_2 = 1)$ with probability $\frac{1}{2}\cos^2\frac{\pi}{8}$.
Similarly:

$$P\left(|\alpha_\perp, \alpha = 0\rangle \otimes |\beta_\perp, \beta = -\pi/8\rangle\right) = \frac{1}{2}\cos^2\left(0 + \frac{\pi}{8}\right) = \frac{1}{2}\cos^2\frac{\pi}{8} \tag{3-37}$$

The state $|\alpha_\perp, \alpha = 0\rangle \otimes |\beta_\perp, \beta = -\pi/8\rangle$ corresponds to $a(x_1) = 1$, $b(x_2) = 1$. Hence, $a(x_1) \oplus b(x_2) = 1 \oplus 1 = 0 = xy = 0 \times 1 = 0$ when $(x_1 = 0, x_2 = 1)$ with probability $\frac{1}{2}\cos^2\frac{\pi}{8}$

Combining Equation 3-36 and Equation 3-37, we can say when $(x_1 = 0, x_2 = 1)$, Alice and Bob have a $\cos^2\frac{\pi}{8} = 0.85$ probability of winning.

Proceeding similarly one can deduce using the adopted strategy, Alice and Bob have a $\cos^2\frac{\pi}{8}$ or 0.85 probability of winning for the remaining two conditions $(x_1 = 1, x_2 = 0)$ and $(x_1 = 1, x_2 = 1)$ as well. Readers are advised to do the maths for these two conditions and validate that the claim is true.

Hence, using the adopted strategy for all possible combination of bits x_1 and x_2, Alice and Bob manage to send back $a(x_1)$ and $b(x_2)$ so as to ensure $a(x_1) \oplus b(x_2) = x_1 x_2$ with probability of $\cos^2\frac{\pi}{8}$ or 0.85. This is higher than the maximum probability of winning achievable in the classical setup, which stands at 0.75.

We implement Bell's inequality in `Cirq` by modeling the cooperation game between Alice and Bob in Listing 3-10. The cooperation game is using the strategy that we just discussed.

Listing 3-10. Bell's Inequality

```python
import cirq
import numpy as np

def bell_inequality_test_circuit():
    """
    Define 4 qubits
    0th qubit - Alice
    1st qubit - contains the bit sent to Alice by the referee
    2nd qubit - Bob's qubit
    3rd qubit - contains the bit sent to Bob by the referee
        :return: cirq circuit
    """
    qubits - [cirq.LineQubit(i) for i in range(4)]
    circuit = cirq.Circuit()
    # Entangle Alice and Bob to the Bell state
    circuit.append([cirq.H(qubits[0]),
            cirq.CNOT(qubits[0], qubits[2])])
    # Apply X^(-0.25) on Alice's Qubit
    circuit.append([cirq.X(qubits[0])**(-0.25)])
    # Apply Hadamard transform to the referee Qubits
    # for Alice and Bob
    # This is done to randomize the qubit
    circuit.append([cirq.H(qubits[1]), cirq.H(qubits[3])])
    # Perform a Conditional X^0.5 on Alice and Bob
    # Qubits based on corresponding referee qubits
    circuit.append([cirq.CNOT(qubits[1], qubits[0])**0.5])
    circuit.append([cirq.CNOT(qubits[3], qubits[2])**0.5])
    # Measure all the qubits
    circuit.append(cirq.measure(qubits[0], key='A'))
    circuit.append(cirq.measure(qubits[1], key='r_A'))
    circuit.append(cirq.measure(qubits[2], key='B'))
    circuit.append(cirq.measure(qubits[3], key='r_B'))
    return circuit
```

```python
def main(iters=1000):
    # Build the Bell inequality test circuit
    circuit = bell_inequality_test_circuit()
    print("Bell Inequality Test Circuit")
    print(circuit)
    #Simulate for several iterations
    sim = cirq.Simulator()
    result = sim.run(circuit, repetitions=iters)
    A = result.measurements['A'][:, 0]
    r_A = result.measurements['r_A'][:, 0]
    B = result.measurements['B'][:, 0]
    r_B = result.measurements['r_B'][:, 0]

    win = (np.array(A) + np.array(B)) % 2 == (np.array(r_A)
        & np.array(r_B))
    print(f"Alice and Bob won {100*np.mean(win)} %
        of the times")

if __name__ == '__main__':
    main()
```

output

Bell Inequality Test Circuit

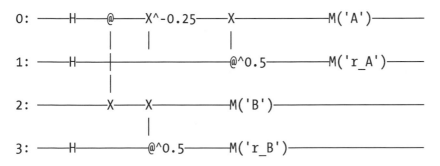

Alice and Bob won 85.7 % of the times

Simon's Algorithm

In Simon's problem, we are given a function $f(x)$ whose access is restricted to queries through a black-box transformation U_f much like in the Deutsch–Jozsa and Bernstein–Vajirani algorithms. As part of the Simon problem, we need to do the following:

1. Find out whether the function is a one-to-one function, i.e., each value of input maps to a unique output.

2. Find out whether the function is two-to-one function, i.e., each value of input maps to exactly two inputs. When the function is two to one, then there is a secret binary string s that ties each pair of inputs x_1 and x_2 that have the same output, i.e., $f(x_1) = f(x_2)$ if and only if $x_1 \oplus x_2 = s$. We need to determine the secret string s for the identified two-to-one function.

3. Further, it is given that the input function will always be either a one-to-one or two-to-one function.

Simon's algorithm is the precursor to other important algorithms such as Shor's algorithm for the prime factorization of the integers. Figure 3-5 illustrates the high-level flow diagram of Simon's algorithm.

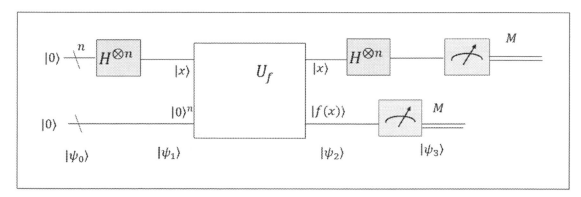

Figure 3-5. *Simon's algorithm*

The following are the steps associated with the Simon's algorithm:

1. We start with n input qubits based on the domain of the problem. Also, we define a set of n qubits as the target qubits to hold the value of $f(x)$. All the qubits are initialized to zero. The initial state of the $2n$ qubits can be written as follows:

$$|\psi_0\rangle = |0\rangle^{\otimes n}|0\rangle^{\otimes n} \tag{3-38}$$

2. We apply the Hadamard transform on each of the input qubits to create an equal superposition state for the inputs. The combined state of the $2n$ qubits after Hadamard transforms is given by the following:

$$|\psi_1\rangle = H^{\otimes n}|0\rangle^{\otimes n} \otimes |0\rangle^n = \frac{1}{2^{\frac{n}{2}}} \sum_{x \in \{0,1\}^n} |x\rangle \otimes |0\rangle^{\otimes n} \tag{3-39}$$

3. In the next stage, we apply the function $f(x)$ to each of the computation basis states $x = x_o\, x_1...x_{n-1}$ through the Oracle transform U_f. So for each computational basis state $|x\rangle$ we have this:

$$U_f|x\rangle|y\rangle = |x\rangle|f(x) \oplus y\rangle \tag{3-40}$$

In Equation 3-40, $|y\rangle$ is the initial state of the each of the n target qubits and hence $y = 0$. This gives us the new state $|\psi_2\rangle$ as follows:

$$|\psi_2\rangle = U_f|\psi_1\rangle = \frac{1}{2^{\frac{n}{2}}} \sum_{x \in \{0,1\}^n}^{2^n-1} |x\rangle \otimes |f(x)\rangle \tag{3-41}$$

Do note that unlike the previous algorithms, there is no *phase kickback* in Simon's algorithm since we have set the initial state of the target qubits $y = 0$.

We apply the Hadamard transform on the input qubits to get the final state $|\psi_3\rangle$ as follows:

$$|\psi_3\rangle = H^{\otimes n}|\psi_2\rangle = \frac{1}{2^n} \sum_{z=\{0,1\}^n} \sum_{x \in \{0,1\}^n} (-1)^{x \odot z} |z\rangle \otimes |f(x)\rangle \tag{3-42}$$

4. Now let's see what happens when the secret string $s = 0000...0$, i.e., the function is one to one. When the function is a one-to-one function, then each value of $f(x)$ is tied to a specific input string x. So, if we measure the target qubits and observe $|f(x)\rangle$, we will get only one corresponding x. For each input $|z\rangle$ state, the probability amplitude given that we have observed the state of the target qubits as $|f(x)\rangle$ is given by $\frac{1}{2^{\frac{n}{2}}}(-1)^{x \odot z}$. Hence the corresponding probability of $|z\rangle$ state given, we have observed the state of the target qubits as $|f(x)\rangle$ is given by $P(z) = \left\| \frac{1}{2^{\frac{n}{2}}}(-1)^{x \odot z} \right\|_2^2 = \frac{1}{2^n}$. Since the probability is the same for all z, we get a uniform distribution over the input states z for each target qubit state $f(x)$.

5. Now let's discuss the case when the secret string s is not all zeros; i.e., the function is a two-to-one function. Once we have measured the target qubits and observed the state $|c\rangle$, there would be two values of x, say, x_1 and x_2 that would give $f(x_1) = f(x_2) = c$. For each measured state c of the target qubits, the probability amplitude of each of the input qubit states $|z\rangle$ is given by the following:

$$\frac{1}{2^{\frac{n}{2}+\frac{1}{2}}}[(-1)^{x_1 \odot z} + (-1)^{x_2 \odot z}] \tag{3-43}$$

For any state $|z\rangle$ to have a nonzero probability amplitude, the following should hold true:

$$(-1)^{x_1 \odot z} = (-1)^{x_2 \odot z} \rightarrow x_1 \odot z = x_2 \odot z \tag{3-44}$$

For a two-to-one function, we know that x_1 and x_2 are bound by the relation $x_1 \oplus x_2 = s$, which also implies $x_2 = x_1 \oplus s$.

Let's now simplify $x_1 \odot z = x_2 \odot z$ by replacing $x_2 = (x_1 \oplus s)$.

$$x_1 \odot z = x_2 \odot z$$
$$= (x_1 \oplus s) \odot z$$
$$= x_1 \odot z \oplus s \odot z \tag{3-45}$$

Since we have $x_1 \odot z$ on both sides, the identify simplifies to $s \odot z = 0$.

This means when we get a nonzero probability of measuring any input state z, then $s \odot z = 0$.

We can measure the input qubits and observe n different z values. Based on the observed z values, we can solve a set of n equations as shown here to find the secret strings:

$$s \odot z_1 = 0$$
$$s \odot z_2 = 0$$
$$.$$
$$.$$
$$s \odot z_n = 0 \tag{3-46}$$

The n equations can be solved conveniently by algorithms such as Gaussian elimination.

Listing 3-11 illustrates the detailed implementation of Simon's algorithm. The secret string 110 is used to demonstrated the Simon's Algorithm in the implementation.

Listing 3-11. Simon's Algorithm

```
import cirq
import numpy as np

def oracle(input_qubits, target_qubits, circuit):
    # Oracle for Secret Code 110
    circuit.append(cirq.CNOT(input_qubits[2],target_qubits[1]))
    circuit.append(cirq.X(target_qubits[0]))
    circuit.append(cirq.CNOT(input_qubits[2], target_qubits[0]))
    circuit.append(cirq.CCNOT(input_qubits[0],input_qubits[1],
    target_qubits[0]))
    circuit.append(cirq.X(input_qubits[0]))
    circuit.append(cirq.X(input_qubits[1]))
    circuit.append(cirq.CCNOT(input_qubits[0], input_qubits[1],
    target_qubits[0]))
    circuit.append(cirq.X(input_qubits[0]))
    circuit.append(cirq.X(input_qubits[1]))
```

```python
    circuit.append(cirq.X(target_qubits[0]))
    return circuit

def simons_algorithm_circuit(num_qubits=3,copies=1000):
    """
    Build the circuit for Simon's Algorithm
    :param num_qubits:
    :return: cirq circuit
    """
    input_qubits = [cirq.LineQubit(i) for
                            i in range(num_qubits)]
    target_qubits = [cirq.LineQubit(k) for
                k in range(num_qubits, 2 * num_qubits)]
    circuit = cirq.Circuit()
    # Create Equal Superposition state for the
    # Input qubits through Hadamard Transform
    circuit.append([cirq.H(input_qubits[i]) for
                        i in range(num_qubits)])
    # Pass the Superposition state through the oracle
    circuit = oracle(input_qubits, target_qubits, circuit)
    # Apply Hadamard transform on the input corners
    circuit.append([cirq.H(input_qubits[i]) for
                            i in range(num_qubits)])
    # Measure the input and the target qubits
    circuit.append(cirq.measure(*(input_qubits
                        + target_qubits), key='Z'))
    print("Circuit Diagram for Simons Algorithm follows")
    print(circuit)
    #Simulate Algorithm
    sim = cirq.Simulator()
    result = sim.run(circuit,repetitions=copies)
    out = dict(result.histogram(key='Z'))
    out_result = {}
    for k in out.keys():
```

```
        new_key =  "{0:b}".format(k)
        if len(new_key) < 2*num_qubits:
            new_key = (2*num_qubits -
                        len(new_key))*'0' + new_key
        out_result[new_key] = out[k]
    print(out_result)

if __name__ =='__main__':
    simons_algorithm_circuit()
```

output

```
Circuit Diagram for Simons Algorithm follows
```

```
{'110110': 62, '110010': 69, '000100': 56, '111010': 59, '111000': 71,
'001110': 66, '110100': 65, '001010': 59, '001000': 62, '111110': 68,
'000010': 68, '000000': 57, '001100': 63, '110000': 46, '111100': 73,
'000110': 56}
```

Based on the output of Simon's algorithm, one can find the secret string easily by just choosing two outcomes where the $f(x)$ value (that is stored in the last 3 bits of the combined $|x\rangle|f(x)\rangle$ state) matches. If we take the two outcomes 111010 and 001010, we can see the output bits for both the outcomes are the same and equal to 010. Therefore, if we do modulo 2 addition with the two inputs 111 and 001, we will get our secret code. So, the secret code is 111 $\oplus$ 001, which gives us 110, which matches with the secret code we have chosen. Readers are advised to write a small function to automate the secret key finding procedure using similar logic.

Grover's Algorithm

One of the potential advantages of quantum computing over classical computing is the speed in which it can access database elements. Grover's algorithm is one such algorithm that can provide a quadratic speedup in searching items from a database. Grover's algorithm uses the *amplitude amplification trick*, which not only helps in database search tasks but can be widely used in several applications.

Suppose we have $N = 2^n$ items in the database and we want to search the item indexed by k, which we term as the *winner*. We can define the N items by the computational basis states $|x\rangle$ corresponding to n input qubits. The oracle works on each of the computational basis states $|x\rangle \in \{0, 1\}^n$ and returns a function output $f(x) = 1$ for the winner item and 0 for the remaining items. In the quantum computing paradigm, we can think of the oracle U_f as the unitary operator that works on the computational basis state $|x\rangle$, as shown here:

$$U_f|x\rangle = (-1)^{f(x)}|x\rangle \tag{3-47}$$

For the winner item referenced by the computational basis state $|k\rangle$, the effect of the Oracle transformation is as shown here:

$$U_f|k\rangle = (-1)^{f(k)}|k\rangle = -1^1|k\rangle = -|k\rangle \tag{3-48}$$

Now that we have some information about the oracle, let's look at the steps in Grover's algorithm:

1. Based on the number of items $N = 2^n$ in the database, we define an equal superposition state over n qubits initialized to $|0\rangle^{\otimes n}$ using the Hadamard transformations, i.e., $|\psi_{in}\rangle = H^{\otimes n}|0\rangle^n = \frac{1}{\sqrt{N}} \sum_{0}^{N-1} |x\rangle$.

   We also take a target qubit initialized at $|0\rangle$ to the minus state, which we use to implement the *phase kickback trick*. This gives us the combined state $|\psi_1\rangle$ of the input and target qubits as follows:

$$|\psi_1\rangle = \frac{1}{\sqrt{N}} \sum_0^{N-1} |x\rangle \otimes \frac{1}{\sqrt{2}}(|0\rangle - |1\rangle) \tag{3-49}$$

2. In the next step, we implement the oracle U_f which works on the computational basis states of the input and target as $U_f|x\rangle\,|y\rangle = |x\rangle\,|f(x) \oplus y\rangle$ where y is the target qubit state. Applying U_f on $|\psi_1\rangle$ gives us $|\psi_2\rangle$ through the *phase kickback trick* that we have illustrated in the Deutsch–Jozsa algorithm. The state $|\psi_2\rangle$ after the transformation by the oracle unitary U_f is given by the following:

$$|\psi_2\rangle = U_f|\psi_1\rangle = \frac{1}{\sqrt{N}} \sum_0^{N-1} |x\rangle(-1)^{f(x)} \otimes \frac{1}{\sqrt{2}}(|0\rangle - |1\rangle) \tag{3-50}$$

As we can see, the target qubit state remains unchanged, and we are able to get the function value $f(x)$ in the phase corresponding to every computational basis state $|x\rangle$. Hence, going forward, we can discard the target qubit and think of the transformation of the oracle U_f on any computational basis state as $U_f|x\rangle = (-1)^{f(x)}|x\rangle$. Now that we have established the Oracle function solely in terms of the input qubits, we will no more refer to the target qubit. The oracle in a sense implements the function $f(x)$, which is 1 when x is the winner state and 0 elsewhere.

3. We can think of the equal superposition state $|\psi_{in}\rangle = \frac{1}{\sqrt{N}} \sum_0^{N-1} |x\rangle$ as a linear combination of two vectors that are mutually orthogonal: the *searched* or *the winner item* that we denote by $|k\rangle$ and the vector $|c\rangle$ that is the unit vector obtained by removing the component of the vector $|k\rangle$ from the equal superposition state $|\psi_{in}\rangle$. Figure 3-6(a) illustrates this.

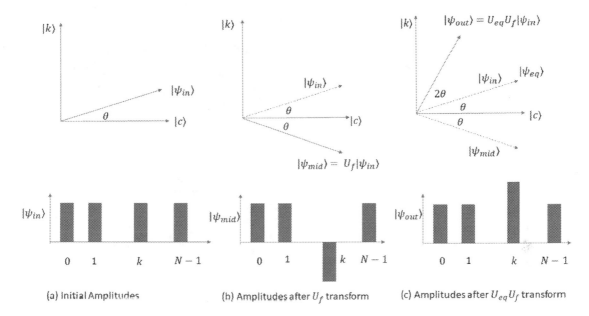

(a) Initial Amplitudes   (b) Amplitudes after U_f transform   (c) Amplitudes after $U_{eq}U_f$ transform

Figure 3-6. *Geometrical interpretation of Grover's algorithm*

This allows us to write $|\psi_{in}\rangle$ in the span of two vectors $|k\rangle$ and $|c\rangle$ (see Figure 3-6(a)) as follows:

$$|\psi_{in}\rangle = sin\theta\,|k\rangle + cos\theta\,|c\rangle \tag{3-51}$$

In Equation 3-51, we have $cos\theta = \dfrac{1}{\sqrt{N}}$ and $sin\theta = \dfrac{\sqrt{(N-1)}}{\sqrt{N}}$.

4. Now once we apply the oracle transformation U_f on the state $|\psi_{in}\rangle$, the phase corresponding to the winner item state $|k\rangle$ gets multiplied by -1, and hence the output state $|\psi_{mid}\rangle$ can be expressed as follows:

$$|\psi_{mid}\rangle = U_f|\psi_{in}\rangle = -sin\theta\,|k\rangle + cos\theta\,|c\rangle \tag{3-52}$$

So, the unitary oracle transform U_f basically has the effect of applying a reflection about the vector $|c\rangle$, as we can see from Figure 3-6(b). The reflections have the effect of negating the amplitude of the winner state $|k\rangle$.

5. Finally, we reflect the vector $|\psi_{mid}\rangle$ over the vector $|\psi_{eq}\rangle$ where $|\psi_{eq}\rangle$ is the equal superposition state for n qubits, i.e., $\frac{1}{\sqrt{N}}\sum_{0}^{N-1}|x\rangle$. The reflection along a vector $|\psi_{eq}\rangle$ is given by the following: the transformation $U_{\psi_{eq}} = 2|\psi_{eq}\rangle\langle\psi_{eq}|-I$. In this two-dimensional basis of $|c\rangle$ and $|k\rangle$, we can write $|\psi_{eq}\rangle$ as $|\psi_{eq}\rangle = \begin{bmatrix} cos\theta \\ sin\theta \end{bmatrix}$.

This makes the unitary transform $U_{\psi_{eq}}$ as follows:

$$U_{\psi_{eq}} = 2|\psi_{eq}\rangle\langle\psi_{eq}|-I = \begin{bmatrix} \cos 2\theta & \sin 2\theta \\ \sin 2\theta & -\cos 2\theta \end{bmatrix} \tag{3-53}$$

Applying the unitary transform $U_{\psi_{eq}}$ to $|\psi_{mid}\rangle$, which is $[cos\theta - sin\theta]^T$ in the two-dimensional basis of $|c\rangle$ and $|k\rangle$, we get $|\psi_{out}\rangle$ as shown here:

$$|\psi_{out}\rangle = U_{\psi_{eq}}|\psi_{mid}\rangle = \begin{bmatrix} \cos 2\theta & \sin 2\theta \\ \sin 2\theta & -\cos 2\theta \end{bmatrix}\begin{bmatrix} cos\theta \\ -sin\theta \end{bmatrix}$$

$$= \begin{bmatrix} \cos 2\theta cos\theta - \sin 2\theta sin\theta \\ \sin 2\theta cos\theta + \cos 2\theta sin\theta \end{bmatrix}$$

$$= \begin{bmatrix} \cos 3\theta \\ \sin 3\theta \end{bmatrix} = \sin 3\theta|k\rangle + \cos 3\theta|c\rangle \tag{3-54}$$

So, with successive unitary transform U_f followed by $U_{\psi_{eq}}$, we have gone from the state $|\psi_{in}\rangle = sin\theta|k\rangle + cos\theta|c\rangle$ to $|\psi_{out}\rangle = sin\,3\theta|k\rangle + cos\,3\theta|c\rangle$. Since sin is monotonically increasing and cos is monotonically decreasing in the first quadrant, it is not difficult to see that the amplitude of $|k\rangle$ given by the sin term has increased from $sin\theta$ to $sin3\theta$ while the amplitude of the remaining states given by $|c\rangle$ has decreased from $cos\theta$ to $cos3\theta$.

6. Applying the unitary transformation U_f followed by $U_{\psi_{eq}}$ in succession iteratively allows us to converge to the winner state $|k\rangle$ by amplifying the amplitude toward it. We can combine the two transforms as $U_{\psi_{eq}}U_f$ and call it Grover's transform G. So, if we apply Grover's transform for m iterations, the final output state $\left(U_{\psi_{eq}}U_f\right)^m|\psi_{in}\rangle$ will be very close to $|k\rangle$.

When we work with two-input qubits that pertain to an oracle with four items, i.e. $N = 4$, we have the following:

$$sin\theta = \frac{1}{\sqrt{N}} = \frac{1}{\sqrt{4}} = \frac{1}{2} \tag{3-55}$$

So, the initial amplitude of the winning item is ½ with a corresponding probability of ¼. Since $sin\theta = \frac{1}{2}$, that implies $\theta = 30°$. After the unitary transform U_f followed by U_{eq}, the new amplitude for the winning item is $sin3\theta = sin(3 \times 30°) = sin90° = 1$. This implies that the starting state $|\psi_{in}\rangle$ has been transformed to the wining item state $|k\rangle$ in just one iteration.

7.   The U_f transformation provided by the oracle is the same as in the Deutsch–Jozsa and Bernstein–Vajıranı algorithms.

8.   We need a way to come up with the unitary transform $U_{\psi_{eq}}$ in terms of the quantum operators. In terms of the Hadamard gate, $U_{\psi_{eq}}$ can be written as follows:

$$U_{\psi_{eq}}\rangle = H^{\otimes n}\left(2|0\rangle^{\otimes n}\langle 0|^{\otimes n} - I\right)H^{\otimes n} \tag{3-56}$$

As we discussed earlier, the role of $U_{\psi_{eq}}$ is to reflect a vector about the equal superposition state $|\psi_{eq}\rangle = \frac{1}{\sqrt{N}}\sum_{0}^{N-1}|x\rangle$. We can simplify $U_{\psi_{eq}}$ as shown here:

$$U_{\psi_{eq}} = H^{\otimes n}\left(2|0\rangle^{\otimes n}\langle 0|^{\otimes n} - I\right)H^{\otimes n}$$

$$= 2(H^{\otimes n}|0\rangle^{\otimes n})(\langle 0|^{\otimes n}H^{\otimes n}) - H^{\otimes n}IH^{\otimes n}$$

$$= 2(H^{\otimes n}|0\rangle^{\otimes n})(\langle 0|^{\otimes n}H^{\otimes n}) - (H^2)^{\otimes n} \tag{3-57}$$

Now $H^{\otimes n}|0\rangle^{\otimes n}$ is nothing, but the equal superposition state for n qubits and hence $H^{\otimes n}|0\rangle^{\otimes n} = \frac{1}{\sqrt{N}}\sum_{0}^{N-1}|x\rangle$ where $N = 2^n$. Also, with the Hadamard transform H being idempotent, we have $H^2 = I$. Using this information, we can rewrite Equation 3-57 as shown here:

$$U_{\psi_{eq}} = 2\left(\frac{1}{\sqrt{N}}\sum_{0}^{N-1}|x\rangle\right)\left(\frac{1}{\sqrt{N}}\sum_{0}^{N-1}\langle x|\right) - I$$

$$= 2|\psi_{eq}\rangle\langle\psi_{eq}| - I \tag{3-58}$$

$2|\psi_{eq}\rangle\langle\psi_{eq}| - I$ is precisely the reflection transform about the vector $\langle\psi_{eq}|$.

Now that we have proved $H^{\otimes n}(2|0\rangle^{\otimes n}\langle 0|^{\otimes n} - I)H^{\otimes n}$ is indeed the unitary transform for reflection about $|\psi_{eq}\rangle$, the only thing left is to find a way to achieve the transformation $(2|0\rangle^{\otimes n}\langle 0|^{\otimes n} - I)$ using standard gates.

9. To see how, we can achieve $(2|0\rangle^{\otimes n}\langle 0|^{\otimes n} - I)$ let's see what this transformation does to a basis state $|x\rangle$.

a) When the basis state is $|x\rangle = |0\rangle^{\otimes n}$:

$$\left(2|0\rangle^{\otimes n}\langle 0|^{\otimes n} - I\right)|0\rangle^{\otimes n} = |0\rangle^{\otimes n}$$

b) When the basis state is $|x\rangle \neq |0\rangle^{\otimes n}$:

$$\left(2|0\rangle^{\otimes n}\langle 0|^{\otimes n} - I\right)|x\rangle$$

$$= \left(2|0\rangle^{\otimes n}\langle 0|^{\otimes n}|x\rangle - |x\rangle\right)$$

$$= 2|0\rangle^{\otimes n}.0 - |x\rangle = -|x\rangle$$

So, the transformation flips the phase when the basis state is other than $|0\rangle^{\otimes n}$.

This conditional phase flip operator can be achieved by using a combination of CNOT, X, and H gates, as we will see during the Grover's algorithm implementation for two qubits.

10. Please note that the input state to Grover's transform $|\psi_{in}\rangle$ equals $|\psi_{eq}\rangle$ only in the first iteration of Grover's transform. You should not assume that in every iteration that would be the case since from the second iteration onward the $|\psi_{in}\rangle$ state to Grover's iteration would be different.

Now that we have discussed all the different aspects of Grover's algorithm in detail, we can put together the high-level flow diagram of Grover's algorithm in Figure 3-7.

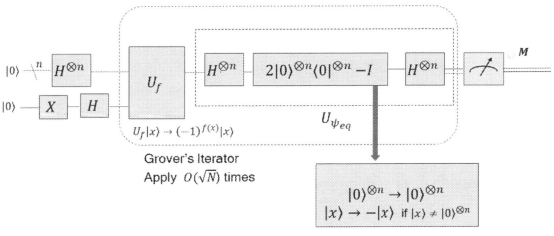

Figure 3-7. *High-level flow diagram of Grover's algorithm*

As discussed earlier, we implement Grover's algorithm using a database size of 4. Also, we build oracle U_f to search for the element **01** for our illustration. For the generalized implementation of the oracle, we invert the state of the input qubits corresponding to which the winner element bits are zero. This ensures the winner computational basis state is converted to all 1s states given by $|1\rangle^{\otimes n}$, where n is the number of input qubits. In the next step, we apply a conditional NOT transform on the target qubit based on all the input qubits as control qubits. Since the winner computational basis state is $|1\rangle^{\otimes n}$, the conditional NOT transform on the target qubit is only going to set $f(x) = 1$ for the winner state. Setting $f(x) = 1$ for the winner computational state is going to bring in the desired -1 flip factor in its amplitude because of the *phase kickback*. The conditional NOT transform is achieved by using the `Toffoli` gate. Once the desired flip is achieved, we need to undo the conditional NOT operations so that the winner computation basis state is restored to its original value from $|1\rangle^{\otimes n}$.

145

The other important part of the algorithm is building the reflection operator $U_{\psi_{eq}}$ that will reflect the state $|\psi_{mid}\rangle$ achieved after the oracle transform U_f about the equal superposition state $|\psi_{eq}\rangle$. We can implement this as illustrated in the circuit diagram for Grover's algorithm in Figure 3-8 for a database size of 4. The oracle U_f and the flection operator $U_{\psi_{eq}}$ forms the Grover iterator. With a few rounds of application of the Grover iterator, one should be able to measure the winner state with high probability. For a database consisting of four items indexed using the computational basis state of two qubits, we converge to the winner state in one Grover iterator.

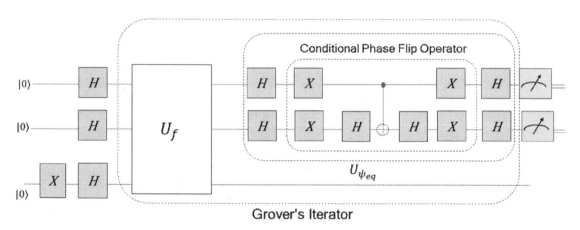

Figure 3-8. *Grover's algorithm circuit for a four-item database*

Readers are advised to take in different basis states including $|00\rangle$ and verify whether the conditional phase flip operator is working as expected. One iteration of Grover's algorithm is sufficient to converge to the winner state 01 as we saw earlier in Figure 3-8. Please see the detailed implementation in Listing 3-12.

Listing 3-12. Grover's Algorithm

```
import cirq
import numpy as np

def oracle(input_qubits, target_qubit,
        circuit, secret_element='01'):
    print(f"Element to be searched: {secret_element}")
```

```python
    # Flip the qubits corresponding to the bits containing 0
    for i, bit in enumerate(secret_element):
        if int(bit) == 0:
            circuit.append(cirq.X(input_qubits[i]))
    # Do a Conditional NOT using all input qubits as control
    # qubits
    circuit.append(cirq.TOFFOLI(*input_qubits, target_qubit))
    # Revert the input qubits to the state prior to Flipping
    for i, bit in enumerate(secret_element):
        if int(bit) == 0:
            circuit.append(cirq.X(input_qubits[i]))
    return circuit

def grovers_algorithm(num_qubits=2, copies=1000):
    # Define input and Target Qubit
    input_qubits = [cirq.LineQubit(i)
            for i in range(num_qubits)]
    target_qubit = cirq.LineQubit(num_qubits)
    # Define Quantum Circuit
    circuit = cirq.Circuit()
    # Create equal Superposition State
    circuit.append([cirq.H(input_qubits[i])
            for i in range(num_qubits)])
    # Take target qubit to minus state |->
    circuit.append([cirq.X(target_qubit)
        ,cirq.H(target_qubit)])
    # Pass the qubit through the Oracle
    circuit = oracle(input_qubits, target_qubit, circuit)
    # Construct Grover operator.
    circuit.append(cirq.H.on_each(*input_qubits))
    circuit.append(cirq.X.on_each(*input_qubits))
    circuit.append(cirq.H.on(input_qubits[1]))
    circuit.append(cirq.CNOT(input_qubits[0]
            ,input_qubits[1]))
```

```python
        circuit.append(cirq.H.on(input_qubits[1]))
        circuit.append(cirq.X.on_each(*input_qubits))
        circuit.append(cirq.H.on_each(*input_qubits))

        # Measure the result.
        circuit.append(cirq.measure(*input_qubits, key='Z'))
        print("Grover's algorithm follows")
        print(circuit)
        sim = cirq.Simulator()
        result = sim.run(circuit, repetitions=copies)
        out = result.histogram(key='Z')

        out_result = {}
        for k in out.keys():
            new_key = "{0:b}".format(k)
            if len(new_key) < num_qubits:
                new_key = (num_qubits - len(new_key))*'0'
                            + new_key
            out_result[new_key] = out[k]
        print(out_result)

if __name__ =='__main__':
    grovers_algorithm(2)
```

output

```
Element to be searched: 01
Grover's algorithm follows
0: ——H——X——@——X——H——X——@——X——H——————————M('Z')————
            |           |           |
1: ——H————————@——H——X——H——X——H——X——H——M——————————
            |
2: ——X——H——X————————————————————————————————————————
{'01': 1000}
```

From the output we can see that Grover's algorithm has converged to the winner item with 100 percent probability.

Summary

With this, we come to the end of Chapter 3. In this chapter, we got familiar with the quantum computing programming paradigm in `Cirq` and to some extent in `Qiskit`. Throughout this chapter, we looked at various quantum computing algorithms such as the Deutsch–Jozsa algorithm, the Bernstein-Vajirani algorithm, Bell's inequality, Grover's algorithm, and Simon's algorithm. All these quantum algorithms are computationally more efficient than their classical counterparts by taking advantage of the quantum mechanical properties of superposition, entanglement, interference, and other subtleties related to quantum mechanics. Readers are advised to thoroughly go through the different algorithms and their underlying maths for a better understanding of the quantum paradigm of computation.

In the next chapter, we will look at quantum Fourier transform–based algorithms that form the backbone of an important set of algorithms in quantum computing as well as in quantum machine learning paradigm. Looking forward to your participation!

CHAPTER 4

Quantum Fourier Transform and Related Algorithms

"The distinction between past, present and future is only a stubbornly persistent illusion."

—Albert Einstein

In this chapter, we will study the quantum Fourier transform and its application in different quantum algorithms. Problems such as *factoring an integer* into prime numbers or *period finding* are computationally intractable problems for a classical computer because of the exponentially large number of operations involved. Integer factoring and period finding can be efficiently solved using the quantum phase estimation algorithm that is heavily based on the quantum Fourier transform. Alternately, since quantum phase estimation aims to find the eigenvalue corresponding to an eigenvector of a unitary operator, it is backbone of important algorithms in optimization such as the HHL algorithm (named for Hassim, Harrow, and Lloyd), which serves as the matrix inversion routine in quantum computing. We start this chapter by revising our concepts of the Fourier transform and its discrete counterpart, the *discrete Fourier transform*, and then move on to the exciting domain of the quantum Fourier transform and the quantum phase estimation algorithm. We follow this up with a discussion and implementation of the few quantum Fourier transform–related algorithms such as factoring a number and period finding. At the end of the chapter, we briefly introduce the basics of group theory with an attempt to explain the hidden subgroup problem and how it relates to several of the Fourier transform–based algorithms.

© Santanu Pattanayak 2021
S. Pattanayak, *Quantum Machine Learning with Python*, https://doi.org/10.1007/978-1-4842-6522-2_4

Fourier Series

A periodic function of a real variable can be expanded as a Fourier series in terms of sines and cosines or in general in terms of the complex exponential functions. We can express such a periodic function $f(x)$ that repeats itself after a period of length L in the Fourier series expansion form as follows:

$$f(x) = \frac{1}{\sqrt{L}} \sum_{k=-\infty}^{+\infty} f_k e^{\frac{2\pi i k x}{L}} \tag{4-1}$$

Any function $f(x)$ can be thought of as a vector of function values over different values of x in its domain. If x is real, then there are an infinite number of values of x in any given interval, and the function can be thought of as an infinite dimensional vector. The exponential functions $e^{\frac{2\pi i k x}{L}}$ in Equation 4-1 obtained by substituting different values of k act as basis functions just like a vector basis. The dot product in this functional space for any two functions f and g over the domain interval $[a, b]$ where $L = b - a$ is given by the following:

$$\langle f, g \rangle = \int_a^b f(x)^* g(x) dx \tag{4-2}$$

where $f(x)^*$ denotes the complex conjugate function of $f(x)$.

Let's evaluate the dot product for two complex exponential functions g_{k_1} and g_{k_2} corresponding to the value of $k = k_1$ and $k = k_2$.

$$\langle g_{k_1}, g_{k_2} \rangle = \int_a^b g_{k_1}(x)^* g_{k_2}(x) dx$$

$$= \int_a^b e^{-\frac{2\pi i k_1 x}{L}} e^{\frac{2\pi i k_2 x}{L}} dx = \int_a^b e^{\frac{2\pi i (k_2 - k_1) x}{L}} dx$$

$$= L \left[\frac{e^{2\pi i (k_2 - k_1) x}}{2\pi i (k_2 - k_1)} \right]_a^b$$

$$= L \left[\frac{e^{\frac{2\pi i (k_2 - k_1) b}{L}} - e^{\frac{2\pi i (k_2 - k_1) a}{L}}}{2\pi i (k_2 - k_1)} \right]$$

$$= Le^{\frac{2\pi i(k_2 - k_1)a}{L}} \left[\frac{e^{\frac{2\pi i(k_2 - k_1)(b-a)}{L}} - 1}{2\pi i(k_2 - k_1)} \right]$$

$$= Le^{\frac{2\pi i(k_2 - k_1)a}{L}} \left[\frac{e^{2\pi i(k_2 - k_1)} - 1}{2\pi i(k_2 - k_1)} \right] \tag{4-3}$$

Since k_1, k_2 are real discrete values, $k_2 - k_1 = t$ is always an integer for all possible values of k_1 and k_2. There are two possibilities as highlighted here.

Case 1:

When $k_2 \neq k_1$, $k_2 - k_1$ is a nonzero integer. For any nonzero integer values of $k_2 - k_1$, $e^{2\pi i(k_2 - k_1)} = 1$. This makes the dot product expression in Equation 4-3 zero.

$$\left\langle f_{k_1}, f_{k_2} \right\rangle = 0, \text{ when } k_1 \neq k_2 \tag{4-4}$$

Case 2:

When $k_2 = k_1$, $k_2 - k_1 = 0$. We cannot directly substitute $k_2 - k_1 = 0$ in Equation 4-3 since substituting the denominator $k_2 - k_1$ by 0 would make the expression undefined. What we can evaluate instead is the limit of $\left\langle g_{k_1}, g_{k_2} \right\rangle$ as $k_1 - k_2 \to 0$.

$$\lim_{k_2 - k_1 \to 0} \left\langle g_{k_1}, g_{k_2} \right\rangle = \lim_{k_2 - k_1 \to 0} e^{\frac{2\pi i(k_2 - k_1)a}{L}} \left[\frac{e^{2\pi i(k_2 - k_1)} - 1}{2\pi i(k_2 - k_1)} \right] \tag{4-5}$$

$$= Le^0 \lim_{k_2 - k_1 \to 0} \left[\frac{e^{2\pi i(k_2 - k_1)} - 1}{2\pi i(k_2 - k_1)} \right]$$

$$= Le^0 \lim_{k_2 - k_1 \to 0} \left[\frac{e^{2\pi i(k_2 - k_1)} - 1}{2\pi i(k_2 - k_1)} \right]$$

$$= L \because \lim_{x \to 0} (e^x - 1)/x = 1 \tag{4-6}$$

We can infer from Equation 4-4 and Equation 4-6 that the complex exponential functions $g_k(x) = e^{\frac{2\pi i k x}{L}}$ form an orthogonal basis for all periodic functions with a fundamental period length L. Also, we noticed from Equation 4-6 that the square of the norm of g_k given by $\langle g_k, g_k \rangle = \|g_k\|^2$ is L. We can normalize $g_k(x)$ by its norm $\sqrt{L}$ so that the exponential basis functions given by $h_k(x) = \frac{1}{\sqrt{L}} e^{\frac{2\pi i k x}{L}}$ are of unit norm and hence form an orthonormal basis.

The term k can be interpreted as some form of frequency. Different values of k lead to different harmonics in a periodic function with several frequencies.

The coefficients for each of the harmonics corresponding to the different frequencies k can be computed as the dot product of $f(x)$ with the unit basis vector $h_k(x)$ as follows:

$$f_k = \langle h_k, f \rangle = \int_{x=a}^{b} h_k(x)^* f(x) dx = \int_{x=a}^{b} \frac{1}{\sqrt{L}} e^{-\frac{2\pi i k x}{L}} f(x) dx \tag{4-7}$$

Fourier Transform

Fourier transform is a natural extension to Fourier series where we try to represent an aperiodic function in terms of the complex exponential functions. You can think of an aperiodic function as one with a period length $L \to \infty$, and hence the lower and upper bounds for its one period L denoted by a and b tends to $-\infty$ and $+\infty$, respectively. Similarly, the harmonics in an aperiodic function are no longer discrete but take up continuous frequencies. The Fourier transform representation of an aperiodic function can be written as a limiting case of Fourier series, as shown here:

$$f(x) = \lim_{L \to 0} \frac{1}{\sqrt{L}} \sum_{k=-\infty}^{+\infty} f_k e^{\frac{2\pi i k x}{L}} \tag{4-8}$$

One can make the substitution $\dfrac{k}{L} \to m$ to get the Fourier transform representation as follows:

$$f(x) = \int_{m=-\infty}^{\infty} \tilde{f}(m) e^{2\pi i m x} dm \tag{4-9}$$

In the pursuit to refer to the frequency variable consistently across different transforms with k, let's change the variable m to k again and express the Fourier transform of the aperiodic function $f(x)$ as follows:

$$f(x) = \int_{k=-\infty}^{\infty} \tilde{f}(k) e^{2\pi i k x} dk \tag{4-10}$$

The coefficient function for the harmonics $\tilde{f}(k)$ is in the continuous domain now, and it relates to $f(x)$ as follows:

$$\tilde{f}(k) = \int_{-\infty}^{\infty} f(x)e^{-2\pi ikx}dx \tag{4-11}$$

In general, the coefficients $\tilde{f}(k)$ are called the *frequency response* of the function $f(x)$. The transformation from $f(x)$ to its frequency response $\tilde{f}(k)$ is called the Fourier transform $\mathcal{F}$ and is represented as follows:

$$\mathcal{F}(f(x)) = \tilde{f}(k) \tag{4-12}$$

Similarly, one can apply the inverse Fourier transform to go from the frequency response of a function to the function itself as shown below.

$$\mathcal{F}^{-1}(\tilde{f}(k)) = f(x) \tag{4-13}$$

One thing to note is that the Fourier transform of a periodic function would turn out to be its Fourier series representation.

Discrete Fourier Transform

The Fourier transform that we defined earlier is applicable only for continuous functions. If we have a function f_n over a discrete input variable, we can use a discrete Fourier transform instead. Any function $f_0, f_1, f_2..., f_{N-1}$ can be represented in terms of its discrete Fourier transform (DFT) expansion as follows:

$$f_n = \frac{1}{\sqrt{N}} \sum_{k=0}^{N-1} \tilde{f}_k e^{\frac{2\pi ikn}{N}} \tag{4-14}$$

The frequency response function $\tilde{f}_k$ for a discrete Fourier transform is given as follows:

$$\tilde{f}_k = \frac{1}{\sqrt{N}} \sum_{n=0}^{N-1} x_i e^{\frac{-2\pi ikn}{N}} \tag{4-15}$$

Kronecker Delta Function

The Kronecker delta δ_{nm} (see Figure 4-1) is a function that is equal to 1 only for value m of the discrete variable n. At all other values of n, the function has value 0.

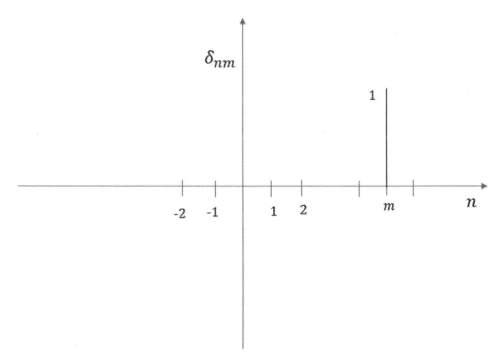

Figure 4-1. *Kronecker delta function*

The Kronecker delta functions can be thought of N-dimensional vectors that assume a value of 1 only at one discrete value of n. The dot product of two Kronecker delta function δ_{nm} and δ_{no} is 0 for $m \neq o$, while the norm of the Kronecker delta, i.e., dot product of δ_{nm}, with itself is 1. Hence, Kronecker delta functions can be used to define an orthonormal basis for representing discrete functions in the nonfrequency domain. For instance, a discrete function f_n can be represented as a linear sum of its representative Kronecker delta functions, as shown here:

$$f_n = f_0\delta_{n0} + f_1\delta_{n1} + \ldots f_{N-1}\delta_{n(N-1)} = \sum_{j=0}^{N-1} f_j\delta_{nj} \qquad (4\text{-}16)$$

Now if we want to retrieve the value of the function at any $n = j$, only $\delta_{nj} = 1$, and hence we get back the function value of f_j.

We can in fact write the Kronecker delta functions δ_{nj} as unit vectors $|j\rangle$. This simplifies the representation of the discrete function f_n in Equation 4-16 to the following:

$$f_n = \sum_{j=0}^{N-1} f_j |j\rangle \tag{4-17}$$

This vector representation of the Kronecker delta will come in handy in the quantum Fourier transform formulation.

Motivating the Quantum Fourier Transform Using the Kronecker Delta Function

The frequency response of the Kronecker delta function can be computed as follows using Equation 4-15:

$$\tilde{f}_k = \frac{1}{\sqrt{N}} \sum_{n=0}^{N-1} \delta_{nm} e^{\frac{-2\pi ikn}{N}} = \frac{1}{\sqrt{N}} e^{\frac{-2\pi ikm}{N}} \tag{4-18}$$

Based on the frequency response, we can write δ_{nm} using the discrete Fourier transform expansion (see Equation 4-14) as follows:

$$\delta_{nm} = \frac{1}{\sqrt{N}} \sum_{k=0}^{N-1} \frac{1}{\sqrt{N}} e^{\frac{-2\pi ikm}{N}} e^{\frac{2\pi ikn}{N}} \tag{4-19}$$

Like in a Fourier series, the complex exponential function $h_k = \frac{1}{\sqrt{N}} e^{\frac{2\pi ikn}{N}}$ forms an orthonormal basis even in the case of the discrete Fourier transform for different values of k. We can represent these complex exponential functions h_k as N-dimensional basis vectors of unit norm and represent them using Dirac notations as $|k\rangle$. In other words, we have this:

$$h_k = \frac{1}{\sqrt{N}} e^{\frac{2\pi ikn}{N}} = |k\rangle \tag{4-20}$$

This vector representation of the complex exponential functions allows us to simplify the function δ_{nm} representation in Equation 4-19 as follows:

$$\delta_{nm} = \frac{1}{\sqrt{N}} \sum_{k=0}^{N-1} e^{\frac{-2\pi ikm}{N}} |k\rangle \tag{4-21}$$

157

Alternately, we can represent the δ_{nm} as $|m\rangle$ in the Kronecker delta basis, and hence Equation 4-21 can be written in an all basis equation, as shown here:

$$|m\rangle = \frac{1}{\sqrt{N}} \sum_{k=0}^{N-1} e^{\frac{-2\pi ikm}{N}} |k\rangle \tag{4-22}$$

A quantum Fourier transform is viewed as the transformation between two sets of basis functions: the spatial or time domain basis functions given by the Kronecker delta $\delta_{nm} = |m\rangle$ and the frequency basis functions given by exponentials $\frac{1}{\sqrt{N}} e^{\frac{2\pi ikn}{N}} = |k\rangle$.

In this regard, Equation 4-22 is an important representation since the quantum Fourier transform is the unitary transform U that takes any generalized spatial or time domain basis function given by $|m\rangle$ and represents it in frequency domain basis $|k\rangle$, as shown here:

$$U|m\rangle = \frac{1}{\sqrt{N}} \sum_{k=0}^{N-1} e^{\frac{-2\pi ikm}{N}} |k\rangle \tag{4-23}$$

Since the Fourier transform unitary operator U is linear, the Fourier transform of any discrete function can be computed as a linear sum of the Fourier series transform on its basis functions, as shown here:

$$Uf_n = U \sum_{j=0}^{N-1} f_j |j\rangle = \sum_{j=0}^{N-1} f_j U|j\rangle \tag{4-24}$$

Substituting for $U|j\rangle$ based on Equation 4-23 in 4-24, we have:

$$Uf_n = \sum_{j=0}^{N-1} f_j \frac{1}{\sqrt{N}} \sum_{k=0}^{N-1} e^{\frac{-2\pi ikj}{N}} |k\rangle = \sum_{k=0}^{N-1} \frac{1}{\sqrt{N}} \sum_{j=0}^{N-1} f_j e^{\frac{-2\pi ikj}{N}} |k\rangle \tag{4-25}$$

Now $\frac{1}{\sqrt{N}} \sum_{j=0}^{N-1} e^{\frac{-2\pi ikj}{N}}$ is the Fourier frequency response for frequency k, which we can denote by $\tilde{f}_k$. Substituting for $\tilde{f}_k = \frac{1}{\sqrt{N}} \sum_{j=0}^{N-1} e^{\frac{-2\pi ikj}{N}}$, we see that Equation 4-25 can be written as follows:

$$Uf_n = \sum_{k=0}^{N-1} \tilde{f}_k |k\rangle \tag{4-26}$$

By writing $\sum_{j=0}^{N-1} f_j |j\rangle$ in the Kronecker delta basis, we can rewrite Equation 4-26 as follows:

$$U : \sum_{j=0}^{N-1} f_j |j\rangle \rightarrow \sum_{k=0}^{N-1} \tilde{f}_k |k\rangle \tag{4-27}$$

Equation 4-27 gives us a generalized way to perform a Fourier transformation of any given discrete function by understanding the basis function relation between the spectral/time and frequency domains. One thing to note is that the unitary transform U just changes the basis of representation for a function undergoing a Fourier transform. This approach to Fourier transforms is all we need to understand and to perform a quantum Fourier transform, as we will see through the rest of the chapter.

Quantum Fourier Transform

In this section, we will look at the quantum Fourier transformation circuit to understand how exactly the Fourier transform works in the quantum computing domain. Using n qubits, we can define the computational basis of the form $|x_1 x_2 ... x_n\rangle = |x\rangle$ where x is the decimal expansion of the binary string $x_1 x_2 ... x_n$ given by the following:

$$x = x_1 2^{n-1} + x_2 2^{n-2} + ... + x_n 2^0 \tag{4-28}$$

With n qubits, we can get $N = 2^n$ number of computation basis states.

Just to be explicit, the computational basis state for each qubit is represented by $x_i \in \{0, 1\}$.

You need to understand the transformation of any generalized computational basis state $|x\rangle = |x_1 x_2 ... x_n\rangle$ by the Fourier transformation circuit in Figure 4-2. The computational basis states $|x\rangle$ are nothing but the Kronecker delta functions δ_{nx}.

The gates used in the quantum circuit are the Hadamard gate H and the rotation gate R_n given as follows:

$$R_m = \begin{bmatrix} 1 & 0 \\ 0 & e^{-\frac{2\pi i}{2^m}} \end{bmatrix} \tag{4-29}$$

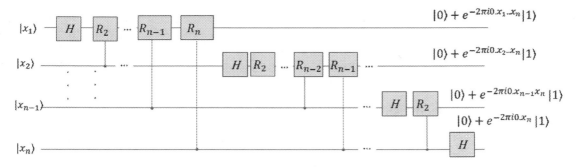

Figure 4-2. *Quantum Fourier transformation circuit*

We start with the first qubit and see the transformation of its state by various gates in the circuit.

The Hadamard gate H changes the state of the qubit from $|x_1\rangle$ to $\frac{1}{\sqrt{2}}\left(|0\rangle+(-1)^{x_1}|1\rangle\right)$.

We can replace the value of -1 with $e^{-\pi i}$ or more conveniently as $e^{2\pi i\left(\frac{1}{2}\right)}$. This lets us rewrite the state of the qubit as follows:

$$H|x_1\rangle = \frac{1}{\sqrt{2}}\left(|0\rangle+e^{-2\pi i\left(\frac{x_1}{2}\right)}|1\rangle\right) \qquad (4\text{-}30)$$

Now just like we write a binary string $x_1x_2...x_n$ in integer form as $x = x_1 2^{n-1} + x_2 2^{n-2} + ... + x_n 2^0$, similarly we can adopt the notation $0.x_1x_2...x_n$ to represent a binary fraction as follows:

$$x = 0.x_1x_2...x_n = x_1 2^{-1} + x_2 2^{-2} + ... + x_n 2^{-n} \qquad (4\text{-}31)$$

Using this notation, we can write $e^{-2\pi i\left(\frac{x_1}{2}\right)}$ as $e^{-2\pi i 0.x_1}$ and hence the state of qubit 1 after the Hadamard product (in Equation 4-31) can be rewritten as follows:

$$H|x_1\rangle = \frac{1}{\sqrt{2}}\left(|0\rangle+e^{-2\pi i 0.x_1}|1\rangle\right) \qquad (4\text{-}32)$$

The rotation matrices R_m are applied next in succession conditioned on the value of the mth qubit with the state $|x_m\rangle$. The transform by R_m conditioned on the value of the m-th qubit in the state $|x_m\rangle$ can be expressed as follows:

$$\tilde{R}_m = \begin{bmatrix} 1 & 0 \\ 0 & e^{-\frac{2\pi i x_m}{2^m}} \end{bmatrix} \qquad (4\text{-}33)$$

If the qubit m is in state $|0\rangle$, the exponential term $e^{-\frac{2\pi i x_m}{2^m}}$ becomes 1, and hence the conditional transform $\tilde{R}_m$ becomes the identity transform. Using Equation 4-32, the state of the first qubit after the conditional transform by the second qubit can be written as follows:

$$\begin{bmatrix} 1 & 0 \\ 0 & e^{-\frac{2\pi i x_2}{2^2}} \end{bmatrix} \frac{1}{\sqrt{2}}\left(|0\rangle + e^{-2\pi i 0.x_1}|1\rangle\right)$$

$$= \frac{1}{\sqrt{2}}\left(|0\rangle + e^{-2\pi i\left(0.x_1 + \frac{x_2}{2^2}\right)}|1\rangle\right) \tag{4-34}$$

Now $\frac{x_2}{2^2}$ can be written as $0.0x_2$. Hence, $0.x_1 + \frac{x_2}{2^2}$ simplifies to $0.\,x_1 x_2$, and the state of the first qubit after the rotation R_2 conditioned on the second qubit becomes the following:

$$|x_1\rangle \rightarrow \frac{1}{\sqrt{2}}\left(|0\rangle + e^{-2\pi i 0.x_1 x_2}|1\rangle\right) \tag{4-35}$$

Proceeding in this way, the state of qubit 1 after all the conditional rotations can be expressed as follows:

$$|x_1\rangle \rightarrow \frac{1}{\sqrt{2}}\left(|0\rangle + e^{-2\pi i 0.x_1 x_2 \ldots x_n}|1\rangle\right) \tag{4-36}$$

Now we shift our focus to the transformation on the second qubit. If we observe Figure 4-2, we would see that the same transformation pattern as qubit 1 is repeated for qubit 2. Hence, by induction, we can write the transform on qubit 2 as follows:

$$|x_2\rangle \rightarrow \frac{1}{\sqrt{2}}\left(|0\rangle + e^{-2\pi i 0.x_2 x_3 \ldots x_n}|1\rangle\right) \tag{4-37}$$

In general, for any qubit m, the transformation can be written as follows:

$$|x_m\rangle \rightarrow \frac{1}{\sqrt{2}}\left(|0\rangle + e^{-2\pi i 0.x_m x_{m-1} \ldots x_n}|1\rangle\right) \tag{4-38}$$

Combining the transformation on all qubits, we can write the overall transformation on the basis vector $|x_1 x_2 \ldots x_n\rangle$ as follows:

$$|x_1 x_2 \ldots x_n\rangle \rightarrow \frac{1}{2^{\frac{n}{2}}} \left(|0\rangle + e^{-2\pi i 0.x_1 x_2 \ldots x_n} |1\rangle\right) \left(|0\rangle + e^{-2\pi i 0.x_2 x_3 \ldots x_n} |1\rangle\right) ..$$

$$\left(|0\rangle + e^{-2\pi i 0.x_n} |1\rangle\right) \tag{4-39}$$

Next we use the SWAP operator to swap the state of the qubits such that any qubit represented by index m swaps its state with the qubit with index $n - m$ (see Figure 4-3). After the SWAP operations, the overall state of the qubits is as follows:

$$|x_1 x_2 \ldots x_n\rangle \rightarrow \frac{1}{2^{\frac{n}{2}}} \left(|0\rangle + e^{-2\pi i 0.x_n} |1\rangle\right) \left(|0\rangle + e^{-2\pi i 0.x_{n-1} x_n} |1\rangle\right) .. \left(|0\rangle + e^{-2\pi i 0.x_1 x_2 \ldots x_n} |1\rangle\right) \tag{4-40}$$

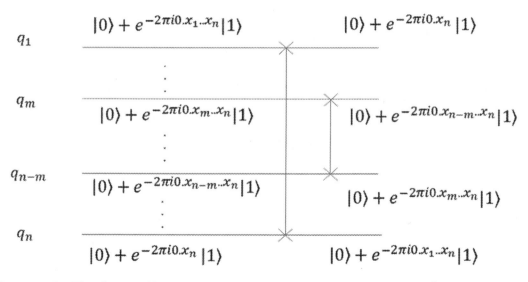

Figure 4-3. *Final state SWAP operation in quantum Fourier transformation circuit*

We saw earlier (Equation 4-22) that the Fourier transform on any basis vector $\delta_{nx} = |x\rangle$ allows us to represent it in the complex exponential frequency basis as follows:

$$|x\rangle \rightarrow \frac{1}{\sqrt{N}} \sum_{k=0}^{N-1} e^{\frac{-2\pi i k x}{N}} |k\rangle \tag{4-41}$$

By substituting $N = 2^n$ and $x = x_1 x_2 ... x_n$, we have the following:

$$|x_1, x_2, ..x_n\rangle \rightarrow \frac{1}{2^{\frac{n}{2}}} \sum_{k=0}^{2^n-1} e^{\frac{-2\pi i k x}{2^n}} |k\rangle \tag{4-42}$$

Now $k = k_1 2^{n-1} + k_2 2^{n-2} + ... + k_n 2^0$, and hence $\dfrac{k}{2^n} = k_1 2^{-1} + k_2 2^{-2} + .. k_n 2^{-n} = \sum_{p=1}^{n} \dfrac{k_p}{2^p}$.

Substituting this into Equation 4-42, we get the following:

$$|x_1 x_2 ... x_n\rangle \rightarrow \frac{1}{2^{\frac{n}{2}}} \sum_{k_1=0}^{1} .. \sum_{k_n=0}^{1} e^{-2\pi i x \left(\sum_{p=1}^{n} \frac{k_p}{2^p} \right)} |k_1 k_2 ... k_n\rangle \tag{4-43}$$

We can express the state $|k\rangle = |k_1 k_2 ... k_n\rangle$ in the tensor product of states formed as $\otimes_{p=1}^{n} |k_p\rangle$, and hence we have this:

$$|x_1 x_2 ... x_n\rangle \rightarrow \frac{1}{2^{\frac{n}{2}}} \sum_{k_1=0}^{1} .. \sum_{k_n=0}^{1} \prod_{p=1}^{n} e^{-2\pi i x k_p 2^{-p}} \otimes_{p=1}^{n} |k_p\rangle \tag{4-44}$$

The summations in Equation 4-44 can be taken inside to run over each qubit basis state, while the product of the exponential terms can be attached to each qubit. This simplifies Equation 4-44 to the following:

$$|x_1 x_2 ... x_n\rangle \rightarrow \frac{1}{2^{\frac{n}{2}}} \otimes_{p=1}^{n} \left(\sum_{k_p=0}^{1} e^{-2\pi i x k_p 2^{-p}} |k_p\rangle \right) \tag{4-45}$$

Expanding the summation over the basis state for each qubit and writing out each term of tensor product, we get this:

$$|x_1 x_2 ... x_n\rangle \rightarrow \frac{1}{2^{\frac{n}{2}}} \otimes_{p=1}^{n} \left(|0\rangle + e^{-2\pi i x 2^{-p}} |1\rangle \right)$$

$$= \frac{1}{2^{\frac{n}{2}}} \left(|0\rangle + e^{-2\pi i x 2^{-1}} |1\rangle \right) \left(|0\rangle + e^{-2\pi i x 2^{-2}} |1\rangle \right) .. \left(|0\rangle + e^{-2\pi i x 2^{-n}} |1\rangle \right) \tag{4-46}$$

Now $x = x_1 2^{n-1} + x_2 2^{n-2} + ... + x_n 2^0$, and hence $x 2^{-p}$ becomes

$$x 2^{-p} = x_1 2^{n-1-p} + x_2 2^{n-2-p} + ... + x_n 2^{-p} \tag{4-47}$$

Let's compute $x 2^{-p}$ by substituting different values of p in Equation 4-47.

When $p = 1$,

$$x2^{-1} = x_1 2^{n-2} + x2^{n-3} + x_{n-1}0 + x_n 2^{-1} \tag{4-48}$$

Except for the last term, all terms are greater than or equal to 1. Substituting $x2^{-1}$ from Equation 4-48 in the expression $e^{2\pi i x 2^{-1}}$, we get the following:

$$e^{-2\pi i x 2^{-1}} = e^{-2\pi i\left(x_1 2^{n-2} + x2^{n-3} + x_{n-1}0 + x_n 2^{-1}\right)}$$

Since all the terms except the last term $x_n 2^{-1}$ is greater than or equal to 1, they would contribute to a factor of 1 since we know $e^{-2\pi i m}$ is 1 for any integer value of m. This simplifies $e^{-2\pi i x 2^{-1}}$ to the following:

$$e^{-2\pi i x 2^{-1}} = e^{-2\pi i x_n 2^{-1}} = e^{-2\pi i 0.x_n} \tag{4-49}$$

Similarly, when $p = 2$, we would have $x2^{-2} = x_1 2^{n-3} + x2^{n-4} + x_{n-1}2^{-1} + x_n 2^{-2}$, which means we would have integer values from all except the last two terms. Hence, we have this:

$$e^{-2\pi i x 2^{-2}} = e^{-2\pi i\left(x_{n-1}2^{-1} + x_n 2^{-2}\right)} = e^{-2\pi i 0.x_{n-1}x_n} \tag{4-50}$$

Using the observations from Equation 4-49 and Equation 4-50, we can simplify Equation 4-46 as follows:

$$\frac{1}{2^{\frac{n}{2}}}\sum_{k=0}^{N-1}e^{\frac{-2\pi i k x}{2^n}}|k\rangle = \frac{1}{2^{\frac{n}{2}}}\left(|0\rangle + e^{-2\pi i 0.x_n}|1\rangle\right)\left(|0\rangle + e^{-2\pi i 0.x_{n-1}x_n}|1\rangle\right)..\left(|0\rangle + e^{-2\pi i 0.x_1 x_2..x_n}|1\rangle\right) \tag{4-51}$$

Thus, we see the Fourier transform expansion for $|x_1 x_2...x_n\rangle$ in the complex exponential or frequency basis derived from the definition in Equation 4-51 exactly matches the Fourier transform expansion achieved through the quantum Fourier transform circuit (see Equation 4-39).

One thing to note is that when we talk about Fourier transforms in general (outside quantum computing), we talk about the complex coefficients or weights of each of the complex exponential basis $\frac{1}{\sqrt{N}}e^{\frac{2\pi i k x}{2^n}}$ that are represented by $|k\rangle$. In quantum Fourier transform circuits, these coefficients are tied to their complex basis states $|k\rangle$ in a superposition. The superposition is advantageous since it combines the Fourier coefficients along with their bases in a sum form, which turns out to be input function signal representation in the complex exponential basis $|k\rangle$. So, the quantum transform on basis $|x_1x_2...x_n\rangle$ turns out be the Fourier expansion of $|x_1x_2...x_n\rangle$ in the complex exponential or frequency basis. The Fourier transform of a function and the Fourier transform expansion of the function in the frequency basis might be used interchangeably at times. The important thing to remember is that the Fourier transform on $|x_1x_2...x_n\rangle$ allows us to write $|x_1x_2...x_n\rangle$ itself as an expansion in the complex exponential or frequency basis.

The proof that the quantum Fourier circuit is doing the same transformation as the discrete Fourier transform has been a long and rigorous exercise. Readers are advised to go through this deduction in minute detail since it forms the backbone of several algorithms related to the quantum Fourier transform.

QFT Implementation in Cirq

We implement the Fourier transform in a modular way so that we can reuse it for other Fourier transform–based implementations. The class QFT can take in each basis state through the input basis_to_transform and output its Fourier transform. Alternately, it can take in a superposition state of a given number of qubits and implement its Fourier transform. We build the quantum Fourier transform circuit iteratively using the qft_circuit function in class QFT. The swap_qubits function swaps the state of the qubits once the qubit states have been altered through the Hadamard transforms and the subsequent rotations conditioned on the other qubits. In qft_circuit, we use the inverse functionality in cirq to create an inverse Fourier transform circuit by using the quantum Fourier transformation circuit. We reuse the inverse quantum Fourier transform (IQFT) for quantum phase estimation and its related implementations. In this QFT implementation, we use IQFT to validate the correctness of the QFT circuit.

Listing 4-1 illustrates the implementation of the QFT algorithm and the output of QFT on the basis state $|0000\rangle$ by using the QFT circuit.

Listing 4-1. Quantum Fourier Transform Implementation

```
import cirq
import numpy as np
import fire
from elapsedtimer import ElapsedTimer
```

```python
class QFT:
    """

    Quantum Fourier Transform
    Builds the QFT circuit iteratively
    """

    def __init__(self, signal_length=16,
                 basis_to_transform='',
                 validate_inverse_fourier=False,
                 qubits=None):

        self.signal_length = signal_length
        self.basis_to_transform = basis_to_transform

        if qubits is None:
            self.num_qubits = int(np.log2(signal_length))
            self.qubits = [cirq.LineQubit(i)
                    for i in range(self.num_qubits)]
        else:
            self.qubits = qubits
            self.num_qubits = len(self.qubits)

        self.qubit_index = 0
        self.input_circuit = cirq.Circuit()

        self.validate_inverse_fourier = validate_inverse_fourier
        self.circuit = cirq.Circuit()
        # if self.validate_inverse_fourier:
        self.inv_circuit = cirq.Circuit()

        for k, q_s in enumerate(self.basis_to_transform):
            if int(q_s) == 1:
                # Change the qubit state from 0 to 1
                self.input_circuit.append(cirq.X(self.qubits[k]))
```

In qft_circuit_iter, we go through the qubits one by one, and for each qubit at index k we apply the conditional rotational on the $(k - 1)$ qubits prior to it. We follow this up by the Hadamard transform of the qubit at index k.

```python
def qft_circuit_iter(self):

    if self.qubit_index > 0:
        # Apply the rotations on the prior qubits
        # conditioned on the current qubit
        for j in range(self.qubit_index):
            diff = self.qubit_index - j + 1
            rotation_to_apply = -2.0 / (2.0 ** diff)
            self.circuit.append(cirq.CZ(self.qubits[
            self.qubit_index],
            self.qubits[j]) ** rotation_to_apply)
    # Apply the Hadamard Transform
    # on current qubit
            self.circuit.append(cirq.H(self.qubits[
            self.qubit_index]))
    # set up the processing for next qubit
    self.qubit_index += 1
```

The function qft_circuit calls qft_circuit_iter to build the circuit through the conditional rotations and the Hadamard transforms. After that, the qubit states are swapped using the swap_qubits function. Finally, we define a quantum inverse Fourier transform circuit by invoking the cirq.inverse method on the defined quantum Fourier transform circuit.

```python
def qft_circuit(self):

    while self.qubit_index < self.num_qubits:
        self.qft_circuit_iter()
        # See the progression of the Circuit built
        print(f"Circuit after processing
                Qubit: {self.qubit_index - 1} ")
        print(self.circuit)
    # Swap the qubits to match qft definititon
    self.swap_qubits()
```

```python
        print("Circuit after qubit state swap:")
        print(self.circuit)
        # Create the inverse Fourier Transform Circuit
        self.inv_circuit = cirq.inverse(self.circuit.copy())

    def swap_qubits(self):
        # Swap the states of pair of qubits whose indices sum to n
        for i in range(self.num_qubits // 2):
            self.circuit.append(cirq.SWAP(self.qubits[i], self.qubits[self.
            num_qubits - i - 1]))

    def simulate_circuit(self):
        sim = cirq.Simulator()
        result = sim.simulate(self.circuit)
        return result

def main(signal_length=16,
         basis_to_transform='0000',
         validate_inverse_fourier=False):

    # Instantiate QFT Class
    _qft_ = QFT(signal_length=signal_length,
            basis_to_transform=basis_to_transform,
            validate_inverse_fourier=validate_inverse_fourier)

    # Build the QFT Circuit
    _qft_.qft_circuit()

    # Create the input Qubit State

    if len(_qft_.input_circuit) > 0:
        _qft_.circuit = _qft_.input_circuit + _qft_.circuit

    if _qft_.validate_inverse_fourier:
        _qft_.circuit += _qft_.inv_circuit

    print("Combined Circuit")
    print(_qft_.circuit)
    # Simulate the circuit
```

```
    output state = _qft_.simulate_circuit()
    # Print the Results
    print(output_state)

if __name__ == '__main__':
    with ElapsedTimer('Execute Quantum Fourier Transform'):
        fire.Fire(main)
```

As part of this exercise, we perform a quantum Fourier transform on the state $|0000\rangle$ pertaining to four qubits.

output

Combined Circuit

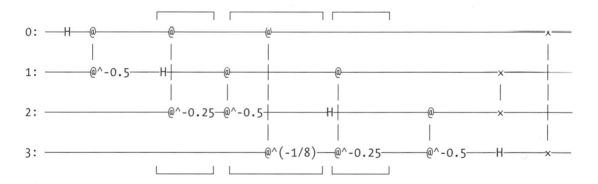

Output Vector

```
[0.24999997+0.j 0.24999997+0.j 0.24999997+0.j 0.24999997+0.j
 0.24999997+0.j 0.24999997+0.j 0.24999997+0.j 0.24999997+0.j
 0.249999 97+0.j 0.24999997+0.j 0.24999997+0.j 0.24999997+0.j
 0.24999997+0.j 0.24999997+0.j 0.24999997+0.j 0.24999997+0.j]
```

From the output, you can see that the QFT routine returns the equal superposition state as expected. The equal superposition is over the complex exponential frequency basis functions.

Also, we perform a quantum Fourier transform followed by an inverse quantum Fourier transform on another basis state $|0011\rangle$ to validate whether we can recover the input correctly in a pursuit to check the correctness of the QFT implementation. We send in 0011 through the basis_to_transform input and also set the validate_inverse_ fourier to True to conduct this experiment.

output

```
output vector: |0011⟩
```

We can see from the output that we have been able to recover the basis state |0011⟩ successfully by applying QFT and inverse QFT in succession on the input basis state.

Hadamard Transform as a Fourier Transform

It may be noted that the Hadamard transform is a Fourier transformation on a discrete signal of length 2, i.e., $N = 2$. The Fourier transform of any basis state of n qubits is given as follows:

$$|x\rangle \rightarrow \frac{1}{2^{\frac{n}{2}}} \sum_{k=0}^{2^n-1} e^{\frac{-2\pi ikx}{2^n}} |k\rangle \tag{4-52}$$

The Fourier transform for qubit state |0⟩ can be obtained by substituting x by 0 and n by 1 in Equation 4-52, as shown here:

$$|0\rangle \rightarrow \frac{1}{2^{\frac{1}{2}}} \sum_{k=0}^{2^1-1} e^{\frac{-2\pi ik0}{2^1}} |k\rangle = \frac{1}{\sqrt{2}}\left(|0\rangle + |1\rangle\right) \tag{4-53}$$

Similarly substituting x by 1 in Equation 4-52, we get the Fourier transform on state |1⟩ as follows:

$$|1\rangle \rightarrow \frac{1}{2^{\frac{1}{2}}} \sum_{k=0}^{2^1-1} e^{\frac{-2\pi ik1}{2^n}} |k\rangle$$

$$= \frac{1}{\sqrt{2}}\left(e^{\frac{-2\pi i0\times1}{2^1}} |0\rangle + e^{\frac{-2\pi i1\times1}{2^1}} |1\rangle\right)$$

$$= \frac{1}{\sqrt{2}}\left(|0\rangle - |1\rangle\right) \tag{4-54}$$

From Equation 4-53 and Equation 4-54 we can see the Fourier transform on states $|0\rangle$ and $|1\rangle$ is the same as the Hadamard transform on states $|0\rangle$ and $|1\rangle$.

In fact, the Hadamard transform on n qubits can be thought of as an n-dimensional discrete Fourier transform on individual dimensions of size 2.

Quantum Phase Estimation

One of the most important algorithms that uses a quantum Fourier transform is the quantum phase estimation. The quantum phase estimation algorithm in turn is a key component of many complex algorithms such as period finding and factoring of numbers, which are both difficult problems for a classical computer to solve. The quantum phase estimation algorithm on a high level tries to estimate the eigenvalue given the eigenvector of a unitary transform. The eigenvalues of a unitary matrix are of unit norm. So, for a known unitary matrix U, if we have an eigenvector $|u\rangle$ and a corresponding eigenvalue of $e^{-2\pi i\phi}$, then the goal of quantum phase estimation is to estimate the phase ϕ. Figure 4-4 is an initial circuit for the quantum phase estimation algorithm.

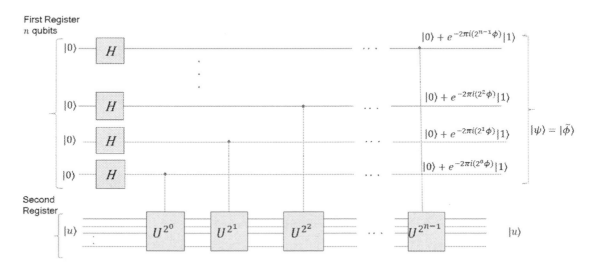

Figure 4-4. *Initial circuit of quantum phase estimation*

The quantum phase estimation algorithm uses two registers (see Figure 4-4). The second register holds the eigenvector $|u\rangle$ for which we desire to find the eigenvalue phase ϕ. The first register consists of n qubits. The choice of n for the first register is based on the level of accuracy we desire for the estimate of ϕ and the probability with which we want the quantum phase estimation algorithm to succeed.

The quantum phase algorithm requires an Oracle that can conditionally apply the unitary transform U on the eigenvector $|u\rangle$ based on the first register qubits. The following are the steps in the quantum phase algorithm:

1. *Initialize the qubit registers*: Initialize the qubits in the first register to the $|0\rangle$ state. The qubits in the first register are often referred to as *ancilla qubits*. The second register should contain the state of the eigenvector $|u\rangle$ for which we want to find the eigenvalue.

2. *Equal superposition state of the first register*: We perform a Hadamard transform on each of the qubits q_i in the first register such that each qubit is in the equal superposition state $|q_i\rangle = \frac{1}{\sqrt{2}}\big(|0\rangle + |1\rangle\big)$. Alternately, all the qubits in the first register are in an equal superposition state given by $\sum_{i=0}^{2^n-1}|k\rangle$.

3. *Unitary transformation on the eigenvector*: For each qubit q_m, the unitary operator U is applied 2^{n-m} times to the second register eigenvector $|u\rangle$. The overall state of the q_m registers after the application of the unitary transform on the eigenvector 2^{n-m} times is shown here:

$$U^{2^{n-m}}|u\rangle \otimes \frac{1}{\sqrt{2}}\big(|0\rangle + |1\rangle\big) = \frac{1}{\sqrt{2}}\Big(|u\rangle|0\rangle + U^{2^{n-m}}|u\rangle|1\rangle\Big) \tag{4-55}$$

Since we are applying the unitary transform based on q_i, as the control qubit, only for the $|1\rangle$ state the unitary transform U would be applied on the eigenvector $|u\rangle$ in the second register. For each application of the unitary transform to the eigenvector $|u\rangle$, the eigenvalue $e^{-2\pi i\phi}$ is going to come out and get associated with the state $|1\rangle$, as shown here:

$$\frac{1}{\sqrt{2}}\Big(|u\rangle|0\rangle + U^{2^{n-m}}|u\rangle|1\rangle\Big) = \frac{1}{\sqrt{2}}\Big(|u\rangle|0\rangle + e^{-2\pi i\phi 2^{n-m}}|u\rangle|1\rangle\Big)$$

$$= |u\rangle \otimes \frac{1}{\sqrt{2}}\Big(|0\rangle + e^{-2\pi i\phi 2^{n-m}}|1\rangle\Big) \tag{4-56}$$

The unitary transform $U^{2^{n-m}}$ doesn't change the state of the eigenvector u but only accumulates phase. Hence, it can be thought of changing the state of the register qubit q_m from the $\frac{1}{\sqrt{2}}\left(|0\rangle + |1\rangle\right)$ to the $\frac{1}{\sqrt{2}}\left(|0\rangle + 2^{-2\pi i \phi 2^{n-m}}|1\rangle\right)$ state. We can say the general state of any qubit q_m after the unitary transformation is as follows:

$$|q_m\rangle = \frac{1}{\sqrt{2}}\left(|0\rangle + e^{-2\pi i \phi 2^{n-m}}|1\rangle\right) \qquad (4\text{-}57)$$

We can think of ϕ having an exact n bit binary expansion as follows:

$$\phi = 0.\phi_1\phi_2\ldots\phi_{n-1} = \phi_1 2^{-1} + \phi_2 2^{-2} + \ldots \phi_m 2^{-m} + \ldots + \phi_n 2^{-n} = \sum_{i=1}^{n}\phi_i 2^{-i} \qquad (4\text{-}58)$$

For the qubit q_1 the value of $\phi 2^{n-m} = \phi 2^{n-1} = \phi_1 2^{n-2} + \phi_2 2^{n-3} + \ldots + \phi_{n-1} 2^0 + \phi_n 2^{-1}$, which means that except $\phi_n 2^{-1}$, all terms have integer values greater than 1. All the integer terms greater than or equal to 1 contribute to a factor of 1 because $e^{-2\pi i t} = 1$ for integer $t \geq 1$. Hence, we have this:

$$e^{-2\pi i \phi 2^{n-1}} = e^{-2\pi i\left(\phi_n 2^{-1}\right)} = e^{-2\pi i (0.\phi_n)}$$

Similarly, for the qubit q_2 in $\phi 2^{n-m} = \phi 2^{n-2} = \phi_1 2^{n-3} + \phi_2 2^{n-4} + \ldots + \phi_{n-1} 2^{-1} + \phi_n 2^{-2}$, all terms except $\phi_{n-1} 2^{-1} + \phi_n 2^{-2}$ are integer values greater than 1, and hence we have this:

$$e^{-2\pi i \phi 2^{n-2}} = e^{-2\pi i\left(\phi_{n-1} 2^{-1} + \phi_n 2^{-2}\right)} = e^{-2\pi i (0.\phi_{n-1}\phi_n)}$$

In general, for the qubit m we would have this:

$$e^{-2\pi i \phi 2^{n-m}} = e^{-2\pi i\left(\phi_{n-m-1} 2^{-1} + \ldots + \phi_n 2^{-m}\right)} = e^{-2\pi i (0.\phi_{n-m-1}\phi_{n-1}\phi_n)} \qquad (4\text{-}59)$$

Based on Equation 4-59, we can write the state of the qubit q_m after unitary transformation as follows:

$$|q_m\rangle = \frac{1}{\sqrt{2}}\left(|0\rangle + e^{-2\pi i (0.\phi_{n-m-1}\phi_{n-1}\phi_n)}|1\rangle\right) \qquad (4\text{-}60)$$

So, the combined state $|\psi\rangle = |q_1 q_2 \ldots q_n\rangle$ of all the n qubits of the first register after the unitary transformations is as follows:

$$|\psi\rangle = \frac{1}{2^{\frac{n}{2}}}\left(|0\rangle + e^{-2\pi i (0.\phi_n)}|1\rangle\right)\left(|0\rangle + e^{-2\pi i (0.\phi_{n-1}\phi_n)}|1\rangle\right)\left(|0\rangle + e^{-2\pi i (0.\phi_1\ldots\phi_n)}|1\rangle\right) \qquad (4\text{-}61)$$

From Equation 4-51 derived earlier, we can see the expression in Equation 4-61 is equal to $\dfrac{1}{2^{\frac{n}{2}}}\displaystyle\sum_{k=0}^{N-1} e^{\frac{-2\pi ik\phi}{2^{n}}}|k\rangle$ and is actually the Fourier transform of the phase ϕ that we intend to estimate. If we represent the Fourier transform of phase ϕ as $|\tilde{\phi}\rangle$, we can write Equation 4-61 as follows:

$$|\psi\rangle = |\tilde{\phi}\rangle = \frac{1}{2^{\frac{n}{2}}}\sum_{k=0}^{N-1} e^{\frac{-2\pi ik\phi}{2^{n}}}|k\rangle \tag{4-62}$$

Figure 4-4 provides us with an implementation-level view of the transformation involved to get to this Fourier transform of the phase $|\phi\rangle$ that we see in Equation 4-59 by considering each qubit in the first input register. This Fourier transformation realization on a high level can be simplified to a large extent by looking at the transformation on the n qubit basis states $|k\rangle$ in superposition, as in Figure 4-5. The Hadamard transforms on the $|0\rangle$ state initialized n qubits create an equal superposition state $\dfrac{1}{2^{\frac{n}{2}}}\displaystyle\sum_{i=0}^{2^{n-1}}|k\rangle$. For each basis $|k\rangle$ where $k \in \{0, 2^{n-1}\}$, we apply the unitary transform U k times on the eigenvector $|u\rangle$ as follows:

$$|k\rangle U^{k}|u\rangle = |k\rangle\left(e^{-2\pi i\phi}\right)^{k}|u\rangle = |k\rangle e^{-2\pi i\phi k}|u\rangle \tag{4-63}$$

Considering the combined unitary transform based on all 2^{n} basis states we get from Equation 4-63:

$$\frac{1}{2^{\frac{n}{2}}}\sum_{k=0}^{2^{n}-1}|k\rangle e^{-2\pi i\phi k}|u\rangle = \left(\frac{1}{2^{\frac{n}{2}}}\sum_{k=0}^{2^{n}-1}e^{-2\pi i\phi k}|k\rangle\right)|u\rangle \tag{4-64}$$

Now $(\dfrac{1}{2^{\frac{n}{2}}}\displaystyle\sum_{k=0}^{2^{n}-1}e^{-2\pi i\phi k}|k\rangle)|u\rangle$ is nothing but the Fourier transform of the phase ϕ, and hence Equation 4-64 can be rewritten as follows:

$$\frac{1}{2^{\frac{n}{2}}}\sum_{k=0}^{2^{n}-1}e^{-2\pi i\phi k}|k\rangle|u\rangle = |\tilde{\phi}\rangle|u\rangle \tag{4-65}$$

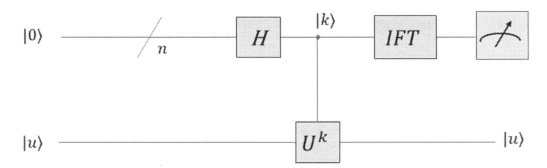

Figure 4-5. *High-level diagram of quantum phase estimation*

Readers looking for a denominator of 2^n in the exponential power $\dfrac{1}{2^{\frac{n}{2}}}\displaystyle\sum_{k=0}^{2^n-1}e^{-2\pi i\phi k}\left|k\right\rangle$ should know that it is merely a difference of notation. When we measure ϕ through a quantum circuit, we do not measure the binary fraction but rather the computation basis state vector $\left|\phi\right\rangle = \left|\phi_1, \phi_2.\,.\,\phi_n\right\rangle$ associated with it. The basis state vector can be represented as an integer value from 0 to 2^n as $\phi = 2^{n-1}\phi_1 + 2^{n-2}\phi_2.....+ 2^0\phi_n$ instead of the binary fraction $\phi = 2^{-1}\phi_1 + 2^{-2}\phi_2.....+ 2^n\phi_n$. The integer representation of the phase ϕ_I and the binary fraction representation of the phase ϕ_F relates to each other by the factor 2^n, as shown here:

$$\phi_F = \frac{\phi_I}{2^n} \tag{4-66}$$

When we say the Fourier transform of the basis vector $\left|\phi\right\rangle$ representation phase ϕ is $\displaystyle\sum_{k=0}^{2^n-1}e^{-2\pi i\phi k}\left|k\right\rangle$, the ϕ referred to in the Fourier expansion is the binary representation of $\left|\phi\right\rangle$. We can represent the same Fourier expansion by the integer representation of ϕ by using the relation in Equation 4-66, as shown here:

$$\left|\tilde{\phi}\right\rangle=\frac{1}{2^{\frac{n}{2}}}\sum_{k=0}^{2^n-1}e^{-2\pi i\phi_F k}\left|k\right\rangle=\frac{1}{2^{\frac{n}{2}}}\sum_{k=0}^{2^n-1}e^{-\frac{2\pi i\phi_I}{2^n}k}\left|k\right\rangle \tag{4-67}$$

4. *Inverse Fourier Transform:* In the final stage, we apply an inverse Fourier transform (IFT in Figure 4-5) on the state $\left|\psi\right\rangle=\left|\tilde{\phi}\right\rangle$ to get the desired state $\left|\phi_1\phi_2.\,.\,\phi_n\right\rangle= \phi=\displaystyle\sum_{i=1}^{n}\phi_i 2^{-i}$. One can run the quantum Fourier transform circuit in reverse to implement the inverse quantum Fourier transform, as we will see in the phase estimation algorithm implementation.

Quantum Phase Estimation Illustration in Cirq

In this section, we implement a simplistic version of quantum phase estimation (QPE) to illustrate the concept. The implementation complexity stems from the size and complexity of the unitary operator whose eigenvalues we want to estimate. In the later sections, we will implement QPE for more complex unitary operators for period finding and integer factoring applications.

We define a `quantum_phase_estimation` class that uses the QFT implemented in the earlier section for performing an inverse quantum Fourier transformation in the second stage of the quantum phase estimation algorithm. Phase 1 of the QPE circuit that applies the unitary transforms U on the eigenvector conditioned on the first register qubits is implemented through the function `phase_1_create_circuit_iter` in the `quantum_phase_estimation` class. Also, the inverse Fourier transform to get the phase of the eigenvalue is implemented through the function `inv_qft` using the inverse Fourier transform functionality of the QFT class from the earlier section.

We perform quantum phase estimation for the eigenvector $|u\rangle = |1\rangle$ of the unitary matrix $Z = \begin{bmatrix} 1 & 0 \\ 0 & -1 \end{bmatrix}$.

This Pauli matrix Z has two eigenvectors $|0\rangle$ and $|1\rangle$ corresponding to eigenvalues of 1 and −1. The phase ϕ corresponding to −1 can be determined by the relation $e^{-2\pi i\phi} = -1$, which gives us our ϕ as 0.5. Now for a two-qubit ancilla, the state $|q_1 q_2\rangle$ should measure $|10\rangle$ since it stands for the fraction 0. $q_1 q_2 = 0.10 = 1 \times 2^{-1} + 0 \times 2^{-2}$. Listing 4-2 illustrates the detailed implementation of the quantum phase estimation.

Listing 4-2. Quantum Phase Estimation

```
import cirq
import numpy
from quantum_fourier_transform import QFT

class quantum_phase_estimation:

    def __init__(self, num_input_state_qubits=1,
                 num_ancillia_qubits=2,
                 unitary_transform=None,
                 U=None,
                 input_state=None):
```

```python
self.num_ancillia_qubits = num_ancillia_qubits

self.output_qubits = [cirq.LineQubit(i)
        for i in range(self.num_ancillia_qubits)]

self.input_circuit = cirq.Circuit()
self.input_state = input_state

if self.input_state is not None:
    self.num_input_qubits = len(self.input_state)
else:
    self.num_input_qubits = num_input_state_qubits

self.input_qubits = [cirq.LineQubit(i) for i in
            range(self.num_ancillia_qubits,
      self.num_ancillia_qubits + num_input_state_qubits)]

if self.input_state is not None:

    for i, c in enumerate(self.input_state):
        if int(c) == 1:
          self.input_circuit.append(
            cirq.X(self.input_qubits[i]))

self.unitary_transform = unitary_transform
if self.unitary_transform is None:
    self.U = cirq.I
elif self.unitary_transform == 'custom':
    self.U = U
elif self.unitary_transform == 'Z':
    self.U = cirq.CZ
elif self.unitary_transform == 'X':
    self.U = cirq.CX
else:
    raise NotImplementedError(f"self.unitary
     transform not Implemented")

self.circuit = cirq.Circuit()
```

The function phase_1_create_circuit_iter builds the phase 1 circuit wherein we first get the "first register" qubits to be in the equal superposition state using the Hadamard transform and then apply the unitary transforms on the eigenvector based on each of the basis states in the equal superposition state of the "first register."

```
def phase_1_create_circuit_iter(self):

    for i in range(self.num_ancillia_qubits):
        self.circuit.append(cirq.H(self.output_qubits[i]))
        _pow_ = 2**(self.num_ancillia_qubits - 1 - i)
        #_pow_ = 2 ** (i)
        for k in range(self.num_input_qubits):
            print(self.U)
            self.circuit.append(self.U(
              self.output_qubits[i],
              self.input_qubits[k])**_pow_)
```

The state of the "first register" qubits after the transformation by the phase 1 circuit is equal to the Fourier transform of the phase ϕ of the eigenvalue of the form $e^{-2\pi i\phi}$. So, we apply the following inverse Fourier transform routine inv_qft to get the required phase ϕ:

```
def inv_qft(self):
    self._qft_ = QFT(qubits=self.output_qubits)
    self._qft_.qft_circuit()

def simulate_circuit(self, circ):
    sim = cirq.Simulator()
    result = sim.simulate(circ)
    return result

def main(num_input_state_qubits=1,
              num_ancillia_qubits=2,
              unitary_transform='Z',
              U=None,input_state='1'):

  _QP_ = quantum_phase_estimation(num_ancillia_qubits=
          num_ancillia_qubits,
          num_input_state_qubits=num_input_state_qubits,
```

```
            unitary_transform=unitary_transform,
            input_state=input_state)
    _QP_.phase_1_create_circuit_iter()

    _QP_.inv_qft()

    circuit = _QP_.circuit  + _QP_._qft_.inv_circuit
    if len(_QP_.input_circuit) > 0:
        circuit = _QP_.input_circuit + circuit

    print(circuit)
    result = _QP_.simulate_circuit(circuit)
    print(result)

if __name__ == '__main__':
    main()
```

output

```
Circuit after processing Qubit: 0
0: ————H————
Circuit after processing Qubit: 1
0: ————H————@————————————————
                 |
1: ————————@^-0.5————————H————

Circuit after qubit state swap:
0: ————H————@——————————————————x——
                 |                        |
1: ————————@^-0.5————H————x——
0: ————————H—@————————————x————————@————————H————
                  |              |           |
1: ——————H—|————@————x————H——@^0.5————————
                  |     |
2: ——X————@^0————@————————————————————————
measurements: (no measurements)
output vector: |101⟩
```

We can see from the output that the measured state is $|101\rangle$ where the first two qubits are the "first register" qubits, and the third qubit corresponds to the eigenvector $|1\rangle$ whose eigenvalue we want to determine. The state of the "first register" returned by the QPE algorithm is in fact $|10\rangle$, which stands for phase 0.5.

Error Analysis in the Quantum Phase Estimation

In the quantum phase algorithm implementation shown previously, we assumed that phase ϕ has an exact n-bit binary expansion so that the basis state $|\phi\rangle = |\phi_1\phi_2 . . \phi_n\rangle$ measured after the inverse Fourier transformation appears with 100 percent probability. Let's now analyze the general case where the phase ϕ measurement does not have an exact n-bit expansion. We want to analyze in these cases whether we can measure the best possible n-bit expansion of ϕ, say, $\phi_{approx} = 0. v_1v_2.... v_n$ with high probability.

The state of the n qubits after the controlled unitary transforms is given here:

$$|\psi\rangle = \frac{1}{2^{\frac{n}{2}}} \sum_{k=0}^{2^n-1} e^{-2\pi i\phi k} |k\rangle \tag{4-68}$$

On applying the inverse Fourier transform on $|\psi\rangle$, we get the state $|\psi_{IFT}\rangle$ as follows:

$$|\psi_{IFT}\rangle = \frac{1}{2^n} \sum_{x=0}^{2^n-1} \sum_{k=0}^{2^n-1} e^{-2\pi i\phi k} e^{\frac{2\pi ixk}{2^n}} |x\rangle \tag{4-69}$$

$$= \frac{1}{2^n} \sum_{x=0}^{2^n-1} \sum_{k=0}^{2^n-1} e^{-2\pi ik\left(\phi-\frac{x}{2^n}\right)} |x\rangle \tag{4-70}$$

The amplitude corresponding to each of the basis state $|x\rangle$ is given as follows:

$$\alpha_x = \frac{1}{2^n} \sum_{k=0}^{2^n-1} e^{-2\pi ik\left(\phi-\frac{x}{2^n}\right)} \tag{4-71}$$

The sum in the amplitude is a geometric series with common ratio $r = e^{-2\pi i\left(\phi-\frac{x}{2^n}\right)}$ and initial term $a = \frac{1}{2^n} e^{-2\pi ik\left(\phi-\frac{x}{2^n}\right)} \Big|_{k=0} = \frac{1}{2^n}$. Hence, we have this:

$$\alpha_x = \frac{a\left(1-r^{2^n}\right)}{1-r} = \frac{1}{2^n} \frac{\left(1-r^{2^n}\right)}{1-r} \tag{4-72}$$

Based on the amplitude, the probability of measuring the state $|x\rangle$ is given by the following:

$$P(x) = |\alpha_x|^2 = \frac{1}{2^{2n}} \left| \frac{\left(1 - r^{2^n}\right)}{1-r} \right|^2 \tag{4-73}$$

Now let's investigate two cases.

Case 1: Phase ϕ can be completely represented by the binary fraction expansion of a basis state x.

In this case, the phase in binary fraction $\phi = \dfrac{x}{2^n}$, where $x \in \{0, 2^n\}$ is an integer based on the expansion $= x_1 2^{n-1} + x_2 2^{n-2} + \dots + x_n$. Since $\phi = \dfrac{x}{2^n}$, the common ratio $r = e^{-2\pi i 0} = 1$. From Equation 4-73, the probability of $\phi = \dfrac{x}{2^n}$ is given by the following:

$$P\left(\frac{x}{2^n} = \phi\right) = \lim_{r \to 1} \frac{1}{2^{2n}} \left| \frac{\left(1 - r^{2^n}\right)}{1-r} \right|^2 = \frac{1}{2^{2n}} \lim_{r \to 1} \left| \frac{\left(1 - r^{2^n}\right)}{1-r} \right|^2 \tag{4-74}$$

Since the denominator tends to 0, we can use L'Hopital's rule and differentiate both the numerator and denominator with respect to r. This gives us the following:

$$P\left(\frac{x}{2^n} = \phi\right) = \frac{1}{2^{2n}} \lim_{r \to 1} \left| \frac{-2^n r^{2^n - 1}}{-1} \right|^2 = \frac{1}{2^{2n}} \left| 2^n \right|^2 = \frac{2^{2n}}{2^{2n}} = 1 \tag{4-75}$$

Hence, we see when phase ϕ has an exact n-bit expansion, we measure ϕ with 100 percent probability.

Case 2: Phase ϕ does not have a binary expansion, and the nearest n-bit expansion is given by the state $x = \phi_{approx} = 0. \, v_1 v_2 \dots v_n$. In this case, the absolute error would be less than $\dfrac{1}{2^{n-1}}$ since ϕ_{approx} can represent ϕ accurately up to n bits. The error $\delta = \phi - \dfrac{x}{2^n}$ would in this case be bounded as $0 \le |\delta| \le \dfrac{1}{2^{n+1}}$. In this case, the common ratio r is equal to $e^{-2\pi i \delta}$. We want to compute the bound of the probability of measuring the state $\dfrac{x}{2^n} = \phi_{approx}$. Given the context, the probability for this is as follows:

$$P\left(\frac{x}{2^n} = \phi_{approx}\right) = \frac{1}{2^{2n}} \left| \frac{\left(1 - e^{-2\pi i \delta 2^n}\right)}{1 - e^{-2\pi i \delta}} \right|^2 \tag{4-76}$$

181

Let's try to bound the probability in Equation 4-72 by viewing the complex exponentials in a complex plan of unit radius. Let's take $e^{-2\pi i \delta 2^n} = x + iy = z$ in Figure 4-6.

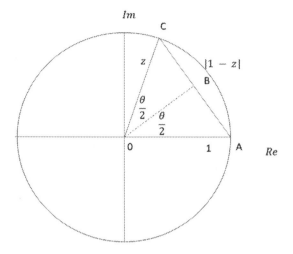

Figure 4-6. *Complex plan demonstration of minor arc length to chord length ratio*

Hence, angle $\theta = -2\pi\delta 2^n$. If we take the amplitude $\left|1 - e^{-2\pi i \delta 2^n}\right|$ in the denominator, it can be expressed as follows:

$$\left|1 - e^{-2\pi i \delta 2^n}\right|$$

$$= |1 - z|$$

$$= |1 - (x + iy)|$$

$$= \sqrt{(1-x)^2 + y^2} \tag{4-77}$$

From Figure 4-6, we can clearly see that $|1 - z|$ is nothing but the chord AC. If we draw a perpendicular from origin O to B, it will bisect the angle θ as well as the chord AC. Hence, we have this:

$$\frac{BC}{OC} = \sin\left(\frac{\theta}{2}\right) \tag{4-78}$$

Now $OC = 1$ and $BC = |1 - z|$. Substituting the values of OC and BC in Equation 4-78, we get the following:

$$\frac{|1-z|}{2} = \sin\left(\frac{\theta}{2}\right)$$

$$\rightarrow |1-z| = 2\sin\left(\frac{\theta}{2}\right) \tag{4-79}$$

Hence, the chord AC length $= |1 - z| = 2\sin\left(\frac{\theta}{2}\right)$. The minor arc AC length is θ.

The ratio of the minor arc AC length to the chord AC length is as follows:

$$\frac{arc(AC)}{chord(AC)} = \frac{\theta}{2\sin\left(\frac{\theta}{2}\right)} \tag{4-80}$$

The previous ratio achieves its maximum value of $\frac{\pi}{2}$ when $\theta = \pi$. Hence, we have the following inequality:

$$\frac{arc(AC)}{chord(AC)} = \frac{\theta}{2\sin\left(\frac{\theta}{2}\right)} \leq \frac{\pi}{2} \tag{4-81}$$

Since $arc(AC) = \theta = -2\pi\delta 2^n$ and $chord(AC) = |1-z| = \left|1 - e^{-2\pi i \delta 2^n}\right|$, we have the following from Equation 4-81:

$$\frac{-2\pi\delta 2^n}{\left|1 - e^{-2\pi i \delta 2^n}\right|} \leq \frac{\pi}{2}$$

$$\rightarrow \frac{4\pi^2\delta^2 2^{2n}}{\left|1 - e^{-2\pi i \delta 2^n}\right|^2} \leq \frac{\pi^2}{4}$$

$$\rightarrow \left|1 - e^{-2\pi i \delta 2^n}\right|^2 \geq 4^2 \delta^2 2^{2n} \tag{4-82}$$

Again, if we consider $e^{-2\pi i\delta} = z$, then we have $\theta = -2\pi\delta$. The minor arc length as before would be θ, and the chord length would be $|1 - z| = |1 - e^{-2\pi i\delta}|$. The minor arc length is at least as much as the chord length, which gives us the following:

$$\theta \geq |1 - z|$$

$$\rightarrow -2\pi\delta \geq |1 - e^{-2\pi i\delta}|$$

$$\rightarrow 4\pi^2\delta^2 \geq |1 - e^{-2\pi i\delta}|^2 \qquad (4\text{-}83)$$

Combining Equation 4-82 and Equation 4-83, we get the following:

$$P\left(\frac{x}{2^n} = \phi_{approx}\right) \geq \frac{4^2\delta^2 2^{2n}}{2^{2n}4\pi^2\delta^2} = \frac{4}{\pi^2} > 0.4 \qquad (4\text{-}84)$$

The probability that we will get the best state corresponding to the n-bit approximation of the phase is greater than 0.4, which is a high lower bound of success.

Shor's Period Finding Algorithm and Factoring

Now that we have the technical understanding of the quantum Fourier transform and quantum phase estimation, we are well equipped to apply these concepts to different applications. The Fourier transform tries to extract different frequencies within a function, and hence it can be well utilized for determining the periodicity of functions. Finding the periodicity of modular exponential functions popularly known as *order finding* is an important component to factor large integers. Shor's algorithm combines the quantum order finding algorithm along with some classical computational steps to make the overall factoring problem algorithm of polynomial complexity in its inputs.

Modular Exponentiation Function

Let's define a function of the form $g(x) = a^x$. The modular exponential function is obtained by dividing the function $g(x)$ by N and obtaining the remainder. Such a function can be written as follows:

$$f(x) = a^x \pmod{N}. \qquad (4\text{-}85)$$

We need to find the order r of the function $f(x)$ such that $f(x + r) = f(x)$. Using Equation 4-85, we get the following:

$$f(x+r) = f(x).\qquad(4\text{-}86)$$

$$\rightarrow a^{x+r}\left(mod\ N\right) = a^{x}\left(mod\ N\right).\qquad(4\text{-}87)$$

Let's suppose each of the terms $a^{x+r} mod N$ and $a^{x} mod N$ equals k where $k < N$. Then we can rewrite $a^{x+r} = k + m_1 N$ and $a^{x} = k + m_2 N$ where m_1 and m_2 are two integers.

Subtracting a^x from a^{x+r}, we get the following:

$$a^{x+r} - a^{x} = \left(m_1 - m_2\right)N \rightarrow a^{x}\left(a^{r} - 1\right) = \left(m_1 - m_2\right)N\qquad(4\text{-}88)$$

Now we know that a^x is not divisible by N since $a^x = k + m_2 N$. Therefore, from Equation 4-88, $(a^r - 1)$ must be divisible by N. In terms of modulo division, we can thus write the following:

$$a^{r} - 1 \equiv 0\left(mod\ N\right).\qquad(4\text{-}89)$$

$$\rightarrow a^{r} \equiv 1\left(mod\ N\right)\qquad(4\text{-}90)$$

So, for a modular exponential function $f(x) = a^x (mod\ N)$, the order is defined to be the smallest integer r that satisfies the relation in Equation 4-90, i.e., $a^r = 1$.

Motivating the Order Finding Problem as a Quantum Phase Estimation Problem

As part of the order finding problem, given an element a and an N, we would like to find the order r of the element a such that $a^r \equiv 1\ mod\ N$. Alternately, we can find the period r of the discrete function $f(x) = a^x\ mod\ N$ where $f(x) = f(x + r)$ and $r \leq N$.

Since the $f(x)$ involves a modulo N division, the range of $f(x)$ is limited to the values $\{0, 1, .., N - 1\}$. We can define an operator U_a that works on any element $y \leq (N - 1)$ as follows:

$$U_a |y\rangle = |ay\ mod\ N\rangle.\qquad(4\text{-}91)$$

The idea here is to have an operator that when applied to an element r times produces the element itself. Operator U_a precisely does that.

$$U^r|y\rangle = U^{r-1}|ay\,(mod\,N)\rangle$$
$$= U^{r-k}|a^k y\,(mod\,N)\rangle$$
$$= |a^r y\,(mod\,N)\rangle = |y\rangle \qquad (4\text{-}92)$$

One can think of the action of operator U_a on the element y as multiplication by the element a and then dividing the product by N. Applying the operator U_a r times is analogous to multiplying a^r to y. Since the element a has an order of r, the component $a^r\,(mod\,N)$ resets to 1, and we are left with the element y. Do note that the elements from 0 through $N-1$ are represented as quantum basis states. We have conveniently named the operator U_a. Since it's operating on the quantum states, it ought to be unitary.

Now let's find the eigenvectors of the unitary operator that would contain eigenvalues of interest to us. Specifically, we want to have eigenvectors that contain the period r in their phase so that we can use the quantum phase estimation algorithm conveniently to extract them. With this motivation, let's look at how the unitary operator U_a works on the state vector $|y\rangle = 1$ for different powers of it.

$$U_a|1\rangle = |a\,mod\,N\rangle$$
$$U_a^2|1\rangle = |a^2\,mod\,N\rangle$$
$$\cdots$$
$$U_a^{r-1}|1\rangle = |a^{r-1}\,mod\,N\rangle$$
$$U_a^r|1\rangle = |1\rangle \qquad (4\text{-}93)$$

Figure 4-7 is an example of the application of U_a on the state $|1\rangle$ where $a = 7$ and $N = 15$. The periodicity r in this case of the element $a\,mod\,N$ is 4.

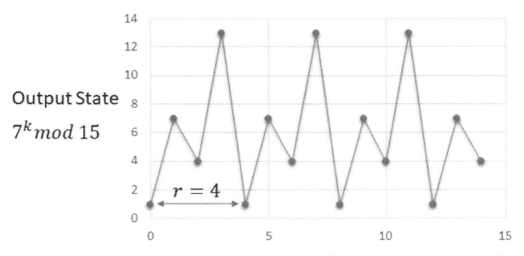

Figure 4-7. *Periodicity of element 7 mod 15 through operator U_7*

One of the points to note here is that since the period of function $f(x) = a^x \ mod \ N$ is r, all the r states in Equation 4-93 of the form $|u_s\rangle = |a^s \ mod \ N\rangle$ where $s \in \{0, 1..., r-1\}$ are unique. We can combine all these r states as the superposition state $|u\rangle$.

$$|u\rangle = \frac{1}{\sqrt{r}} \sum_{k=0}^{r-1} |a^k \ mod \ N\rangle \tag{4-94}$$

It is not hard to see that the state $|u\rangle$ is an eigenvector of U_a.

$$U_a|u\rangle = \frac{1}{\sqrt{r}} U_a\left(|1\rangle + |a \ mod \ N\rangle .. + |a^{r-1} \ mod \ N\rangle\right)$$

$$= \frac{1}{\sqrt{r}}\left(|a \ mod \ N\rangle + |a^2 \ mod \ N\rangle .. + |a^r \ mod \ N\rangle\right)$$

$$= \frac{1}{\sqrt{r}}\left(|a \ mod \ N\rangle + |a^2 \ mod \ N\rangle .. + |1\rangle\right) = |u\rangle \tag{4-95}$$

From Equation 4-95 we see that $|u\rangle = \sum_{k=0}^{r-1} |a^k \ mod \ N\rangle$ is an eigenvector of U_a but not an interesting one for us since its eigenvalue is 1, which doesn't contain the period r in its expression.

We can add a phase to each of the computational basis states $|a^k \bmod N\rangle$ that are proportional to k and that contain the period r, as shown here:

$$|u\rangle = \frac{1}{\sqrt{r}} \sum_{k=0}^{r-1} e^{\frac{2\pi i k}{r}} |a^k \bmod N\rangle \qquad (4\text{-}96)$$

Let's see if $|u\rangle$ in Equation 4-96 still makes it as an eigenvector of operator U_a.

$$U_a|u\rangle = \frac{1}{\sqrt{r}} U_a \left(e^{\frac{2\pi i 0}{r}} |1\rangle + e^{\frac{2\pi i 1}{r}} |a \bmod N\rangle .. + e^{\frac{2\pi i (r-1)}{r}} |a^{r-1} \bmod N\rangle \right)$$

$$= \frac{1}{\sqrt{r}} \left(e^{\frac{2\pi i 0}{r}} |a \bmod N\rangle + e^{\frac{2\pi i 1}{r}} |a^2 \bmod N\rangle .. + e^{\frac{2\pi i (r-1)}{r}} |a^r \bmod N\rangle \right)$$

$$= \frac{1}{\sqrt{r}} e^{\frac{-2\pi i}{r}} \left(e^{\frac{2\pi i 1}{r}} |a \bmod N\rangle + e^{\frac{2\pi i 2}{r}} |a^2 \bmod N\rangle .. + e^{2\pi i} |1\rangle \right)$$

$$= e^{\frac{-2\pi i}{r}} \frac{1}{\sqrt{r}} \left(e^{\frac{2\pi i 1}{r}} |a \bmod N\rangle + e^{\frac{2\pi i 2}{r}} |a^2 \bmod N\rangle .. + |1\rangle \right)$$

$$= e^{\frac{-2\pi i}{r}} |u\rangle \qquad (4\text{-}97)$$

We can see that $|u\rangle = \frac{1}{\sqrt{r}} \sum_{k=0}^{r-1} e^{\frac{2\pi i k}{r}} |a^k \bmod N\rangle$ is in fact the eigenvector of the unitary operator U_a with eigenvalue $e^{\frac{-2\pi i}{r}}$. However, U_a is only one such eigenvector. In general, we can express the eigenvectors as follows:

$$|u_s\rangle = \frac{1}{\sqrt{r}} \sum_{k=0}^{r-1} e^{\frac{2\pi i k s}{r}} |a^k \bmod N\rangle \qquad (4\text{-}98)$$

In Equation 4-98, $s \in \{0, 1, 2 .. r-1\}$ since for any value of $s \geq r$ the phases would repeat themselves and so too the vectors. The corresponding eigenvalues of $|u_s\rangle$ would be of the form $e^{\frac{-2\pi i s}{r}}$. Although there are phases in the eigenvalues of the form $e^{\frac{-2\pi i s}{r}}$, we cannot really do quantum phase estimation with $|u_s\rangle$ since it contains the unknown period r. As you would recall, we need a known eigenvector $|u\rangle$ in the quantum Fourier estimation. How about we take the equal superposition of the eigenvectors $|u_s\rangle$ defined next and see if it would be useful? Do note that we want a state $|u\rangle$ that is totally known prior to starting the quantum phase estimation.

$$|u\rangle = \frac{1}{\sqrt{r}}\sum_{s=0}^{r-1}|u_s\rangle \tag{4-99}$$

Substituting the expression for $|u_s\rangle$ from Equation 4-98 in Equation 4-99, we get the following:

$$|u\rangle = \frac{1}{\sqrt{r}}\sum_{s=0}^{r-1}\frac{1}{\sqrt{r}}\sum_{k=0}^{r-1}e^{\frac{2\pi iks}{r}}|a^k mod\, N\rangle$$

$$= \frac{1}{r}\sum_{s=0}^{r-1}\left(e^{\frac{2\pi i0s}{r}}|a^0\ mod\, N\rangle + e^{\frac{2\pi i1s}{r}}|a^1\ mod\, N\rangle + .. + e^{\frac{2\pi i(r-1)s}{r}}|a^{r-1}\ mod\, N\rangle\right)$$

$$= \frac{1}{r}\sum_{s=0}^{r-1}\left(|1\rangle + e^{\frac{2\pi i1s}{r}}|a^1 mod\, N\rangle + .. + e^{\frac{2\pi i(r-1)s}{r}}|a^{r-1} mod\, N\rangle\right)$$

$$= |1\rangle + \sum_{s=0}^{r-1}e^{\frac{2\pi i1s}{r}}|a\ mod\, N\rangle + ... + \sum_{s=0}^{r-1}e^{\frac{2\pi i(r-1)s}{r}}|a^{r-1}\ mod\, N\rangle \tag{4-100}$$

$$= |1\rangle + \sum_{k=1}^{r-1}|a^k mod\, N\rangle\sum_{s=0}^{r-1}e^{\frac{2\pi iks}{r}} \tag{4-101}$$

Except for the state initial state $|1\rangle$, the phases in each state $|a^k\ mod\, N\rangle$ is a geometric series with initial term $b = 1$ and common ratio $m = e^{\frac{2\pi ik}{r}}$. The geometric series sum corresponding to each values of $k \geq 1$ is as follows:

$$\sum_{s=0}^{r-1}e^{\frac{2\pi iks}{r}} = \frac{e^{\frac{2\pi ik}{r}}\left(e^{\frac{2\pi ik.r}{r}}-1\right)}{e^{\frac{2\pi ik}{r}}-1} = \frac{e^{\frac{2\pi ik}{r}}\left(e^{2\pi ik}-1\right)}{e^{\frac{2\pi ik}{r}}-1} = 0 \tag{4-102}$$

Hence, the state $|u\rangle = \frac{1}{\sqrt{r}}\sum_{s=0}^{r-1}|u_s\rangle = |1\rangle$, which is good for us since it's a known vector that we can feed to the quantum phase estimation algorithm. Since $|u\rangle$ is the superposition of the eigenvectors $|u_0\rangle, |u_1\rangle, ...\,|u_{r-1}\rangle$ with eigenvalues $1, e^{\frac{-2\pi i}{r}}, ..., e^{\frac{-2\pi i(r-1)}{r}}$ instead of quantum phase estimation, giving one phase, it would give a superposition of the phases corresponding to all the eigenvectors $|u_0\rangle, |u_1\rangle, ..\,|u_{r-1}\rangle$.

Hence, the state that we will get at the end of the inverse Fourier transform stage of QPE is as follows:

$$|\phi\rangle = \frac{1}{\sqrt{r}}\left(\left|\frac{0}{r}\right\rangle + \left|\frac{1}{r}\right\rangle + \ldots\left|\frac{1-r}{r}\right\rangle\right) = \frac{1}{\sqrt{r}}\sum_{s=0}^{r-1}\left|\frac{s}{r}\right\rangle \qquad (4\text{-}103)$$

Now on measuring $|\phi\rangle$, we will get any of the phases $\frac{s}{r}$ with equal probability where s is a random number from 0 to $(r-1)$.

We know the measurements of the phases $\frac{s}{r}$ where $s \in \{0, 1, .. r-1\}$ would be a rational number. However, the value of phase $\frac{s}{r}$ that we would get might be a real number that is a close approximation of $\frac{s}{r}$ based on the number of "first register" qubits defined and because of the rounding approximations. We can use the continued fractions algorithm to convert the real numbers to rational numbers of the form $\frac{b}{c}$ where b and c are co-prime to each other. We know that $\frac{r-1}{r}$ is the maximum value among the measured phase. Hence, after applying the continued fractions algorithm on the maximum phase measured, if we could get two integers b and c such that $c - b = 1$, we know for sure the desired period $r = c$.

Continued Fractions Algorithm

The continued fractions algorithm is an effective way to get to a rational number representation for any given real number. Given a real number x, we can represent it in terms of integers alone using the expression of the following form:

$$x \approx [b_0, b_1, \ldots b_m] = b_o + \cfrac{1}{b_1 + \cfrac{1}{\ldots + b_m}} \qquad (4\text{-}104)$$

The expression of x in Equation 4-104 forms a converging series for different values of m. Infact when x is a rational number, we converge to x for a finite value of m.

For instance, let's express 0.67 as a rational number using the continued fractions method.

In this case,

- $b_0 = 0$ since 0.67 is less than 1 and hence the remainder $r_0 = 0.67$.

- $b_1 = integer\left(\dfrac{1}{r_0}\right) = integer\left(\dfrac{1}{0.67}\right) = 1$. The remainder $r_1 = \dfrac{1}{r_0} - b_1 = 0.49257$.

- $b_2 = integer\left(\dfrac{1}{r_1}\right) = integer\left(\dfrac{1}{0.49257}\right) = 2$. The remainder

$r_2 = \dfrac{1}{r_1} - b_2 = 0.030168$.

If we leave the remainder r_2, the rational number approximation of 0.67 is $\dfrac{2}{3}$, as we can see here:

$$0.67 = b_0 + \cfrac{1}{b_1 + \cfrac{1}{b_2}} = 0 + \cfrac{1}{1 + \cfrac{1}{2}} = \frac{2}{3}$$

Now that we have gone through the heuristics associated in turning the period finding problem as a quantum phase estimation problem, we will proceed with the implementation of it for different values of $a \leq N$ where we chose $N = 15$. Figure 4-8 shows the high-level diagram of the period finding problem.

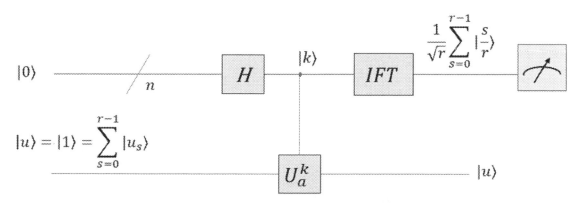

Figure 4-8. *High-level diagram of quantum phase estimation*

Period Finding Implementation in Cirq

We implement the period finding algorithm through the PeriodFinding class in which we perform the quantum phase estimation algorithm with the input vector $|u\rangle = |1\rangle$. The input vector $|u\rangle$ is a superposition of eigenvectors of the unitary transform U_a. The unitary transform U_a operates on a state $|y\rangle$ to produce the state $|ay \bmod N\rangle$.

The core of the period finding algorithm is building the unitary operator U_a, which we have implemented through the periodic_oracle function in the PeriodFinding class. The periodic_oracle function uses a bunch of SWAP operations to implement the unitary operation U_a. We discuss its implementation in detail at the end of the code. We established earlier that a elements that are factors of N or share common factors with N would not have periodic functions of the form a^x mod N. In general, only a elements that are relatively prime or co-prime to N would have periodic function of the form a^x mod N. To check whether the element a passed to the program is relatively co-prime to N, we use the function euclid_gcd that returns the greatest common divisor between a and N. The state at the end of the periodic finding implementation is an equal superposition of the states $\left|\dfrac{s}{r}\right\rangle$ where r is the period and $s \in \{0, 1, 2. ., r-1\}$. So, on measurement, we will get one of the states from the uniform distribution of $\dfrac{0}{r}, \dfrac{1}{r}, \ldots, \dfrac{r-1}{r}$.

We use the measurement_to_period function to come up with the final period. Listing 4-3 shows the detailed implementation of the period finding algorithm.

Listing 4-3. Period Finding Implementation

```
import cirq
from quantum_fourier_transform import QFT
import numpy as np

def euclid_gcd(a, b):
    if b == 0:
        return a
    else:
        return euclid_gcd(b, a % b)

"""

The Period Finding Class computes the Period of functions
```

```
of the form f(x) = a^x mod N using Quantum Phase Estimation
Alternately we can say the algorithm finds the period of
the element a mod N
"""

class PeriodFinding:

    def __init__(self,
                 ancillia_precision_bits=4,
                 func_domain_size=16,
                 a=7,
                 N=15
                 ):

        self.ancillia_precision_bits = ancillia_precision_bits
        self.func_domain_size = func_domain_size
        self.num_output_qubits = self.ancillia_precision_bits
        self.num_input_qubits =
                int(np.log2(self.func_domain_size))
        self.output_qubits = [cirq.LineQubit(i)
                for i in range(self.num_output_qubits)]
        self.input_qubits = [cirq.LineQubit(i)
            for i in range(self.num_output_qubits,
            self.num_output_qubits + self.num_input_qubits)]

        self.a = a

        self.N = N
        if self.N is None:
            self.N = func_domain_size - 1

        self.circuit = cirq.Circuit()
```

The periodic_oracle function implements the unitary transform U_a that takes a state $|y\rangle$ and outputs $|ay \bmod N\rangle$. If the period of the function is r, then r times the application of U_a on $|y\rangle$ would yield the state $|y\rangle$ again. We implement the unitary transform U_a through a bunch of SWAP and NOT gates. The implementation steps are outlined in the next section in detail. Readers are advised to refer to it while implementing the period finding algorithm for better clarity.

```python
def periodic_oracle(self, a, m, k):
    """

    Implement an oracle U_a that takes in the state
    input state |y> and outputs |ay mod N>
    """

    for i in range(m):
        if a in [2, 13]:
            self.circuit.append(cirq.SWAP(
                self.input_qubits[0],
                self.input_qubits[1]).controlled_by(
                self.output_qubits[k]))
            self.circuit.append(cirq.SWAP(
                self.input_qubits[1],
                self.input_qubits[2]).controlled_by(
                self.output_qubits[k]))
            self.circuit.append(cirq.SWAP(
                self.input_qubits[2],
                self.input_qubits[3]).controlled_by(
                self.output_qubits[k]))

        if a in [7, 8]:
            self.circuit.append(cirq.SWAP(
                self.input_qubits[2],
                self.input_qubits[3]).controlled_by(
                self.output_qubits[k]))

            self.circuit.append(cirq.SWAP(
                self.input_qubits[1],
                self.input_qubits[2]).controlled_by(
                self.output_qubits[k]))

            self.circuit.append(cirq.SWAP(
                self.input_qubits[0],
                self.input_qubits[1]).controlled_by(
                self.output_qubits[k]))
```

```python
        if a in [4, 11]:
            self.circuit.append(cirq.SWAP(
                self.input_qubits[1],
                self.input_qubits[3]).controlled_by(
                self.output_qubits[k]))

            self.circuit.append(cirq.SWAP(
                self.input_qubits[0],
                self.input_qubits[2]).controlled_by(
                self.output_qubits[k]))

        # 7 is 8 (mod 15). So, for both 7 and 8
        # we apply the Implementation for 8. Finally
        # we reverse the state of inputs for 7 to
        # perform mod 15
        # We do likewise for 11 which is (4 mod 15)
        # and for 13 which is (2 mod 15)
        if a in [7, 11, 13]:
            for j in range(self.num_input_qubits):
                self.circuit.append(cirq.X(
                self.input_qubits[j]).controlled_by(
                self.output_qubits[k]))

def build_phase_1_period_finding_circuit(self):

    # Apply Hadamard Transform on each output qubit

    self.circuit.append([cirq.H(self.output_qubits[i])
            for i in range(self.num_output_qubits)])

    # Set input qubits to state |0001>
    self.circuit.append(cirq.X(self.input_qubits[-1]))

    if euclid_gcd(self.N, self.a) != 1:
        print(f"{self.a} is not co-prime to {self.N}")
        co_primes = []
        for elem in range(2, self.N):
            if euclid_gcd(self.N, elem) == 1:
                co_primes.append(elem)
```

```
        print(f"Select a from the list of co-primes to {self.N}:
        {co_primes} ")

    else:
        print(f"Trying period of element a
                    = {self.a} mod {self.N}")
        a = self.a

    for q in range(self.num_output_qubits):
        _pow_ = 2 ** (self.num_output_qubits - q - 1)
        self.periodic_oracle(a=a, m=_pow_, k=q)

def inv_qft(self):
    """

    Inverse Fourier Transform
    :return:
    IFT circuit
    """

    self._qft_ = QFT(qubits=self.output_qubits)
    self._qft_.qft_circuit()

def simulate_circuit(self, circ):
    """

    Simulates the Period Finding Algorithm
    :param circ: Circuit to Simulate
    :return: Output results of Simulation
    """

    circ.append([cirq.measure(*self.output_qubits, key='Z')])
    sim = cirq.Simulator()
    result = sim.run(circ, repetitions=1000)
    out = dict(result.histogram(key='Z'))
    out_result = {}

    for k in out.keys():
        new_key = "{0:b}".format(k)
```

```
    if len(new_key) < self.num_output_qubits:
        new_key = (self.num_output_qubits
                        - len(new_key)) * '0' + new_key
    out_result[new_key] = out[k]
```

```
return out_result
```

We determine the period of the function in the following measurement_to_period routine using the continued fractions algorithm that we have illustrated earlier.

```python
def measurement_to_period(self, results, denom_lim=15):

    #convert a state to Phase as a binary fraction
    #|x_1,x_2..x_n>-> x_1*2^-1 + x_2*2^-2 + ..+x_n*2^-n

    measured_states = list(results.keys())

    measured_phase = []
    measured_phase_rational = []

    for s in measured_states:
        phase = int(s, 2)/(2**len(s))
        #Implements continued fractions algorithm
        phase_rational = Fraction(phase).limit denominator(denom_lim)
        measured_phase.append(phase)
        measured_phase_rational.append(phase_rational)

    print(f"--------------------------------")
    print(f"Measured  |   Real   |    Rational")
    print(f"State     |   Phase  |    Phase  ")
    print(f"--------------------------------")
    for i in range(len(measured_phase)):
        print(f"    {measured_states[i]}  |
{measured_phase[i]}    |  {measured_phase_rational[i]}")
        print(f"-----------------------------")
    print('\n')

    max_phase_index = np.argmax(np.array(measured_phase))
    max_phase_rational = measured_phase_rational[
                                        max_phase_index]
```

```
        max_phase_numerator = max_phase_rational.numerator
        max_phase_denominator = max_phase_rational.denominator
        if (max_phase_denominator - max_phase_numerator) == 1 :
            period = max_phase_denominator
        else:
            print(f"Period cannot be determined")
            period = np.inf

        return period

def period_finding_routine(func_domain_size=16,
        ancillia_precision_bits=4,
        a=7,
        N=15):
    """

    :param func_domain_size:
        States in the Domain of the function.
    :param ancillia_precision_bits:
        Precision bits for Phase Measurement
    :param N: Number for Modulo division
    :param a:   Element whose periodicity mod N
                is to be computed
    :return: Period r of the element a mod N
     """

    _PF_ = PeriodFinding(
            ancillia_precision_bits=ancillia_precision_bits,
            func_domain_size=func_domain_size,
            a=a,
            N=N)

    _PF_.build_phase_1_period_finding_circuit()

    _PF_.inv_qft()

    circuit = _PF_.circuit + _PF_._qft_.inv_circuit
```

```
    print(circuit)
    result = _PF_.simulate_circuit(circuit)
    print(result)
    period = _PF_.measurement_to_period(result, denom_lim=_PF_.N)
    print(f"Period of {a} mod {N} is: {period} ")

if __name__ == '__main__':
    period_finding_routine()
```

output

Trying period finding of element a = 7 mod 15

Measurement Histogram Results follow
{'0000': 271, '0100': 251, '1000': 244, '1100': 234}

```
----------------------------------
Measured  |   Real   |   Rational
State     |  Phase   |    Phase
----------------------------------
  0000  |   0.0    |  0
----------------------------------
  0100  |   0.25   |  1/4
----------------------------------
  1000  |   0.5    |  1/2
----------------------------------
  1100  |   0.75   |  3/4
----------------------------------
```

Period of 7 mod 15 is: 4

See Figure 4-9.

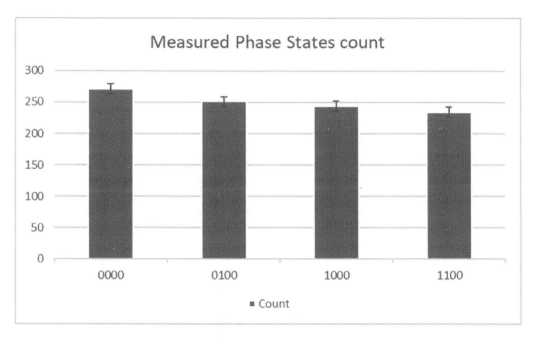

Figure 4-9. *Count of measured phase states*

We can see from the output that all four possible phases have been sampled with almost equal probability. From the measurements, we extract the period from the rational representation of the largest phase. This is because we know that for the largest phase the numerator and denominator always differ by 1, and hence the denominator will always be the period.

Implementing the Unitary Operator Through Quantum Circuits

We saw earlier in the code implementation section that the core of the period finding algorithm is in constructing the unitary operator U_a using a quantum circuit. We have implemented the same in the `periodic_oracle` function within the `PeriodFinding` class by using `SWAP` operators. Since we have `N=15`, the unitary operator is implemented for all numbers that are co-prime to 15, i.e., `2, 4, 7, 8,11, 13`.

We illustrate the unitary operator U_a implementation for `a=2`. For any other value of a, the approach remains same. The unitary operator U_a takes an element in state $|y\rangle$

to the state $|\,ay\,mod\,N\rangle$. For a=2 and N=15, the action of the operator can be defined as follows:

$$U_2|y\rangle=|2y\,mod\,15\rangle \qquad (4\text{-}105)$$

Now each of the computation basis states $|y\rangle$ is represented by four qubits (for N =15) as $|y\rangle = |\,y_1, y_2, y_3, y_4\rangle$ where y_1 through y_4 stands for the computation basis state of the individual qubits. The state $|y_1, y_2, y_3, y_4\rangle$ can be represented as an integer state through the binary expansion as follows:

$$|y\rangle=|y_1,y_2,y_3,y_4\rangle=|8y_1+4y_2+2y_3+y_4\rangle \qquad (4\text{-}106)$$

Using the binary expansion of y from Equation 4-106, the transformed state $|2y\,mod\,15\,\rangle$ can be written as follows:

$$|2y\,mod\,15\rangle$$
$$=|2(8y_1+4y_2+2y_3+y_4)mod\,15\rangle$$
$$=|(16y_1+8y_2+4y_3+2y_4)mod\,15\rangle \qquad (4\text{-}107)$$

Now $16y_1$ mod 15 is nothing but y_1. The maximum value of rest of the terms would not exceed 15, and hence we can rewrite Equation 4-107 as follows:

$$|2y\,mod\,15\rangle=|y_1+8y_2+4y_3+2y_4\rangle \qquad (4\text{-}108)$$

All the terms on the right side of the equation in Equation 4-108 are multiples of the power of 2. By arranging them in decreasing order of the powers of 2, we have the following:

$$|2y\,mod\,15\rangle=|8y_2+4y_3+2y_4+y_1\rangle \qquad (4\text{-}109)$$

Now $8y_2 + 4y_3 + 2y_4 + y_1$ is nothing but the integer expansion of the binary string $y_2y_3y_4y_1$, and hence we have the following:

$$|2y\,mod\,15\rangle=|y_2,y_3,y_4,y_1\rangle \qquad (4\text{-}110)$$

Using Equation 4-110, we can express the operation of the unitary operator U_2 as follows:

$$U_2 |y_1, y_2, y_3, y_4\rangle = \langle y_2, y_3, y_4, y_1|$$

(4-111)

From Equation 4-111, we can see that all the unitary operator U_2 is doing is interchanging the states of the four qubits. This can be effectively implemented using SWAP operators in a quantum circuit, as illustrated in Figure 4-10.

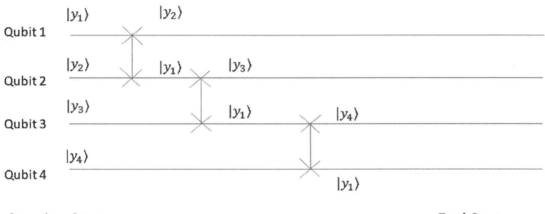

Starting State

$$|y_1, y_2, y_3, y_4\rangle$$

End State

$$|y_2, y_3, y_4, y_1\rangle$$

Figure 4-10. *Quantum circuit implementation of operator U_2*

The operator for $a = 13$; i.e., U_{13} can be constructed easily from U_2 since 13 is the complement of 2 in a modulo division by 15. The unitary operator U_{13} action on a state y can be expressed as follows:

$$U_{13}|y\rangle = |13y \bmod 15\rangle$$

(4-112)

We can replace 13 by $(15 - 2)$ and rewrite Equation 4-112 as follows:

$$U_{13}|y\rangle = |(15-2)y \bmod 15\rangle$$
$$= |(15y - 2y) \bmod 15\rangle$$
$$= |-2y \bmod 15\rangle$$

(4-113)

Since we are performing modulo 15 division, we can conveniently add 15 to the state value. Also, we know from Equation 4-109 that $2y \bmod 15 = y_1 + 8y_2 + 4y_3 + 2y_4$. Making these substitutions in Equation 4-113, we get the following:

$$
\begin{aligned}
U_{13}|y\rangle &= |-2y \bmod 15\rangle \\
&= |15 - 2y \bmod 15\rangle \\
&= |8 + 4 + 2 + 1 - (y_1 + 8y_2 + 4y_3 + 2y_4)\rangle \\
&= |8(1 - y_2) + 4(1 - y_3) + 2(1 - y_4) + (1 - y_1)\rangle \\
&= |1 - y_2, 1 - y_3, 1 - y_4, 1 - y_1\rangle
\end{aligned}
\tag{4-114}
$$

Now each of the qubits state is given as $|1 - y_i\rangle$, which is basically the complementary basis state to the state $|y_i\rangle$. For instance, if $|y_i\rangle = |1\rangle$, then the complementary state $|1 - y_i\rangle = |0\rangle$, and vice versa.

So, U_{13} takes the state $|y\rangle = |y_1, y_2, y_3, y_4\rangle$ to the output state $|1 - y_2, 1 - y_3, 1 - y_4, 1 - y_1\rangle$, whereas U_2 takes the same state $|y_1, y_2, y_3, y_4\rangle$ to the output state $|y_2, y_3, y_4, y_1\rangle$. The state $|1 - y_2, 1 - y_3, 1 - y_4, 1 - y_1\rangle$ can be obtained from the state $|y_2, y_3, y_4, y_1\rangle$ by applying the quantum NOT gate X on each of the qubits. Hence, the quantum circuit for U_{13} transformation can be obtained from the U_2 circuit by passing each of the qubits through the quantum NOT gate X, as shown in Figure 4-11.

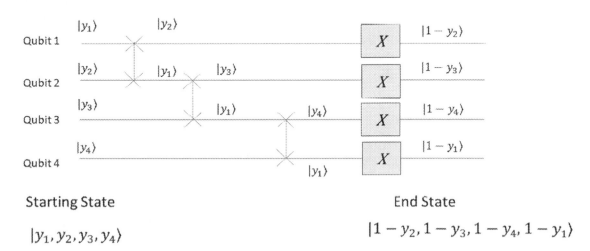

Figure 4-11. *Quantum circuit implementation of operator U_{13}*

Factoring Algorithm

Given a compositive number N, the factoring problem tries to express the same in a product form of primes as shown below:

$$N = p_1^{e_1} p_2^{e_2} .. p_n^{e_n} = \prod_{i=1}^{n} p_i^{e_i} \qquad (4\text{-}115)$$

The elements p_1 through p_n in the previous expression in Equation 4-115 are prime numbers. For instance, we can factor 60 as $2^2 \times 3^1 \times 5^1$. One of the most important factoring problems is when N is a factor of two odd primes p and q where the primes are very close in length to each other. This ensures that the primes are as large as possible, thus making factoring such a number N a difficult task. The RSA cryptosystem builds keys as product of such large prime numbers.

The key to factoring such a number $N = pq$ where p and q are prime numbers is to find a number x with the following properties:

Property 1:

$$x^2 \equiv 1 \left(mod\ N \right) \qquad (4\text{-}116)$$

Property 2:

$$x \neq \pm 1 \left(mod\ N \right) \qquad (4\text{-}117)$$

Now let's see how such a number x with properties 1 and 2 help in factorizing N into primes p and q. From property 1, we have the following:

$$x^2 \equiv 1 \left(mod\ N \right)$$
$$\rightarrow\ x^2 - 1 \equiv 0 \left(mod\ N \right)$$

$$\rightarrow (x-1)(x+1) \equiv \left(0\ mod\ N \right) \qquad (4\text{-}118)$$

From Equation 4-112, it is clear that N divides $(x-1)(x+1)$. However, from property 2, we know that N does not divide either $(x-1)$ or $(x+1)$ since $x \neq \pm 1\ (mod\ N)$. Then for N to divide $(x-1)(x+1)$, one of the primes p should divide either $(x-1)$ or $(x+1)$. Say, p divides $(x-1)$; then q should divide $(x+1)$. Hence, the primes p and q can be obtained by finding the greatest common divisor (gcd) between N and factors $(x \pm 1)$.

$$p = \gcd(N, x+1)$$

$$q = \gcd(N, x-1) \qquad (4\text{-}119)$$

Let's illustrate this with an example wherein we want to factorize $N = 15$. We will take take random numbers from 2 to 14 as x and see whether we can get any such numbers with properties 1 and 2 and work through the factorization.

Let's choose $x = 2$ to begin with. We have the following:

$$x^2 = 4 \equiv 4 \, mod \, 15$$

$$x \equiv 2 \, mod \, 15 \neq \pm 1 \, (mod \, 15) \qquad (4\text{-}120)$$

We see $x = 2$ satisfies property 2 but not property 1 and hence is not our desired x. Now let's try our luck with $x = 4$.

$$x^2 = 16 \equiv 1 \, (mod \, 15)$$

$$x = 4 \equiv 4 \, (mod \, 15) \neq \pm 1 \, (mod \, 15) \qquad (4\text{-}121)$$

We see that $x = 4$ satisfies both property 1 and property 2. Hence, we can find the two prime numbers p and q by computing the greatest common divisor of N with $(x + 1) = (4 + 1) = 5$ and $(x - 1) = (4 - 1) = 3$.

$$p = \gcd(N, x+1) = (15, 5) = 5$$

$$q = \gcd(N, x-1) = (15, 3) = 3 \qquad (4\text{-}122)$$

Now that we are convinced that a number x that satisfies properties 1 and 2 would help us factorize N as a product of two primes, p and q, the next obvious question is how to derive such an x given N. This is where the quantum period finding algorithm comes in handy. Through quantum period finding, we aim to find the periodicity r of elements $a \, (mod \, N)$ where $a < N$ and a and N are co-primes to each other. The periodicity relation of such an element can be expressed as follows:

$$a^r \equiv 1 \, (mod \, N) \qquad (4\text{-}123)$$

Say for a given co-prime a with respect to N we can find its period r through quantum period finding. We have two possibilities.

Period r is even:

When r is even, we can write Equation 4-123 as follows:

$$a^r \equiv 1 \left(mod\ N \right)$$

$$\rightarrow \left(a^{\frac{r}{2}} \right)^2 \equiv 1 \left(mod\ N \right) \tag{4-124}$$

So, when r is even, property 1 is satisfied. If also $a^{\frac{r}{2}} \neq 1 \left(mod\ N \right)$, i.e., property 2 is also satisfied, we get our desired $= a^{\frac{r}{2}}$. The prime factors of N can be found as follows:

$$p = \gcd \left(N, a^{\frac{r}{2}} + 1 \right)$$

$$q = \gcd \left(N, a^{\frac{r}{2}} - 1 \right) \tag{4-125}$$

If property 2 is not satisfied, we try period finding with a different co-prime a with respect to N.

Period r is odd:

If period r is odd, property 1 would not be satisfied since we would not be able to get integer value for $a^{\frac{r}{2}}$. In this case, also we should try period finding with a different co-prime a with respect to N.

Factoring Implementation in Cirq

Now that we have gone through the factoring algorithm, we implement it to factorize numbers that are the product of two primes. We import the quantum period finding implementation `period_finding_routine` that uses the `PeriodFinding` class. The `period_finding_routine` computes the period of the numbers of the form $a \left(mod\ N \right)$ where $a < = N$ and N is the number that we want to factorize. Once the period is determined to be even, we use classical logic to check whether properties 1 and 2 are met for the number N to be factored. If the required properties are not met or the period is determined to be odd, we try order finding for a different value of a and repeat the process until we factorize N successfully. Listing 4-4 shows the Cirq implementation for this.

Listing 4-4. Factoring Implementation

```
import cirq
from period_finding import period_finding_routine
from period_finding import euclid_gcd
import numpy as np
```

The `factoring` implementation chooses different co-factors a of the number to be factorized N and uses the period finding algorithm we implemented in the earlier section to come up with periods r of the functions of the form $f_a(x) = a^x mod N$. For each such function, $f_a(x)$ pertaining to the co-factor, once the period r is determined, we check whether $a^{\frac{r}{2}}$ satisfies property 1 and property 2. If both the properties are satisfied, we get our two factors as $\gcd\left(N, a^{\frac{r}{2}} + 1\right)$ and $\gcd\left(N, a^{\frac{r}{2}} - 1\right)$. If both the properties are not satisfied, we try with a different co-factor a.

```
class Factoring:
    """

    Find the factorization of number N = p*q
    where p and q are prime to each other
    """

    def __init__(self, N):
        self.N = N

    def factoring(self):

        prev_trials_for_a = []
        factored = False

        while not factored:
            new_a_found = False

            # Sample a new "a" not already sampled
            while not new_a_found:
                a = np.random.randint(2, self.N)
```

```
            if a not in prev_trials_for_a:
                new_a_found = True

        # "a" not co-prime to N are not periodic
        if euclid_gcd(self.N, a) == 1:

        # Call the period_finding_routine
        #from PeriodFinding Implementation

            period = period_finding_routine(a=a, N=self.N)

            # Check if the period is even.
            # It period even (a^(r/2))^2 = 1 mod (N)
            # for integer, a^(r/2)

            if period % 2 == 0:

                # Check if a^(r/2) != +/- 1 mod(N)
                # if condition satisfied number gets
                # factorized in this iteration

                if a ** (period / 2) % self.N not
                                    in [+1, -1]:
                    prime_1 = euclid_gcd(self.N,
                                    a**(period/2) + 1)
                    prime_2 = euclid_gcd(self.N,
                                    a**(period / 2) - 1)
                    factored = True
                    return prime_1, prime_2
        else:

            # If we have exhausted all "a"s and
            # still have not got prime factors recheck
            # input

            if len(prev_trials_for_a) == self.N - 2:
                raise ValueError(f"Check input
                        is a product of two primes")
```

```python
if __name__ == '__main__':

    fp = Factoring(N=15)
    factor_1, factor_2 = fp.factoring()

    if factor_1 is not None:
        print(f"The factors of {fp.N} are {factor_1}
                                and {factor_2}")
    else:
        print(f"Error in factoring")
```

The period finding algorithm implemented earlier selects the co-primes a in a random manner until it can find a suitable one with a suitable period that factorizes the number. We ran the algorithm twice, and the two outputs from the following factorization correspond to that.

output

first Run

```
-----------------------------------
Measured   |   Real    |   Rational
State      |   Phase   |   Phase
-----------------------------------
0000       |   0.0     |   0
-----------------------------------
1100       |   0.75    |   3/4
-----------------------------------
0100       |   0.25    |   1/4
-----------------------------------
1000       |   0.5     |   1/2
-----------------------------------
```

Period of 7 mod 15 is: 4
The factors of 15 are 5.0 and 3.0

2nd run

```
-----------------------------------
Measured  |   Real   |   Rational
State     |   Phase  |   Phase
-----------------------------------
000       |  0.0     |  0
-----------------------------------
1000      |  0.5     |  1/2
-----------------------------------
```

```
Period of 11 mod 15 is: 2
The factors of 15 are 3.0 and 5.0
```

As we can see from the first run, the algorithm factorized using a= 7 (mod 15), which has a period of 4. In the second run, the algorithm factorized using a = 11 (mod 15), which has a period of 2. In both cases, it factorized 15 properly as the product of the primes 3 and 5.

Hidden Subgroup Problem

Another interesting application of the quantum Fourier transform is the hidden subgroup problem in the field of group theory. In fact, several quantum algorithms that we have already implemented fall under the category of the hidden subgroup problem, as we will see later in this section. For readers who are not too familiar with group theory, we will quickly go through some preliminary concepts before diving into the problem.

Definition of a Group

On a set G, a law of composition can be defined as a rule for combining two elements a, $b \in G$ to get an element $c \in G$. For example, addition and multiplication of any two real numbers produce another real number. Hence, the law of composition can be thought of as a map from $G \times G \to G$. A law of composition can be anything such as multiplication and addition for real numbers or matrix multiplication on square matrices, to name a few. We will use the notation $\circ$ to represent any generalized law of composition.

A set G along with a law of composition denoted by $\circ$ is said to form a group $(G, \circ)$ if the following holds true:

- **Closure**: For any two elements as follows:

$$a, b \in G, a \circ b \in G \tag{4-126}$$

- **Identity**: There exists an element $e \in G$ as follows:

$$a \circ e = e \circ a = a \tag{4-127}$$

- **Inverse**: For each element $a \in G$ there exists an inverse element a^{-1} as follows:

$$a \circ a^{-1} = a^{-1} \circ a = e \tag{4-128}$$

- **Associativity**: For any three elements $a, b, c \in G$ the below holds true:

$$(a \circ b) \circ c = a \circ (b \circ c) \tag{4-129}$$

Now that we have defined a group, let's look into some examples of groups.

- The real line $\mathbb{R}$ forms a group $(\mathbb{R}, +)$ under the composition law of addition. Hence, the notation $\circ$ for composition is addition $(+)$ in this case. It is easy to see that the identity in this group is the element 0 since if we take the any element, say $5.01 \in \mathbb{R}$, we have $5.01 + 0 = 0 + 5.01 = 5.01$. The inverse of the element 5.01 in this group is -5.01 since $5.01 - 5.01 = 0$.

- The 2×2 square and invertible matrices under the composition law of matrix multiplication forms a group. The identity element in this group is the 2×2 Identity Matrix $I_{2 \times 2}$.

- The 2×2 Pauli matrices X, Y, Z together with the identity matrix I form a group where the elements are $\{\pm I, \pm iI, \pm X, \pm iX, \pm Y, \pm iY, \pm Z, \pm iZ\}$. The law of composition for the group is matrix multiplication.

For the ease of reference, we will often refer to the set G of the group $(G, \circ)$ as the group itself.

Abelian Group

The composition law in general is not commutative in nature. For instance, if we take the group G of 2×2 square invertible matrices under the composition law of matrix multiplication in general for any two matrices $A, B \in G$ as follows:

$$AB \neq BA$$

$$(4\text{-}130)$$

A group $(G, \circ)$ is said to be an abelian group if its elements commute under the law of composition. Hence, in an abelian group, any two elements $a, b \in G$ follows.

$$a \circ b = b \circ a$$

$$(4\text{-}131)$$

The group $(\mathbb{R}, +)$ and $(\mathbb{Z}, +)$ are abelian groups. If we take elements $5, 7 \in \mathbb{Z}$, they commute since $5 + 7 = 7 + 5$.

Subgroups

Given a group $(G, \circ)$, a subset H of G is a subgroup of the set G if it is a group in its own right and thus obeys the properties of closure, identity, inverse, and associatively.

For example, for the group $(\mathbb{Z}, +)$, all multiples of 2 denoted by $2\mathbb{Z}$ form a subgroup $(2\mathbb{Z}, +)$. This subgroup contains 0 as the identity, and for any two elements denoted by $2a, 2b \in 2\mathbb{Z}$ we know that $2a + 2b \in 2\mathbb{Z}$.

Cosets

If H is the subgroup of a group $(G, \circ)$ and $a \in G$, then the subset $a \circ H$ where

$$a \circ H = \{a \circ h \mid h \in H\}$$

$$(4\text{-}132)$$

is called a *left coset*. Similarly, $H \circ a$ is called a *right coset*. Do note that the cosets themselves are not subgroups in general except for the coset $e \circ H = H$. Unless explicitly specified by a coset we would mean a left coset.

The cosets of H in G forms a partition of group G. For any two elements $a, b \in G$, the following is true:

$$a \circ H = b \circ H \; if \; a = b \circ h \; for \; some \; h \in H \tag{4-133}$$

Now let's try to prove the previous claim in Equation 4-133. If $a \circ H = b \circ H$, then there exists two elements $h_1, h_2 \in H$.

$$a \circ h_1 = b \circ h_2 \tag{4-134}$$

Operating with h_1^{-1} on both sides of Equation 4-134, we get the following:

$$a \circ h_1 \circ h_1^{-1} = b \circ h_2 \circ h_1^{-1}$$

$$\rightarrow a = b \circ \left(h_2 \circ h_1^{-1} \right) \tag{4-135}$$

Since $h_1, h_2, h_1^{-1} \in H$, as per the closure property of a group, the element $h = h_2 \circ h_1^{-1} \in H$. Hence, by replacing $\left(h_2 \circ h_1^{-1} \right)$ by the element $h \in H$, we have the following:

$$a = b \circ h_2 \tag{4-136}$$

Also, when the two cosets given by $a \circ H$ and $b \circ H$ equal each other, i.e., $a \circ H = b \circ H$, the elements a and b should belong to the same coset. This is because since H contains the identity element, $a \circ H$ must contain element a, while $b \circ H$ must contain the element b. This gives us another important relationship as follows:

$$(a \circ H = b \circ H = S) \rightarrow a, b \in S \tag{4-137}$$

For example, for the group $G = (\mathbb{Z}, +)$ and its corresponding subgroup $H = (3\mathbb{Z}, +)$, let's look at the different cosets of the form $\{g + H| g \in G\}$.

We start with $g = 0$, and the corresponding coset is $0 + H = H$. The set H consists of the integer multiples of 3 as its elements and hence $H = \{3k| k \in \mathbb{Z}\}$.

For $g = 1$, the corresponding coset is $1 + H = \{3k + 1 | k \in \mathbb{Z}\}$.

For $g = 2$, the corresponding coset is $2 + H = \{3k + 2 | k \in \mathbb{Z}\}$.

For $g = 3$, the corresponding coset is $3 + H = \{3k + 3 | k \in \mathbb{Z}\} = \{3k'| k' \in \mathbb{Z}\} = H$.

We see that there are in fact three cosets given by $H, (1 + H), (2 + H)$. Also, we see that the cosets $(3 + H) = (0 + H)$. As per the claim in Equation 4-133, $(a + H) = (b + H)$

if $a = (b + h)$ where $h \in H$. For our case, we can take $a = 3$ and $b = 0$ and hence $h = (a - b) = 3$. The element 3 is indeed an element of the subgroup H, which consists of integer multiples of 3.

Normal Subgroup

A subgroup $(H, \circ)$ of $(G, \circ)$ is said to be a normal subgroup if its left coset $g \circ H$ equals its right coset $H \circ g$ for each element $g \in G$. Hence, for a normal subgroup H, we can write the following:

$$g \circ H = H \circ g \quad \forall g \in G \tag{4-138}$$

Operating with g^{-1} on both sides of Equation 4-138, we get this:

$$H = g^{-1} \circ H \circ g \quad \forall g \in G \tag{4-139}$$

For any element $g \in G$, $g^{-1} \circ H \circ g$ is the set $\{g^{-1} \circ h \circ g \,|\, h \in H\}$. The operation $g^{-1} \circ h \circ g$ by the element g on h is called *conjugation*, and as per Equation 4-139 the element $g^{-1} \circ h \circ g$ should belong to the normal subgroup H.

So, we can define a normal subgroup H as one that remains invariant under conjugation by any element $g \in G$. In summary conjugation of the normal subgroup H by any element $g \in G$ merely reorders the elements of H.

The set of cosets of a normal subgroup H forms a group Q where the elements are the cosets themselves. Such a group is defined as follows:

$$Q = \{g \circ H = H \circ g | g \in G\} \tag{4-140}$$

The identity of the group Q is the coset H itself, and for any two cosets $a \circ H$, $b \circ H \in Q$ the closure is defined as follows:

$$(a \circ H) \circ (b \circ H) = (a \circ b) \circ H \tag{4-141}$$

The relation in Equation 4-141 is true since for normal subgroup H the left coset $b \circ H$ equals its right coset $H \circ b$, which allows us to write $(a \circ H) \circ (b \circ H)$ as follows:

$$(a \circ H) \circ (b \circ H) = (a \circ H) \circ (H \circ b)$$

$$= a \circ (H \circ H) \circ b \tag{4-142}$$

For any group G, we have $G \circ G = G$ because of the closure property of groups, and hence Equation 4-142 simplifies to the following:

$$(a \circ H) \circ (b \circ H) = a \circ H \circ b$$

$$= a \circ b \circ H \tag{4-143}$$

Group Homomorphism

Given two groups $(G_1, \circ)$ and $(G_2, *)$, a group homomorphism from $(G_1, \circ)$ to $(G_2, *)$ is a mapping $f: G_1 \to G_2$ such that for every pair of $x, y \in G_1$ we have this:

$$f(x \circ y) = f(x) * f(y) \tag{4-144}$$

Do note that the laws of composition for G_1 and G_2 are in general different, and hence we have denoted them by $\circ$ and $*$, respectively.

Here are some observations:

- The identity element e_1 in G_1 maps to identity element e_2 in G_2; i.e., $f(e_1) = e_2$.

  This can be proved by substituting $y = e_1$ in Equation 4-143. Doing so we get the following:

$$f(x \circ e_1) = f(x) * f(e_1)$$

$$\to f(x) = f(x) * f(e_1) \qquad \because x \circ e_1 = x \tag{4-145}$$

  Now $f(x)$ and $f(e_1)$ are elements of group G_2, and for the composition of two elements to be equal to one of them, the other has to be the identity. Hence, as per Equation 4-145, $f(e_1)$ should be the identity e_2 of the group G_2.

$$f(e_1) = e_2 \tag{4-146}$$

- Also, in group homomorphism, an inverse of an element in
  G_1 maps to an inverse in G_2. To derive the expression for it, we can
  substitute $y = x^{-1}$ in Equation 4-144 and get this:

$$f\left(x \circ x^{-1}\right) = f(x) * f\left(x^{-1}\right)$$
$$\rightarrow f(e_1) = f(x) * f\left(x^{-1}\right)$$
$$\rightarrow e_2 = f(x) * f\left(x^{-1}\right) \tag{4-147}$$

Now the composition of elements $f(x)$ and $f(x^{-1})$ in G_2 equals the
identity e_2 in G_2, and hence $f(x^{-1})$ should be equal to the inverse of $f(x)$.

$$f\left(x^{-1}\right) = f(x)^{-1} \tag{4-148}$$

The following are a few examples of homomorphism between
groups:

- The exponential function $f(x) = e^x$ defines a group homomorphism
  from the group $(\mathbb{R}, +)$ to $(\mathbb{R} > 0, \times)$. Since the laws of composition for
  the groups $(\mathbb{R}, +)$ and $(\mathbb{R} > 0, \times)$ are $+$ and $\times$, respectively, the group
  homomorphism property that should be obeyed in this example is as
  follows:

$$f(x + y) = f(x) \times f(y) \tag{4-149}$$

For the exponential function map $f(x) = e^x$, this is obeyed since the
following holds true:

$$e^{x+y} = e^x \times e^y \tag{4-150}$$

- The determinant map det $GL_n(\mathbb{R}) \rightarrow (R_{\neq 0}, \times)$ where $GL_n(\mathbb{R})$ represents the
  group of $n \times n$ square invertible matrices with real entries with the law of
  composition as matrix multiplication and $(\mathbb{R}_{\neq 0}, \times)$ represents the group
  of real numbers except 0 with the law of composition as multiplication.
  The rule of homomorphism to be satisfied here is as follows:

$$f(AB) = f(A) \times f(B) \tag{4-151}$$

The same is obeyed since for any two matrices A and B the product of their determinant can be expressed as follows:

$$det(AB) = det(A) \times det(B) \tag{4-152}$$

Kernel of Homomorphism

For a group homomorphism from $(G_1, {}^\circ)$ to $(G_2, *)$, the identity element e_1 of $(G_1, {}^\circ)$ maps to the identity element e_2 of $(G_2, *)$. If the map for the group homomorphism is f, then from Equation 4-146 we have $f(e_1) = e_2$. In fact, there may be elements other than e_1 in G_1 that also map to the identity element $e_2 \in G_2$. The set K of all such elements $k \in G$ such that $f(k) = e_2$ is called the *kernel* of the homomorphism.

$$K = \{k \in G | f(k) = e_2\} \tag{4-153}$$

The kernel K of the group homomorphism is actually a normal subgroup of the group G_1. We have earlier discussed that a normal subgroup is one that remains invariant under conjugation. We take an element $g \in G_1$ and let g work on any generalized element $k \in K$ through conjugation to produce the generalized element $g^{-1} \circ k \circ g$. We need to prove $g^{-1} \circ k \circ g \in K$ to prove that K is a normal subgroup of G_1. Since all elements in the kernel K map to the identity e_2 in G_2, all we need to prove is that $f(g^{-1} \circ k \circ g) = e_2$. The following is the proof:

$$f\left(g^{-1} \circ k \circ g\right) = f\left(g^{-1}\right) * f(k) * f(g)$$

$$= f\left(g^{-1}\right) * f(g) = f(g)^{-1} f(g) = e_2 \tag{4-154}$$

We see that $f(g^{-1} \circ k \circ g) = e_2$, and hence the kernel of homomorphism of kernel K has to be a normal subgroup of G_1.

Figure 4-12 shows group homomorphism from G_1 to G_2 where we see the kernel of the homomorphism K is mapped to the identity element e_2 of G_2.

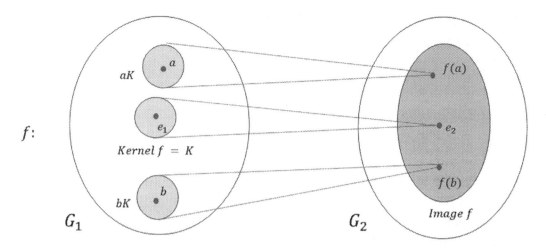

Figure 4-12. *Group homomorphism*

Also, we can see in Figure 4-12 that the coset $aK = \{a \circ k = k \circ a| k \in K\}$ maps to $f(a)$. This is true because of the following:

$$f(aK) = \{f(a \circ k)| k \in K\} = \{f(a) * f(k)| k \in K\}$$
$$= \{f(a) * e_2| k \in K\}$$
$$= \{f(a)| k \in K\} = f(a) \qquad (4\text{-}155)$$

So, each coset of the kernel K maps to the same value, and hence the function f is constant over each coset.

Hidden Subgroup Problem

Now that we have a preliminary understanding of the group theory basics, let's look at what the hidden subgroup problem is.

Given a group $(G, \circ)$, a subgroup $(H, \circ)$ where $H \subseteq G$, and a set X, a function $f : G \to X$ is said to hide the group H if the function is constant over different cosets of the subgroup H. For Equation 4-137, we know any two elements g_1 and g_2 are set to be in the same coset if $g_1 H = g_2 H$. So, for a function f, which hides the subgroup H given any two elements $g_1, g_2 \in G$.

$$f(g_1) = f(g_2) \text{ iff } g_1 H = g_2 H \qquad (4\text{-}156)$$

The goal of the hidden subgroup problem is to determine the subgroup H. A special case of the hidden subgroup problem is one in which G and X are both groups and $f: G \rightarrow X$ defines a group homomorphism. In such cases, the subgroup H we are interested in turns out to be the kernel of the homomorphism.

Several problems we have done already fall under the category of the hidden subgroup problems, as noted here:

- *Period finding*: The period finding application falls under the hidden subgroup problem. In a period finding application, given an element a that is co-prime to N, we define a function from the group of non-negative integers $Z_{\geq 0}$ to the set S of co-primes of N as $f(x) = a^x mod N$. The goal is to find the periodicity r of the function such that $f(x + r) = f(x)$. The periodicity r of the function divides the number of co-primes of N that is generally denoted by $\phi(N)$. Hence, $r | \phi(N)$.

Since the function repeats with periodicity r, the different cosets are as follows:

- Hidden subgroup $H = \{0, r, 2r, ...\}$. The function $f(x) = 1; \forall x \in H$.

- Every other coset is of the form $g + H$ where $1 \leq g \leq r - 1$. The function $f(x) = a^g mod N; \forall x \in g + H$.

The generators of a group are the minimal set of elements required to create a group through composition. Since r alone can generate the entire group, we say $H = \langle r \rangle$. Finding the hidden subgroup H is analogous to finding the period r since r generates the subgroup H. This is precisely what we derived in the period finding algorithm using quantum phase estimation and a quantum inverse Fourier transform.

If we take $N = 15$ and $a = 2$, then the set of co-primes of N is $S = \{1, 2, 4, 7, 8, 11, 13, 14\}$. The function $f(x) = 2^x \, mod \, 15$ has periodicity $r = 4$ as can be found out by substituting different values of $x = 0, 1, 2, ...$.

The hidden subgroup in this case is $H = \{0, 4, 8, ...\}$, while the other cosets are

$$1 + H = \{1, 5, 9, ...\}, \quad 2 + H = \{2, 6, 10, ...\} \quad \text{and } 3 + H = \{3, 7, 11, ...\}.$$

- *Simon's algorithm*: The Simon's algorithm that we have implemented in Chapter 2 also falls under the hidden subgroup problem umbrella. In Simon's algorithm, we are given an unknown black-box function f, which is either one to one ($1:1$), which maps one input to exactly one output, or two to one ($2:1$), which maps two inputs to the same output. In the second case, there is a binary string s such that if $f(x_1) = f(x_2)$, then $x_1 \oplus x_2 = s$. Hence, the cosets in this case are of size 2, and the elements in the cosets are tied together by the relation $x_1 \oplus x_2 = s$.

Summary

With this, we come to the end of Chapter 4. In this chapter, we not only investigated the quantum Fourier transformation and its important applications in great detail but also worked through its associated mathematics with great rigor. Readers are advised to understand the underlying mathematics behind the techniques as much as possible to be able to apply them to a wide range of problems with subtle customizations. Some of the algorithms such as quantum phase estimation are widely used for several quantum computing–based and machine learning–based algorithms such as the HHL algorithm for matrix inversion. Further, we looked at the period finding and the factoring problems in great detail, which will have huge potential in several real-world applications soon. At the end of the chapter, we introduced readers to the basics of group theory and explained the hidden subgroup problem and how it relates to several of the Fourier transform–based algorithms that we deployed. Readers are advised to go through the topics in great detail since Fourier transform–based applications form a major portion of the quantum computing paradigm. The next chapter will cover the particularly exciting avenue of quantum machine learning.

CHAPTER 5

Quantum Machine Learning

"The distinction between past, present, and future is only a stubbornly persistent illusion."

—Albert Einstein

In this chapter and the next one, we will explore the exciting areas of quantum machine learning and quantum deep learning. Machine learning and deep learning have seen great success in recent years because of the increase in the computational power at our disposal and because of the high-end research in these fields. Quantum machine learning presents an exciting opportunity to increase the computational efficiency of the existing machine learning algorithms as well as presents a way to tackle some of the more computationally intractable problems. In this chapter, we start with the Harrow-Hassidim-Lloyd algorithm, popularly known as HHL, which acts as the matrix inversion routine in the quantum computing domain. Hence, HHL will be the default choice for algorithms such as linear regression and least square support vector machines. Subsequently, we touch upon quantum linear regression and support vector machines in detail in this chapter. We will then move on to implementing quantum routines such as quantum dot product and quantum Euclidean distances since they are integral to several machine learning algorithms such as the k-means clustering and nearest neighbor methods. In this regard, we will implement the k-means clustering method in detail. Also, we will discuss how Grover's algorithm can be used to optimize quantum objectives by illustrating its usage in the cluster assignment in the k-means algorithm. Principal component analysis is an important machine learning technique, and we will walk through its quantum implementation in great detail.

221

© Santanu Pattanayak 2021
S. Pattanayak, *Quantum Machine Learning with Python*, https://doi.org/10.1007/978-1-4842-6522-2_5

HHL Algorithm

The Harrow-Hassidim-Lloyd algorithm involves finding a solution to a set of linear equations using a quantum implementation. Finding a solution to a set of linear equations is analogous to solving the matrix inversion problem. Given a matrix A and a vector b, the matrix inversion problem aims to find the vector x.

$$Ax = b \qquad (5\text{-}1)$$

Classically, we can solve for x as $A^{-1}b$ given that the inverse of A exists. However, matrix inversion can be intractable for large matrices. Such inversion problems are hence solved through methods such as Gaussian elimination, which has $O(N^3)$ computational complexity for a matrix of dimension $N \times N$. If the matrix A has sparsity s where s denotes the proportion of elements in A with 0 values and condition number κ where κ denotes the ratio of the maximum eigenvalue to the minimum eigenvalue, then algorithms such as conjugate gradient can solve the matrix inversion problem in $O(Ns\kappa \log(1/\epsilon))$ time where epsilon is the desired error bound. Using HHL, we can achieve a logarithmic reduction in compute by solving the matrix inverse problem in $O\left(logNs^2\kappa^2 \log\left(\frac{1}{\epsilon}\right) \right)$ time in most cases.

This algorithm is critical for quantum machine learning purposes since several machine learning algorithms learn their parameter θ by solving the matrix inversion problem of the form $A\theta = b$. Generally, the matrix A in such problems is a function of the input features of training data points represented by the data matrix X. The vector b is a function of both data matrix X and the target vector Y for the training data points. For instance, for linear regression where we model output $y = \theta^T x$, finding the θ boils down to solving the matrix inversion problem given by the following:

$$\left(X^T X \right)\theta = X^T Y \qquad (5\text{-}2)$$

As you can see, $A = X^T X$ while $b = X^T Y$ for linear regression. We will discuss quantum linear regression in more detail in the subsequent sections.

In HHL we need to find one or more operators that can transform the state $|b\rangle$ to our solution vector θ. It is obvious that we would have to factor in $A = X^T X$ in one of the operators. We cannot choose A as the quantum operator unless A is unitary. Instead, we can choose A to the Hamiltonian H of the quantum system provided A is Hermitian. Just to refresh your memory, a matrix or linear operator H is Hermitian if it equals its complex conjugate transpose $H^\dagger$. Even if A is not Hermitian, we can define a Hermitian operator $\tilde{A}$ as shown here:

$$\tilde{A} = \begin{bmatrix} 0 & A^\dagger \\ A & 0 \end{bmatrix} \tag{5-3}$$

Now since $\tilde{A}$ is Hermitian, it has an eigenvalue decomposition given by the following:

$$\tilde{A} = \sum_i \lambda_i |u_i\rangle \langle u_i| \tag{5-4}$$

where the eigenvectors $|u_i\rangle$ forms an orthonormal basis. The vector $|b\rangle$ can be represented in the orthonormal basis $|u_i\rangle$ as shown here:

$$|b\rangle - \sum_i \beta_i |u_i\rangle \tag{5-5}$$

The solution to the inverse problem is then given by the following:

$$|x\rangle = \tilde{A}^{-1}|b\rangle \tag{5-6}$$

Since $\tilde{A}$ is a Hermitian matrix with spectral decomposition $\tilde{A} = \sum_i \lambda_i |u_i\rangle\langle u_i|$, its inverse is given by the following:

$$\tilde{A}^{-1} = \sum_i \frac{1}{\lambda_i} |u_i\rangle \langle u_i| \tag{5-7}$$

Substituting the value of $\tilde{A}^{-1}$ from Equation 5-7 and $|b\rangle$ from Equation 5-5 in Equation 5-6, we get the solution $|x\rangle$, as shown here:

$$|x\rangle = \sum_i \frac{1}{\lambda_i} |u_i\rangle \langle u_i| \sum_j \beta_j |u_j\rangle$$

$$= \sum_j \frac{\beta_j}{\lambda_j} |u_j\rangle \tag{5-8}$$

We can see from Equation 5-8 that if we could go from the eigenstates $|u_i\rangle$ to $\frac{1}{\lambda_i}|u_i\rangle$, we would be closer to the solution. One way to achieve this is to perform quantum phase estimation using the unitary operator $U = e^{-i\tilde{A}t}$ on the state $|b\rangle$ expressed as the superposition state of the basis states $|u_i\rangle$ since it would take the eigenstates $|u_i\rangle$ to $\lambda_i | u_i\rangle$. Finally, through controlled rotation, we can invert the eigenvalues to take the eigenstates from $\lambda_i|u_i\rangle$ to $\dfrac{1}{\lambda_i}|u_i\rangle$. Please do note that the state $|b\rangle$ needs to be of unit norm before quantum phase estimate can be applied on state $|b\rangle$.

Although we now have a high-level understanding of the HHL algorithm, we need to go over each of the steps in a little more detail for an end-to-end implementation. The following are the steps of the HHL algorithm.

Initializing the Registers

We start HHL with three registers.

- The ancilla register of one qubit initialized at $|0\rangle_{ANC}$.

- The work register to hold the eigenvalues from quantum phase estimation. The number of qubits for the work registers depends on the level of accuracy to which we want to measure the eigenvalues. The register starts at the initialized $|0\rangle_W$ state.

- The final register holds the value of the state $|b\rangle$. As discussed, for quantum phase estimation to work, $|b\rangle$ should be of unit norm, and hence we load the final register with the following:

$$|\tilde{b}\rangle = \frac{|b\rangle}{\langle b|b\rangle^{\frac{1}{2}}} = \frac{1}{\langle b|b\rangle^{\frac{1}{2}}}\sum_j b_j |u_j\rangle = \sum_j \tilde{b}_j |u_j\rangle \tag{5-9}$$

In Equation 5-9, the normalized coefficient $\tilde{b}_j = \dfrac{b_j}{\langle b|b\rangle^{\frac{1}{2}}}$. So, the initial state of the three registers is given by the following:

$$|\psi\rangle_0 = |0\rangle_{ANC} \otimes |0\rangle_W \otimes |\tilde{b}\rangle = |0\rangle_{ANC} \otimes \sum_j \tilde{b}_j |0\rangle_W \otimes |u_j\rangle \tag{5-10}$$

Performing Quantum Phase Estimation

Apply quantum phase estimate using the unitary operator $e^{-i\tilde{A}t}$. Since $\tilde{A}$ has a spectral decomposition given by $\tilde{A} = \sum_i \lambda_i |u_i\rangle \langle u_i|$, the spectral decomposition of $e^{i\tilde{A}t}$ is given by the following:

$$e^{-i\tilde{A}t} = \sum_j e^{-i\lambda_j t} |u_j\rangle\langle u_j| \tag{5-11}$$

In Equation 5-11, $e^{-i\lambda_j t}$ is the eigenvalue corresponding to the eigenvector $|u_j\rangle$ of the operator $e^{-i\tilde{A}t}$. The eigenvalues can be written as follows:

$$e^{-i\lambda_j t} = e^{-2\pi i \left(\frac{\lambda_j t}{2\pi} \right)} \tag{5-12}$$

So, on performing quantum estimation using $e^{-i\tilde{A}t}$ on $|\tilde{b}\rangle$, we would get phases $\tilde{\lambda}_j = \frac{\lambda_j t}{2\pi}$ in the work register.

So, the overall state of the system after quantum phase estimation is given by the following:

$$|\psi\rangle_1 = |0\rangle_{ANC} \otimes \sum_j \tilde{b}_j |\tilde{\lambda}_j\rangle_W \otimes |u_j\rangle = \sum_j |0\rangle_{ANC} \otimes \tilde{b}_j |\tilde{\lambda}_j\rangle_W \otimes |u_j\rangle \tag{5-13}$$

Inverting the Eigenvalues

We need to invert the normalized eigenvalues $\tilde{\lambda}_j$. This can be done by rotating the ancilla qubit state around the y-axis conditioned on the states $|\tilde{\lambda}_j\rangle$. The angle of rotation θ_j and the rotational operator pertaining to each of the eigenvectors $|u_j\rangle$ are given by the following:

$$\theta_j = 2 \sin^{-1} \frac{C}{\lambda_j} \tag{5-14}$$

Thus, the rotational operator around the y-axis for each angle θ_j can be expressed as follows:

$$R_y(\theta_j) = e^{-\frac{iY\theta_j}{2}} \tag{5-15}$$

Since the Pauli matrix $Y = \begin{bmatrix} 0 & -i \\ i & 0 \end{bmatrix}$ is idempotent, i.e., satisfies the relation $Y^2 = I$, $R_y(\theta_j)$ can be written also as follows:

$$R_y(\theta_j) = I\cos\left(\frac{\theta_j}{2}\right) - iY\sin\left(\frac{\theta_j}{2}\right) = \begin{bmatrix} \cos\left(\dfrac{\theta_j}{2}\right) & -\sin\left(\dfrac{\theta_j}{2}\right) \\ \sin\left(\dfrac{\theta_j}{2}\right) & \cos\left(\dfrac{\theta_j}{2}\right) \end{bmatrix} \tag{5-16}$$

The rotation matrix would change the state of the ancillary bit at $|0\rangle_{ANC}$ to the following:

$$R_y(\theta_j)|0\rangle_{ANC} = \begin{bmatrix} \cos\left(\dfrac{\theta_j}{2}\right) & -\sin\left(\dfrac{\theta_j}{2}\right) \\ \sin\left(\dfrac{\theta_j}{2}\right) & \cos\left(\dfrac{\theta_j}{2}\right) \end{bmatrix} \begin{bmatrix} 1 \\ 0 \end{bmatrix} = \begin{bmatrix} \cos\left(\dfrac{\theta_j}{2}\right) \\ \sin\left(\dfrac{\theta_j}{2}\right) \end{bmatrix}$$

$$= \cos\left(\frac{\theta_j}{2}\right)|0\rangle_{ANC} + \sin\left(\frac{\theta_j}{2}\right)|1\rangle_{ANC} \tag{5-17}$$

From Equation 5-14, we have $\theta_j = 2\sin^{-1}\dfrac{C}{\tilde{\lambda}_j}$, which makes $\sin\left(\dfrac{\theta_j}{2}\right) = \dfrac{C}{\tilde{\lambda}_j}$ and $\cos\left(\dfrac{\theta_j}{2}\right) = \sqrt{1 - \dfrac{C^2}{\tilde{\lambda}_j^2}}$. Hence, Equation 5-17 simplifies to the following:

$$R_y(\theta_j)|0\rangle_{ANC} = \sqrt{1 - \frac{C^2}{\tilde{\lambda}_j^2}}|0\rangle_{ANC} + \frac{C}{\tilde{\lambda}_j}|1\rangle_{ANC} \tag{5-18}$$

So, the combined state $|\psi_3\rangle$ of the three registers after the ancilla qubit rotation is given by the following:

$$|\psi_3\rangle = \sum_j \left(\sqrt{1 - \frac{C}{\tilde{\lambda}_j}}|0\rangle_{ANC} + \frac{C}{\tilde{\lambda}_j}|1\rangle_{ANC} \right) \otimes \tilde{b}_j |\tilde{\lambda}_j\rangle_W \otimes |u_j\rangle \tag{5-19}$$

Uncomputing the Work Registers

Once we have done the conditional rotation based on the eigenvalue states in the work register, we do not really need them. We can apply the inverse of the quantum phase estimation transform to what we have applied earlier to uncompute the work register. Essentially, this uncompute step would change the state of the work register to $|0\rangle_W$ for every $|\tilde{\lambda}_j\rangle_W$ state.

So, the state of the three registers after the uncompute step is given by the following:

$$|\psi_4\rangle = \sum_j \left(\sqrt{1 - \frac{C^2}{\tilde{\lambda}_j^2}} |0\rangle_{ANC} + \frac{C}{\tilde{\lambda}_j} |1\rangle_{ANC} \right) \otimes \tilde{b}_j |0\rangle_W \otimes |u_j\rangle$$

$$= |0\rangle_W \otimes \sum_j \left(\sqrt{1 - \frac{C}{\tilde{\lambda}_j}} |0\rangle_{ANC} + \frac{C}{\tilde{\lambda}_j} |0\rangle_{ANC} \right) \otimes \tilde{b}_j |u_j\rangle \qquad (5\text{-}20)$$

Now that the work register has been reset to the $|0\rangle_W$ state, we can ignore the work register since it no longer would be entangled unfavorably with the qubit states that matter. Hence, we can concentrate on the combined state of the ancilla qubit and input-output register qubits, which is given by the following:

$$|\psi_5\rangle = \sum_j \left(\sqrt{1 - \frac{C^2}{\tilde{\lambda}_j^2}} |0\rangle_{ANC} + \frac{C}{\tilde{\lambda}_j} |1\rangle_{ANC} \right) \otimes \tilde{b}_j |u_j\rangle$$

$$= \sum_j \left(\tilde{b}_j \sqrt{1 - \frac{C^2}{\tilde{\lambda}_j^2}} |0\rangle_{ANC} \otimes |u_j\rangle + C\frac{\tilde{b}_j}{\tilde{\lambda}_j} |1\rangle_{ANC} \otimes |u_j\rangle \right) \qquad (5\text{-}21)$$

Measuring the Ancilla Qubit

In the final step, we measure the ancilla qubit. When the ancilla qubit measures the state $|1\rangle$, the post-measurement input-output register state is given by the following:

$$|\psi_6\rangle = C \sum_j \frac{\tilde{b}_j}{\tilde{\lambda}_j} |u_j\rangle \qquad (5\text{-}22)$$

Now $\tilde{b}_j = \dfrac{b_j}{\langle b|b \rangle^{1/2}}$ and $\tilde{\lambda}_j = \dfrac{\lambda_j t}{2\pi}$, and hence we can rewrite Equation 5-22 as follows:

$$|\psi_6\rangle = C \times \frac{2\pi}{t\langle b|b\rangle^{1/2}} \sum_j \frac{b_j}{\lambda_j} |u_j\rangle \tag{5-23}$$

The state $|\psi_6\rangle$ is nothing but the solution state $|x\rangle = \sum_j \dfrac{b_j}{\lambda_j}|u_j\rangle$ up to some

proportionality factor given by $C \times \dfrac{2\pi}{t\langle b|b\rangle^{1/2}}$. The proportionality constant C and t can be

chosen appropriately to reduce the factor $C \times \dfrac{2\pi}{t\langle b|b\rangle^{1/2}}$ to 1.

HHL Algorithm Implementation Using Cirq

Listing 5-1 shows the HHL algorithm implemented in a structural way. We first go through the illustration of the HHL class, which uses the `hamiltonian_simulator`, `QuantumPhaseEstimation`, and `EigenValueInversion` classes to be illustrated later as building blocks. The `QuantumPhaseEstimation` class is used to transform the state $|b\rangle$ into the superposition of the tensor product of the eigenvectors and their corresponding eigenvalues by applying the unitary transform $e^{-i\tilde{A}t}$, as illustrated in the "Performing Quantum Phase Estimation" section earlier. The unitary transform $e^{-i\tilde{A}t}$ is simulated using the `HamiltonianSimulation` class, while the `EigenValueInversion` class is used to invert the eigenvalues by conditional ancilla bit rotation.

Listing 5-1. HHL Implementation

```
import cirq
from hamiltonian_simulator import HamiltonianSimulation
from QuantumPhaseEstimation import QuantumPhaseEstimation
from EigenValueInversion import EigenValueInversion
import numpy as np
import sympy

class HHL:

    def __init__(self,
            hamiltonian,
            initial_state=None,
```

```
            initial_state_transforms=None,
            qpe_register_size=4,
            C=None, t=1):
    """

    :param hamiltonian: Hamiltonian to Simulate
    :param C: hyper parameter to Eigen Value Inversion
    :param t: Time for which Hamiltonian is simulated
    :param initial_state: |b>
    """

    self.hamiltonian = hamiltonian
    self.initial_state = initial_state
    self.initial_state_transforms = initial_state_transforms
    self.qpe_register_size = qpe_register_size
    self.C = C
    self.t = t

    const = self.t/np.pi
    self.t = const*np.pi
    if self.C is None:
        self.C = 2*np.pi / (2**self.qpe_register_size * t)

def build_hhl_circuit(self):
    self.circuit = cirq.Circuit()
    self.ancilla_qubit = cirq.LineQubit(0)
    self.qpe_register = [cirq.LineQubit(i)
            for i in range(1, self.qpe_register_size+1)]
    if self.initial_state is None:
        self.initial_state_size =
    int(np.log2(self.hamiltonian.shape[0]))
        if self.initial_state_size == 1:
            self.initial_state =
                [cirq.LineQubit(self.qpe_register_size + 1)]
        else:
            self.initial_state = [cirq.LineQubit(i) for i in
                    range(self.qpe_register_size + 1,
                        self.qpe_register_size + 1
                        + self.initial_state_size)]
```

```
for op in list(self.initial_state_transforms):
    self.circuit.append(op(self.initial_state[0]))

# Define Unitary Operator simulating the Hamiltonian
self.U = HamiltonianSimulation(_H_=
                            self.hamiltonian, t=self.t)
# Perform Quantum Phase Estimation
_qpe_ = QuantumPhaseEstimation(
        input_qubits=self.initial_state, output_qubits=self.qpe_register,
        U=self.U)
_qpe_.circuit()
self.circuit += _qpe_.circuit
# Perform EigenValue Inversion
_eig_val_inv_ = EigenValueInversion(
                num_qubits=self.qpe_register_size + 1,
                C=self.C, t=self.t)
self.circuit.append(_eig_val_inv_(*(self.qpe_register +
                            [self.ancilla_qubit])))
#Uncompute the qpe_register to |0..0> state
self.circuit.append(_qpe_.circuit**(-1))
self.circuit.append(
cirq.measure(self.ancilla_qubit,key='a'))
self.circuit.append([
    cirq.PhasedXPowGate(
    exponent=sympy.Symbol('exponent'),
    phase_exponent=
    sympy.Symbol('phase_exponent'))(*self.initial_state),
    cirq.measure(*self.initial_state, key='m')
])
```

The following simulate function runs the HHL simulation. The output state we are interested in cannot be measured since it would collapse the state. Hence, in applications that use HHL, the solution state is to be fed to an inference circuit directly. For our verification purposes, we measure the expectation of the solution state using the

Pauli *X, Y,* and *Z* matrices as measurement operators (see the following) and validate these expectation values to precomputed numbers.

```python
def simulate(self):
    simulator = cirq.Simulator()

    params = [{
        'exponent': 0.5,
        'phase_exponent': -0.5
    }, {
        'exponent': 0.5,
        'phase_exponent': 0
    }, {
        'exponent': 0,
        'phase_exponent': 0
    }]

    results = simulator.run_sweep(self.circuit, params, repetitions=5000)

    for label, result in zip(('X', 'Y', 'Z'),list(results)):
        expectation = 1 - 2 *np.mean
        (result.measurements['m'][result.measurements['a']
          == 1])
    print('{} = {}'.format(label, expectation))
```

We have learned about quantum phase estimation in great detail in an earlier chapter. We'll illustrate it here again for ease of reference. Readers are advised to study quantum phase estimation in details as it forms the basis for several machine learning algorithms.

```python
import cirq
from quantum_fourier_transform import QFT

class ControlledUnitary(cirq.Gate):

    def __init__(self, num_qubits, num_input_qubits, U):
        self._num_qubits = num_qubits
        self.num_input_qubits = num_input_qubits
```

```python
        self.num_control_qubits = num_qubits
                        - self.num_input_qubits
        self.U = U

    def num_qubits(self) -> int:
        return self._num_qubits

    def _decompose_(self, qubits):
        qubits = list(qubits)
        input_state_qubit =
                    qubits[:self.num_input_qubits]
        control_qubits = qubits[self.num_input_qubits:]

        for i,q in enumerate(control_qubits):
            _pow_ =2**(self.num_control_qubits - i - 1)
            #yield self.U(q, *input_state_qubit)**_pow_
            yield
                cirq.ControlledGate(self.U**_pow_)
            (q, *input_state_qubit)

class QuantumPhaseEstimation:

    def __init__(self,
                    U,
                    input_qubits,
                    num_output_qubits=None,
                    output_qubits=None,
                    initial_circuit=[],
                    measure_or_sim=False):

        self.U = U
        self.input_qubits = input_qubits
        self.num_input_qubits = len(self.input_qubits)
        self.initial_circuit = initial_circuit
        self.measure_or_sim = measure_or_sim

        if output_qubits is not None:
            self.output_qubits = output_qubits
            self.num_output_qubits
                = len(self.output_qubits)
```

```
    elif num_output_qubits is not None:
        self.num_output_qubits = num_output_qubits
        self.output_qubits = [cirq.LineQubit(i)
            for i in range(self.num_input_qubits,
                self.num_input_qubits
                +self.num_output_qubits)]
    else:
        raise ValueError("Atleast one of num_output_qubits or
        output_qubits to be specified")

    self.num_qubits = self.num_input_qubits+
                        self.num_output_qubits

def inv_qft(self):
    self._qft_= QFT(qubits=self.output_qubits)
    self._qft_.qft_circuit()
    self.QFT_inv_circuit =  self._qft_.inv_circuit

def circuit(self):
    self.circuit = cirq.Circuit()
    self.circuit.append(cirq.H.on_each(
                *self.output_qubits))
    print(self.circuit)
    print(self.output_qubits)
    print(self.input_qubits)
    print((self.output_qubits + self.input_qubits))
    self.qubits = list(self.input_qubits
        + self.output_qubits)
    self.circuit.append(ControlledUnitary(
        self.num_qubits, self.num_input_qubits,
        self.U)(*self.qubits))
    self.inv_qft()
    self.circuit.append(self.QFT_inv_circuit)
    if len(self.initial_circuit) > 0 :
        self.circuit = self.initial_circuit
            + self.circuit
```

```
        def measure(self):
            self.circuit.append(cirq.measure(
            *self.output_qubits,key='m'))

        def simulate_circuit(self, measure=True):
            sim = cirq.Simulator()
            if measure == False:
                result = sim.simulate(self.circuit)
            else:
                result = sim.run(self.circuit,
                repetitions=1000).histogram(key='m')
            return result
```

The following is a `HamiltonianSimulation` class that simulates the unitary transform e^{-iAt} given a Hamiltonian operator A.

```
import cirq
import numpy as np

class HamiltonianSimulation(cirq.EigenGate, cirq.SingleQubitGate):
    """
    This class simulates the Hamiltonian evolution for
    a Single qubit. For a Hamiltonian given by H the
    Unitary Operator simulated for time t is
    given by e**(-iHt). An Eigenvalue of lambda for the
     Hamiltonian H corresponds to the
     Eigenvalue of e**(-i*lambda*t).
     The EigenGate takes in an Eigenvalue of the
     form e**(i*pi*theta) as theta and the corresponding Eigenvector
     as |v><v|
    """

    def __init__(self, _H_, t, exponent=1.0):
        cirq.SingleQubitGate.__init__(self)
        cirq.EigenGate.__init__(self, exponent=exponent)
        self._H_ = _H_
        self.t = t
        eigen_vals, eigen_vecs = np.linalg.eigh(self._H_)
```

```
        self.eigen_components = []
        for _lambda_, vec in zip(eigen_vals, eigen_vecs.T):
            theta = -_lambda_*t / np.pi
            _proj_ = np.outer(vec, np.conj(vec))
            self.eigen_components.append((theta, _proj_))

    def _with_exponent(self, exponent):
        return HamiltonianSimulation(self._H_, self.t, exponent)

    def _eigen_components(self):
        return self.eigen_components
```

Finally, we illustrate the EigenValueInversion class that is used to invert the eigenvalues by conditional ancilla bit rotation.

```
import cirq
import numpy as np
import math

class EigenValueInversion(cirq.Gate):
    """

    Rotates the ancilla bit around the Y axis
    by an angle theta = 2* sin inv(C/eigen value)
    corresponding to each Eigen value state basis |eigen value>.
    This rotation brings the factor (1/eigen value) in
    the amplitude of the basis |1> of the ancilla qubit
    """

    def __init__(self, num_qubits, C, t):
        super(EigenValueInversion, self)
        self._num_qubits = num_qubits
        self.C = C
        self.t = t
        # No of possible Eigen values self.N
        self.N = 2**(num_qubits-1)

    def num_qubits(self):
        return self._num_qubits
```

```python
def _decompose_(self, qubits):
    """

    Apply the Rotation Gate for each possible
    # Eigen value corresponding to the Eigen
    # value basis state. For each input basis state
    # only the Rotation gate corresponding to it would be
    # applied to the ancilla qubit
    """

    base_state = 2**self.N - 1

    for eig_val_state in range(self.N):
        eig_val_gate = self._ancilla_rotation(eig_val_state)

        if (eig_val_state != 0):
            base_state = eig_val_state - 1
        # XOR between successive eigen value states to
        # determine the qubits  to flip
        qubits_to_flip = eig_val_state ^ base_state

        # Apply the flips to the qubits as determined
        # by the XOR operation

        for q in qubits[-2::-1]:

            if qubits_to_flip % 2 == 1:
                yield cirq.X(q)
            qubits_to_flip >>= 1

            # Build controlled ancilla rotation
            eig_val_gate = cirq.ControlledGate(eig_val_gate)
        # Controlled Rotation Gate with the 1st
            # (num_qubits -1) qubits as
        # control qubit and the last qubit as the target qubit(ancilla)

        yield eig_val_gate(*qubits)

def _ancilla_rotation(self, eig_val_state):
    if eig_val_state == 0:
        eig_val_state = self.N
```

```
        theta = 2*math.asin(self.C * self.N * self.t / (2*np.pi * eig_val_
        state))
        # Rotation around the y axis by angle theta
        return cirq.ry(theta)

def test(num_qubits=5):
    num_input_qubits = num_qubits - 1
    # Define ancilla qubit
    ancilla_qubit = cirq.LineQubit(0)
    input_qubits = [cirq.LineQubit(i) for i in range(1, num_qubits)]
    #Define a circuit
    circuit = cirq.Circuit()
    # Set the state to equal superposition of |00000> and |00001>
    circuit.append(cirq.X(input_qubits[-4]))
    # t is set to 1
    t = 0.358166*np.pi
    # Set C to the smallest Eigen value that can be measured
    C = 2 * np.pi / ((2 ** num_input_qubits) * t)
    circuit.append(EigenValueInversion(num_qubits,C,t)(*(input_qubits +
    [ancilla_qubit])))
    # Simulate circuit
    sim = cirq.Simulator()
    result = sim.simulate(circuit)
    print(result)
```

We run the HHL simulation with a Hermitian matrix A and the initial state b given by initial_state_transforms. The expected output of the exercise is the expectation of the solution state with regard to the measurement operators X, Y, and Z.

```
if __name__ == '__main__':
    A = np.array([[4.30213466 - 6.01593490e-08j,
                    0.23531802 + 9.34386156e-01j],
                   [0.23531882 - 9.34388383e-01j,
                    0.58386534 + 6.01593489e-08j]])
    t = 0.358166 * np.pi
    C = None
    qpe_register_size = 4
```

```
initial_state_transforms = [cirq.rx(1.276359), cirq.rz(1.276359)]
_hhl_ = HHL(hamiltonian=A,
            initial_state_transforms=initial_state_transforms
            ,qpe_register_size=4)
_hhl_.build_hhl_circuit()
_hhl_.simulate()
```

xx - output -xx

X = 0.19398258115597788
Y = 0.4172494172494172
Z = -0.8893219017926735

The expectation values of the solution state with regard to the X, Y, and Z operators match approximately to the classically computed values. Readers are advised to tally the expectation values given by HHL by computing these expectations through traditional methods.

Quantum Linear Regression

In any regression problem, we try to predict the continuous value of a variable $y_i \in \mathbb{R}$ given a set of input features $x^{(1)}, x^{(2)}...x^{(N)}$ that can be represented as an N-dimensional input vector $x \in \mathbb{R}^N$. In linear regression, we consider the output to be a linear combination of the input features with some irreducible error component e_i, as follows:

$$y_i = \theta_1 x^{(1)} + \theta_2 x^{(2)} + ...\theta_N x^{(N)} + b + e_i$$

$$= \sum_{i=1}^{N} \theta_i x^{(i)} + b + e_i \tag{5-24}$$

The θ_i corresponding to each feature and the intercept b are the parameters to the model that we want to learn. If we represent the parameters θ_i; $i \in \{1, 2, .. N\}$ by the vector $\theta \in \mathbb{R}^N$, then we can simplify the linear relationship in Equation 5-24 as follows:

$$y_i / x_i = \theta^T x_i + b + e_i \tag{5-25}$$

The expression y_i/x_i stands for the value of y_i conditioned on x_i. Now e_i is the irreducible component that shares zero correlation with the input features and hence is not learnable. We can, however, given x_i, completely determine the term $\theta^T x_i + b$. The error e_i is assumed to follow a normal distribution with zero mean and finite standard deviation σ, and hence we can write the following:

$$e_i \sim N\left(0, \sigma^2\right) \tag{5-26}$$

The term $\theta^T x_i + b$ is constant given the value of feature vector x_i, and we can say this:

$$\theta^T x_i + b + e_i \sim N\left(\theta^T x_i + b, \sigma^2\right)$$

$$\rightarrow y_i/x_i \sim N\left(\theta^T x_i + b, \sigma^2\right) \tag{5-27}$$

So, the target label y_i given the input feature follows a normal distribution with mean $\theta^T x_i + b$ and standard deviation σ. In linear regression, we take the conditional mean of the distribution as our prediction, as shown here:

$$\hat{y}_i = \mathbb{E}\left[y_i/x_i\right] = \theta^T x_i + b \tag{5-28}$$

The parameters of the model, θ and b, can be determined by minimizing the sum of the square of the error term e_i for each data point. For the ease of notation, we can consume the bias term b as a parameter within the θ parameter vector corresponding to the constant feature of 1. This makes the prediction $\hat{y}_i = \theta^T x_i$ where both θ and x_i are $N + 1$ dimensional vectors. With this simplification, the system of equations for the M data points can be written in matrix notation, as shown here:

$$\begin{bmatrix} x_1^T \rightarrow \\ x_2^T \rightarrow \\ .. \\ x_i^T \rightarrow \\ .. \\ x_M^T \rightarrow \end{bmatrix} \theta = \begin{bmatrix} \hat{y}_1 \\ \hat{y}_2 \\ .. \\ \hat{y}_i \\ .. \\ \hat{y}_M \end{bmatrix} \tag{5-29}$$

If we represent the matrix with the input feature vectors in Equation 5-29 as $X \in \mathbb{R}^{M \times (N+1)}$ and the prediction vector as $\hat{Y}_i \in \mathbb{R}^M$, then 5-29 can be written as follows:

$$X\theta = \hat{Y} \tag{5-30}$$

Now if we let the actual targets y_i for all the M data points be represented by vector $Y \in \mathbb{R}^M$, then we have the error vector $e \in \mathbb{R}^M$ as follows:

$$e = Y - \hat{Y} = Y - X\theta \tag{5-31}$$

The loss objective can be written as the mean of the squared errors in prediction for each data point.

$$L(\theta) = \frac{1}{M} \sum_{i=1}^{M} e_i^2 \tag{5-32}$$

The previous loss is nothing but the average of the dot product of the error vector $e \in \mathbb{R}^M$ with itself. This allows us to write the loss completely in matrix notations, as shown here:

$$L(\theta) = \frac{1}{M} \sum_{i=1}^{M} e_i^2$$

$$= \frac{1}{M} e^T e$$

$$= \frac{1}{M} (Y - X\theta)^T (Y - X\theta) \tag{5-33}$$

To determine the parameter θ, we need to minimize the loss $L(\theta)$ with respect to θ. To determine the minima, we can take the gradient of the loss $L(\theta)$ with respect to θ and set it to zero vector as shown here:

$$\nabla_\theta = -\frac{2}{M} X^T (Y - X\theta) = 0$$

$$\rightarrow (X^T X)\theta = X^T Y \tag{5-34}$$

The matrix (X^TX) is Hermitian in nature and hence can be treated as Hamiltonian for a quantum system. We can solve the matrix inversion problem in Equation 5-34 to find the model parameter θ by using the HHL algorithm that we discussed earlier.

Quantum Swap Test Subroutine

The quantum swap test is an effective subroutine that computes the dot product of two quantum states in terms of the probability of measuring an ancilla qubit in state $|0\rangle$. Since computing the dot product is an essential requirement in all machine learning algorithms, the swap test subroutine will be central in the implementation of their quantum machine learning counterparts. We take two unit-norm vectors $|a\rangle$ and $|b\rangle$ and illustrate how we can use the circuit in Figure 5-1 to compute the dot product between them. The circuit also has an ancilla qubit initialized at state $|0\rangle$. The state vectors $|a\rangle$ and $|b\rangle$ can be represented by $\log_2 n$ qubits where n is the dimension of these state vectors.

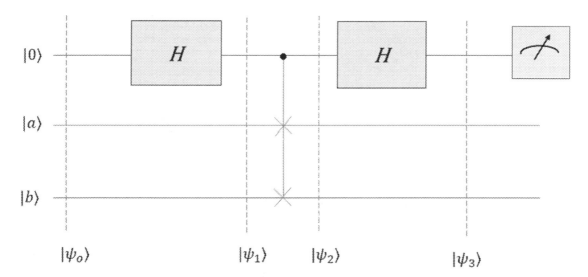

Figure 5-1. *Swap test to compute dot product*

We will look at the combined state of the qubits at each stage of the swap test subroutine to understand the series of transformations involved in computing the dot product.

Initial State

The initial state of the system is given by the following:

$$|\psi_o\rangle = |0\rangle \otimes |a\rangle \otimes |b\rangle \qquad (5\text{-}35)$$

Hadamard Gate on the Ancilla Qubit

After the application of the Hadamard gate on the ancilla qubit, the combined state of the system changes to the following:

$$|\psi_1\rangle = \frac{1}{\sqrt{2}}(|0\rangle + |1\rangle) \otimes |a\rangle \otimes |b\rangle \qquad (5\text{-}36)$$

Controlled Swap Operation

In this step, the two state vectors are swapped conditioned on the ancilla qubit. If the ancilla qubit is in state $|0\rangle$, the states $|a\rangle$ and $|b\rangle$ are left unchanged, while if the ancilla qubit is in state $|1\rangle$, then the two states are swapped. Hence, the combined state of the system $|\psi_2\rangle$ after the controlled SWAP operation is as follows:

$$|\psi_2\rangle = \frac{1}{\sqrt{2}}(|0\rangle \otimes |a\rangle \otimes |b\rangle + |1\rangle \otimes |b\rangle \otimes |a\rangle) \qquad (5\text{-}37)$$

Hadamard Gate on the Control Qubit

The Hadamard gate on the control qubit after the Controlled SWAP Operation changes the combined state to $|\psi_3\rangle$, as shown here:

$$|\psi_3\rangle = \frac{1}{2}(|0\rangle + |1\rangle) \otimes |a\rangle \otimes |b\rangle \;\; + \frac{1}{2}(|0\rangle - |1\rangle) \otimes |b\rangle \otimes |a\rangle$$

$$= \frac{1}{2}|0\rangle(|a\rangle \otimes |b\rangle + |b\rangle \otimes |a\rangle) + \frac{1}{2}|1\rangle(|a\rangle \otimes |b\rangle - |b\rangle \otimes |a\rangle) \qquad (5\text{-}38)$$

In the state $|\psi_3\rangle$, the probability of the ancilla qubit in the state $|0\rangle$ is given by the square of the l^2 norm of the state $|\phi_0\rangle = \frac{1}{2}\left(|a\rangle \otimes |b\rangle + |b\rangle \otimes |a\rangle\right)$ attached to it.

$$P(|0\rangle) = \langle \phi_0 | \phi_0 \rangle$$

$$= \frac{1}{4}\left(\langle b| \otimes \langle a| + \langle a| \otimes \langle b|\right)\left(|a\rangle \otimes |b\rangle + |b\rangle \otimes |a\rangle\right)$$

$$= \frac{1}{4}\left(\langle b|\langle a|a\rangle|b\rangle + \langle b|\langle a|b\rangle|a\rangle + \langle a|\langle b|a\rangle|b\rangle + \langle a|\langle b|b\rangle|a\rangle\right)$$

$$= \frac{1}{4}\left(1 + 2\langle a|b\rangle^2 + 1\right) = \frac{1}{2} + \frac{1}{2}\langle a|b\rangle^2 \tag{5-39}$$

If we measure the ancilla qubit to be in the state $|0\rangle$ with probability 0.5, then the states $|a\rangle$ and $|b\rangle$ are mutually orthogonal to each other since their dot product $\langle a|b\rangle$ in this case turns out to be 0 as per Equation 5-39. Similarly, when the states $|a\rangle$ and $|b\rangle$ are the same, the dot product $\langle a|b\rangle = 1$ and the probability of the ancilla qubit in state $|0\rangle$ turns out to be 1. The good thing about the swap test approach of computing the dot product over classical methods is the time complexity does not scale with the number of qubits required to represent each state.

Swap Test Implementation

In this section, we implement the swap test for two unit vectors using Cirq. The SwapTest class that implements the dot product of the two quantum states takes as input prepare_input_states, input_state_dim, and nq. When prepare_input_states is set to True, the routine defines the required qubits based on input_state_dim and creates the required input states based on the input_1_transforms and input_2_transforms that feeds as inputs to the build_circuit function. When prepare_input_states is set to False, the input states are fed directly as input_1 and input_2 in the build_circuit function. The input nq is used to specify the number of qubits already defined prior to the call of the swap test routine so that the qubits can be defined in the swap test with the required offset. Listing 5-2 shows the implementation.

Listing 5-2. Implementation of Swap Test for Dot Product Computation

```python
import cirq
import numpy as np

class SwapTest:
    def __init__(self,prepare_input_states=False,
input_state_dim=None,nq=0,
measure=False,copies=1000):
        self.nq = nq
        self.prepare_input_states = prepare_input_states
        self.input_state_dim = input_state_dim
        if input_state_dim is not None:
            self.num_qubits_input_states
            = int(np.log2(self.input_state_dim))
            print(self.num_qubits_input_states)

        self.measure = measure
        self.copies = copies
        self.ancilla_qubit = cirq.LineQubit(self.nq)
        self.nq += 1

        if self.prepare_input_states:
            if input_state_dim is None:
                raise ValueError("Please enter a
                valid dimension for input states to compare")
            else:
                self.num_qubits_input_states
                = int(np.log2(self.input_state_dim))
                self.input_1 = [cirq.LineQubit(i)
for i in range(self.nq, self.nq +self.num_qubits_input_states)]
                self.nq += self.num_qubits_input_states
                self.input_2 = [cirq.LineQubit(i)
for i in range(self.nq, self.nq + self.num_qubits_input_states)]
                self.nq += self.num_qubits_input_states
```

In build_circuit, the two input states $|a\rangle$ and $|b\rangle$ for which we want to compute the dot product can be directly fed through input_1 and input_2 or be constructed by using the set of unitary transforms specified in input_1_transforms and input_2_transforms. Next we perform the Hadamard transform H on the ancilla qubit and follow that up with controlled swap (based on the ancilla qubit) of the qubits corresponding to the input states $|a\rangle$ and $|b\rangle$. Finally, we measure the ancilla qubit.

```
def build_circuit(self,input_1=None,
input_2=None,input_1_transforms=None,
input_2_transforms=None):

    self.circuit = cirq.Circuit()
    if input_1 is not None:
        self.input_1 = input_1
    if input_2 is not None:
        self.input_2 = input_2
    if input_1_transforms is not None:
        for op in input_1_transforms:
            print(op)
            print(self.input_1)
            self.circuit.append(op.on_each(self.input_1))
    if input_2_transforms is not None:
        for op in input_2_transforms:
            self.circuit.append(op.on_each(self.input_2))

    # Ancilla in + state
    self.circuit.append(cirq.H(self.ancilla_qubit))
    # Swap states conditoned on the ancilla
    for i in range(len(self.input_1)):
        self.circuit.append(cirq.CSWAP(
        self.ancilla_qubit, self.input_1[i], self.input_2[i]))
    # Hadamard Transform on Ancilla
    self.circuit.append(cirq.H(self.ancilla_qubit))
```

```
    if self.measure:
        self.circuit.append(cirq.measure(
        self.ancilla_qubit,key='m'))
    print(self.circuit)
```

In the `simulate` function defined next, we simulate the swap circuit several times, and based on the number of the times the ancilla qubit measures as state $|0\rangle$, we estimate the probability $P(|0\rangle)$. The square of the dot product between the two states $|a\rangle$ and $|b\rangle$ is computed as $(2P(|0\rangle)) - 1$.

```
    def simulate(self):
        sim = cirq.Simulator()
        results = sim.run(self.circuit,repetitions=self.copies)
        results = results.histogram(key='m')
        prob_0 = results[0]/self.copies
        dot_product_sq = 2*(max(prob_0 - .5,0))
        return prob_0,dot_product_sq

def main(prepare_input_states=True,input_state_dim=4,
                input_1_transforms=[cirq.H],
                input_2_transforms=[cirq.I],
                measure=True,copies=1000):
    st = SwapTest(prepare_input_states=prepare_input_states,input_state_
    dim=input_state_dim,measure=measure,copies=copies)
    st.build_circuit(input_1_transforms=input_1_transforms,
                    input_2_transforms=input_2_transforms)
    prob_0, dot_product_sq = st.simulate()
    print(f"Probability of zero state {prob_0}")
    print(f"Sq of Dot product  {dot_product_sq}")
    print(f"Dot product  {dot_product_sq**0.5}")

if __name__ == '__main__':
    main()
```

x output x

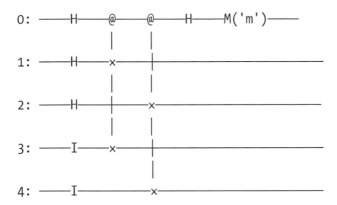

```
Probability of zero state 0.644
Sq of Dot product  0.28800000000000003
Dot product  0.5366563145999496
```

In the swap test implementation, we test the dot product between the equal superposition state $|a\rangle = \frac{1}{2}(|00\rangle + |01\rangle + |10\rangle + |11\rangle)$ achieved by applying the Hadamard transform on two qubits initialized at $|00\rangle$ and the state $|b\rangle = |00\rangle$. The swap test circuit gives a dot product of 0.53, which is close to the expected value of 0.5. The probability of the ancilla qubit being 1 from measurement is also reported for reference.

Quantum Euclidean Distance Calculation

Much like the dot product, the Euclidean distance is a core component of several machine learning algorithms such as k-means clustering and K nearest neighbors.

Classical data represented by vector $\vec{a}$ is generally encoded as a quantum state by unit vector $|a\rangle$, as shown here:

$$|a\rangle = \frac{\vec{a}}{\|\vec{a}\|} = \|\vec{a}\|^{-1} \sum_{i=0}^{N-1} a_i |i\rangle \tag{5-40}$$

In machine learning, we are interested in finding out the Euclidean distance between vectors that are not unit vectors in general. Let's try to compute the Euclidean distance between two general vectors represented by $\vec{a}$ and $\vec{b}$ whose l^2 norms are not necessarily 1. As it turns out, we can use the swap test intelligently to compute the Euclidean distance between $\vec{a}$ and $\vec{b}$.

We create the two quantum states $|a\rangle$ and $|b\rangle$ by normalizing $\vec{a}$ and $\vec{b}$, as illustrated in Equation 5-40. Now using $|a\rangle$ and $|b\rangle$ and another qubit, we can create two states $|\psi\rangle$ and $|\phi\rangle$ as shown here:

$$|\psi\rangle = \frac{1}{\sqrt{2}}\left(|0\rangle \otimes |a\rangle + |1\rangle \otimes |b\rangle\right)$$

$$|\phi\rangle = \frac{1}{\sqrt{Z}}\left(\|\vec{a}\|\,|0\rangle - \|\vec{b}\|\,|1\rangle\right) \tag{5-41}$$

In Equation 5-41, Z is the sum of the square of the l^2 norm of $\vec{a}$ and $\vec{b}$. In other words, $Z = \|\vec{a}\|^2 + \|\vec{b}\|^2$.

Performing a swap test with $|\psi\rangle$ and $|\phi\rangle$, we will get the dot product $\langle\psi|\phi\rangle$ from Equation 5-39 in terms of the probability of measuring the ancilla qubit in state $|0\rangle$, as shown here:

$$P(|0\rangle) = \frac{1}{2} + \frac{1}{2}\langle\psi|\phi\rangle^2 \tag{5-42}$$

Now the dot product $\langle\psi|\phi\rangle$ can be simplified as follows:

$$\langle\psi|\phi\rangle = \frac{1}{\sqrt{2}}\left(\langle a|\langle 0| + \langle b|\langle 1|\right)\frac{1}{\sqrt{Z}}\left(\|\vec{a}\|\,|0\rangle - \|\vec{b}\|\,|1\rangle\right)$$

$$= \frac{1}{\sqrt{2Z}}\left(\|\vec{a}\|\langle a|\langle 0|0\rangle - \|\vec{b}\|\langle a|\langle 0|1\rangle + \|\vec{a}\|\langle b|\langle 1|0\rangle - \|\vec{b}\|\,|b\rangle\langle 1|1\rangle\right.$$

$$= \frac{1}{\sqrt{2Z}}\left(\|\vec{a}\|\langle a| - \|\vec{b}\|\langle b|\right) = \frac{1}{\sqrt{2Z}}\left(\vec{a} - \vec{b}\right)^T \tag{5-43}$$

Substituting the expression for $\langle\psi|\phi\rangle$ in Equation 5-42, we get the following:

$$P(|0\rangle) = \frac{1}{2} + \frac{1}{2}\|\frac{1}{\sqrt{2Z}}\left(\vec{a} - \vec{b}\right)\|^2$$

$$= \frac{1}{2} + \frac{1}{4}\frac{1}{Z}\|(\vec{a} - \vec{b})\|^2 \tag{5-44}$$

So, from Equation 5-44, we can see that the square of the Euclidean distance can be computed from the probability of measuring the ancilla qubit in state $|0\rangle$ and known value of Z, as shown here:

$$\|(\vec{a}-\vec{b})\|^2 = 4Z\big(P(|0\rangle)-0.5\big) \tag{5-45}$$

Creating the Initial States Without QRAM

The creation of the initial state $|\psi\rangle = \dfrac{1}{\sqrt{2}}\big(|0\rangle \otimes |a\rangle + |1\rangle \otimes |b\rangle\big)$ is easy to perform using a QRAM infrastructure. Since we do not really have QRAM at our disposal, we would have to find an alternative method to create this state. The following is a circuit (see Figure 5-2) that can be used to create the initial state $|\psi\rangle$. As depicted in Figure 5-2, we start with four-qubit registers $|q_0\rangle_A$, $|q_1\rangle_W$, $|q_2\rangle_{INP_1}$, and $|q_3\rangle_{INP_2}$. The first register $|q_0\rangle_A$ has one qubit and is suffixed with A since it acts as an ancilla qubit. The second register $|q_1\rangle_W$ is a work register that will hold the state of the input states. The tensor state of the ancilla and the work register $|q_0\rangle_A \otimes |q_1\rangle_W$ is going to hold the state $\dfrac{1}{\sqrt{2}}\big(|0\rangle \otimes |a\rangle + |1\rangle \otimes |b\rangle\big)$ at the end of the circuit. Once the required state $\dfrac{1}{\sqrt{2}}\big(|0\rangle \otimes |a\rangle + |1\rangle \otimes |b\rangle\big)$ has been created

using the ancilla qubit and the work register, we need to uncompute the state of qubit q_2 and q_3 that holds the input states $|a\rangle$ and $|b\rangle$ to the initialized state $|0\rangle$ so that they don't remain entangled with the ancilla and work registers.

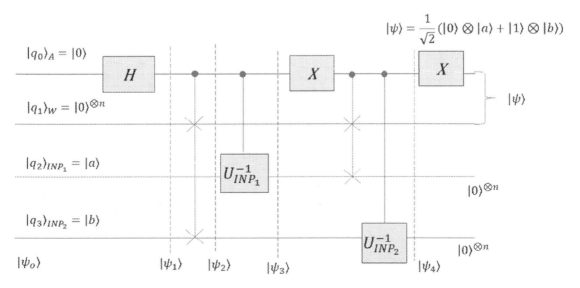

Figure 5-2. *Initial state creation circuit for Euclidean distance computation*

Quantum Euclidean Distance Compute Routine Implementation

We implement the quantum Euclidean distance compute routine in this section using the swap test routine already implemented in the chapter. Given two vectors $\vec{a}$ and $\vec{b}$, whose Euclidean distance we want to compute, the routine first constructs two states

$$|\psi\rangle = \frac{1}{\sqrt{2}}\left(|0\rangle \otimes |a\rangle + |1\rangle \otimes |b\rangle\right) \text{ and } |\phi\rangle = \frac{1}{\sqrt{Z}}\left(\|\vec{a}\|\,|0\rangle - \|\vec{b}\|\,|1\rangle\right) \text{ where } |a\rangle \text{ and } |b\rangle \text{ are}$$

unit vectors corresponding to $\vec{a}$ and $\vec{b}$. The term Z is equal to the sum of the square of the l^2 norm of $\vec{a}$ and $\vec{b}$. Once the states $|\psi\rangle$ and $|\phi\rangle$ are constructed, we feed them to the already implemented swap test routine SwapTest to compute $\langle\psi|\phi\rangle$. The square of the distance $\|(\vec{a}-\vec{b})\|^2$ can then be estimated as $4Z\langle\psi|\phi\rangle^2$. Listing 5-3 shows the detailed implementation.

Listing 5-3. Implementation of Quantum Euclidean Distance Computation

```
import cirq
import numpy as np
import math
from swap_test import SwapTest

class Euclidean_distance:
    def __init__(self, input_state_dim
  ,prepare_input_states=False,
  copies=10000):
        self.prepare_input_states = prepare_input_states
        self.input_state_dim = input_state_dim
        self.copies = copies
        self.nq = 0
        self.control_qubit = cirq.LineQubit(0)
        self.nq += 1
```

```
self.num_qubits_per_state
= int(np.log2(self.input_state_dim))
self.state_store_qubits = [cirq.LineQubit(i) for i
                    in range(self.nq,
                    self.nq +self.num_qubits_per_state)]
self.nq += self.num_qubits_per_state

if self.prepare_input_states:

    self.input_1 = [cirq.LineQubit(i)
            for i in range(self.nq, self.nq +
                    self.num_qubits_per_state)]
    self.nq += self.num_qubits_per_state

    self.input_2 = [cirq.LineQubit(i)
            for i in range(self.nq, self.nq +
                    self.num_qubits_per_state)]
    self.nq += self.num_qubits_per_state

self.other_state_qubits = [cirq.LineQubit(i)
            for i in range(self.nq,self.nq + 1 +
                    self.num_qubits_per_state)]
self.nq += 1 + self.num_qubits_per_state
self.circuit = cirq.Circuit()
```

The main activity in the dist_circuit function is to create the states $|\psi\rangle$ and $|\phi\rangle$ from the input states $|a\rangle$ and $|b\rangle$ before feeding them to the SwapTest routine for computing $\langle\psi|\phi\rangle$.

```
def dist_circuit(self, input_1_norm=1, input_2_norm=1,
                input_1=None,
                    input_2=None,
                input_1_transforms=None,
                input_2_transforms=None,
                    input_1_circuit=None,
        input_2_circuit=None):

    self.input_1_norm = input_1_norm
```

```
        self.input_2_norm = input_2_norm
        self.input_1_circuit = input_1_circuit
        self.input_2_circuit = input_2_circuit

        if input_1 is not None:
            self.input_1 = input_1

        if input_2 is not None:
            self.input_2 = input_2

        if input_1_transforms is not None:

            self.input_1_circuit = []

            for op in input_1_transforms:
                self.circuit.append(op.on_each(self.input_1))
                self.input_1_circuit.append(op.on_each(
                self.input_1))
        if input_2_transforms is not None:
            self.input_2_circuit = []
            for op in input_2_transforms:
                self.circuit.append(op.on_each(self.input_2))
                self.input_2_circuit.append(
                op.on_each(self.input_2))

        self.input_1_uncompute = cirq.inverse(self.input_1_circuit)
        self.input_2_uncompute = cirq.inverse(self.input_2_circuit)

        # Create the required state 1

        self.circuit.append(cirq.H(self.control_qubit))

        for i in range(len(self.input_2)):
            self.circuit.append(cirq.CSWAP(self.control_qubit,
                    self.state_store_qubits[i],
                    self.input_2[i]))
        self.circuit.append(cirq.X(self.control_qubit))

        for i in range(len(self.input_1)):
            self.circuit.append(cirq.CSWAP(self.control_qubit,
```

```
            self.state_store_qubits[i],
            self.input_1[i]))
    for c in self.input_2_uncompute:
        self.circuit.append(c[0].controlled_by(
                        self.control_qubit))
    self.circuit.append(cirq.X(self.control_qubit))
    for c in self.input_1_uncompute:
        self.circuit.append(c[0].controlled_by(
        self.control_qubit))

    # Prepare the other state qubit
    self.Z = self.input_1_norm**2 + self.input_2_norm**2
    print(self.Z)
    theta = 2*math.acos(self.input_1_norm/np.sqrt(self.Z))
    self.circuit.append(cirq.ry(theta)
    (self.other_state_qubits[0]))
    self.circuit.append(cirq.Z(self.other_state_qubits[0]))

    self.st = SwapTest(prepare_input_states=False,
                input_state_dim=4,nq=self.nq,measure=False)

    print(self.other_state_qubits)
    self.state = [self.control_qubit] +
    self.state_store_qubits
    self.st.build_circuit(input_1=self.state,
    input_2=self.other_state_qubits)
    self.circuit += self.st.circuit
    self.circuit.append(cirq.measure(
    self.st.ancilla_qubit, key='k'))
    print(self.circuit)

def compute_distance(self):
    sim = cirq.Simulator()
    results = sim.run(self.circuit,
        repetitions=self.copies).histogram(key='k')
    results = dict(results)
    print(results)
    results = dict(results)
```

```
        prob_0 = results[0]/self.copies
        print(prob_0)
        Euclidean_distance = 4*self.Z*max((prob_0 - 0.5),0)
        print("Euclidean distance",Euclidean_distance)

if __name__ == '__main__':

    dist_obj = Euclidean_distance(input_state_dim=2,
    prepare_input_states=True,copies=100000)
    dist_obj.dist_circuit(
    input_1_transforms=[cirq.H], input_2_transforms=[cirq.H])
    dist_obj.compute_distance()
```

x output x

We initially compute the Euclidean distance between two vectors, both of which are in the equal superposition state $\frac{1}{\sqrt{2}}(|0\rangle+|1\rangle)$. We pass the Hadamard transforms to the input_1_tranforms to create the equal superposition state from the input qubits initialized at $|0\rangle$ state. Figure 5-3 shows the circuit for this.

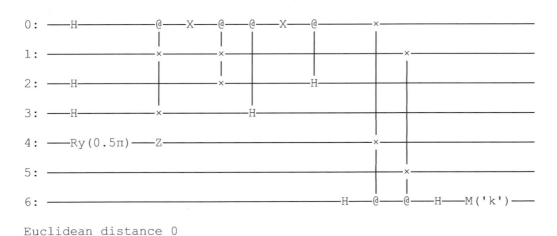

```
Euclidean distance 0
```

Figure 5-3. *Euclidean distance computation circuit*

As expected, the Euclidean distance is 0.

Quantum K-Means Clustering

The quantum implementation of k-means clustering can be achieved using the Euclidean distance calculation routine along with Grover's search algorithm routine that we used in Chapter 2. The steps are the same as the classical k-means algorithm with the individual steps being carried out by quantum routines rather than through classical ones. The following sections outline the steps.

Initialize

Initialize the k cluster centroids $\mu_1, \mu_2...\mu_k \in \mathbb{R}^n$ using a heuristic similar to that in the classical version of k-means. For instance, one can randomly choose k data points as the initial clusters.

Until Convergence

Here are the steps:

a) For each data point $x_i \in \mathbb{R}^n$ represented by its magnitude $\|\vec{x_i}\|_2$ stored classically and by its unit norm $|x_i\rangle$ stored as a quantum state, we compute its distance using the quantum Euclidean distance calculation routine with each of the k cluster centroids as follows:

$$d(i,j) = \|(x_i - u_j)\|^2 = 4Z(P(|0\rangle) - 0.5) \quad j \in \{1, 2, .. k\} \tag{5-46}$$

b) Use Grover's search algorithm to assign each data point x_i to one of the k clusters. The oracle for the Grover's search algorithm should be able to take the distance $d(i,j)$ and assign the correct cluster c_i as shown below.

$$c_i = \underset{j}{argmin} \ \|(x_i - u_j)\|^2 \quad c_i \in \{1, 2, .. k\} \tag{5-47}$$

c) Once each of the data points x_i is assigned its cluster $c_i \in \{1, 2, ...k\}$, the mean or centroid of each cluster is computed as follows:

$$u_j = \frac{1}{N_j} \sum_{c_i=j} x_i \tag{5-48}$$

In the previous equation, N_j denotes the number of data points that belong to the cluster j.

The algorithm converges when the data points stop changing clusters over each subsequent iteration. The classical k-means clustering has a complexity of $O(MNk)$ in each iteration. The distance computational complexity for each data point to a cluster is of $O(N)$ where N is the number of features of the data points. Since there are k clusters, for each data point the complexity is $O(Nk)$. Also since each of the M data points would have complexity of $O(Nk)$, the overall complexity for the algorithm for each iteration comes out to be $O(MNk)$. Where we score in the quantum k-means is the fact that the quantum Euclidean distance computation for each data point from a cluster is of the order $O(logN)$ for a large value of the feature dimension N, giving an overall complexity of $Mlog(N)k$. One thing to note here is that the complexities of assigning each data point to the appropriate cluster based on distance minimization is not taken into consideration for both classical and quantum k-means. In this regard, Grover's algorithm, used for assigning the data points to their appropriate clusters, can provide a further speedup if designed properly.

Quantum K-Means Clustering Using Cosine Distance

In this section, we implement the quantum k-means clustering algorithm using cosine distance as the distance matrix. The cosine similarity between two vectors $\vec{x}$ and $\vec{y}$ is defined as the distance between the unit vectors $|x\rangle$ and $|y\rangle$ in the direction of the given vectors. Since unit vectors have unit norm, they can be mapped directly to quantum states. The square of the Euclidean distance between the unit vectors $|x\rangle$ and $|y\rangle$ is given by the following:

$$||\,|x\rangle - |y\rangle\,||^2 = \langle x|x\rangle + \langle y|y\rangle - 2\langle x|y\rangle = 2 - 2\langle x|y\rangle = 2\left(1 - \langle x|y\rangle\right) \tag{5-49}$$

From the swap test, we know the probability of measuring the ancilla state as 0 is given by $\frac{1}{2} + \frac{1}{2}\langle x|y\rangle^2$, which gives us the probability of measuring the state 1 as follows:

$$P(1) = \frac{1}{2} - \frac{1}{2}\langle x|y\rangle^2 = \frac{1}{2}(1 - \langle x|y\rangle^2) = \frac{1}{2}(1 - \langle x|y\rangle)(1 + \langle x|y\rangle) \tag{5-50}$$

Although the measured probability of the ancilla bit being 1 is not exactly equal to the cosine distance, it shares a high correlation with it as is obvious from Equation 5-49 and Equation 5-50. In fact, the distance measure given by $P(1)$ treats both positive and negative correlation in the same way because of the square term $\langle x|y\rangle^2$. This might be favorable for several applications where only the magnitude of the correlation is important. In this exercise, we use the swap test routine to compute the dot product between the unit vectors pertaining to the given vectors and use the probability of the ancilla qubit being 1 as our distance measure. The dataset used in this implementation (see Listing 5-4) contains the annual income and spending score of customers as features. We are going to use these two features to create pertinent customer clusters. Listing 5-4 shows the detailed implementation.

Listing 5-4. Quantum K-Means Clustering

```
import cirq
from swap_test import SwapTest
import pandas as pd
import math
import numpy as np
import matplotlib
import matplotlib.pyplot as plt

class QuantumKMeans:

    def __init__(self,data_csv,num_clusters,
    features,copies=1000,iters=100):
        self.data_csv = data_csv
        self.num_clusters = num_clusters
        self.features = features
        self.copies = copies
        self.iters = iters
```

The two-features once normalized to unit vector $|x\rangle = [x_1 x_2]^T$ can be presented by a one-qubit state. We compute the direction of the unit vectors by measuring the angle θ, which the feature vector makes with the qubit basis state $|0\rangle$. This lets us represent the unit vector as $|x\rangle = [cos\theta\ sin\theta]^T$.

```
    def data_preprocess(self):
        df = pd.read_csv(self.data_csv)
        print(df.columns)
        df['theta'] = df.apply(lambda x:
```

```
math.atan(x[self.features[1]]/
x[self.features[0]]), axis=1)
self.X = df.values[:,:2]
self.row_norms = np.sqrt((self.X**2).sum(axis=1))
self.X = self.X/self.row_norms[:, np.newaxis]
self.X_q_theta = df.values[:,2]
self.num_data points = self.X.shape[0]
```

We can take a qubit in state $|0\rangle$ to the state $\cos\left(\dfrac{\phi}{2}\right)|0\rangle + \sin\left(\dfrac{\phi}{2}\right)|1\rangle$ by applying a

unitary transformation given by $U(\phi) = e^{\frac{-iY\phi}{2}} = \dfrac{\cos\phi}{2} I - i\sin\left(\dfrac{\phi}{2}\right)Y$ where Y is the Pauli

matrix given by $Y = \begin{bmatrix} 0 & -i \\ i & 0 \end{bmatrix}$.

Hence, to prepare the qubit state $|x\rangle = [\cos\theta \ \sin\theta]^T$, we can apply a unitary transformation $U(2\theta)$. We apply the same using `cirq.ry`, as shown in the distance function defined next. The two unit vectors for which we need the distance to be measured are defined by the arguments x and y to the _distance_ function. Here, x and y are the angle of rotations to the unitary transform provided by `cirq.ry`. These unitary transforms will first be applied to the two qubits initialized at $|0\rangle$ to achieve states $|x\rangle$ and $|y\rangle$, and then the swap test will be used to compute the distance between them.

```
def distance(self,x,y):
    st = SwapTest(prepare_input_states=True, input_state_dim=2, measure=True,
                  copies=self.copies)
    st.build_circuit(input_1_transforms=[cirq.ry(x)],
                     input_2_transforms=[cirq.ry(y)])
    prob_0, _ = st.simulate()
    _distance_ = 1 - prob_0
    del st
    return _distance_
```

The rest of the code deals implements the k-means algorithm using the distance computed from the swap test, as illustrated earlier. The distance is basically used to assign a data point represented as a unit vector state to the nearest cluster.
Here, the assignment is being done classically using `numpy argmin` functionality in `assign_clusters`.

```python
def init_clusters(self):
    self.cluster_points=np.random.randint(
    self.num_data points,
    size=self.num_clusters)
    self.cluster_data points = self.X[self.cluster_points,:]
    self.cluster_theta = self.X_q_theta[self.cluster_points]
    self.clusters = np.zeros(len(self.X_q_theta))

def assign_clusters(self):
    self.distance_matrix = np.zeros((self.num_data points,
    self.num_clusters))

    for i,x in enumerate(list(self.X_q_theta)):
        for j,y in enumerate(list(self.cluster_theta)):
            sclf.distance_matrix[i, j] = self.distance(x,y)
    self.clusters = np.argmin(self.distance_matrix,axis=1)
```

Based on the assigned clusters for each data point, the update_clusters routine computes the centroid of each cluster.

```python
def update_clusters(self):
    updated_cluster_data points = []
    updated_cluster_theta = []
    for k in range(self.num_clusters):

        centroid = np.mean(self.X[self.clusters == k],axis=0)
        centroid_theta = math.atan(centroid[1]/centroid[0])
        updated_cluster_data points.append(centroid)
        updated_cluster_theta.append(centroid_theta)

    self.cluster_data points= np.array(updated_cluster_data points)
    self.cluster_theta = np.array(updated_cluster_theta)

def plot(self):
    fig = plt.figure(figsize=(8, 8))
    colors = ['red', 'green', 'blue', 'purple','yellow','black']
```

```
        plt.scatter(self.X[:,0],self.X[:,1],c=self.clusters,
                    cmap=matplotlib.colors.ListedColormap(colors[:self.
                    num_clusters]))
        plt.savefig('Clusters.png')

    def run(self):
        self.data_preprocess()
        self.init_clusters()
        for  i in range(self.iters):
            self.assign_clusters()
            self.update_clusters()
        self.plot()

if __name__ == '__main__':
    data_csv = '/home/santanu/Downloads/DataForQComparison.csv'
    num_clusters = 4
    qkmeans = QuantumKMeans(data_csv=data_csv, num_clusters=num_clusters,
                iters=10,features=['Annual Income_k$','0'])
    qkmeans.run()
```

output

The circuit to measure the distance has been illustrated for a pair of data points.

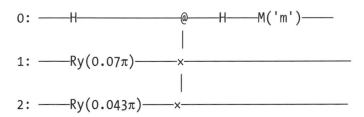

```
0:  ──H──────────────@────H────M('m')────

1:  ──Ry(0.07π)──────×──────────────────

2:  ──Ry(0.043π)────×──────────────────
```

We use the matplotlib function to plot the results of clustering. Since we have normalized the data to be of unit norm in a pursuit to treat that as quantum states, all the data points lie on a unit circle (see Figure 5-4). Hence, the state vectors with high cosine similarity should be in the same clusters. We create four customer clusters for this dataset.

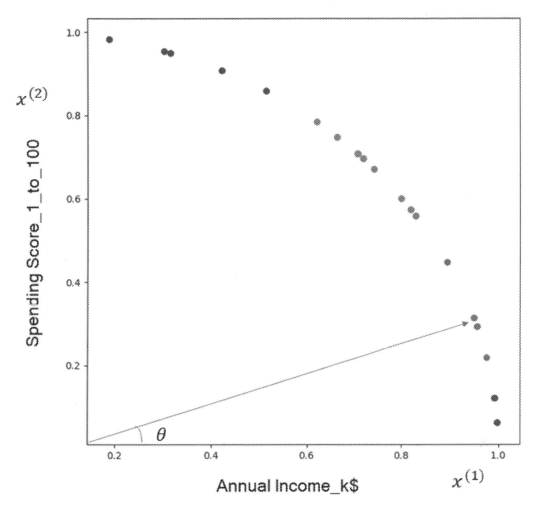

Figure 5-4. *Quantum k-means clusters*

Quantum Principal Component Analysis

Principal component analysis (PCA) is one of the widely used machine learning algorithms for dimensionality reduction of input data. Given M data points x_i of dimensionality N, the goal of principal component analysis is to use the eigenvectors of the covariance matrix of the data as new dimensions for the data. For highly correlated data, the variability in the entire dataset is almost captured by projecting the data along the first few eigenvectors having high variability. The eigenvalues give the variability of the data along the different eigenvectors where larger eigenvalues correspond to larger variability in data along their corresponding eigenvectors. One can reduce the dimensionality of the data by choosing only the first few eigenvectors with the highest eigenvalues. These chosen eigenvectors are called *principal components* in the context of PCA. As you probably realize, the crux of the PCA algorithm lies in performing eigenvalue decomposition of the covariance matrix efficiently.

Quantum principal component analysis aims to perform the eigenvalue decomposition using quantum algorithms to reduce the computational complexity in comparison to its classical counterparts. To be specific, the quantum phase estimation algorithm is used to determine the eigenvectors of the covariance matrix, which acts as the Hamiltonian of a simulated quantum system. The following are the steps of the quantum principal algorithm.

Preprocessing and Transforming the Classical Data to Quantum States

The first step in quantum principal component analysis is to transform the classical data into quantum states. Suppose we have M data points $x_i \in \mathbb{R}^N$. We first subtract the mean vector from each of the data points to make them zero centered, as shown here:

$$x_i \to x_i - \sum_{i=1}^{M} x_i \tag{5-51}$$

Once mean centered, we divide each of the data points x_i by their l^2 norm $\|x_i\|_2$ such that each has unit norm and hence can be treated as a quantum state $|x_i\rangle$.

$$|x_i\rangle \to \|x_i\|^{-1} x_i \tag{5-52}$$

The Mixed Density Matrix or the Covariance Matrix Creation

Given the quantum state $|x_i\rangle$, the density matrix for each data point is given by the following:

$$\rho_i = |x_i\rangle \langle x_i| \qquad (5\text{-}53)$$

Now for a mixed quantum system that can exist in any of the M states with equal classical probability, the density matrix is given by the following:

$$\rho = \frac{1}{M} \sum_{i=1}^{M} |x_i\rangle \langle x_i| \qquad (5\text{-}54)$$

The N dimensional state vectors $|x_i\rangle$ can be represented in the orthonormal basis $|k\rangle$ where $k \in \{0, 1, 2, .. N-1\}$, as follows:

$$|x_i\rangle = \sum_{i=0}^{N-1} x_{ik} |k\rangle \qquad (5\text{-}55)$$

Substituting the expression for the state vector $|x_i\rangle$ from Equation 5-55 to Equation 5-54, we get the following:

$$\rho = \frac{1}{M} \sum_{i=1}^{M} \sum_{k=0}^{N-1} x_{im}^{*} \, x_{ik} |m\rangle \langle k| \qquad (5\text{-}56)$$

We generally deal with real data in principal component analysis and hence x_{im} is equal to its complex conjugate x_{im}^{*}. Hence we can rewrite Equation 5-56 as follows:

$$\rho = \frac{1}{M} \sum_{i=1}^{M} \sum_{m=0}^{N-1} \sum_{k=0}^{N-1} x_{im} x_{ik} |m\rangle \langle k| \qquad (5\text{-}57)$$

Since the data is already zero centered, the expression for ρ in Equation 5-57 is nothing but the covariance matrix in which the entry corresponding to the row m and the column k is given by the outer product $|m\rangle\langle k|$. Hence, ρ in Equation 5-57 can be written as follows:

$$\rho = \frac{1}{M}\sum_{i=1}^{M}\begin{bmatrix} \sum_i x_{i0}^2 & \sum_i x_{i0}x_{i1} & \cdots & \sum_i x_{i0}x_{i(N-1)} \\ \sum_i x_{i1}x_{i0} & \sum_i x_{i1}^2 & \cdots & \sum_i x_{i1}x_{i(N-1)} \\ \cdots & \cdots & & \cdots \\ \sum_i x_{i(N-1)}x_{i0} & \sum_i x_{i(N-1)}x_{i1} & \cdots & \sum_i x_{i(N-1)}^2 \end{bmatrix} \tag{5-58}$$

Density Matrix as a Hamiltonian

The density matrix being the covariance matrix is symmetrical or Hermitian in general and hence has an orthonormal set of eigenvectors with real eigenvalues. Therefore, the density matrix can be treated as a Hamiltonian of a quantum system. Using the density matrix as the Hamiltonian, we can simulate a quantum system using the unitary operator $U = e^{-i\rho t}$.

Quantum Phase Estimation for Spectral Decomposition of the Unitary Operator

We can use the quantum phase estimation algorithm intelligently to perform the spectral decomposition of the unitary operator and eventually the density matrix. For the quantum phase estimation, our unitary operator is $= e^{-i\rho t}$. Generally, in quantum phase estimation, given a unitary operator and one of its eigenvector states, we compute its corresponding eigenvalue. Since in this problem we are required to find the eigenvalues and their corresponding eigenvectors, we cannot start with a known eigenvector state. If the density matrix ρ has a spectral decomposition given by $\rho = \sum_j \lambda_j |\phi_j\rangle \langle\phi_j|$, then the unitary operator has a spectral decomposition given by the following:

$$e^{-i\rho t} = \sum_{j=1}^{M} e^{-i\lambda_j t} |\phi_j\rangle \langle\phi_j| = \sum_{j=1}^{M} e^{-2\pi i\left(\lambda_j t/2\pi\right)} |\phi_j\rangle \langle\phi_j| \tag{5-59}$$

If we use a n-qubit work register for quantum phase estimation, then quantum phase estimation with any eigenstate $|\phi_j\rangle$ would fetch us the eigenvalue phase $\tilde{\lambda}_j = \left(\lambda_j t/2\pi\right)$, as shown here:

$$QPE : |0\rangle_w^{\otimes n} |\phi_j\rangle \rightarrow |\tilde{\lambda}_j\rangle_w |\phi_j\rangle \tag{5-60}$$

Now since we do not know the eigenvalues, we can start with a data point state $|x_i\rangle$, which can be expressed as a superposition of the eigenvalue states as $|x_i\rangle = \sum_j x_{ij}|\phi_j\rangle$.

$$x_{ij} = \langle\phi_j|x_i\rangle \tag{5-61}$$

Hence, the quantum phase estimation on the data point state $|x_i\rangle$ can be expressed as follows:

$$QPE:|0\rangle_w^{\otimes n}|x_i\rangle \rightarrow |y_i\rangle = \sum_{j=1}^{M} x_{ij}|\tilde{\lambda}_j\rangle_w|\phi_j\rangle \tag{5-62}$$

Instead of the data point $|x_i\rangle$, we can think of the quantum phase estimation on the density matrix $|x_i\rangle\langle x_i|$. If the output of quantum phase estimation on $|x_i\rangle$ is $|y_i\rangle$ (see Equation 5-62), then the quantum phase estimation on $|x_i\rangle\langle x_i|$ is $|y_i\rangle\langle y_i|$, as shown here:

$$\gamma_i = |y_i\rangle\langle y_i| = \sum_{j=1}^{M} |x_{ij}|^2 |\tilde{\lambda}_j\rangle_w \langle\tilde{\lambda}_j|_w \otimes |\phi_j\rangle\langle\phi_j| \tag{5-63}$$

Now that we have the result of quantum phase estimation of the density matrix $|x_i\rangle\langle x_i|$ for the data point state $|x_i\rangle$, we can extend it to the mixed state $\rho = \dfrac{1}{M}\sum_{i=1}^{M}|x_i\rangle\langle x_i|$ of all the data points. The same can be expressed as shown here:

$$QPE:\rho \rightarrow \eta = \sum_{i=1}^{M}\sum_{j=1}^{M} |x_{ij}|^2 |\tilde{\lambda}_j\rangle_w \langle\tilde{\lambda}_j|_w \otimes |\phi_j\rangle\langle\phi_j| \tag{5-64}$$

Now let's see if we can simplify the expression in Equation 5-64. We have $x_{ij} = \langle\phi_j|x_i\rangle$ and hence the following:

$$|x_{ij}|^2 = \langle\phi_j|x_i\rangle\langle x_i|\phi_j\rangle \tag{5-65}$$

Taking the mean of $|x_{ij}|^2$ over the M data points, we have the following:

$$\frac{1}{M}\sum_{i=1}^{M}|x_{ij}|^2 = \frac{1}{M}\sum_{i=1}^{M}\langle\phi_j|x_i\rangle\langle x_i|\phi_j\rangle$$

$$= \langle\phi_j|(\frac{1}{M}\sum_{i=1}^{M}|x_i\rangle\langle x_i|)|\phi_j\rangle$$

$$= \langle\phi_j|\rho|\phi_j\rangle \tag{5-66}$$

Since $|\phi_j\rangle$ is the eigenvector of ρ, we have $\langle\phi_j|\rho|\phi_j\rangle = \lambda_j$. This reduces Equation 5-66 to the following:

$$\frac{1}{M}\sum_{i=1}^{M}\left|x_{ij}\right|^2 = \lambda_j \tag{5-67}$$

Substituting $\dfrac{1}{M}\displaystyle\sum_{i=1}^{M}\left|x_{ij}\right|^2$ from Equation 5-67 in Equation 5-64, the quantum phase estimation of the density matrix ρ simplifies to the following:

$$QPE: \rho \to \eta = \sum_{j=1}^{M}\lambda_j \,|\tilde{\lambda}_j\rangle_w \,\langle\tilde{\lambda}_j|_w \otimes |\phi_j\rangle\langle\phi_j| \tag{5-68}$$

Extracting the Principal Components

The final state η has the eigenvalue states entangled with the corresponding eigenvectors, and hence by making measurements on the final state, we will get the eigenvector $|\phi_j\rangle$ and the eigenvalue λ_j with probability λ_j. Hence, if we do m measurements, the principal component vector $|\phi_j\rangle$ would get sampled approximately $m\lambda_j$ times.

We can compute the projection s_{ij} of a given data point $|x_i\rangle$ along the j-th principal component $|\phi_j\rangle$ by using the swap test.

$$s_{ij} = \langle\phi_j|x_i\rangle \tag{5-69}$$

Based on the number of principal components k we want to retain, the $|x_i\rangle$ state vector can be expressed in the basis, consisting of the k principal components as follows:

$$|x_i\rangle = \left[s_{i1}\ s_{i2}\ .....s_{ik}\right]^T \tag{5-70}$$

Building the operator $e^{-i\rho t}$ has $O(logN)$ complexity where N is the number of features for each data point. Assuming there are k principal components that account for almost 100 percent of the variability in the data, the cost of final state sampling is given by $O(klogN)$. Quantum principal components would be beneficial to use if the number of principal components k is fewer than the number of features N of each data point.

Quantum Support Vector Machines

Support vector machine, popularly known as SVM, is one of the widely used supervised machine learning algorithm techniques. SVM tries to find a hyperplane in the input feature space that separates two classes. At times, finding a good hyperplane in the given input space might not be most optimal. By using various kernel methods one can aim to find a hyperplane in a higher-dimensional input feature space without explicitly defining the higher-dimensional feature space. Kernels define the dot product of given input feature vectors in a higher-dimensional feature vector space. Since the solution to finding the hyperplane depends on the dot product of input feature vectors and not explicitly on the input features, SVMs work well with different kernels to render nonlinearity in the decision boundary with respect to the input features. In brief, kernels help project the vectors in the input feature space to a higher-dimensional vector space where it is possible to get a linear decision boundary to separate the two classes. Based on the kernel function used in the SVM formulation, the optimization objective of learning the hyperplane can be convex or nonconvex. Nonconvex optimization may lead the solution to converge at a local minima leading to suboptimal performance. In this regard, we can use the quantum minimization subroutine of Grover's algorithm to solve for the global minima of the nonconvex optimization problem. See Figure 5-5.

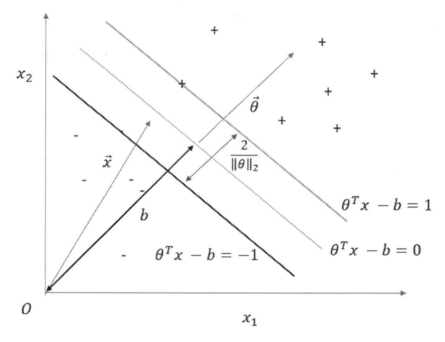

Figure 5-5. *Support vector machine hyperplanes*

Given that our hyperplane orientation is defined by the parameter vector $\vec{\theta} \in \mathbb{R}^n$ perpendicular to the hyperplane and by the bias b that defines the distance of the hyperplane from the origin, the feature vectors $\vec{x} \in \mathbb{R}^n$ that lie on the hyperplane can be defined as follows:

$$\theta^T x = b \rightarrow \theta^T x - b = 0 \qquad (5\text{-}71)$$

In SVMs we try to build the hyperplane in a way such that one class of data points, say, having label $y = 1$, satisfy the following relation:

$$\theta^T x - b \geq 1; \forall y = 1$$

$$\rightarrow y\left(\theta^T x - b\right) \geq 1 \qquad (5\text{-}72)$$

The other class of data points having label $y = -1$ should satisfy the following relation:

$$\theta^T x - b \leq 1; \forall y = -1$$

$$\rightarrow y\left(\theta^T x - b\right) \geq 1 \qquad (5\text{-}73)$$

As we can see, we are not satisfied by having the hyperplane $\theta^T x - b = 0$ separate the two classes but instead want to have some additional separation between the two classes by defining two more hyperplanes given by $\theta^T x - b = \pm 1$.

In SVM what we want to do is choose the parameters of the model in such a way that the distance between the boundary of the two classes defines by the hyperplanes $\theta^T x - b = \pm 1$ is maximized. We take two points, x_+ lying on hyperplane $\theta^T x - b = 1$ and belonging to class 1, and point x_- lying on hyperplane $\theta^T x - b = -1$ and belonging to class -1. Since these points lie on the hyperplanes, they satisfy the following:

$$\theta^T x^+ - b = 1$$

$$\theta^T x^- - b = -1 \tag{5-74}$$

One can subtract the two equations in Equation 5-53 and get the following:

$$\theta^T \left(x^+ - x^- \right) = 2$$

$$\rightarrow \left\| \theta^T \left(x^+ - x^- \right) \right\| = 2$$

$$\rightarrow \left\| \theta \right\| \left\| x^+ - x^- \right\| = 2$$

$$\rightarrow \left\| x^+ - x^- \right\|_2 = \frac{2}{\left\| \theta \right\|_2} \tag{5-75}$$

The distance between the two hyperplanes is nothing but the distance $\| x_+ - x_- \|$ between the two points x_+ and x_-.

To learn the parameters for the hyperplane in SVM, we maximize the distance between the hyperplanes $\| x^+ - x^- \|_2$ so that the classes are as distant as possible. Maximizing the distance between the hyperplanes is analogous to minimizing the norm of the parameter θ, as is obvious from Equation 5-75. However, maximizing the separation infinitely without any constraint is going to lead to misclassifications. To see that the data points are classified properly, we need to adhere to the constraints in Equation 5-72 and Equation 5-73 for each data point (x_i, y_i), as summarized here:

$$y_i \left(\theta^T x_i - b \right) \geq 1$$

$$\rightarrow y_i \left(\theta^T x_i - b \right) - 1 \geq 0 \tag{5-76}$$

So, the optimization problem can be written as follows:

$$\min_{\theta} \frac{1}{2} \|\theta\|_2^2 \tag{5-77}$$

It is subject to the following constraint:

$$y_i \left(\theta^T x_i - b \right) - 1 \geq 0; \forall i = \{1, 2, \ldots M\}$$

Since it is a constrained optimization problem, we can use the Lagrangian multipliers along with Karush-Kuhn-Tucker (KKT) conditions to solve the problem. Using the Lagrangian multipliers $\alpha_i \geq 0$ for each data point (x_i, y_i) in the training dataset of size M, the overall objective function can be formulated as follows:

$$L(\theta, b, \alpha) = \frac{1}{2} \|\theta\|_2^2 - \sum_{i=1}^{M} \alpha_i \left(y_i \left(\theta^T x_i - b \right) - 1 \right) \tag{5-78}$$

The Lagrangian multipliers determine the support vectors in an SVM. The data points with nonzero α_i only influence the model prediction and are called *support vectors*. The data points with $\alpha_i = 0$ do not influence the model parameters and hence the prediction.

In the previous expression, α is the vector of the Lagrangian multipliers for all the M data points. The optimized parameters θ^*, b^*, α^* can be obtained by the minmax optimization of the objective in Equation 5-78 as follows:

$$\theta^*, b^*, \alpha^* = \underbrace{argmin}_{\theta, b} \; \underbrace{argmax}_{\alpha} \; L(\theta, b, \alpha) \tag{5-79}$$

We generally do the optimization in two steps. First, we minimize the objective with respect to θ and b and substitute the value of the derived θ and b in Equation 5-79. To do so, we take the gradient of $L(\theta, b, \alpha)$ with respect to θ and b and set it to zero. The gradient of the objective with respect to θ yields the following:

$$\nabla_{\theta} L(\theta, b, \alpha) = \theta - \sum_{i=1}^{M} \alpha_i y_i x_i = 0$$

$$\rightarrow \theta = \sum_{i=1}^{M} \alpha_i y_i x_i \tag{5-80}$$

Similarly, we set the derivative of objective with respect to b to zero and obtain the following:

$$\frac{\partial L(\theta,b,\alpha)}{\partial b} = \sum_{i=1}^{M} \alpha_i y_i = 0 \tag{5-81}$$

Substituting the value of θ from Equation 5-80, we get the following:

$$L(\theta,b,\alpha) = \frac{1}{2}\sum_{i=1}^{M}\alpha_i y_i x_i^T \sum_{j=1}^{M}\alpha_j y_j x_j - \sum_{i=1}^{M}\alpha_i y_i \theta^T x_i + \sum_{i=1}^{M}\alpha_i y_i b + \sum_{i=1}^{M}\alpha_i$$

$$= \frac{1}{2}\sum_{i=1}^{M}\sum_{j=1}^{M}\alpha_i \alpha_j y_i y_j x_i^T x_j - \sum_{i=1}^{M}\alpha_i y_i \sum_{j=1}^{M}\alpha_j y_j x_j^T x_i + \sum_{i=1}^{M}\alpha_i y_i b + \sum_{i=1}^{M}\alpha_i$$

$$= \frac{1}{2}\sum_{i=1}^{M}\sum_{j=1}^{M}\alpha_i \alpha_j y_i y_j x_i^T x_j - \sum_{i=1}^{M}\sum_{j=1}^{M}\alpha_i \alpha_j y_i y_j x_i^T x_j + \sum_{i=1}^{M}\alpha_i y_i b + \sum_{i=1}^{M}\alpha_i \tag{5-82}$$

The third term in Equation 5-82 is zero as per Equation 5-81, and hence we can simplify our objective to the following:

$$L(\alpha) = \sum_{i=1}^{M}\alpha_i - \frac{1}{2}\sum_{i=1}^{M}\sum_{j=1}^{M}\alpha_i \alpha_j y_i y_j \left(x_i^T x_j\right) \tag{5-83}$$

Now our objective is exclusively in terms of the Lagrangian multipliers α_i, and hence we enter the second stage of optimization where we need to solve the dual optimization problem as defined here:

$$\max_{\alpha} L(\alpha) = \sum_{i=1}^{M}\alpha_i - \frac{1}{2}\sum_{i=1}^{M}\sum_{j=1}^{M}\alpha_i \alpha_j y_i y_j \left(x_i^T x_j\right) \tag{5-84}$$

It is subject to these constraints:

$$\alpha_i \geq 0; \forall i = 1,2,\ldots M$$

$$\sum_{i=1}^{M}\alpha_i y_i = 0$$

As you can see in Equation 5-84, the dual formulation contains only the dot product between the feature vectors, so we can use kernel function to replace the dot products to learn a nonlinear decision boundary. This is because the function of the kernel between two feature vector is to define their dot product in a higher dimension. For example, the Gaussian kernel between two feature vectors x_i and x_j is defined as follows:

$$k\left(x_i, x_j\right) = \phi\left(x_i\right)^T \phi\left(x_j\right) = e^{-\frac{\|x_i - x_j\|_2^2}{\sigma}} \tag{5-85}$$

The function $\phi(.)$ in Equation 5-85 projects the feature vector into a higher dimension, but we do not need to learn it. As we can see from the dual formulation, we are only interested in the dot product, and the same is provided by the kernel $k(.,.)$ without having to explicitly learn $\phi(.)$. However, the nature of the projection to a higher dimension would be defined by the kernel chosen, and hence based on the problem, one may need to choose the optimal kernel. So, in general, the objective in the dual formulation can be rewritten in terms of the kernel function as follows:

$$\min_\alpha L\left(\alpha\right) = \frac{1}{2}\sum_{i=1}^{M}\sum_{j=1}^{M}\alpha_i\alpha_j y_i y_j k\left(x_i, x_j\right) - \sum_{i=1}^{M}\alpha_i \tag{5-86}$$

Do note that in Equation 5-86 we have changed the maximization problem to a minimization problem by multiplying the objective by -1.

One thing to note is that the decision function during classification of the binary classes is not as rigid, and we let the hyperplane $\theta^T x - b = 0$ do the class discrimination instead of the hyperplanes $\theta^T x - b = \pm 1$. Hence, the decision function can be written as follows:

$$f_{\theta, b}\left(x\right) = \theta^T x - b \tag{5-87}$$

From Equation 5-80, we have $\theta = \sum_{i=1}^{M}\alpha_i y_i x_i$. Substituting this into Equation 5-87, we get the updated decision boundary as follows:

$$f_{\alpha, b}\left(x\right) = \sum_{i=1}^{M}\alpha_i y_i x_i^T x - b \tag{5-88}$$

Much like the training objective, the decision boundary for prediction is dependent on the dot product of the predicted data point x and the data points x_i in training. Hence, we can generalize the decision boundary by the replacing the dot product with a kernel function, as shown here:

$$f_{\alpha,b}(x) = \sum_{i=1}^{M} \alpha_i y_i k(x_i, x) - b \tag{5-89}$$

The quantum SVM version by Anquita et al. solves this dual formulation by attempting a discrete solution where the Lagrangian multipliers are assumed to be either 0 or 1. This readily allows the Lagrangian multiplier vectors to be represented as basis states $|\alpha\rangle = |\alpha_1\alpha_2...\alpha_M\rangle$ for an M-qubit system. There would be 2^M basis states for an M-qubit system, and they provide the exhaustive set of Lagrangian multiplier vector set possibilities for the optimization problem. The idea is to solve this dual problem of finding the most optimal Lagrangian multiplier vector $|\alpha^*\rangle$ using the Grover optimization algorithm.

An oracle O that executes the function $L(\alpha)$ and outputs 1 for the most optimal α^* needs to be implemented as part of this quantum SVM formulation. The input to Grover's algorithm is equal superposition of all possible Lagrangian multipliers $|\psi\rangle = \frac{1}{2^M} \sum_{k=1}^{2^M} |\alpha_k\rangle$, and the desired output is the most optimal Lagrangian multiplier $|\alpha^*\rangle$ with high probability.

The Grover algorithm provides a global optima for the objective function in Equation 5-64 and also decreases the time complexity from $O(N)$ to $O(\sqrt{N})$. However, implementing such a quantum SVM algorithm does have its own limitations. Note that building an oracle that implements the objective function $L(\alpha)$ having complex kernels might be a very challenging task.

Quantum Least Square SVM

As we discussed, the quantum SVM proposal by Anquita et al. might not be a practical way of implementing SVM because of the complexities in designing the quantum oracle that would return the best Lagrangian multiplier vector. A different formulation known as *least square SVM* that avoids having to build a quantum oracle has gained popularity as the SVM formulation of choice in the quantum machine learning paradigm.

The quantum least square SVM algorithm is known as qSVM, and it uses the HHL algorithm by Harrow, Hassidim, and Lloyd discussed earlier to determine the parameters of the model.

The least square SVM formulation uses a different approach than the dual formulation by converting the inequality constraints $y_i(\theta^T x_i - b) \geq 1$ for each data point (x_i, y_i) into an equality constraint by introducing error slack terms $e_i \geq 0$ for each data point, as shown here:

$$y_i\left(\theta^T x_i - b\right) = 1 - e_i \tag{5-90}$$

As part of the optimization, we minimize the sum of the square of the errors e_i^2 for each data point as a regularizer along with the cost objective $\frac{1}{2}\|\theta\|^2$ associated in maximizing the distance between the hyperplanes $(\theta^T x_i - b) = \pm 1$. The optimization problem should also obey the equality constraint in Equation 5-90 for each data point. The overall objective of the least square SVM can be written as follows:

$$\min_{\theta} L(\theta, b) = \frac{1}{2}\theta^T \theta + \frac{\gamma}{2}\sum_{i=1}^{M} e_i^2$$

It is subject to the constraint:

$$y_i\left(\theta^T x_i - b\right) = 1 - e_i \; ; \; \forall i \in \{1, 2, \dots M\} \tag{5-91}$$

In SVM, the binary classes are labeled as +1 or −1, and hence $y_i^2 = 1$. By multiplying y_i on either side of the equality in Equation 5-91, we have the following:

$$y_i^2\left(\theta^T x_i - b\right) = y_i - y_i e_i$$

$$\rightarrow \theta^T x_i - b = y_i - y_i e_i$$

$$\rightarrow y_i e_i = y_i - \left(\theta^T x_i - b\right) \tag{5-92}$$

Since $y_i \in \{-1, +1\}$ for SVM, the quantity $y_i e_i$ is going to be $+e_i$ for positive classes and $-e_i$ for negative classes. We can in general relax the $e_i \geq 0$ constraint and replace the $y_i e_i$ by an e_i such that $e_i \in \mathbb{R}$. This allows us to rewrite Equation 5-92 as follows:

$$y_i - \left(\theta^T x_i - b\right) = e_i \tag{5-93}$$

The overall objective in least square SVM can thus be written as follows:

$$\min_{\theta} L(\theta, b) = \frac{1}{2}\theta^T\theta + \frac{\gamma}{2}\sum_{i=1}^{M}e_i^2$$

It is subject to the following constraint:

$$y_i - \left(\theta^T x_i - b\right) = e_i \; ; \; \forall i \in \{1, 2, ...M\} \tag{5-94}$$

The constraints for each data point (x_i, y_i) can be combined in the existing objective using Lagrangian multipliers α_i as shown here:

$$L(\theta, b, \alpha, e) = \frac{1}{2}\theta^T\theta + \frac{\gamma}{2}\sum_{i=1}^{M}e_i^2 - \sum_{i=1}^{M}\alpha_i\left[\left(\theta^T x_i - b\right) - y_i + e_i\right] \tag{5-95}$$

The conditions for optimality are as follows:

$$\nabla_\theta L = \theta - \sum_{i=1}^{M}\alpha_i x_i = 0 \rightarrow \theta = \sum_{i=1}^{M}\alpha_i x_i$$

$$\frac{\partial L}{\partial b} = \sum_{i=1}^{M}\alpha_i = 0$$

$$\nabla_e L = \gamma e - \alpha = 0 \rightarrow \alpha = \gamma e$$

$$\frac{\partial L}{\partial \alpha_i} = \left(\theta^T x_i - b\right) - y_i + e_i = 0 \; ; \; \forall i \in \{1, 2, ...M\} \tag{5-96}$$

We can get rid of the θ and the error slack terms e_i by solving for the previous four set of equations (see Equation 5-96) pertaining to the optimality. This leaves us with a system of linear equations expressed as follows:

$$\begin{bmatrix} 0 & 1^T \\ 1 & K+\gamma^{-1} \end{bmatrix}\begin{bmatrix} -b \\ \alpha \end{bmatrix} = \begin{bmatrix} 0 \\ Y \end{bmatrix} \tag{5-97}$$

In Equation 5-97, K is the kernel matrix of dimension $M \times M$, and Y is the vector of target labels y_i for all the M data points arranged in a column matrix. The generalized kernel matrix entry is $k(x_i, x_j)$ where i and j are the row and column numbers of the matrix K. We can solve for the system of equations represented in Equation 5-73 to derive α and b using the HHL algorithm. The decision boundary for classification would continue to be as follows:

$$f_{\alpha,\,b}(x) = \sum_{i=1}^{M} \alpha_i y_i k(x_i, x) - b \tag{5-98}$$

SVM Implementation Using Qiskit

In this section, we will execute the quantum SVM implementation from IBM Qiskit and see how it fares on a breast cancer dataset classification task. For this task, we first do a standard Z scaling on the given data and then perform principal component analysis to reduce the data dimensionality to 2. This will allow us to represent the data using two qubits. Qiskit also offers a way to project the data in high dimension. We use the SecondOrderExpansion capabilities of Qiskit to create second-order features. The entangler_map allows you to create interaction between features while creating the SecondOrderExpansion features. The second-order feature data points are fed to the QSVM routine for training the model.

```
from sklearn import datasets
from sklearn.model_selection import train_test_split
from sklearn.preprocessing import StandardScaler, MinMaxScaler
from sklearn.decomposition import PCA
from qiskit import Aer
from qiskit.aqua.components.feature_maps
     import SecondOrderExpansion,FirstOrderExpansion
from qiskit.aqua.algorithms import QSVM
from qiskit.aqua import QuantumInstance
import numpy as np
import matplotlib.pyplot as plt

class QSVM_routine:

    def __init__(self,
                 feature_dim=2,
                 feature_depth=2,
```

```
                  train_test_split=0.3,
                  train_samples=5,
                  test_samples=2,
                  seed=0,
                  copies=5):
        self.feature_dim = feature_dim
        self.feature_depth = feature_depth
        self.train_test_split = train_test_split
        self.train_samples = train_samples
        self.test_samples = test_samples
        self.seed = seed
        self.copies = copies

# Create train test datasets

def train_test_datasets(self):
        self.class_labels = [r'A', r'B']
        data, target = datasets.load_breast_cancer(True)
        train_X, test_X, train_y, test_y =
                        train_test_split(data, target,
                          test_size=self.train_test_split,
                          random_state=self.seed)
        # Mean std normalization
        self.z_scale = StandardScaler().fit(train_X)
        self.train_X_norm = self.z_scale.transform(train_X)
        self.test_X_norm = self.z_scale.transform(test_X)

        # Project the data into dimensions equal to the
        # number of qubits
        self.pca = PCA(n_components=self.feature_dim).fit(self.train_X_norm)
        self.train_X_norm = self.pca.transform(self.train_X_norm)
        self.test_X_norm = self.pca.transform(self.test_X_norm)

        # Scale to the range (-1,+1)
        X_all = np.append(self.train_X_norm,
                        self.test_X_norm, axis=0)
        minmax_scale = MinMaxScaler((-1, 1)).fit(X_all)
```

```
        self.train_X_norm = minmax_scale.transform(self.train_X_norm)
        self.test_X_norm = minmax_scale.transform(self.test_X_norm)

        # Pick training and test number of data point
        self.train = {key: (self.train_X_norm[train_y == k,
                        :])[:self.train_samples] for k, key in
                    enumerate(self.class_labels)}
        self.test ={key:(self.test_X_norm[test_y == k,
                      :])[:self.test_samples]
                      for k, key in
                    enumerate(self.class_labels)}

    # Train the QSVM Model
    def train_model(self):
        backend = Aer.get_backend('qasm_simulator')
        feature_expansion = SecondOrderExpansion(feature_dimension=
        self.feature_dim,
            depth=self.feature_depth,
            entangler_map=[[0, 1]])
        # Model definition
        svm = QSVM(feature_expansion, self.train, self.test)
        #svm.random_seed = self.seed
        q_inst = QuantumInstance(backend, shots=self.copies)

        # Train the SVM
        result = svm.run(q_inst)
        return svm, result

    # Analyze the training and test results

    def analyze_training_and_inference(self, result, svm):
        data_kernel_matrix = result['kernel_matrix_training']
        image = plt.imshow(np.asmatrix(data_kernel_matrix),
                        interpolation='nearest',
                        origin='upper', cmap='bone_r')
        plt.show()
        print(f"Test Accuracy: {result['testing_accuracy']}")
```

```
def main(self):
    self.train_test_datasets()
    svm, result = self.train_model()
    self.analyze_training_and_inference(svm, result)

if __name__ == '__main__':
    qsvm = QSVM_routine()
    qsvm.main()
```

xx - output - xx
Test Accuracy: 0.9

You can see that we get an impressive classification accuracy of 0.9 with the quantum SVM implementation from IBM's Qiskit.

Summary

In this chapter, we implemented some of the frequently used machine learning algorithms from supervised and unsupervised methods using quantum machine learning approaches. Also, we discussed the computational advantages of these methods over their classical counterparts once these quantum methods become mainstream. The field of machine learning at this time is to some extent constrained by the unavailability of a suitable QRAM aka. quantum RAM, that presents an easy way to project classical data as complicated quantum states. Once the QRAM implementations stabilize the field of quantum machine learning should see a boost in the number of usable machine learning algorithms.

The next chapter covers the exciting field of quantum deep learning and how it can leverage quantum computation in its various formulations. Looking forward to your participation.

CHAPTER 6

Quantum Deep Learning

"The more we delve into quantum mechanics the stranger the world becomes; appreciating this strangeness of the world, whilst still operating in that which you now consider reality, will be the foundation for shifting the current trajectory of your life from ordinary to extraordinary. It is the Tao of mixing this cosmic weirdness with the practical and physical, which will allow you to move, moment by moment, through parallel worlds to achieve your dreams."

—Kevin Michel

In the past decade, deep learning has had a profound impact on machine learning and artificial intelligence in general. Around the same time, quantum algorithms have proven to be effective in solving some of the intractable problems on classical computers. Quantum computing can provide a much more efficient framework for deep learning than the existing classical regime by providing better optimization of the underlying objective function. The field of quantum deep learning attempts to build neural networks that can benefit from the quantum information flow through the network. In summary, quantum deep learning networks are accompanied by quantum layers consisting of quantum gates.

In this chapter, we will introduce readers to the field of quantum deep learning by studying two classes of quantum deep learning networks. The first class of quantum deep learning models contains both classical and quantum components, and the category is referred to as *hybrid quantum-classical neural networks*. In the second class, we look at deep learning architectures that are totally quantum in their formulation and hence use only quantum gates in their construction.

© Santanu Pattanayak 2021
S. Pattanayak, *Quantum Machine Learning with Python*, https://doi.org/10.1007/978-1-4842-6522-2_6

Hybrid Quantum-Classical Neural Networks

A hybrid quantum-classical neural network has quantum hidden layers in the form of parameterized quantum circuits. A parameterized quantum circuit consists of quantum gates that operate on qubits defining a quantum layer. The quantum gates rotate the state of the qubits in a given layer based on outputs from a classical circuit preceding it, which acts as parameters to the rotation gates.

Figure 6-1 is a stepwise illustration of how hybrid quantum-classical neural networks work.

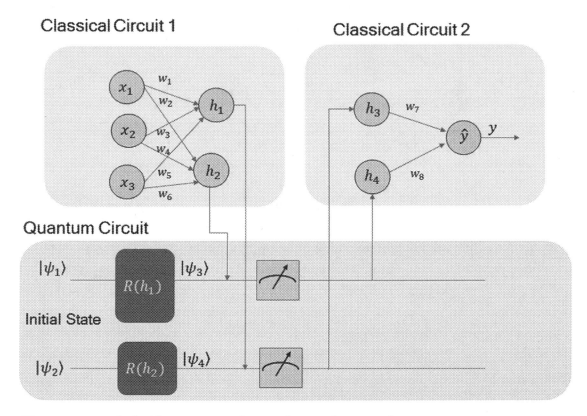

Figure 6-1. *A hybrid quantum-classical neural network*

The inputs $[x_1, x_2, x_3]^T$ to the hybrid quantum-classical neural network are converted to the hidden layer activations $[h_1, h_2]^T$ by the classical circuit 1.

$$h_1 = \sigma\left(x_1 w_1 + x_2 w_3 + x_3 w_5\right)$$

$$h_2 = \sigma\left(x_1 w_2 + x_2 w_4 + x_3 w_6\right) \tag{6-1}$$

In the above equation $\sigma(.)$ stands for the sigmoid activation function. In general, σ can be any activation function.

The hidden activations h_1 and h_2 act as the rotational angle parameters to the gates R_1 and R_2 in the quantum circuit, and they change the initial states $|\psi_1\rangle$ and $|\psi_2\rangle$ of the two qubits as follows:

$$|\psi_3\rangle = R(h_1)|\psi_1\rangle$$

$$|\psi_4\rangle = R(h_2)|\psi_2\rangle \qquad (6\text{-}2)$$

The unitary transforms in Equation 6-2 are followed by the measurement of the qubits in the appropriate basis. The measurement collapses the quantum information stored in the two qubits to classical information given by h_3 and h_4, respectively. The information in h_3 and h_4 is used to produce the final predicted output $\hat{y}$ as follows:

$$\hat{y} = \sigma\left(h_3 w_7 + h_4 w_8\right) \qquad (6\text{-}3)$$

Through this illustration you can see how to construct quantum deep learning networks using classical and quantum computing components.

Backpropagation in the Quantum Layer

Deep learning models are trained through backpropagation, which allows the models to compute the gradient of a loss function with respect to the weights in a given layer through the chain rule. The gradient of the weights at a given layer depends on the gradient of the loss with respect to the weights and the activations in the layers prior to it if the network is viewed from the output layer towards the input layer. If you consider the cost objective to be C and the parameters of the quantum circuit to be vector θ, then you can use the *parameter shift rule* to compute the gradient of the objective with respect to θ, as shown here:

$$\nabla_\theta(\theta) \approx \frac{\left[C(\theta + s) - C(\theta - s)\right]}{2s} \qquad (6\text{-}4)$$

The idea is simple: we evaluate the cost of the quantum circuit at two different parameter values $(\theta + s)$ and $(\theta - s)$ and then take the normalized difference $\dfrac{\left[C(\theta + s) - C(\theta - s)\right]}{2s}$ as the gradient. The parameter s is called the *shift coefficient*.

MNIST Classification Using Hybrid Quantum-Classical Neural Network

In this section, we implement an MNIST classifier on the two digits 0 and 1 using a hybrid quantum-classical neural network. Figure 6-2 illustrates the network architecture.

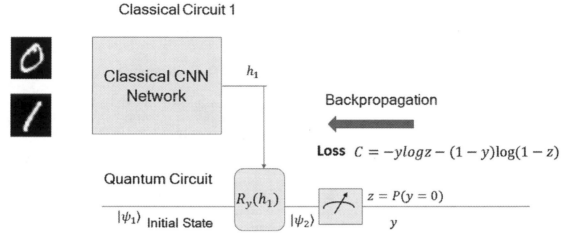

Figure 6-2. *MNIST classifier using hybrid quantum-classical neural network*

The network in Figure 6-2 starts off with a classical CNN network consisting of convolution and maxpooling layers and finally outputs a hidden activation h_1. The hidden activation h_1 feeds as angle of rotation to a quantum rotation gate R_y around the *y*-axis.

Based on the angle of rotation h_1, a unitary transform $R_y(h_1) = \begin{bmatrix} \cos\dfrac{h_1}{2} & -\sin\dfrac{h_1}{2} \\ \sin\dfrac{h_1}{2} & \cos\dfrac{h_1}{2} \end{bmatrix}$

takes the qubit in the initial state $|\psi_1\rangle$ to the state $|\psi_2\rangle$, as shown here:

$$R_y(h_1)|\psi_1\rangle = |\psi_2\rangle \tag{6-5}$$

We then measure the qubit in the $|0\rangle$ and $|1\rangle$ computational basis, and based on the number of 0 and 1 states revealed through measurement, we estimate the probability of $P(y = 0)$. For instance, if we make N measurements and the $|0\rangle$ state comes up m times, then we can estimate the probability of state $|0\rangle$ that represents MNIST digit 0, as follows:

$$P(y = 0) = z = \frac{m}{N} \tag{6-6}$$

If the actual label of the image is y and we predict the probability of the image being of digits 0 as $P(y = 0) = z$, then the log loss C for the image is given by the following:

$$C = -y \log\big(p(y=0)\big) - (1-y)\log\big(1 - P(y=0)\big)$$

$$= -y \log z - (1-y)\log(1-z) \qquad (6\text{-}7)$$

The model is trained by backpropagating the log loss C. Please note that the loss is illustrated for only one training data point. Neural networks are trained using mini-batches, and hence for a minibatch of size k, the log loss needs to be summed up for all k data points and backpropagated.

Gradient in the Quantum Layer

Backpropagation, as discussed earlier, requires the gradient of each layer output with respect to its inputs. The input to the quantum layer in Figure 6-2 is h_1, and the output of the quantum layer is the probability that the image is the digit 0 given by $P(0) = z$. If the parameters of the classical CNN network are represented by W, then h_1 is some function of W, and we can write the following:

$$h_1 = f(W) \qquad (6\text{-}8)$$

The gradient of the loss C with respect to W can be written using a chain rule, as follows:

$$\nabla_W C = \left(\frac{\partial C}{\partial z}\right)\left(\frac{\partial z}{\partial h_1}\right)\nabla_W h_1 \qquad (6\text{-}9)$$

The gradients $\left(\dfrac{\partial C}{\partial z}\right)$ and $\nabla_W h_1$ deal with classical data, and hence common deep learning packages such as PyTorch and TensorFlow automatically compute them. We need to come up with a way to compute the gradient $\left(\dfrac{\partial z}{\partial h_1}\right)$ in the quantum layer so that backpropagation can compute the gradient of the loss with respect to the parameter W.

This is where we apply the parameter shift rule and evaluate z at two values of h_1 given by $(h_1 + s)$ and $(h_1 - s)$. If the values of z at these two values of h_1 are $z(h_1 + s)$ and $z(h_1 - s)$, the gradient $\left(\dfrac{\partial z}{\partial h_1}\right)$ can be approximated as follows:

$$\left(\frac{\partial z}{\partial h_1}\right) = \frac{z(h_1 + s) - z(h_1 - s)}{2s} \tag{6-10}$$

One thing to note is that to evaluate $\left(\dfrac{\partial z}{\partial h_1}\right)$, we need to simulate the quantum circuit twice corresponding to the two different values of h_1.

The MINIST classifier has been implemented in this section using PyTorch as the deep learning framework and Qiskit as the quantum computing framework.

The following shows the detailed implementation:

```
import numpy as np
import matplotlib.pyplot as plt
import torch
from torch.autograd import Function
from torchvision import datasets, transforms
import torch.optim as optim
import torch.nn as nn
import torch.nn.functional as F
import qiskit
from qiskit.visualization import *
```

The class `QuantumCircuit` defines the quantum circuit for the quantum layer where `theta` is the rotation angle for the qubits coming from the classical circuit and hence defined as a parameter in the __init__ function. The quantum circuit is defined using Qiskit modules. In the first step of the circuit, Hadamard gates take the qubits from the $|0\rangle^{\otimes n}$ state to the equal superposition state $|\psi_1\rangle = \dfrac{1}{\sqrt{2}}\left(|0\rangle + |1\rangle\right)^{\otimes n}$. This is followed by the rotation using the `cirq.ry` gate where the angle of rotation is theta. Finally, the qubits are measured in the computational basis states $|0\rangle$ and $|1\rangle$.

The `run` function executes the circuit based on the value of theta received from the classical circuit. Based on the measurements of several simulations of the quantum state, the expectation of the different basis states is computed. If the quantum circuit consists of only one qubit, then the expectation gives the probability of the state $|1\rangle$.

```python
class QuantumCircuit:
    """

    The class implements a simple Quantum Block
    """

    def __init__(self, num_qubits, backend, copies: int = 1000):
        self._circuit_ = qiskit.QuantumCircuit(num_qubits)
        self.theta = qiskit.circuit.Parameter('theta')
        self._circuit_.h([i for i in range(num_qubits)])
        self._circuit_.barrier()
        self._circuit_.ry(self.theta,
        [i for i in range(num_qubits)])
        self._circuit_.measure_all()

        self.backend = backend
        self.copies = copies

    def run(self, theta_batch):
        job = qiskit.execute(self._circuit_,
                             self.backend,
                             shots=self.copies,
                             parameter_binds=[
                                 {self.theta: theta}
                                 for theta in theta_batch])
        result = job.result().get_counts(self._circuit_)

        counts = np.array(list(result.values()))
        states = np.array(list(result.keys())).astype(np.float32)
        probs = counts / self.copies
        expectation = np.array([np.sum(np.multiply(probs, states))])
        return expectation
```

QuantumFunction implements the forward and backward functions required for the quantum layer for the backpropagation using PyTorch. The forward function executes the quantum circuit and computes the expectation based on the measurement. The expectation will give the probability of the state $|1\rangle$ for a quantum layer circuit. The backward method computes the gradient through the quantum layer using the shift method illustrated earlier.

```python
class QuantumFunction(Function):
    """ Hybrid quantum - classical function definition """

    @staticmethod
    def forward(ctx, input, q_circuit, shift):
        """ Forward pass computation """
        ctx.shift = shift
        ctx.q_circuit = q_circuit
        theta_batch = input[0].tolist()
        expectation = ctx.q_circuit.run(theta_batch=theta_batch)
        result = torch.tensor([expectation])
        ctx.save_for_backward(input, result)
        return result

    @staticmethod
    def backward(ctx, grad_output):
        """ Backward pass computation """
        input, expectation = ctx.saved_tensors
        theta_batch = np.array(input.tolist())

        shift_right = theta_batch +
        np.ones(theta_batch.shape) * ctx.shift
        shift_left = theta_batch -
        np.ones(theta_batch.shape) * ctx.shift

        gradients = []
        for i in range(len(theta_batch)):
            expectation_right = ctx.q_circuit.run(shift_right[i])
            expectation_left = ctx.q_circuit.run(shift_left[i])

            gradient = torch.tensor([expectation_right])
            - torch.tensor([expectation_left])
            gradients.append(gradient)
        gradients = np.array([gradients]).T
        return torch.tensor([gradients]).float()*
                    grad_output.float(), None, None
```

The QuantumLayer class is defined next using the QuantumCircuit and QuantumFunction class capabilities. This class will be called to define quantum layers while defining an end-to-end classical quantum network.

```python
class QuantumLayer(nn.Module):
    """ Hybrid quantum - classical layer definition """

    def __init__(self,num_qubits, backend, shift, copies=1000):
        super(QuantumLayer, self).__init__()
        self.q_circuit = QuantumCircuit(num_qubits, backend, copies)
        self.shift = shift

    def forward(self, input):
        return QuantumFunction.apply(input,
        self.q_circuit, self.shift)
```

Now that we have all the ingredients for defining a quantum layer, we can go ahead and create a classical quantum neural network. The QCNNet class does exactly that. It first defines the different convolution, linear, and the quantum layer in the __init__ function. In the forward function, the defined layers are put together to create a network. The network starts with couple of pair of convolution and maxpooling layers followed by a couple of fully connected layers. The output of the final fully connected layer self.fc2 is a hidden unit of dimension 1 that feeds as the angle of rotation to the rotation gate in the quantum layer self.q_layer. The output of the quantum layer is the probability corresponding to state $|1\rangle$. The forward function returns the probability of both state $|1\rangle$ and state $|0\rangle$.

```python
class QCNNet(nn.Module):
    def __init__(self, num_qubits=1, backend=
                qiskit.Aer.get_backend('qasm_simulator'),
                shift=np.pi/2,
                copies=1000):
        super(QCNNet, self).__init__()
        self.conv1 = nn.Conv2d(1, 6, kernel_size=5)
        self.conv2 = nn.Conv2d(6, 16, kernel_size=5)
        self.dropout = nn.Dropout2d()
```

```python
        self.fc1 = nn.Linear(256, 64)
        self.fc2 = nn.Linear(64, 1)
        self.q_layer = QuantumLayer(num_qubits=num_qubits,
                                    backend=backend,
                                    shift=shift,
                                    copies=copies)

    def forward(self, x):
        x = F.relu(self.conv1(x))
        x = F.max_pool2d(x, 2)
        x = F.relu(self.conv2(x))
        x = F.max_pool2d(x, 2)
        x = self.dropout(x)
        x = x.view(1, -1)
        x = F.relu(self.fc1(x))
        x = self.fc2(x)
        x = self.q_layer(x)
        return torch.cat((x, 1 - x), -1)
```

In the train_test_dataloaders functions shown next, we define the train and test data loaders for training and inference purposes:

```python
# Define the train test data loaders
def train_test_dataloaders(train_samples=1000,
                           test_samples=500,
                           train_batch_size=1,
                           test_batch_size=1):
    X_train = datasets.MNIST(root='./data',
            train=True, download=True,
               transform=transforms.Compose(
               [transforms.ToTensor()]))

    # Extracting only MNIST labels 0 and 1
    idx = np.append(np.where(X_train.targets
```

```
       == 0)[0][:train_samples], np.where(X_train.targets
       == 1)[0][:train_samples])

       X_train.data = X_train.data[idx]
       X_train.targets = X_train.targets[idx]

       train_loader = torch.utils.data.DataLoader(X_train,
       batch_size=train_batch_size, shuffle=True)

       X_test = datasets.MNIST(root='./data',
       train=False, download=True, transform=transforms.Compose(
       [transforms.ToTensor()]))

       idx = np.append(np.where(X_test.targets
       == 0)[0][:test_samples], np.where(X_test.targets
       == 1)[0][:test_samples])

       X_test.data = X_test.data[idx]
       X_test.targets = X_test.targets[idx]

       test_loader = torch.utils.data.DataLoader(X_test,
       batch_size=test_batch_size, shuffle=True)
       return train_loader, test_loader
```

In the main function we put together, we train the model followed by inference. We start by creating the model using the QCNNet class followed by train and test data loader creation using train_test_dataloaders. Finally, we train the model for a specified number of epochs as in num_epochs followed by inference on the test dataset. The model is trained using log loss or the negative log likelihood loss using the PyTorch-defined nn.NLLLoss(). We use adaptive moment estimation or Adam as the optimizer for training.

```
def main(num_epochs=20,
         lr=.001,
         train_samples=1000,
         test_samples=500,
         train_batch_size=1,
         test_batch_size=1):
```

```python
model = QCNNet()
optimizer = optim.Adam(model.parameters(), lr=lr)
loss_func = nn.NLLLoss()

train_loader, test_loader = train_test_dataloaders(
                                    train_samples,
                                    test_samples,
                                    train_batch_size,
                                    test_batch_size)

loss_list = []

model.train()

for epoch in range(num_epochs):
    total_loss = []

    for batch_idx, (data, target) in enumerate(train_loader):
        optimizer.zero_grad()
        # Take the Forward pass
        output = model(data)
        # Calculate the log loss
        loss = loss_func(output, target)
        # Take the Backward pass
        loss.backward()
        # Update the Model weights
        optimizer.step()
        total_loss.append(loss.item())

    loss_list.append(sum(total_loss) / len(total_loss))

    print('Training [{:.0f}%]\tLoss: {:.4f}'.format(
        100. * (epoch + 1) / num_epochs, loss_list[-1]))

plt.plot(loss_list)
plt.title('Hybrid ConvNet Training Convergence')
plt.xlabel('Training Iterations')
plt.ylabel('Neg Log Loss')
```

```
    model.eval()
    with torch.no_grad():
        correct = 0
        for batch_idx, (data, target) in enumerate(test_loader):
            output = model(data)

            pred = output.argmax(dim=1, keepdim=True)
            correct += pred.eq(target.view_as(pred)).sum().item()

            loss = loss_func(output, target)
            total_loss.append(loss.item())

        print('Inference on test data:\n\tLoss: {:.4f}\n\tAccuracy:
        {:.1f}%'.format(
            sum(total_loss) / len(total_loss),
            correct / len(test_loader) * 100)
        )

if __name__ == '__main__':
    main()

-x- output -x-

Training [80%] Loss: -0.9968
Training [85%] Loss: -0.9971
Training [90%] Loss: -0.9966
Training [95%] Loss: -0.9966
Training [100%] Loss: -0.9965

Inference on test data:
        Loss: -0.9974
    Accuracy: 100.0%
```

As you can see from the output, the model has 100 percent accuracy on the test dataset. The training loss profile also seems to suggest the model convergences smoothly over the 20 epochs (Figure 6-3).

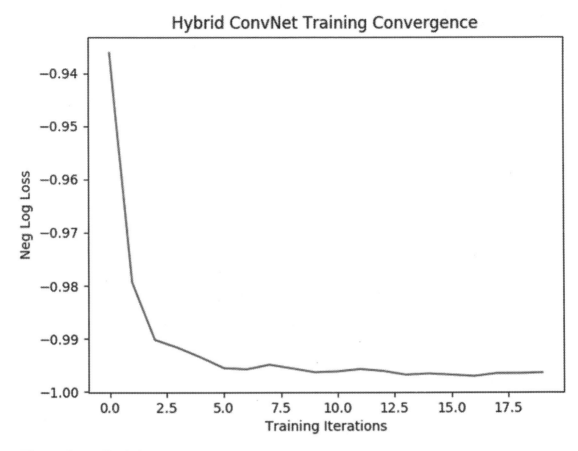

Figure 6-3. *Training convergence*

Quantum Neural Network for Classification on Near-Term Processors

In this section, we will study quantum neural network (QNN) architectures that can solve classification problems for binary input data. This class of QNN was first formulated by Farhi et al. in their paper (`https://arxiv.org/pdf/1802.06002.pdf`). As opposed to the previous architecture of QNN we implemented that has both classical and quantum layers, this architecture consists of only quantum layers, each of which is a unitary gate. If we have a data point with n binary input features $x_1, x_2...x_n$, it can be represented by one of the computational basis states of n qubits $q_1, q_2. . q_n$. Also, we take a readout qubit q_{n+1}, which gets transformed jointly with the input qubits based on the different unitary gates in each quantum layer. For a binary classification, the readout qubit is initialized to the state $|1\rangle$ corresponding to the class label $y = 1$. We can label the other class label $y = -1$ corresponding to the readout state $|0\rangle$. The input qubits are initialized to the $|0\rangle$ or $|1\rangle$ state based on whether the feature corresponding to the qubit is 0 or 1. Each of the unitary transforms $U(\theta_i)$ in a quantum layer i involves only a subset of qubits from the $(n + 1)$ set and is parameterized by the weight θ_i.

If we have l layers in the QNN and the unitary transform in each layer is represented by $U_i(\theta_i)$, then the overall unitary transform $U(\theta)$ can be written as follows:

$$U(\theta) = U_l(\theta_l) U_{l-1}(\theta_{l-1}) \ldots U_1(\theta_1) \tag{6-11}$$

where $\theta = [\theta_L, \theta_{L-1}, \ldots . \theta_1]^T$ is the set of parameters for the QNN.

Figure 6-4 shows a sample QNN network consisting of unitary layers where each of the parameterized unitary gates work on two qubits, one of which is an input qubit and the other the readout qubit. We will implement this QNN in the next section.

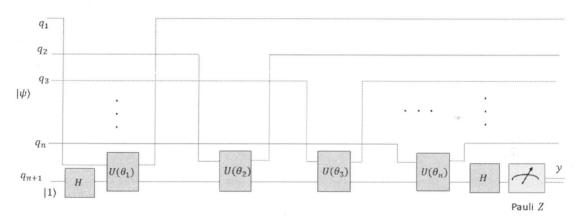

Figure 6-4. *QNN with unitary layers*

The set of $n + 1$ qubits pertaining to a data point is initialized to the computational basis state $|x_1 x_2 \ldots x_n, 1\rangle$, where the last qubit corresponds to the readout qubit. After the unitary transform $U(\theta)$, the state of the qubits will be as follows:

$$U(\theta) | x_1 x_2 \ldots x_n, 1 \rangle \tag{6-12}$$

The hope is that once the model is trained, the unitary transform $U(\theta)$ on the qubits will change the state of the readout qubit enough to align it to its true labels. Since in quantum computation we take measurements on several copies of the simulated circuit, we generally take an expectation of the measurement of the readout qubit with respect to a Pauli matrix as a measurement operator. We can take the measurement operator as the Pauli Z since it has eigenvalues of 1 and −1 pertaining to the states $|0\rangle$ and $|1\rangle$.

Hence, the expectation value will range from −1 to 1. The expectation value $\hat{y}$ that serves as our predicted label can be written as follows:

$$\hat{y} = U(\theta)\langle x_1 x_2 .. x_n, 1|ZU(\theta)|x_1 x_2 .... x_n, 1\rangle \tag{6-13}$$

If the expectation value $\hat{y}$ is less than zero, we can assign the class −1 to the data point, while if the expectation is greater than 0, we can assign the class +1.

As part of training, the goal is to get the predicted class label $\hat{y}$ as close as possible to the true label y. In this regard, we can train the model with hinge loss C, which is given by the following:

$$C = \max(0, 1 - y\hat{y}) \tag{6-14}$$

As we can see from Equation 6-14, when the predicted label $\hat{y}$ is equal to the actual label y, then the loss is zero for both the cases $(y = 1)$ and $(y = -1)$. The maximum loss of 2 occurs when $(y=1, \hat{y}=-1)$ or $(y=-1, \hat{y}=1)$. We cannot incur loss of more than 2 since the predicted value $\hat{y}$ is an expectation based on the measurement operator Z and hence the loss is bounded by its two eigenvalues −1 and +1.

When y and $\hat{y}$ agree on their sign, the loss incurred is $(1-|\hat{y}|)$, while when they do not agree on their sign, the loss is $(1+|\hat{y}|)$. Figure 6-5 is the hinge loss for different values of the product $y\hat{y}$.

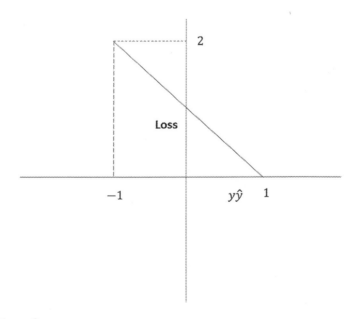

Figure 6-5. *Hinge loss*

You can see from Figure 6-5 that the loss is linear in the range $-1 < y\hat{y} < 1$, with the loss being maximum at $y\hat{y} = -1$ and minimum at $y\hat{y} = 1$.

MNIST Classification Using TensorFlow Quantum

In this section, we will use the TensorFlow Quantum Framework to perform a binary classification of two MNIST digits. The TensorFlow Quantum Framework works with Cirq as the quantum computing library. One of the unique features of the TensorFlow Quantum Framework is the ability to encode classical data represented through Cirq quantum circuits as tensors. These quantum data tensors are of type tf.string.

```
import tensorflow as tf
import tensorflow_quantum as tfq
import cirq
import sympy
import numpy as np
import collections
import matplotlib.pyplot as plt
from cirq.contrib.svg import SVGCircuit
```

This following function extracts the two MNIST digits for setting up the binary classification problem:

```
def extract_specific_digits(X, y, labels_to_extract):
    label_y1 = labels_to_extract[0]
    label_y2 = labels_to_extract[1]

    mask = (y == label_y1) | (y == label_y2)
    X, y = X[mask], y[mask]
    y = (y == label_y1)
    return X, y
```

Each MNIST image is 28 × 28 in size. In this QNN formulation, since we treat each pixel in the image by a qubit, the number of qubits required to represent an MNIST image of dimension 28 × 28 is exceedingly larger. Since the current quantum computers have limited capacity, we downsample the images to a manageable dimension such as 4 × 4.

Because of downsampling, there are chances that two images with different labels might end up having the same downsampled binary representation. We want to remove such duplicates so as to not impact the training adversely.

```python
def remove_sample_with_2_labels(X, y):
    mapping = collections.defaultdict(set)
    # Determine the set of labels for each unique image:
    for _x_, _y_ in zip(X, y):
        mapping[tuple(_x_.flatten())].add(_y_)

    new_x = []
    new_y = []
    for _x_, _y_ in zip(X, y):
        labels = mapping[tuple(_x_.flatten())]
        if len(labels) == 1:
            new_x.append(_x_)
            new_y.append(list(labels)[0])
        else:
            pass

    print("Initial number of examples: ", len(X))
    print("Final number of
non-contradictory examples: ", len(new_x))

    return np.array(new_x), np.array(new_y)
```

The following `data_preprocessing` function does the end-to-end data preprocessing as follows:

1. Normalizes the MNIST pixel values by 255 so that the pixel values lie between 0 and 1.

2. Extracts the two classes for binary classification.

3. Downsamples the images to smaller resolution as per `resize_dim`. We take `resize_dim=4` to downsample the images to 4 × 4.

4. We threshold the image pixel values to be either 0 or 1 based on `binary_threshold`. This is done so that each pixel can be represented by a qubit where the 0 value of a pixel can correspond to the state $|0\rangle$ and 1 value of a pixel can correspond to the state $|1\rangle$.

```python
def data_preprocessing(labels_to_extract,
resize_dim=4,
binary_threshold=0.5):
    # Load the data
    (x_train, y_train), (x_test, y_test)
            = tf.keras.datasets.mnist.load_data()
    # Rescale the images from 0 to 1 range
    x_train = x_train[..., np.newaxis] / 255.0
    x_test = x_test[..., np.newaxis] / 255.0

    print("Number of original training examples:", len(x_train))
    print("Number of original test examples:", len(x_test))

    # Extract on the specified 2 classes  in labels_to_extract
    x_train, y_train = extract_specific digits(x train,
    y_train, labels_to_extract=labels_to_extract)
    x_test, y_test = extract_specific_digits(x_test,
    y_test,labels_to_extract=labels_to_extract)

    print("Number of filtered training examples:", len(x_train))
    print("Number of filtered test examples:", len(x_test))

    # Resize the MNIST Images since 28x28 size image requires as
    # many qubits which is too much for Quantum Computers to
    # allocate. We resize them to 4x4 for keeping the problem
    # tractable in Quantum Computing realm.

    x_train_resize = tf.image.resize(x_train,
                    (resize_dim, resize_dim)).numpy()
    x_test_resize = tf.image.resize(x_test,
                    (resize_dim, resize_dim)).numpy()

    # Because of resizing to such small dimension
    # there is a chance of images with different classes
    #hashing to the same downsampled representation.
    # We remove such duplicate images through
    # remove_sample_with_2_labels
```

```
    x_train_resize, y_train_resize = \
        remove_sample_with_2_labels(x_train_resize, y_train)

    # We represent each pixel in binary by applying a threshold
    x_train_bin = np.array(x_train_resize > binary_threshold
                            ,dtype=np.float32)
    x_test_bin = np.array(x_test_resize > binary_threshold
                            ,dtype=np.float32)

return x_train_bin, x_test_bin, x_train_resize, \
        x_test_resize,y_train_resize, y_test
```

In this function `classical_to_quantum_data_circuit`, we build a quantum circuit using Cirq to represent each binary pixel by a qubit. If the input pixel is 0, we assign it the state $|0\rangle$; otherwise, we assign it the state $|1\rangle$. So, a downsampled MNIST image of size 4×4 would be represented by 16 qubits.

```
# Quantum circuit to represents each 0 valued pixel by |0> state
# and 1 pixel by |1> state.

def classical_to_quantum_data_circuit(image):
    image_flatten = image.flatten()
    qubits = cirq.GridQubit.rect(4, 4)
    circuit = cirq.Circuit()
    for i, val in enumerate(image_flatten):
        if val:
            circuit.append(cirq.X(qubits[i]))
    return circuit
```

The Cirq quantum circuits defined for each of the MNIST images is converted to tensors of the form `tf.string` through the TensorFlow quantum capabilities. If we have binary input data 0101, then as per this formulation we will encode the quantum circuit U in Cirq as the tensor using the TensorFlow Quantum Framework such that $U|0\rangle^{\otimes 4} = |0101\rangle$.

```
# Define circuit for classical to quantum data  for
# all datapoints and transform those circuits to Tensors
# using Tensorflow Quantum
```

```
def classical_data_to_tfq_tensors(x_train_bin, x_test_bin):
    x_train_c = [classical_to_quantum_data_circuit(x)
for x in x_train_bin]
    x_test_c = [classical_to_quantum_data_circuit(x)
for x in x_test_bin]
    x_train_tfc = tfq.convert_to_tensor(x_train_c)
    x_test_tfc = tfq.convert_to_tensor(x_test_c)
    return x_train_tfc, x_test_tfc
```

We implement the QuantumLayer class (see below) to add layers to the quantum neural network. Each quantum layer deals with qubits representing the input image and a qubit as the class readout. In each call of add_layer, each input qubit along with the readout qubit goes through a two-qubit unitary transform parameterized by a weight. Since we are dealing with $4 \times 4 = 16$ input qubits for representing each MNIST image, we have 16 weights pertaining to the 16 unitary transforms. If we consider a two-qubit gate $Z \otimes Z$ applied to the ith input qubit q_i with state $|q_i\rangle$ and readout qubit r with state $|r\rangle$, then the output state of the two qubits after the transformation is given by $Z^{\theta_i}|q_i\rangle \otimes Z^{\theta_i}|r\rangle$. All the other qubit states remain unchanged. Here θ_i is the weight corresponding to the input qubit i.

```
class QuantumLayer:
    def __init__(self, data_qubits, readout):
        self.data_qubits = data_qubits
        self.readout = readout

    def add_layer(self, circuit, gate, prefix):
        for i, q in enumerate(self.data_qubits):
            _w_ = sympy.Symbol(prefix + '-' + str(i))
            circuit.append(gate(q, self.readout) ** _w_)
```

The create_QNN function defined next uses the QuantumLayer class to define the CNN once the input and the readout qubits are defined. We define the qubits pertaining to the input image in a rectangular topology using cirq.GridQubit.rect.

Once the readout qubit is transformed to the state $\frac{1}{\sqrt{2}}(|0\rangle - |1\rangle)$ through Pauli X and Hadamard transforms, we apply two sets of quantum layers having two-qubit transformation gates as $X \otimes X$ and $Z \otimes Z$, respectively. After that, we apply another Hadamard transform on the readout qubit. Finally, we pass the readout qubit with the

301

Pauli Z operator attached to it. Do note that the final Pauli Z operator is attached to the quantum circuit since it acts as a measurement operator for the readout qubit. Hence, the readout qubit will be measured in the $|0\rangle$ and $|1\rangle$ eigenbasis of the Pauli Z matrix, and the expectation value will be computed over its eigenvalues -1 and 1.

```python
def create_QNN(resize_dim=4):
    """Create a QNN model circuit and prediction(readout) """
    data_qubits = cirq.GridQubit.rect(resize_dim, resize_dim)  # a 4x4 grid.
    readout = cirq.GridQubit(-1, -1)  # a single qubit at [-1,-1]
    circuit = cirq.Circuit()

    # Prepare the readout qubit.
    circuit.append(cirq.X(readout))
    circuit.append(cirq.H(readout))

    builder = QuantumLayer(
        data_qubits=data_qubits,
        readout=readout)

    # Apply a series of XX layers followed
    # by a series of ZZ layers
    builder.add_layer(circuit, cirq.XX, "XX")
    builder.add_layer(circuit, cirq.ZZ, "ZZ")

    # Hadamard Gate on the readout qubit
    circuit.append(cirq.H(readout))

    return circuit, cirq.Z(readout)
```

We define the hinge accuracy through the following function where if the expectation of the readout given by y_pred > 0, then we take the predicted class to 1, while if y_pred < 0, we take the predicted class to be -1. We compare the true classes 1 and -1 to the predicted ones to get the hinge loss accuracy. We use this hinge accuracy as a metric in our training while the model is trained with hinge loss given by tf.keras.losses.Hinge.

```python
def hinge_accuracy(y_true, y_pred):
    y_true = tf.squeeze(y_true) > 0.0
    y_pred = tf.squeeze(y_pred) > 0.0
    cost = tf.cast(y_true == y_pred, tf.float32)

    return tf.reduce_mean(cost)
```

The build_model function calls `create_QNN` to define the model circuit and the model readout. We use `tf.keras` to define the model. The TensorFlow quantum `layers.PQC` option is used to define the quantum-based QNN. It takes in the quantum circuit as well as `model_readout` as input. Since the `model_readout` is tied to the Pauli Z measurement operator, we will get the expectation values from -1 and 1.

```python
def build_model(resize_dim=4):
    model_circuit, model_readout = \
create_QNN(resize_dim=resize_dim)
    # Build the model.
    model = tf.keras.Sequential([
        tf.keras.layers.Input(shape=(), dtype=tf.string),
        tfq.layers.PQC(model_circuit, model_readout),
    ])
    return model, model_circuit, model_readout
```

The `main` function puts together the data preprocessing, model definition, model training, and model evaluation to provide an end-to-end pipeline. Do note the target classes 1 and 0 have reassigned to 1 and −1 to align with the hinge loss that we are using to train the model. With respect to training, we train the model for 3 epochs with batch sizes of 32. We use Adam as the optimizer, and as discussed, we train the model with hinge_loss.

```python
def main(labels_to_extract,
         resize_dim,
         binary_threshold,
         subsample,
         epochs=3,
         batch_size=32,
         eval=True):
    # Perform data preprocessing
    x_train_bin, x_test_bin, x_train_resize, x_test_resize, \
    y_train_resize, y_test_resize = \
        data_preprocessing(labels_to_extract=labels_to_extract,
                           resize_dim=resize_dim,
                           binary_threshold=binary_threshold)
```

```python
    x_train_tfc, x_test_tfc = \
        classical_data_to_tfq_tensors(x_test_bin, x_test_bin)

    # Convert labels to -1 or 1 to align with hinge loss
    y_train_hinge = 2.0 * y_train_resize - 1.0
    y_test_hinge = 2.0 * y_test_resize - 1.0

    # build model
    model, model_circuit, model_readout = \
        build_model(resize_dim=resize_dim)

    # Compile Model

    model.compile(
        loss=tf.keras.losses.Hinge(),
        optimizer=tf.keras.optimizers.Adam(),
        metrics=[hinge_accuracy])
    print(model.summary())

    if subsample > 0:
        x_train_tfc_sub = x_train_tfc[:subsample]
        y_train_hinge_sub = y_train_hinge[:subsample]

    qnn_hist = model.fit(
        x_train_tfc_sub,
        y_train_hinge_sub,
        batch_size=batch_size,
        epochs=epochs,
        verbose=1,
        validation_data=(x_test_tfc,
                         y_test_hinge))

    if eval:
        results = model.evaluate(x_test_tfc, y_test_hinge)
        print(results)

if __name__ == '__main__':
    labels_to_extract = [3, 6]
    resize_dim = 4
```

```
    binary_threshold = 0.5
    subsample = 500
    epochs = 3
    batch_size = 32

    main(labels_to_extract=labels_to_extract,
        resize_dim=resize_dim,
        binary_threshold=binary_threshold,
        subsample=subsample,
        epochs=epochs,
        batch_size=batch_size)
```

xx - output -xx

```
Number of original training examples: 60000
Number of original test examples: 10000
Number of filtered training examples: 12049
Number of filtered test examples: 1968
Initial number of examples: 12049
Final number of non-contradictory examples: 11520

Model: "sequential_2"
_____
Laycr (type) Output Shape Param #
=============================================================
pqc_2 (PQC) (None, 1) 32
=============================================================
Total params: 32 Trainable params: 32 Non-trainable params: 0

Train on 11520 samples, validate on 1968 samples
Epoch 1/3
11520/11520 [==============================] - 439s 38ms/sample -
loss: 0.6591 - hinge_accuracy: 0.7385 - val_loss: 0.3611 -
val_hinge_accuracy: 0.8281
Epoch 2/3
11520/11520 [==============================] - 441s 38ms/sample -
loss: 0.3458 - hinge_accuracy: 0.8286 - val_loss: 0.3303 -
val_hinge_accuracy: 0.8281
Epoch 3/3
```

```
11520/11520 [==============================] - 437s 38ms/sample -
loss: 0.3263 - hinge_accuracy: 0.8493 - val_loss: 0.3268 -
val_hinge_accuracy: 0.8564
1968/1968 [==============================] - 3s 2ms/sample - loss:
0.3268 - hinge_accuracy: 0.8564
```

We can see from the output logs that the model has converged to good validation accuracy in only three epochs of training. This is impressive given that the model has only 32 trainable parameters.

Summary

In this chapter, we introduced you to the existing field of quantum deep learning by looking at the two classes of quantum deep learning architectures: one that uses both classical and quantum layers in its formulation and the other that is built using only quantum gates. One of the advantages of quantum deep learning is that we can use fewer parameters in comparison to their classical counterparts if we choose the quantum gates wisely since they provide a lot of prior to the network. You are advised to work through the implementation details of both quantum deep learning architectures to get comfortable with the subtle differences they have from their classical counterparts.

The next chapter covers the advanced methods of quantum-based optimization such as adiabatic optimization and a variation quantum eigensolver. These optimization methods can work on even noisy near-term quantum computers and hence are practical approaches that will disrupt the field of optimization very soon.

CHAPTER 7

Quantum Variational Optimization and Adiabatic Methods

"The history of the universe, is in effect, a huge ongoing quantum computation. The universe is a quantum computer."

—Seth Lloyd

In this chapter, we will take a look at the various optimization techniques that use quantum computing in their formulation. A couple of such algorithms that we are going to work through in great detail are the variational quantum eigensolver, popularly known as VQE, and the quantum approximate optimization algorithm, also known as QAOA. The central idea in both methods is to define cost objectives as an expectation of appropriate Hamiltonians pertaining to quantum systems. Based on the maximization or minimization problem, we look to derive the maximum or minimum eigenvalue state through these optimization techniques. Both of these methods are variational in that they combine both quantum and classical methods for the optimization. Since the topic is centered around Hamiltonians, we will study the popular Ising Hamiltonian model as well in this chapter. Similarly, the QAOA technique is based on the adiabatic evolution of a quantum system, and hence we will study its underlying math in great detail in this chapter.

As an application to VQE, we implement the quantum max-cut algorithm for graph clustering. Finally, we conclude the chapter by working through the graph quantum random walk algorithm. All the optimization techniques in this chapter are approximate, and hence they are perfect for noisy near-term quantum computers. Without further ado, let's get started with the variational quantum eigensolver.

© Santanu Pattanayak 2021
S. Pattanayak, *Quantum Machine Learning with Python*, https://doi.org/10.1007/978-1-4842-6522-2_7

Variational Quantum Eigensolver

The variational quantum eigensolver is a quantum computing algorithm that is well suited for solving optimization problems where the objective can be defined in terms of the Hamiltonian of a quantum system. The Hamiltonian represents the energy of the quantum system in different quantum basis states, and we are interested in the basis state that has the minimum energy. The expected energy of a quantum system in the state $|\psi\rangle$ with a Hamiltonian H is given by the expectation of the Hamiltonian operator as follows:

$$\langle H \rangle = \langle \psi | H | \psi \rangle \tag{7-1}$$

In the variational quantum eigensolver, we want to choose the state $|\psi*\rangle$ that minimizes the energy of the Hamiltonian as shown here:

$$|\psi *\rangle = arg \min_{\psi} \langle \psi | H | \psi \rangle \tag{7-2}$$

Since the Hamiltonian of the quantum system is Hermitian in nature, it has a spectral decomposition where the eigenvectors form an orthonormal basis and the eigenvalues are real. The eigenvalues of the Hamiltonian stand for the energy of the quantum system at the corresponding eigenstates, and since they are real, they can be arranged in order as shown here:

$$\lambda_0 \leq \lambda_1 \leq \lambda_2 \leq \ldots \lambda_{n-1} \tag{7-3}$$

It is not difficult to see that the minimum Hamiltonian energy is equal to the lowest eigenvalue λ_0 and occurs in the eigenstate $|\phi_0\rangle$ corresponding to the lowest eigenvalue λ_0. To deduce this mathematically, we can minimize the objective in Equation 7-1 with a constraint that the basis state is of unit l^2 norm in accordance with the norm of a quantum state.

$$\min_{\psi} \langle \psi | H | \psi \rangle$$

$$\text{Subject to } \langle \psi | \psi \rangle = 1 \tag{7-4}$$

We can combine the constraint using a Lagrangian multiplier λ to the main objective as shown here:

$$L(\psi) = \langle \psi | H | \psi \rangle - \lambda \langle \psi | \psi \rangle \tag{7-5}$$

To minimize the objective $L(\psi)$, we can take its gradient with respect to the state vector $|\psi\rangle$ and set it to zero as shown here:

$$\nabla_\psi L = 2H|\psi\rangle - 2\lambda|\psi\rangle = 0$$

$$\rightarrow H|\psi\rangle = \lambda|\psi\rangle \tag{7-6}$$

Equation 7-6 tells us that the minimum energy state is an eigenvector of the Hamiltonian H, but we do not yet know which one specifically. As discussed earlier, the Hamiltonian has a spectral decomposition where the eigenvectors are orthonormal and the eigenvalues are real. This allows us to write the Hamiltonian H as follows:

$$H = \sum_{i=0}^{n-1} \lambda_i |\phi_i\rangle\langle\phi_i| \tag{7-7}$$

The quantity to be minimized, $\langle\psi|H|\psi\rangle$, can be written in terms of the spectral decomposition in Equation 7-7 as follows:

$$\langle\psi|H|\psi\rangle = \sum_{i=0}^{n-1} \lambda_i \langle\psi|\phi_i\rangle\langle\phi_i|\psi\rangle \tag{7-8}$$

We have already derived that $|\psi\rangle$ has to be one of the eigenvectors $|\phi_i\rangle$. From Equation 7-8, we can see that the $\langle\psi|H|\psi\rangle$ is minimized when we choose $|\psi\rangle = |\phi_o\rangle$ in which case the Hamiltonian energy turns out to be λ_o.

So, in the quantum variational eigensolver, we attempt to solve minimization problems by first formulating the optimization objective as a suitable Hamiltonian and then solving for the eigenvector corresponding to the lowest eigenvalue of the Hamiltonian. The approach to solve for the eigenvector corresponding to the lowest eigenvalue is attempted through a combination of quantum computing and classical computing steps, and hence the technique falls under the category of variational methods. Figure 7-1 illustrates the steps in optimization using a variational quantum eigensolver.

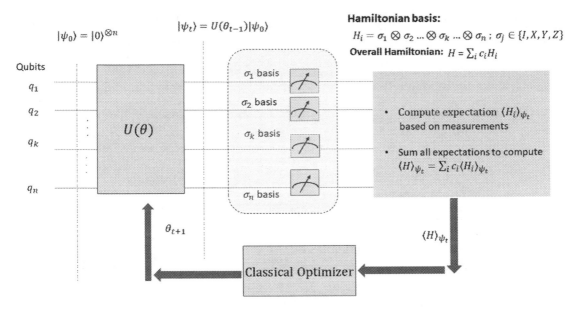

Figure 7-1. *High-level flow diagram of VQE*

Defining the Hamiltonian

In a Variation Quantum Eigensolver we define the Hamiltonian in terms of the Pauli matrices Z, X, Y, and I. Any Hamiltonian or any Hermitian operator in general can be written in terms of the tensor product of the Pauli matrices as the basis. For instance, we can define the Hamiltonian of a two-qubit system in terms of the tensor product of Pauli matrices as the basis as follows:

$$H = \sum_k c_k \left(\sigma_0^{(k)} \otimes \sigma_1^{(k)} \right) = \sum_k c_k \prod_{i=0}^{2-1} \otimes \sigma_i^{(k)} \tag{7-9}$$

In the previous expression, $\left(\sigma_0^{(k)} \otimes \sigma_1^{(k)} \right)$ or $\prod_{i=0}^{2-1} \otimes \sigma_i^{(k)}$ denotes the kth basis and each of $\sigma_i^{(k)} \in \{X, Y, Z, I\}$. The terms c_k are the linear coefficients corresponding to each basis. The index i in $\sigma_i^{(k)}$ denotes that $\sigma_i^{(k)}$ corresponds to the qubit i in the kth basis. We can generalize this expression for an n-qubit system and write its Hamiltonian H as follows:

$$H = \sum_k c_k \prod_{i=0}^{n-1} \otimes \sigma_i^{(k)} = \sum_k H_k \tag{7-10}$$

This Pauli basis representation of the Hamiltonian is advantageous for two reasons.

- It lets us compute the expectation of each Hamiltonian H_k with respect to each basis k independently and then sum them to get the expectation of the overall Hamiltonian. This is because of the linearity of the expectation shown here:

$$\langle \psi | H | \psi \rangle = \sum_k \langle \psi | H_k | \psi \rangle$$

$$\rightarrow \langle H \rangle_\psi = \sum_k \langle H_k \rangle_\psi \tag{7-11}$$

- The eigenvalues and the eigenvectors for Pauli matrices are known up front, and hence we know for a given Hamiltonian base H_k what basis we need to measure the qubits for the expectation computation. For instance, if we are to measure the expectation of a qubit in the state $|\psi\rangle$ for a given Hamiltonian $H_k = -Z$, we can do so by measuring the qubit in the computational basis state $|0\rangle$, $|1\rangle$ since we know the eigenvectors of Z are $|0\rangle$ and $|1\rangle$ corresponding to the eigenvalues of 1 and −1. As the Hamiltonian is given as −Z, the eigenvalues change to −1 and +1 corresponding to the eigenvectors $|0\rangle$ and $|1\rangle$. We can measure the qubit in state $|\psi\rangle$ in the computational basis as $|\psi\rangle = \alpha|0\rangle + \beta|1\rangle$, and based on the estimates of α and β from multiple measurements, we can compute the expectation as follows:

$$\langle -Z \rangle_\psi = \lambda(|0\rangle) * P(|0\rangle) + \lambda(|1\rangle) P(|1\rangle)$$

$$\rightarrow -|\alpha|^2 + |\beta|^2 \tag{7-12}$$

In Equation 7-12, $\lambda(|0\rangle)$ and $\lambda(|1\rangle)$ are the eigenvalues corresponding to the eigen vectors $|0\rangle$ and $|1\rangle$ of the Hamiltonian −Z. Just to check that the expectation computed through measurement of the quantum state matches with the expectation of the operator −Z with respect to state $|\psi\rangle$ based on the operator expectation formula, we compute the latter here:

$$\langle -Z \rangle_\psi = \langle \psi | -Z | \psi \rangle$$

$$\rightarrow -(\alpha^* \langle 0| + \beta^* \langle 1|)(|0\rangle\langle 0| - |1\rangle\langle 1|)(\alpha|0\rangle + \beta|1\rangle)$$

$$\rightarrow -\alpha^* \alpha + \beta^* \beta = -|\alpha|^2 + |\beta|^2 \tag{7-13}$$

So, we see that the expectation for a given Pauli matrix as Hamiltonian can be computed by measuring the state with the eigenvectors of the Pauli matrices as the basis for measurement. This is true for any Hamiltonian. However, when we work with Pauli matrices, we know the eigenvalues and the eigenvectors up front, and hence by measuring the state vector in the known eigen basis, we can compute the expectation. Furthermore, this process can be generalized to the Hamiltonian basis, which is the tensor product of Pauli matrices corresponding to multiple qubits. In the expectation computation section to follow, we will illustrate this for a two-qubit system having a Hamiltonian given by $Z \otimes X$ where Z stands for the Hamiltonian of the first qubit and X stands for the Hamiltonian of the second qubit.

Preparing the Ansatz State Based on the Expectation Optimization

Once we have defined a Hamiltonian whose expectation we want to minimize, our goal is to determine the eigenvector corresponding to the smallest eigenvalue. Based on the Hamiltonian, we define a quantum system with the required number of qubits n having an initial state $|\psi_0\rangle$. The state $|\psi_0\rangle$ is controlled by an unitary transform $U(\theta)$ parameterized by θ that can change the initial state $|\psi_o\rangle$ to $|\psi(\theta)\rangle$ as desired. Such a state $|\psi(\theta)\rangle$ that can be prepared based on the optimized parameter θ from a classical computation block is termed as *ansatz* in the realm of variational methods. In each iteration k of VQE, we compute the expectation of the Hamiltonian H by measuring the state $|\psi(\theta_k)\rangle$ in the Hamiltonian eigen basis and compute the expectation. The expectation values are fed to a classical optimizer such as Nelder–Mead or COYBLA. The classical optimizer comes up with optimized value of θ_{k+1}, that is supposed to improve the expectation with respect to the new state derived as follows:

$$|\psi\rangle(\theta_{k+1})\rangle = U(\theta_{k+1}|\psi_o\rangle \tag{7-14}$$

In summary, we use quantum computation to evolve the state and compute the expectation through measurement in the appropriate basis and use classical computing to optimize the Hamiltonian cost function by giving out the appropriate parameter θ_k. The parameter θ_k given out by the classical optimizer in iteration k corresponds to the optimized state $|\psi(\theta_k)\rangle$ achieved through the unitary transform $U(\theta_k)$ on some initial state.

Expectation Computation

We discussed that the expectation $\langle H \rangle$ computation for the Hamiltonian H is done by breaking up the Hamiltonian as a linear sum of the basis formed by the tensor product of Pauli matrices where the Pauli matrices stand for the Hamiltonian base corresponding to the individual qubits. To illustrate this with an example, let's take a Hamiltonian basis for a two-qubit system as $Z \otimes X$ where Z stands for the Hamiltonian basis for qubit q_1 and X stands for the Hamiltonian basis for qubit q_2. The Hamiltonian for $Z \otimes X$ can be written in matrix form as follows:

$$Z \otimes X = \begin{bmatrix} 1 & 0 \\ 0 & -1 \end{bmatrix} \otimes \begin{bmatrix} 0 & 1 \\ 1 & 0 \end{bmatrix} = \begin{bmatrix} 0 & 1 & 0 & 0 \\ 1 & 0 & 0 & 0 \\ 0 & 0 & 0 & -1 \\ 0 & 0 & -1 & 0 \end{bmatrix} \tag{7-15}$$

Let's take the state $|\psi\rangle = \frac{1}{\sqrt{2}}(|0\rangle + |1\rangle) \otimes \frac{1}{\sqrt{2}}(|0\rangle + |1\rangle) = \frac{1}{2}(|00\rangle + |01\rangle + |10\rangle + |11\rangle)$, which can be written as $\frac{1}{2}[1\,1\,1\,1]^T$ in the usual computation basis. The expectation of $Z \otimes X$ with respect to state $|\psi\rangle$ based on the POVM postulate of measurement is given by the following:

$$\langle Z \otimes X \rangle = \frac{1}{4}[1\,1\,1\,1]\begin{bmatrix} 0 & 1 & 0 & 0 \\ 1 & 0 & 0 & 0 \\ 0 & 0 & 0 & -1 \\ 0 & 0 & -1 & 0 \end{bmatrix}\begin{bmatrix} 1 \\ 1 \\ 1 \\ 1 \end{bmatrix} = 0 \tag{7-16}$$

Now let's compute the expectation by measuring the qubit states in the eigen basis corresponding to the Pauli matrices in $Z \otimes X$. For the qubit q_1, the Hamiltonian matrix is Z, and hence the eigenvalues are 1 and −1 corresponding to eigenvectors $|0\rangle$ and $|1\rangle$. The qubit q_1 represented in the state $|\psi\rangle = \frac{1}{\sqrt{2}}(|0\rangle + |1\rangle) \otimes \frac{1}{\sqrt{2}}(|0\rangle + |1\rangle)$ is in the usual $|0\rangle$ and $|1\rangle$ basis that pertains to the eigenvectors of Z. The state of the qubit q_2 needs to be presented in the $|+\rangle$ and $|-\rangle$ basis where $|+\rangle = \frac{1}{\sqrt{2}}(|0\rangle + |1\rangle)$ and $|-\rangle = \frac{1}{\sqrt{2}}(|0\rangle - |1\rangle)$. This is because the Hamiltonian corresponding to the operator q_2 is X whose eigenvectors are the $|+\rangle$ and $|-\rangle$ states corresponding to the eigen values 1 and -1. So, the combined state of the two qubits represented in the basis of their individual Hamiltonians can be represented as follows:

$$|\psi\rangle = \frac{1}{\sqrt{2}}\left(|0\rangle + |1\rangle\right) \otimes \frac{1}{\sqrt{2}}\left(|0\rangle + |1\rangle\right)$$

$$= \frac{1}{\sqrt{2}}\left(|0\rangle + |1\rangle\right) \otimes |+\rangle \qquad (7\text{-}17)$$

Now suppose we measure the qubits q_1 in the $|0\rangle$ and $|1\rangle$ basis and q_2 in the $|+\rangle$ and $|-\rangle$ basis. The state as represented in Equation 7-17 on measurement will yield either of two eigenstates $\frac{1}{\sqrt{2}}|0\rangle \otimes |+\rangle$ and $\frac{1}{\sqrt{2}}|1\rangle \otimes |+\rangle$ with an equal probability amplitude of $\frac{1}{\sqrt{2}}$. The eigenvalues corresponding to the state $|0\rangle \otimes |+\rangle$ is the product of the individual eigenvalues corresponding to the $|0\rangle$ eigenvector for Hamiltonian Z and the $|+\rangle$ eigenvector for Hamiltonian X. Both of these eigenvalues are 1, and hence the eigenvalue corresponding to $|0\rangle \otimes |+\rangle$ is 1. Similarly, the eigenvalue for the state $|1\rangle \otimes |+\rangle$ is $-1 \times 1 = -1$. Hence, the overall expectation of the Hamiltonian is as follows:

$$\langle Z \otimes X \rangle_\psi = \lambda\left(|0\rangle \otimes |+\rangle\right) * P\left(|0\rangle \otimes |+\rangle\right) + \lambda\left(|1\rangle \otimes |+\rangle\right) P\left(|1\rangle \otimes |+\rangle\right)$$

$$= 1 \times \left(\frac{1}{\sqrt{2}}\right)^2 - 1 \times \left(\frac{1}{\sqrt{2}}\right)^2 = 0 \qquad (7\text{-}18)$$

So, we see the expectation computed by measuring the qubits in the eigen basis corresponding to their Hamiltonian represented by Pauli operators is equivalent to the expectation of $Z \otimes X$ computed with respect to state $|\psi\rangle$ based on the operator expectation formula.

Isling Model and Its Hamiltonian

The Isling model can be looked at as an abstract mathematical framework that consists of several elements arranged in a lattice. The elements of the Isling model can exist in either of the two states $+1$ or -1, and each element interacts with the neighboring elements with varying degrees of magnitude. The interactions between the element states is restricted to only two-way interactions. Given a square lattice of $n \times n$ elements, the elements in the Isling model can be represented as shown in Figure 7-2. If we consider the element q_{10}, it only interacts with the nearest neighbors in the grid; i.e., q_6, q_9, $q_{14,}$ and q_{11}.

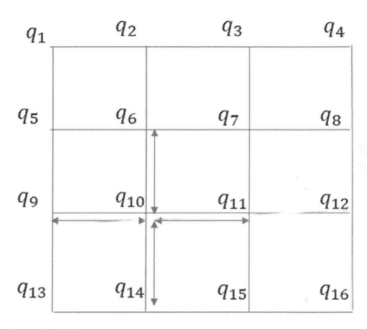

Figure 7-2. *Isling model*

Each of the elements q_i can be treated as a random variable that can take up two states +1 and −1. If we represent the state of the element q_i by the random variable σ_i, then each of $\sigma_i \in \{-1, 1\}$. Let's try to come up with a Hamiltonian that would contain the energy of the system in all the possible configurations of the state of the elements. In an Isling model, two neighboring elements being in the same state are considered a more stable configuration than when the elements contradict in their states. In this regard, the Hamiltonian component for two elements q_i and q_j can be represented as follows:

$$e_{ij} = -c_{ij}\sigma_i\sigma_j \qquad (7\text{-}19)$$

In Equation 7-19, $c_{ij} \geq 0$ denotes the strength of interaction between the two elements q_i and q_j. As you can see, when both σ_i and σ_j are of the same sign i.e. $\sigma_i\sigma_j = 1$, the interaction energy $-c_{ij}$ is negative. For neighboring elements with differing states, this interaction energy is c_{ij}. Hence, Equation 7-19 clearly models an interaction energy, which is lower in magnitude when the states agree than when the states disagree.

$$E_1 = -\sum_{\langle i, j \rangle} c_{ij} \sigma_i \sigma_j \qquad (7\text{-}20)$$

The total interaction energy can be represented by Equation 7-20 where $\langle i, j \rangle$ is the sum over the nearest neighbor pair of elements. The other component of the energy comes from the individual states of the elements and can be expressed as follows:

$$E_2 = -\sum_i b_i \sigma_i \qquad (7\text{-}21)$$

The overall energy of the system in the Isling model is given by the sum of the interaction energy E_1 and the individual energy E_2 as shown here:

$$E = -\sum_{\langle i,j \rangle} c_{ij} \sigma_i \sigma_j - \sum_i b_i \sigma_i \qquad (7\text{-}22)$$

In fact, the Isling model was developed by Wilhelm Lenz to model ferromagnetism. Consider the n elements to be n atoms in the presence of magnetic field of strength B working along direction z. Also suppose each of the atoms q_i represent spin systems where the state $\sigma_i = +1$ represents spin-up, and $\sigma_i = -1$ represents a spin-down system. The total energy of the n atom system contains the interaction energies between the neighboring atoms similar to e_{ij} and also the energy due to the magnetic field B on each of the atoms. We can write down the overall energy of the system as follows:

$$E = -C \sum_{\langle i,j \rangle} \sigma_i \sigma_j - \mu B \sum_i \sigma_i \qquad (7\text{-}23)$$

In Equation 7-23, C is called the *exchange energy*, and μ is called the *magnetic moment*. Since each of the atoms can exist in two states, the total number of configurations for the n atoms is 2^n. The first term in Equation 7-23 suggests that the interaction energy would be minimized when the spin states of the atoms agree with each other. The overall minimization of the energy would depend on the direction of the magnetic field B. When B is negative, the energy would be minimized when all the atoms are in the spin-down state, i.e., $\sigma_i = -1$, whereas when B is positive, then the energy would be minimized when $\sigma_i = 1$ for all the atoms. Although developed with regard to ferromagnetism, the Isling model as discussed earlier works like a mathematical framework to a broader range of physical phenomenon and abstract problems, and hence we would be using the generalized formula in Equation 7-22 to model the energy of a system using the Isling model.

Since the energy function in Equation 7-22 gives the energy of an abstract system in each of its configurations, it can be treated as the Hamiltonian of the system.

Isling Model for a Quantum System

We can extend the Isling model to a system of n qubits where the spin-down and spin-up can be represented by the qubit states $|0\rangle$ and $|1\rangle$ corresponding to the energy labels -1 and $+1$. This energy levels -1 and $+1$ of a qubit can act as the eigenvalues of a Hamiltonian corresponding to the eigenstates $|0\rangle$ and $|1\rangle$. Such a Hamiltonian can be written in the spectral form as follows:

$$H_q = -1|0\rangle\langle 0| + 1|1\rangle\langle 1|$$

$$= -(|0\rangle\langle 0| - |1\rangle\langle 1|) = -\begin{bmatrix} 1 & 0 \\ 0 & -1 \end{bmatrix} = -Z \qquad (7\text{-}24)$$

We can see from Equation 7-24 that the energy associated with the individual states of the qubit can be expressed in terms of the Pauli Z matrix. This is an important relationship since it ties directly to the energy of the individual states of the qubits. Hence, the energy E_2 of the Hamiltonian for the system of n qubits can be expressed as follows:

$$E_2 = -\sum_i b_i Z_i \qquad (7\text{-}25)$$

In Equation 7-25, Z_i is the Pauli Z matrix pertaining to the qubit $i \in \{1, 2, .. n\}$, and b_i is a coefficient pertaining to each qubit. To get a rigorous matrix notation for each Pauli matrix Z_i, we should set the Hamiltonian corresponding to the other $n-1$ qubits as identity $I_{2\times 2}$. For instance, for a three-qubit system, Z_2 should be written as $I_1 \otimes Z_2 \otimes I_3$. However, in Equation 7-25, we chose to write $I_1 \otimes Z_2 \otimes I_3$ as Z_2 to avoid cluttering the notations and will follow the same notation going forward.

Now let's see how we can represent the interaction between neighboring qubits using the appropriate Hamiltonian. As per the Isling model, two neighboring qubits q_i and q_j should have lower energy when their states agree with each other than when they differ in their states. If the interaction energy coefficient between two qubits is given by c_{ij}, then the interaction energy should be as shown in Table 7-1 for different configurations of the two qubits.

Table 7-1. *State to Energy Map for Two-Way Qubit Interaction*

Combined Energy State for q_i and q_j	Energy
$\lvert 00 \rangle$	$-c_{ij}$
$\lvert 01 \rangle$	c_{ij}
$\lvert 10 \rangle$	c_{ij}
$\lvert 11 \rangle$	$-c_{ij}$

Treating the energy levels as the eigenvalues and the energy states as the corresponding eigenvectors, we can write the Hamiltonian for the interaction as follows:

$$H_{qq} = -c_{ij}\lvert 00 \rangle\langle 00 \rvert + c_{ij}\lvert 01 \rangle\langle 01 \rvert + c_{ij}\lvert 10 \rangle\langle 10 \rvert + c_{ij}\lvert 11 \rangle\langle 11 \rvert$$

$$= \begin{bmatrix} -c_{ij} & 0 & 0 & 0 \\ 0 & c_{ij} & 0 & 0 \\ 0 & 0 & c_{ij} & 0 \\ 0 & 0 & 0 & -c_{ij} \end{bmatrix} = -c_{ij}\begin{bmatrix} 1 & 0 & 0 & 0 \\ 0 & -1 & 0 & 0 \\ 0 & 0 & -1 & 0 \\ 0 & 0 & 0 & 1 \end{bmatrix} \tag{7-26}$$

We can see from Equation 7-26 that the Hamiltonian is a diagonal matrix, and the diagonal in order represents the interaction energy of the states $\lvert 00 \rangle$, $\lvert 10 \rangle$, $\lvert 10 \rangle$, and $\lvert 11 \rangle$. We can express the diagonal matrix in terms of the tensor product of the Pauli Z matrices as expressed here:

$$H_{qq} = -c_{ij}\begin{bmatrix} 1 & 0 & 0 & 0 \\ 0 & -1 & 0 & 0 \\ 0 & 0 & -1 & 0 \\ 0 & 0 & 0 & 1 \end{bmatrix}$$

$$= -c_{ij}\begin{bmatrix} 1 & 0 \\ 0 & -1 \end{bmatrix} \otimes \begin{bmatrix} 1 & 0 \\ 0 & -1 \end{bmatrix}$$

$$= -c_{ij}Z_i \otimes Z_j \tag{7-27}$$

So, the interaction Hamiltonian considering all neighbors can be expressed as follows:

$$E_1 = -\sum_{\langle i,j \rangle} c_{ij} Z_i \otimes Z_j \tag{7-28}$$

Combining Equation 7-25 and Equation 7-28, we can write the overall Isling Hamiltonian for the system of n qubits as follows:

$$E = E_1 + E_2 = -\sum_{\langle i,j \rangle} c_{ij} Z_i \otimes Z_j - \sum_i b_i Z_i \tag{7-29}$$

So, we can see from Equation 7-29 that we can express the Isling Hamiltonian for a system of n qubits entirely in terms of the Pauli matrix Z. This is advantageous in algorithms such as VQE and QAOA since we can compute the expectation of the Hamiltonian by solely making measurements with respect to the usual $|0\rangle$ and $|1\rangle$ basis. Also, the Isling model can be generalized to any given set of input qubits or elements, and they need not necessarily have to lie on a grid or lattice. Whether two qubits or elements are neighbors or not can solely be controlled by the interaction coefficient c_{ij} based on the physical system or the problem formulation. For instance, if the elements of the Isling system are nodes in a graph, the edge weight between the nodes as defined in the adjacency matrix could play the role of the interaction coefficient c_{ij}. For a given node i, its neighbors can be determined by looking at all nodes j for which $c_{ij} \neq 0$.

Implementation of the VQE Algorithm

In this section, we implement the VQE algorithm for an Isling Hamiltonian. Listing 7-1 shows the detailed implementation along with an appropriate explanation for each of the important functions.

Listing 7-1. VQE Implementation for Isling Hamiltonian

```
import cirq
import numpy as np
from scipy.optimize import minimize
```

Next we define a setup_vqe function that takes in the bases for the Hamiltonian whose expectation we plan to minimize. The Hamiltonian bases marked as hamiltonian_bases are the tensor products of the Pauli matrices. For instance, for representing a two-qubit Hamiltonian that is the tensor product of the Pauli matrices Z we setup the hamiltonian_bases as ZZ. The setup_vqe also takes in the scale factor for each Hamiltonian through hamiltonian_scales in setup_vqe. Based on the definition of the Hamiltonians fed into setup_vqe, it computes the eigenvalue of the individual base Hamiltonians to be used later for expectation computation.

```python
def setup_vqe(hamiltonian_bases=['ZZZ'],
        hamiltonian_scales=[-1.0]):

    num_qubits = len(hamiltonian_bases[0])
    eigen_values_dict = {}

    for base,scale in zip(hamiltonian_bases,hamiltonian_scales):
        eigen_values = []
        for i, char in enumerate(base):
            if char == 'Z':
                eigens = np.array([1, -1])
            elif char == 'I':
                eigens = np.array([1, 1])
            else:
                raise NotImplementedError(f"The Gate {char}
                  is yet to be implemented")

            if len(eigen_values) == 0:
                eigen_values = eigens
            else:
                eigen_values = np.outer(eigen_values
                            ,eigens).flatten()

        eigen_values_dict_elem = {}

        for i, x in enumerate(list(eigen_values)):
            eigen_values_dict_elem[i] = scale * x

        eigen_values_dict[base] = eigen_values_dict_elem

    return eigen_values_dict, num_qubits
```

We define an ansatz called `ansatz_parameterized` that takes in the parameter `theta` and performs the rotation of the qubits around the *y*-axis based on the parameter in `theta`.

```
def ansatz_parameterized(theta,num_qubits=3):
    """

    Create an Ansatz
    :param theta:
    :param num_qubits:
    :return:
    """

    qubits = [cirq.LineQubit(c) for c in range(num_qubits)]
    circuit = cirq.Circuit()
    for i in range(num_qubits):
        circuit.append(cirq.Ry(theta[i]*np.pi)(qubits[i]))
    circuit.append(cirq.measure(*qubits, key='m'))
    return circuit, qubits
```

The is the expectation computation routine `compute_expectation` based on the measurements of the qubits in the relevant basis pertaining to the Pauli Hamiltonian basis associated with each qubit. The measurement gives the probability of each eigenstate of the Hamiltonian, and this is used to compute the expectation of the eigenvalues of the Hamiltonian.

```
def compute_expectation(circuit, eigen_value_dict={}, copies=10000) -> float:
    sim = cirq.Simulator()
    results = sim.run(circuit, repetitions=copies)
    output = dict(results.histogram(key='m'))
    print('Stats', output)
    _expectation_ = 0
    for base in list(eigen_value_dict.keys()):
        for i in list(output.keys()):
            _expectation_ += eigen_value_dict[base][i]*
            output[i]

    _expectation_ = _expectation_ / copies

    return _expectation_
```

We put together the functions defined thus far in VQE_routine to perform the expected minimization of the given Hamiltonian. VQE_routine uses a classical optimizer to optimize the theta parameters of the ansatz so that the qubits converge to the lowest eigenvalue state of the Hamiltonian. We use the COBYLA method in the scipy.optimize package to perform the optimization. Essentially, the optimizer takes in the expected value of the Hamiltonian computed through measurement pertaining to a given state defined by theta and returns an optimized theta. This iterative process is performed until the theta produces the lowest eigenvalue state of the Hamiltonian.

```python
def VQE_routine(hamiltonian_bases=['ZZZ']
                ,hamiltonian_scales=[1.],
                 copies=1000, vqe_iterations=100,
                 initial_theta=[0.5, 0.5, 0.5], verbose=True):
    eigen_value_dict,num_qubits=
        setup_vqe(hamiltonian_bases=hamiltonian_bases
                  ,hamiltonian_scales=hamiltonian_scales)
    print(eigen_value_dict)
    initial_theta = np.array(initial_theta)

    def objective(theta):
        circuit, qubits = ansatz_parameterized(theta, num_qubits)
        expectation = compute_expectation(circuit
                    ,eigen_value_dict, copies)
        if verbose:
            print(f" Theta: {theta} Expectation:
            {expectation}")

        return expectation

    result = minimize(objective, x0=initial_theta
                    , method='COBYLA')
    print(result)
    return result.x,result.fun
```

Test Hamiltonian: $-Z \otimes Z$

First we will try to optimize the two-qubit system Hamiltonian given by $-Z \otimes Z$. It has two ground states, $|00\rangle$ and $|11\rangle$, pertaining to the eigenvalue of -1. So, it should converge to either of the two eigenstates.

```
if __name__ == '__main__':
    optim_theta, optim_func,hist_stats
            = VQE_routine(hamiltonian_bases=['ZZ'],
                hamiltonian_scales=[-1.0],
                initial_theta=[0.75,0.75])
    print(f"VQE Results: Minimum Hamiltonian
            Energy:{optim_func} at theta: {optim_theta}")
    print(f"Histogram for optimized State:", hist_stats)
```

output

```
VQE Results: Minimum Hamiltonian Energy:-1.0 at theta: [2.01361981 1.99155862]

Histogram for optimized State: {0: 999, 2: 1}
```

We can see from the output that the desired eigenvalue of -1 that denotes the lowest energy of the Hamiltonian $-Z \otimes Z$ has been achieved at one of the desired eigenstates $|00\rangle$ with almost probability 1.

Test Hamiltonian: $-Z \otimes Z - Z \otimes I$

We will try VQE now with the Hamiltonian $-Z \otimes Z - Z \otimes I$. The lowest eigenvalue of the Hamiltonian is -2 pertaining to the eigenstate $|00\rangle$.

```
if __name__ == '__main__':
    optim_theta, optim_func,hist_stats
            = VQE_routine(hamiltonian_bases=['ZZ','ZI'],
                hamiltonian_scales=[-1.0,-1.0],
                    initial_theta=[0.5, 0.5])
    print(f"VQE Results: Minimum Hamiltonian
        Energy:{optim_func} at theta: {optim_theta}")
    print(f"Histogram for optimized State:", hist_stats)
```

output

```
VQE Results: Minimum Hamiltonian Energy:-1.998 at theta: [1.99400595 0.03030307]
Histogram for optimized State: {0: 1000}
```

From the output, you can see that the optimization converged to the desired lowest eigenvalue of -2 corresponding to the state $|00\rangle$ with probability 1.

Quantum Max-Cut Graph Clustering

The max-cut method is a graph partitioning technique that partitions a graph $G = (V, E)$ into two partitions S_1 and S_2 such that the number of edges between the two partitions is maximized. For a weighted graph, the max-cut tries to maximize the sum of the weights of the edges between the two partitions instead of the number of edges. Figure 7-3 is a diagram of a max-cut partition on a graph where the vertices A and B belong to the same partition S_1 while C, D, and E belong to the partition S_2.

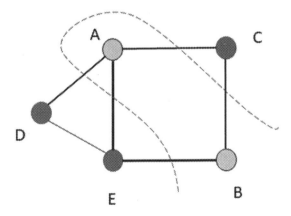

Figure 7-3. *Max-cut*

We can see that the max-cut maximizes the number of edges between the two partitions. Max-cut is often used for clustering the graph into two clusters where the edges represent some form of dissimilarity between two vertices connecting them. By maximizing the number of edges or the sum of the edge weights between the two sets of vertices, we are maximizing the dissimilarity between the two clusters. Alternately, we are minimizing the similarity between the two set of vertices in the two clusters. In this regard, if we consider the edge weights to represent similarity instead of distances, we need to minimize the sum of the edge weights between the vertices of the two clusters. Such a formulation is known as *min-cut clustering*. Based on whether we are using the edges to represent distance or similarity, we can use max-cut or min-cut accordingly to cluster the vertices.

We consider a graph G with n vertices $v_1, v_2, ..., v_n$ whose cluster assignment is given by $z_1, z_2,..., z_n$. So, each of z_i can belong to two clusters, which we label as 1 and -1.

If the edge weight w_{ij} denotes distance between the two vertices i and j, the objective of the max-cut method can be written as follows:

$$C(z_1, z_2...z_n)=\frac{1}{2}\sum_i\sum_{j>i} w_{ij}z_i\left(1-z_j\right) \tag{7-30}$$

As part of the max-cut optimization, we are interested in finding the optimal cluster assignment $z^* =\left[z_1^*, z_2^*...z_n^*\right]^T$.

$$z^* =\underset{z}{\underbrace{argmax}}\frac{1}{2}\sum_i\sum_{j>i}w_{ij}z_i\left(1-z_j\right) \tag{7-31}$$

Let's take the objective $C_{ij} =\frac{1}{2}w_{ij}z_i\left(1-z_j\right)$ corresponding to the interaction between any two vertices i and j and validate that this is in accordance with the goal of max-cut.

Case 1: $w_{ij} = 1$ and $z_i = z_j$.

In this case, the assignment of vertex i and vertex j should be in different clusters since they have the maximum distance. However, since $z_i = z_j$ we have suboptimal value of 0 for the objective. The objective would have had optimal value of $w_{ij} = 1$ had z_i and z_j belonged to different clusters.

Case 2: $w_{ij} = 1$ and $z_i \neq z_j$, say $z_i = 1$ and $z_j = -1$

In this case, the assignment of vertex i and j into different clusters gives us the optimal objective score of $\frac{1}{2}w_{ij}1\left(1-(-1)\right)=w_{ij} =1$.

Case 3: $w_{ij} = 0$

In this case, the objective $C_{ij} = 0$ irrespective of whether vertices i and j belong to the same cluster or not.

Now let's extend the classical objective function to one represented by the Hamiltonian of a quantum system. We can represent each vertex of the graph G by a qubit where the state of the qubit determines the cluster it is assigned to. The objective for every pair of qubits corresponding to vertices i and j can be represented by a cost Hamiltonian given by the tensor product of the Pauli Z matrices as shown here:

$$H_{ij} = w_{ij}\left(I - Z_i \otimes Z_j\right) = w_{ij}I - w_{ij}\begin{bmatrix} 1 & 0 \\ 0 & -1 \end{bmatrix} \otimes \begin{bmatrix} 1 & 0 \\ 0 & -1 \end{bmatrix}$$

$$= w_{ij}\begin{bmatrix} 0 & 0 & 0 & 0 \\ 0 & 1 & 0 & 0 \\ 0 & 0 & 1 & 0 \\ 0 & 0 & 0 & 0 \end{bmatrix} \tag{7-32}$$

The eigenvalues of H_{ij}, which stands for the Hamiltonian cost at different eigenstates, are maximum at w_{ij} when states of the qubits disagree, i.e., for eigenstates $|01\rangle$ and $|10\rangle$. Similarly, when the states of the qubits agree, the Hamiltonian cost is 0. This is in accordance with what we have seen in the classical formulation of max-cut. On those lines, we can write the overall Hamiltonian for the max-cut problem as follows:

$$H = \sum_{\langle i,j \rangle} w_{ij}\left(I - Z_i \otimes Z_j\right) \tag{7-33}$$

In the max-cut problem, we would like to find the combined state of the qubits $|\phi\rangle = |z_1 z_2 \ldots z_n\rangle$ that maximizes the expectation of the Hamiltonian H.

The expectation of H is given by the following:

$$\langle H \rangle = \langle \phi | H | \phi \rangle$$

$$= \sum_{\langle i,j \rangle} w_{ij} \langle \phi | I - Z_i \otimes Z_j | \phi \rangle$$

$$= \sum_{\langle i,j \rangle} w_{ij} \langle \phi | \phi \rangle - \sum_{\langle i,j \rangle} w_{ij} \langle \phi | Z_i \otimes Z_j | \phi \rangle$$

$$= \sum_{\langle i,j \rangle} w_{ij} - \langle \sum_{\langle i,j \rangle} w_{ij} Z_i \otimes Z_j \rangle \phi \tag{7-34}$$

Now for a given graph G, the first term in Equation 7-34 is constant, and hence we can discard it and only maximize the second term $-\langle \sum_{\langle i,j \rangle} w_{ij} Z_i \otimes Z_j \rangle \phi$. Again, instead of maximizing the expectation value of $-\langle \sum_{i,j} w_{ij} Z_i \otimes Z_j \rangle \phi$, we can choose to minimize the negative of it, i.e. $\langle \sum_{\langle i,j \rangle} w_{ij} Z_i \otimes Z_j \rangle \phi$, since the classical optimizers are more aligned to minimizing an objective than maximizing it. That makes the final Hamiltonian H_c whose expectation is to be minimized to get the max-cut solution as follows:

$$H_c = \sum_{\langle i, j \rangle} w_{ij} Z_i \otimes Z_j \qquad (7\text{-}35)$$

Now that we have figured out the Hamiltonian H_c whose expectation is to be minimized, we can do so by feeding in the Hamiltonian H_c into the already implemented VQE routine.

Max-Cut Clustering Implementation Using VQE

In this section, we will implement the max-cut algorithm for a graph with four vertices using the VQE routine we implemented earlier in this chapter. The emphasis in this routine is on defining the Hamiltonian appropriately in terms of the tensor product of the Pauli Z matrices as the basis for the Hamiltonian H_c. The weights of each of the basis is based on the provided graph adjacency matrix.

The graph adjacency matrix gives a measure of similarity. We convert the graph adjacency similarity matrix into a distance matrix to align it to the max-cut problem. For two vertices with a nonzero distance of w_{ij}, we define the Hamiltonian corresponding to the interaction of vertices i and j as $w_{ij} Z_i \otimes Z_j$. The $Z_i \otimes Z_j$ is a Hamiltonian basis, and w_{ij} is the corresponding Hamiltonian coefficient to the vqe_simulation routine. We create such a Hamiltonian basis for every pair of vertices having a nonzero distance.

Listing 7-2 shows the detailed implementation of the max-cut clustering problem.

Listing 7-2. Max-Cut Clustering

```
import cirq
from vqe_cirq import *
import numpy as np
import networkx as nx
import matplotlib.pyplot as plt

class QuantumMaxCutClustering:

    def __init__(self, adjacency_matrix:np.ndarray,
                    invert_adjacency=True):
        self.adjacency_matrix = adjacency_matrix
        self.num_vertices = self.adjacency_matrix.shape[0]
        self.hamiltonian_basis_template = 'I' * self.num_vertices
```

```
    if invert_adjacency:
        self.hamiltonian = 1 - self.adjacency_matrix
    else:
        self.hamiltonian = self.adjacency_matrix
```

In create_max_cut_hamiltonian, for every pair of vertices with a nonzero distance of w_{ij}, we create the Hamiltonian base $Z_i \otimes Z_j$ with the Hamiltonian coefficient w_{ij}. The Hamiltonian bases and their corresponding wieghts coeffecients, called hamiltonian_bases and hamiltonian_coefficients are fed to the vqe_routine from our earlier implementation in the chapter for optimization.

```
def create_max_cut_hamiltonian(self):

    hamiltonian_bases, hamiltonian_coefficients = [], []
    for i in range(self.num_vertices):
        for j in range(i + 1, self.num_vertices):
            if self.hamiltonian[i, j] > 0:
                hamiltonian_coefficients.append(
                  self.hamiltonian[i, j])

                hamiltonian_base = ''
                for k, c in enumerate
                 (self.hamiltonian_basis_template):
                    if k in [i, j]:
                        hamiltonian_base += 'Z'
                    else:
                        hamiltonian_base += self.hamiltonian_basis_
                        template[k]
                hamiltonian_bases.append(hamiltonian_base)
    return hamiltonian_bases, hamiltonian_coefficients

def vqe_simulation(self, hamiltonian_bases,
                hamiltonian_coefficients,
                initial_theta=None,
                copies=10000):
    if initial_theta is None:
        initial_theta = [0.5] * self.num_vertices
```

```
optim_theta, optim_func, hist_stats = \
    VQE_routine(hamiltonian_bases=hamiltonian_bases,
                hamiltonian_scales=
            hamiltonian_coefficients,
                initial_theta=initial_theta,
                copies=copies)
solution_stat = max(hist_stats, key=hist_stats.get)
solution_stat = bin(solution_stat).replace("0b", "")
solution_stat = (self.num_vertices - len(solution_stat)) * "0" +
solution_stat

return optim_theta, optim_func, hist_stats, solution_stat
```

The optimized state derived from the vqe_routine execution in vqe_simulation gives the cluster labels for the vertices. Vertices with the qubit state $|0\rangle$ belong to one cluster, while those with the qubit state $|1\rangle$ belong to the other cluster. We annotate the distance-based graph by coloring the vertices based on their cluster labels.

```
def max_cut_cluster(self, distance_matrix, solution_state):
    print(distance_matrix)
    G = nx.Graph()
    G.add_nodes_from(np.arange(0, self.num_vertices, 1))
    edge_list = []
    for i in range(self.num_vertices):
        for j in range(i + 1, self.num_vertices):
            if distance_matrix[i, j] > 0:
                edge_list.append((i, j, 1.0))
    G.add_weighted_edges_from(edge_list)
    colors = []
    for s in solution_state:
        if int(s) == 1:
            colors.append('r')
        else:
            colors.append('b')
    pos = nx.spring_layout(G)
    default_axes = plt.axes(frameon=True)
```

```
        nx.draw_networkx(G, node_color=colors, node_size=600, alpha=.8,
        ax=default_axes, pos=pos)
        plt.show()

    def main(self):
        hamiltonian_bases, hamiltonian_coefficients
                = self.create_max_cut_hamiltonian()
        print("Hamiltonian bases:", hamiltonian_bases)
        optim_theta, optim_func, \
        hist_stats, solution_state
            = self.vqe_simulation(hamiltonian_bases,
                        hamiltonian_coefficients)

        print(f"VQE Results:
                Minimum Hamiltonian Energy:{optim_func} at theta: {optim_
                theta}")
        print(f"Histogram for optimized State:", hist_stats)
        print(f"Solution state: {solution_state}")
        self.max_cut_cluster(distance_matrix=self.hamiltonian, solution_
        state=solution_state)

if __name__ == '__main__':
    adjacency_matrix = np.array([[1, 0, 0, 0],
                                 [0, 1, 0, 1],
                                 [0, 0, 1, 0],
                                 [0, 1, 0, 1]])

    mc = QuantumMaxCutClustering(
        adjacency_matrix=adjacency_matrix)
    mc.main()
```

From the adjacency matrix, it is clear that vertex 1 and vertex 4 are neighbors since the only connection we have in the graph is between them. The distance matrix based on the adjacency matrix is as follows:

```
[[0, 1, 1, 1],
 [1, 0, 1, 0],
 [1, 1, 0, 1],
 [1, 1, 1, 0]]
```

-x output -x

Based on the distance matrix, the required Hamiltonian bases are as shown here:

Hamiltonian_bases: ['ZZII', 'ZIZI', 'ZIIZ', 'IZZI', 'IIZZ']

```
VQE Results: Minimum Hamiltonian Energy:-2.9956 at theta: [ 0.99548824
-0.0111251   1.01720462   2.00438109]
Histogram for optimized State: {10: 9989, 8: 7, 14: 4}
Solution state: 1010
```

The solution state, as we can see, assigns vertices 1 and 4 in one cluster and vertices 2 and 4 in another cluster (Figure 7-4).

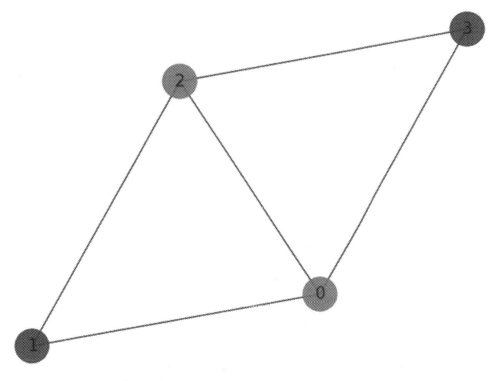

Figure 7-4. *Max-cut cluster assignment*

Quantum Adiabatic Theorem

Let's consider a quantum system whose Hamiltonian is slowly evolved from H_0 to H_f over a period of time T such that the instantaneous Hamiltonian $H(t)$ at any time t can be expressed as the convex combination of the initial Hamiltonian $H(t = 0) = H_0$ and the final Hamiltonian $H(t = T) = H_f$ as shown here:

$$H(t) = \left(1 - \frac{t}{T}\right)H_f + \frac{t}{T}H_0 \tag{7-36}$$

At any time t where $0 \leq t \leq T$, let's say that the instantaneous eigenstates corresponding to the instantaneous Hamiltonian $H(t)$ be represented by $|\phi_n(t)\rangle$.

$$H(t)|\phi_n(t)\rangle = E_n(t)|\phi_n(t)\rangle \tag{7-37}$$

Also, let's consider $E_1(t) < E_2(t) .... < E_n(t) ....$ such that there are no repeated eigenvalues to avoid degeneracies.

If the system at time $t = 0$ is in the state $|\psi(t = 0)\rangle = |\phi_n(0)\rangle$ for some n and the Hamiltonian is slowly changed from H_0 to H_f over a period of time T based on Equation 7-36, then as per the adiabatic theorem at time $t = T$, the state of the system would be $|\psi(t = T)\rangle \cong |\phi_n(T)\rangle$. This essentially means if the system starts off in the nth lowest eigenvalue state $\phi_n(0)\rangle$ corresponding to the starting Hamiltonian H_o, then at time T the system would be in the nth lowest eigenvalue state $\phi_n(T)$ corresponding to the final Hamiltonian H_f if the Hamiltonian is evolved very slowly from H_0 to H_f. See Figure 7-5.

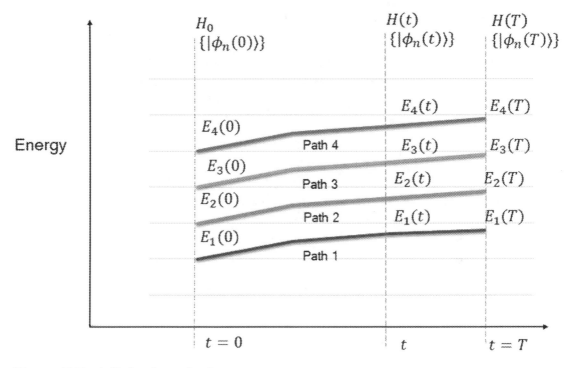

Figure 7-5. *Adiabatic evolution*

This property of quantum systems is advantageous to optimization problems that use the expectation of the Hamiltonian as an optimization objective over a set of possible quantum state configurations. For instance, we may be interested in finding the ground energy E_{1f} and its corresponding eigenstate $|\phi_{1f}\rangle$ of a complicated Hamiltonian H_f. We can solve the problem using adiabatic computing by starting in the ground state $|\phi_{10}\rangle$ with ground energy E_{10} of a known Hamiltonian H_0 and then slowly evolving the quantum system to the desired Hamiltonian H_f over a period of time T.

Proof of the Adiabatic Theorem

The quantum state $|\psi(t)\rangle$ at any time t can be expressed in the eigen basis of the instantaneous Hamiltonian $H(t)$ as follows:

$$|\psi(t)\rangle = \sum_n c_n(t)|\phi_n(t)\rangle \tag{7-38}$$

Note that not only the probability amplitudes $c_n(t)$ but also the basis vectors $|\phi_n(t)\rangle$ are a function of time since the Hamiltonian $H(t)$ changes with time. We can substitute this expression for state $|\psi(t)\rangle$ from Equation 7-38 in the Schrodinger equation. Also, we will drop the reference to the variable t in each of the terms to avoid cluttering up the notation. The time-dependent Schrodinger's equation is given here below:

$$i\hbar|\dot{\psi}(t)\rangle = H(t)|\psi(t)\rangle \tag{7-39}$$

The time derivative of $|\psi(t)\rangle$ can be obtained by differentiating both sides of Equation 7-38 with respect to t as shown here:

$$|\dot{\psi}(t)\rangle = \sum_n \dot{c}_n|\phi_n\rangle + \sum_n c_n|\dot{\phi}_n\rangle \tag{7-40}$$

The term $H(t)|\psi(t)\rangle$ can be expressed in terms of the instantaneous eigen basis as shown here:

$$H(t)|\psi(t)\rangle = \sum_n H c_n|\phi_n\rangle = \sum_n c_n E_n|\phi_n\rangle \tag{7-41}$$

Substituting $|\dot{\psi}(t)\rangle$ and $H(t)|\psi(t)\rangle$ from Equation 7-40 and Equation 7-41, respectively, into the time-dependent Schrodinger's equation in Equation 7-39, we get the following:

$$i\hbar\sum_n \dot{c}_n|\phi_n\rangle + i\hbar\sum_n c_n|\dot{\phi}_n\rangle = \sum_n c_n E_n|\phi_n\rangle \tag{7-42}$$

If we do a dot product with an eigenvector $|\phi_k(t)\rangle$ on either side of Equation 7-42, then we get the following:

$$i\hbar\dot{c}_k + i\hbar\sum_n \langle\phi_k|\dot{\phi}_n\rangle c_n = c_k E_k$$

$$\rightarrow i\hbar\dot{c}_k = c_k E_k - i\hbar\sum_n \langle\phi_k|\dot{\phi}_n\rangle c_n$$

$$\rightarrow i\hbar\dot{c}_k = c_k E_k - i\hbar c_k\langle\phi_k|\dot{\phi}_k\rangle - i\hbar\sum_{n\neq k} \langle\phi_k|\dot{\phi}_k\rangle c_n \tag{7-43}$$

We next differentiate the eigenvalue equation $H(t)|\phi_n(t)\rangle = E_n(t)|\phi_n(t)\rangle$ in Equation 7-37 with respect to t and get the following:

$$\dot{H}|\phi_n\rangle + H|\dot{\phi}_n\rangle = \dot{E}_n|\phi_n\rangle + E_n|\dot{\phi}_n\rangle \tag{7-44}$$

Again, by performing the dot product by $|\phi_k(t)\rangle$ on either side of Equation 7-38 for all n values except $n = k$, we get the following:

$$\langle\phi_k|\dot{H}|\phi_n\rangle + \langle\phi_k|H|\dot{\phi}_n\rangle = \langle\phi_k|\dot{E}_n|\phi_n\rangle + \langle\phi_k|E_n|\dot{\phi}_n\rangle$$

$$\rightarrow \langle\phi_k|\dot{H}|\phi_n\rangle + E_k\langle\phi_k|\dot{\phi}_n\rangle = E_n\langle\phi_k|\dot{\phi}_n\rangle$$

$$\rightarrow \langle\phi_k|\dot{H}|\phi_n\rangle = (E_n - E_k)\langle\phi_k|\dot{\phi}_n\rangle$$

$$\rightarrow \langle\phi_k|\dot{\phi}_n\rangle = \frac{\langle\phi_k|\dot{H}|\phi_n\rangle}{E_n - E_k} \tag{7-45}$$

Substituting the value of $\langle\phi_k|\dot{\phi}_n\rangle$ from Equation 7-45 into Equation 7-43, we get the following:

$$i\hbar\dot{c}_k = c_k E_k - i\hbar c_k\langle\phi_k|\dot{\phi}_k\rangle - i\hbar\sum_{n\neq k}c_n\frac{\langle\phi_k|\dot{H}|\phi_n\rangle}{E_n - E_k} \tag{7-46}$$

Now when the Hamiltonian $H(t)$ is evolved slowly, the derivative of the Hamiltonian $\dot{H}(t)$ will be very small. This will make the value of $\langle\phi_k|\dot{H}|\phi_n\rangle$ close to zero, and hence we can ignore the term proportional to $\langle\phi_k|\dot{H}|\phi_n\rangle$. By throwing away the term proportional to $\langle\phi_k|\dot{H}|\phi_n\rangle$, we get the following:

$$i\hbar\dot{c}_k = c_k E_k - i\hbar c_k\langle\phi_k|\dot{\phi}_k\rangle$$

$$\rightarrow \dot{c}_k = \frac{1}{i\hbar}c_k\left(E_k - i\hbar\langle\phi_k|\dot{\phi}_k\rangle\right)$$

$$\rightarrow \frac{\dot{c}_k}{c_k} = \frac{1}{i\hbar}\left(E_k - i\hbar\langle\phi_k|\dot{\phi}_k\rangle\right)$$

$$\rightarrow \frac{\frac{dc_k(t)}{dt}}{c_k} = \frac{1}{i\hbar}\left(E_k - i\hbar\langle\phi_k|\dot{\phi}_k\rangle\right) \tag{7-47}$$

We can multiply both sides of the equation in Equation 7-47 by dt and integrate to get $c_k(t)$ as shown here. In this regard, the limits of integration will be from $t' = 0$ to $t' = t$.

$$\int_{c_k(0)}^{c_k(t)} \frac{dc_k(t')}{c_k} = \int \frac{1}{i\hbar}\left(E_k - i\hbar\langle\phi_k|\dot\phi_k\rangle\right)dt'$$

$$\rightarrow \log_e c_k(t)/c_k(0) = \int_{t'=0}^{t} \frac{1}{i\hbar}\left(E_k - i\hbar\langle\phi_k|\dot\phi_k\rangle\right)dt'$$

$$\rightarrow c_k(t) = c_k(0) * \exp\left(\int_{t'=0}^{t} \frac{1}{i\hbar}\left(E_k - i\hbar\langle\phi_k|\dot\phi_k\rangle\right)dt'\right)$$

$$\rightarrow c_k(t) = c_k(0)\exp\left(\int_{t'=0}^{t} \frac{1}{i\hbar}E_k\, dt'\right)\exp\left(-\int_{t'=0}^{t}\langle\phi_k|\dot\phi_k\rangle)dt'\right)$$

$$\rightarrow c_k(t) = c_k(0)\exp\left(i\int_{t'=0}^{t} -\frac{1}{\hbar}E_k\, dt'\right)\exp\left(i\int_{t'=0}^{t} i\langle\phi_k|\dot\phi_k\rangle)dt'\right) \tag{7-48}$$

Replacing the integrals $\int_{t'=0}^{t} -\frac{1}{\hbar}E_k\, dt'$ by $\theta_k(t)$ and $\int_{t'=0}^{t} i\langle\phi_k|\dot\phi_k\rangle)dt'$ with $\gamma_k(t)$, we have the following:

$$c_k(t) = c_k(0)e^{i\theta_k(t)}e^{i\gamma_k(t)} \tag{7-49}$$

After some rigorous mathematical deductions, we have finally reached the equation that matters. We see that the probability amplitude of the kth instantaneous eigenstate at time t is essentially the same as the probability amplitude of the kth eigenstate at time $t = 0$ barring a global phase given by $e^{i\theta_k(t)}e^{i\gamma_k(t)}$. Hence, the square of the norm of $c_k(t)$ and $c_k(0)$ are essentially the same, i.e., $|c_k(t)|^2 = |c_k(0)|^2$. If we start the adiabatic evolution with the initial state $|\psi(0)\rangle = |\phi_k(0)\rangle$, then all the probability mass is at the kth eigenstate $|\phi_k(0)\rangle$, and hence $|c_k(0)|^2 = 1$. Since at any time t the probability of the kth eigenstate $|c_k(t)|^2 = |c_k(0)|^2 = 1$, we will continue to be in the kth instantaneous eigenstate throughout the adiabatic evolution.

Quantum Approximate Optimization Algorithm

The quantum approximate optimization algorithm (QAOA) is an optimization technique that leverages adiabatic computing to solve various optimization problems. In QAOA we define our optimization objective in terms of a Hamiltonian H_c whose expectation $\langle H_c \rangle$ we want to optimize. The expectation $\langle H_c \rangle$ is minimized by the eigenstate corresponding to the minimum eigenvalue, as we saw in VQE in the earlier sections. Also, the minimum expectation $\langle H_c \rangle$ equals the minimum eigenvalue of the matric H_c. Alternately, the expectation $\langle H_c \rangle$ is maximized when the state is the eigenstate corresponding to the maximum eigenvalue.

In QAOA we leverage adiabatic computing to determine the required eigenstate for a given Hamiltonian expectation to optimize. For a problem requiring us to minimize the expectation $\langle H_c \rangle$ of the Hamiltonian H_c, we start with the lowest known eigenvalue state $|\phi_0(0)\rangle$ corresponding to an initial Hamiltonian H_0 and then evolve the quantum system, slowly to the desired Hamiltonian H_c over a period of time T. As per the adiabatic theorem at the end of time T, we would be in the lowest eigenvalue state $|\phi_0(T)\rangle$ corresponding to the desired Hamiltonian H_c. Similarly, for a maximization problem, we would start with the maximum eigenvalues state $|\phi_{max}(0)\rangle$ corresponding to the initial Hamiltonian H_0 and then slowly evolve the quantum system to the desired Hamiltonian H_c over a period of time T. The adiabatic theorem will ensure that we reach the maximum eigenvalue state $|\phi_{max}(T)\rangle$ of H_c at time T.

Evolving the Quantum System to the Objective Hamiltonian

As discussed in the earlier section, in QAOA we need to evolve the quantum state of the system from initial Hamiltonian H_0 to the final Hamiltonian we are interested in, i.e., H_c. We can evolve the Hamiltonian slowly over a period of T so that at any time $t \leq T$, the instantaneous Hamiltonian is given by the following:

$$H(t) = \left(1 - \frac{t}{T}\right)H_o + \frac{t}{T}H_c \tag{7-50}$$

Given that the Hamiltonian $H(t)$ changes over time, the unitary evolution for the Hamiltonian $H(t)$ is given by the Schrodinger time-dependent equation as follows:

$$i\hbar\frac{d|\psi(t)\rangle}{dt} = H(t)|\psi(t)\rangle \qquad (7\text{-}51)$$

If we evolve the system under the influence of the Hamiltonian $H(t)$ in Equation 7-50, from time t_1 to t_2 the associated unitary operator $U(t_2, t_1)$ can be found out from the time-dependent Schrodinger's equation in Equation 7-51 as illustrated here:

$$i\hbar\frac{d|\psi(t)\rangle}{dt} = H(t)|\psi(t)\rangle$$

$$\rightarrow \frac{d|\psi(t)\rangle}{|\psi(t)\rangle} = -\frac{i}{\hbar}H(t)dt \qquad (7\text{-}52)$$

Integrating both sides of Equation 7-52 from t_1 to t_2, we get the following:

$$\int_{\psi(t_1)}^{\psi(t_2)}\frac{d|\psi(t)\rangle}{|\psi(t)\rangle} = \int_{t_1}^{t_2}-\frac{i}{\hbar}H(t)dt$$

$$\rightarrow \log_e\frac{|\psi(t_2)\rangle}{|\psi(t_1)\rangle} = \int_{t_1}^{t_2}-\frac{i}{\hbar}H(t)dt$$

$$\rightarrow |\psi(t_2)\rangle = \exp\left(\int_{t_1}^{t_2}-\frac{i}{\hbar}H(t)dt\right)|\psi(t_1)\rangle \qquad (7\text{-}53)$$

From Equation 7-53 we see that the transform $\exp\left(\int_{t_1}^{t_2}-\frac{i}{\hbar}H(t)dt\right)$ takes the state from $|\psi(t_1)\rangle$ to $|\psi(t_2)\rangle$, and hence our required unitary transform $U(t_2, t_1)$ is as follows:

$$U(t_2,t_1) = \exp\left(\int_{t_1}^{t_2}-\frac{i}{\hbar}H(t)dt\right) \qquad (7\text{-}54)$$

We are interested in the unitary transform from $t = 0$ to $t = T$. We can divide the time duration of integral T into p steps of duration $\Delta = \dfrac{T}{p}$ and replace the integral with a sum of the area in the p steps.

$$\int_0^T -\frac{i}{\hbar}H(t)dt = \int_0^\Delta -\frac{i}{\hbar}H(t)dt + \int_\Delta^{2\Delta} -\frac{i}{\hbar}H(t)dt + .. \int_{(p-1)\Delta}^{p\Delta} -\frac{i}{\hbar}H(t)dt \qquad (7\text{-}55)$$

Since the duration Δ of each integral on the right side of Equation 7-55 is small, we can keep the Hamiltonian constant over the duration Δ. Using this simplification, Equation 7-55 can be written as follows:

$$\int_0^T -\frac{i}{\hbar}H(t)dt = \int_0^\Delta -\frac{i}{\hbar}H(t)dt + \int_\Delta^{2\Delta} -\frac{i}{\hbar}H(t)dt + .. \int_{(p-1)\Delta}^{p\Delta} -\frac{i}{\hbar}H(t)dt$$

$$= \int_0^\Delta -\frac{i}{\hbar}H(\Delta)dt + \int_\Delta^{2\Delta} -\frac{i}{\hbar}H(2\Delta)dt + .. \int_{(p-1)\Delta}^{p\Delta} -\frac{i}{\hbar}H(p\Delta)dt$$

$$= -\frac{i\Delta}{\hbar}\big(H(\Delta) + H(2\Delta) + ... + H(p\Delta)\big) \qquad (7\text{-}56)$$

Using Equations 7-56 and 7-54, we can write the unitary transform $U(T,0)$ that will evolve the quantum system from the Hamiltonian H_0 to the desired Hamiltonian H_c as follows:

$$U(T,0) = \exp\left(-\frac{i\Delta}{\hbar}\big(H(\Delta) + H(2\Delta) + ... + H(p\Delta)\big)\right)$$

$$\approx \prod_{k=1}^{p} \exp\left(-\frac{i\Delta II(k\Delta)}{\hbar}\right) \qquad (7\text{-}57)$$

As per Trotter's formula (refer to Chapter 2), when the Δ is small, we can approximate the exponential of the sum of operators to the product of exponentials as we did in Equation 7-57.

The instantaneous Hamiltonian $H(t)$ at any time t is given by Equation 7-50 as $H(t) = \left(1 - \dfrac{t}{T}\right)H_o + \dfrac{t}{T}H_c$. We can discretize the Hamiltonian by looking at its value at Δ time interval such that any generalized time t where we sample the Hamiltonian is represented as $t = k\Delta$. Hence, the generalized representation of the Hamiltonian at the kth timestep is given by the following:

$$H(t) = \left(1 - \frac{t}{T}\right)H_o + \frac{t}{T}H_c$$

$$\rightarrow H(k\Delta) = \left(1 - \frac{k\Delta}{p\Delta}\right)H_0 + \left(\frac{k\Delta}{p\Delta}\right)H_c$$

$$\rightarrow H(k\Delta) = \left(1 - \frac{k\Delta}{p\Delta}\right)H_0 + \left(\frac{k\Delta}{p\Delta}\right)H_c$$

$$\rightarrow H(k\Delta) = \left(1 - \frac{k}{p}\right)H_0 + \frac{k}{p}H_c \qquad (7\text{-}58)$$

Using the expression for $H(k\Delta)$ from Equation 7-58 in Equation 7-57, we get the unitary transform $U(T, 0)$ as follows:

$$U(T, 0) = \prod_{k=0}^{p-1} \exp\left(-\frac{i\Delta H(k\Delta)}{\hbar}\right)$$

$$= \prod_{k=0}^{p-1} \exp\left(-\frac{i\Delta\left(1 - \frac{k}{p}\right)H_0 + i\Delta\frac{k}{p}H_c}{\hbar}\right)$$

$$U(T, 0) \approx \prod_{k=1}^{p} \exp\left(-\frac{i\Delta}{\hbar}\left(1 - \frac{k}{p}\right)H_0\right)\exp\left(-\frac{i\Delta k}{\hbar p}H_c\right) \qquad (7\text{-}59)$$

We can evolve the quantum system in p steps using the unitary transform $U(T, 0)$ as in Equation 7-59 to go from an initial Hamiltonian H_0 to H_c.

Instead of using $\frac{\Delta}{\hbar}\left(1 - \frac{k}{p}\right)$ and $\frac{\Delta k}{\hbar p}$ as in Equation 7-59, we parameterize them as β_k and γ_k and use a classical optimization algorithm to choose the best set of β_k and γ_k that optimizes the expectation of H_c based on the optimization problem. Since we evolve the Hamiltonian in p steps, there are $2p$ number of parameters for the unitary transform $U(T, 0)$ corresponding to the p sets of β_k and γ_k. We can denote all the γ_k parameters, i.e., $\gamma_1, \gamma_2, \ldots, \gamma_p$, by the vector $\vec{\gamma}$ and the β_k parameters, i.e., $\beta_1, \beta_2, \ldots \beta_p$, by the vector $\vec{\beta}$.

Hence, the unitary transform specialized for QAOA can be written in a parameterized form as follows:

$$U\left(\vec{\gamma},\vec{\beta}\right)=\prod_{k=1}^{p}\exp\left(-i\beta_{k}H_{0}\right)\exp\left(-i\gamma_{k}H_{c}\right) \tag{7-60}$$

Starting Hamiltonian for QAOA

For a system of N qubits, the starting Hamiltonian H_o is taken to be the sum of the Pauli matrix X pertaining to each qubit. Hence, we can write H_0 as follows:

$$H_o = \sum_{i=1}^{N} X_i \tag{7-61}$$

The lowest eigenvalue state of the Hamiltonian H_0 is $|+\rangle^{\otimes N}$ where the $|+\rangle$ state is the equal superposition state $\frac{1}{\sqrt{2}}\left(|0\rangle+|1\rangle\right)$. So, for the minimization problem, we take the starting Hamiltonian as $\sum_{i=1}^{N} X_i$ and the starting state as its lowest eigenvalue state $|+\rangle^{\otimes N}$.

Substituting the value of H_0 from Equation 7-54 in $\exp(-i\beta_k H_0)$, we get the following:

$$\exp\left(-i\beta_{k}H_{0}\right)=\exp\left(-i\beta_{k}\sum_{j=1}^{N}X_{j}\right)=\prod_{j=1}^{N}e^{-i\beta_{k}X_{j}} \tag{7-62}$$

We can write Equation 7-55 in a product form since the same Pauli matrix X applies to all qubits and hence they commute. Figure 7-6 is a high-level flow diagram of QAOA.

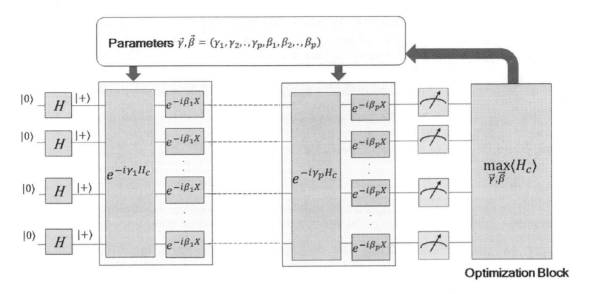

Figure 7-6. *QAOA high-level diagram*

The following are the steps in the quantum approximate optimization algorithm for minimizing the expectation of the Hamiltonian H_c.

Starting Hamiltonian and Initial Eigenstate

As illustrated earlier, we chose the starting Hamiltonian to be $H_o = \sum_{i=1}^{N} X_i$ and the starting state to the lowest eigenvalue state $|+\rangle^{\otimes N}$ corresponding to the Hamiltonian H_c.

Unitary Evolution

The unitary evolution associated with the starting Hamiltonian $\exp(-i\beta_k H_0) = \prod_{j=1}^{N} e^{-i\beta_k X_j}$ is not hard to construct. We can use conditional rotation around the x-axis by an angle $2\beta_k$ for each qubit to construct the transform $\prod_{j=1}^{N} e^{-i\beta_k X_j}$. We also need to construct the unitary transform $e^{-i\gamma_k H_c}$ pertaining to the Hamiltonian H_c whose expectation we are minimizing. If it is an Isling Hamiltonian consisting of only interactions between the qubits, then H_c can be written as follows:

$$H_c = -\sum_{\langle i,j \rangle} Z_i \otimes Z_j \qquad (7\text{-}63)$$

Hence, the unitary transform associated with H_c can be written as follows:

$$\exp\left(-i\gamma_k H_c\right) = \exp\left(i\gamma_k \sum_{\langle i,j \rangle} Z_i \otimes Z_j\right) \qquad (7\text{-}64)$$

Since the $Z_i \otimes Z_j$ Hamiltonian is diagonal for every pair of qubits (i,j), they commute. Hence, the exponential of sums in Equation 7-57 can be rewritten as the product of exponentials as shown here:

$$\exp\left(-i\gamma_k H_c\right) = \exp\left(i\gamma_k \sum_{\langle i,j \rangle} Z_i \otimes Z_j\right) = \prod_{\langle i,j \rangle} \exp\left(i\gamma_k Z_i \otimes Z_j\right) \qquad (7\text{-}65)$$

Once the unitary transforms $\exp(-i\beta_k H_0)$ and $\exp(-i\gamma_k H_c)$ are defined, we evolve the state in p steps by applying the transforms $\exp(-i\gamma_k H_c)$ and $\exp(-i\beta_k H_0)$ alternately.

Measurement and Optimization

Once we have evolved the state of the quantum system in p steps by alternately applying the transforms $\exp(-i\gamma_k H_c)$ and $\exp(-i\beta_k H_0)$, we measure the qubits based on the basis of the Hamiltonian. If the Hamiltonian H_c is defined in terms of Pauli Z matrices as in Equation 7-63, we need to measure the qubits in the standard computational basis. Based on the measurements, the Hamiltonian expectation $\langle H_c \rangle$ is computed. When the parameters $\vec{\gamma}, \vec{\beta}$ are properly optimized, the minimum Hamiltonian expectation $\langle H_c \rangle$ should converge toward the minimum eigenvalue of H_c. Generally, a classical optimizer is used to look at the expectation values $\langle H_c \rangle$ based on measurement in each step and to propose the next best set of parameters for $\vec{\gamma}, \vec{\beta}$ much like what we do in VQE as well. The process is continued until the optimization converges to the optimal values of $\vec{\gamma}^*, \vec{\beta}^*$.

Implementation of QAOA

In this section, we implement the quantum approximate optimization algorithm through the class QAOA for Isling Hamiltonians. The class takes as input a matrix called `hamiltonian_interactions`, which defines the two qubits that interact. The sign of the interaction is also defined in the `hamiltonian_interactions` matrix. We start with the lowest eigenvalue state of a known Hamiltonian H_0 and then adiabatically evolve the quantum system to the desired Hamiltonian H_c over time T. Because of the adiabatic evolution at the end of time T, we would be in the lowest eigenvalue state of H_c. The lowest eigenvalue state of the Hamiltonian is what we are interested in since it minimizes the expectation of the Hamiltonian H_c, which is our cost objective.

```python
import cirq
import numpy as np

class QAOA:

    def __init__(self, num_elems:int,
                    hamiltonian_type:str,
                    hamiltonian_interactions:np.ndarray):
        self.num_elems = num_elems
        self.hamiltonian_type = hamiltonian_type
        self.hamiltonian_interactions = hamiltonian_interactions
        if self.hamiltonian_type not in ['isling']:
            raise ValueError(f"No support for the
                                Hamiltonian type {self.hamiltonian_type}")
        self.qubits = [cirq.LineQubit(x)
            for x in range(num_elems)]
```

The function interaction_gate defines the unitary evolution of the $Z \otimes Z$ Hamiltonian given by $\exp(i\gamma_k Z_i \otimes Z_j)$. This is implemented by using the conditional CZ gate.

```python
@staticmethod
def interaction_gate(q1, q2, gamma=1):
    circuit = cirq.Circuit()
    circuit.append(cirq.CZ(q1, q2)**gamma)
    circuit.append([cirq.X(q2),
            cirq.CZ(q1, q2)**(-gamma), cirq.X(q2)])
    circuit.append([cirq.X(q1),
            cirq.CZ(q1, q2) **(-gamma), cirq.X(q1)])
    circuit.append([cirq.X(q1), cirq.X(q2),
            cirq.CZ(q1, q2) ** gamma, cirq.X(q1), cirq.X(q2)])
    return circuit
```

The `target_hamiltonian_evolution_circuit` function builds the circuit for the unitary evolution of the target Hamiltonian H_c by applying the `interaction_gate` to all pairs of interacting qubits.

```
# Build the Target Hamiltonian based circuit Evolution
    def target_hamiltonian_evolution_circuit(self,gamma):
        circuit = cirq.Circuit()
        # Apply the interaction gates to all the qubit pairs

        for i in range(self.num_elems):

            for j in range(i+1, self.num_elems):
                if self.hamiltonian_interactions[i,j] != 0:
                    circuit.append(self.interaction_gate(
                        self.qubits[i], self.qubits[j],
                            gamma=gamma))
        return circuit
```

The function `starting_hamiltonian_evolution_circuit` implements the starting Hamiltonian unitary evolution given by $\prod_{j=1}^{N} e^{-i\beta_k X_j}$.

```
# Build the Starting Hamiltonian based evolution circuit
    def starting_hamiltonian_evolution_circuit(self, beta):
        for i in range(self.num_elems):
            yield cirq.X(self.qubits[i])**beta
```

The `build_qoaa_circuit` function uses the `starting_hamiltonian_evolution_circuit` and `target_hamiltonian_evolution_circuit` functions to build the overall unitary evolution circuit for the qubits from the starting Hamiltonian H_0 to the target Hamiltonian H_c. The parameters for the function are the `gamma_store` and `beta_store` parameters pertaining to the p iterations of unitary evolution. Also, before the start of the unitary evolution, the qubits initialized to the $|0\rangle$ state are transformed to the $|+\rangle$ state since the state $|+\rangle^{\otimes N}$ is the lowest eigenvalue state of the starting Hamiltonian $H_o = \sum_{i=1}^{N} X_i$ in which we need to start the unitary evolution.

```
    def build_qoaa_circuit(self, gamma_store, beta_store):
        self.circuit = cirq.Circuit()
        # Hadamard gate on each qubit to get an
          equal superposition state
```

```
        self.circuit.append(cirq.H.on_each(*self.qubits))

    for i in range(len(gamma_store)):
        self.circuit.append(
            self.target_hamiltonian_evolution_circuit(
                                    gamma_store[i]))
        self.circuit.append(
            self.starting_hamiltonian_evolution_circuit(
                                    beta_store[i]))
```

The simulate function defined here runs the quantum circuit that we defined:

```
def simulate(self):
    #print(self.circuit)
    sim = cirq.Simulator()
    waveform = sim.simulate(self.circuit)
    return waveform
```

The expectation circuit computes the expectation of the target Hamiltonian H_c with respect to the relevant eigen basis.

```
def expectation(self,waveform):

    expectation = 0
    prob_from_waveform = (np.absolute
            (waveform.final_state))**2
    #print(prob_from_waveform)
    for i in range(len(prob_from_waveform)):
        base = bin(i).replace("0b", "")
        base = (self.num_elems - len(base))*'0' + base
        base_array = []
        for b in base:
            if int(b) == 0:
                base_array.append(-1)
            else:
                base_array.append(1)

        base_array = np.array(base_array)
        base_interactions = np.outer(base_array, base_array)
```

```
        expectation =+
      prob_from_waveform[i]*np.sum(np.multiply(
               base_interactions,
               self.hamiltonian_interactions))
    return expectation
```

If has been theoretically and experimentally verified that choosing $p = 1$ gives a good enough approximation of the required Hamiltonian evolution. Since for $p = 1$, we have to optimize for only two parameters instead of using an optimizer, we perform grid search on the parameter values for beta and gamma to choose the optimal values for them.

```
  def optimize_params(self, gammas, betas, verbose=True):
      expectation_dict = {}
      waveforms_dict  = {}
      for i, gamma in enumerate(gammas):
          for j, beta in enumerate(betas):
              self.build_qoaa_circuit([gamma],[beta])
              waveform = self.simulate()
              expectation = self.expectation(waveform)
              expectation_dict[(gamma,beta)] = expectation
              waveforms_dict[(gamma,beta)]
                   = waveform.final_state
              if verbose:
                  print(f"Expectation
                          for gamma:{gamma},
                          beta:{beta} = {expectation}")
      return expectation_dict, waveforms_dict
```

The main function puts it all together and performs the unitary evolution and subsequent expectation computation for all pairs of gammas and betas defined through the grid search function optimize_params. Finally, we choose the parameters called beta and gamma, which minimize the expectation of the Hamiltonian H_c the most.

```
  def main(self):
      gammas = np.linspace(0, 1,50)
      betas = np.linspace(0, np.pi,50)
      expectation_dict,waveform_dict = self.optimize_params(
                                          gammas, betas)
```

```python
        expectation_vals = np.array(
                    list(expectation_dict.values()))
        expectation_params = list(expectation_dict.keys())
        waveform_vals = np.array(list(waveform_dict.values()))
        optim_param = expectation_params[
                                np.argmin(expectation_vals)]
        optim_expectation = expectation_vals[
                                    np.argmin(expectation_vals)]
        optim_waveform = waveform_vals[
                                np.argmin(expectation_vals)]
        optim_waveform_probs = [np.abs(x)**2 for x
                            in optim_waveform]
        optim_eigen_state = np.argmax(optim_waveform_probs)
        optim_eigen_state =
                bin(optim_eigen_state). replace("0b", "")
        optim_eigen_state = "0"*(self.num_elems
                - len(optim_eigen_state) + optim_eigen_state
        print(f"Optimized parameters\n")
        print(f" gamma,beta = {optim_param[0]}
                            ,{optim_param[1]}")
        print(f"Expectation = {optim_expectation}")

        print(f"Waveform probability = {
                [np.abs(x)**2 for x in optim_waveform]} ")
        Print(f"Lowest Eigen value State : {optim_eigen_state}")
        return expectation_dict

if __name__ == '__main__':
    hamiltonian_interaction = np.array([[0,-1,-1,-1],
                                        [0,0,-1,-1],
                                        [0,0,0,-1],
                                        [0,0,0,0]])
    qaoa_obj = QAOA(num_elems=4,
                    hamiltonian_type='isling',
                    hamiltonian_interactions=hamiltonian_interaction)
    expectation_dict = qaoa_obj.main()
```

As part of the illustration, we will work with a system of four qubits where all qubits interact with each other, and we will get an Isling model Hamiltonian to optimize. We feed this information through `hamiltonian_interaction` where every pair of interactions has been captured once. The lowest Hamiltonian energy occurs in the eigenstates of the Hamiltonian in which all the qubits agree, i.e., the states $|0000\rangle$ and $|1111\rangle$ states. Let's see what QAOA comes up with:

output

```
Optimized parameters
 gamma,beta = 0.12244897959183673, 1.6669675304762166
Expectation = -2.237522542476654
Waveform probability = [0.3729205063992005, 0.009119188393314437,
0.009119186970336424, 0.030200931372814432, 0.009119188393314437,
0.03020092619364334, 0.03020093655198597, 0.009119185547358521,
0.009119188393314437, 0.03020094173115795, 0.030200941/3115795,
0.009119188393314437, 0.030200946910330373, 0.009119189816292561,
0.009119191239270796, 0.3729204336014078]

Lowest Eigen value State : 0000
```

We can see that in the waveform corresponding to the minimum value of the expectation -2.23 the two states $|0000\rangle$ and $|1111\rangle$ have the highest probability of 0.3729, which is in accordance with the expected results. We print one of the two states as the lowest eigenvalue state.

Quantum Random Walk

Quantum random walk is a random walk implementation that leverages the quantum evolution based on a Hamiltonian graph. At the end of the random walk, what we end up with is a probability amplitude vector pertaining to the vertices of the graph. Unlike classical random walk where the walker moves to one of the vertices with some probability, quantum random walks are based on probability amplitudes. Also Quantum random walk do not converge to any limiting distribution like classical random walk does. Superposition and interference causes drastic difference between the quantum and classical random walk. In general quantum random walks spread faster than classical random walk and has faster hitting times. Hitting time h_{AB} is defined as the expected time it takes for the walker starting at vetex A to reach vertex B for the first time.

Coming back to the Hamiltonian graph H_G for a quantum random walk, it is generally an adjacency matrix A. At times it is convenient to add the identity matrix I so that each vertex of the graph has an edge to itself. Such a graph is called a *complete graph*. In such cases, the Hamiltonian graph is given by the following:

$$H_G = A + I \qquad (7\text{-}66)$$

Once we have the Hamiltonian H_G graph, we can use the appropriate number of qubits to define the quantum system. For instance, if we have N vertices in the graph, then we can have a quantum system of $n = log_2(N)$ qubits. The quantum system of n qubits is then evolved as per Schrodinger's equation.

$$i\hbar\frac{d|\psi(t)\rangle}{dt} = H_G|\psi(t)\rangle \qquad (7\text{-}67)$$

The state $|\psi(t)\rangle$ would contain the probability amplitudes of each vertex in the graph. We generally take the normalized Plank's constant value to be 1 and evolve the system using the unitary transform.

$$U(t) = e^{-iH_G t}. \qquad (7\text{-}68)$$

The solution of the Scrodinger's equation for constant Hamiltonian is given by

$$|\psi(t)\rangle = U(t)|\psi(0)\rangle \qquad (7\text{-}69)$$

As discussed earlier, the state $|\psi(t)\rangle$ should contain the probability amplitude of every vertex in the graph at time t.

The unitary transform can be implemented by designing the quantum circuit using the appropriate gates. In this regard, one must note that defining a unitary operator as the exponential of a Hamiltonian can be difficult to implement unless the Hamiltonian is diagonal. It turns out that having a complete graph helps in easy diagonalization using the transform $Q = H^{\otimes n}$ where H is the Hadamard transform. The diagonalization of the Hamiltonian and the unitary operator is given by the following:

$$H_{GD} = Q^\dagger H_G Q$$

$$U_D(t) = Q^\dagger e^{-iH_G t} Q. \qquad (7\text{-}70)$$

The unitary operator contains the time of evolution of the Hamiltonian H_G. This can be treated as a hyperparameter for the graph quantum walk algorithm.

Quantum Random Walk Implementation

In this section, we will implement the quantum random walk implementation using Cirq. We will work with a complete graph of four vertices (Figure 7-7) and create the circuit for the Hamdard diagonalized unitary transform $U_D(t) = Q^{\dagger} e^{-iH_G t} Q$ using a conditional Pauli Z gate.

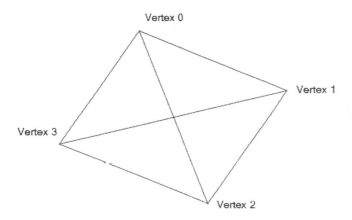

Figure 7-7. *Complete graph with vertices*

This is implemented through the function `diagonal_exponential`. The input to this function is the eigenvalues of the Hamiltonian H_G and the time t of evolution.

We perform a quantum random walk for different time durations of time t up to $t = 4$ seconds.

```
import cirq
import numpy as np
import matplotlib.pyplot as plt
import networkx as nx

class GraphQuantumRandomWalk:

    def __init__(self, graph_hamiltonian, t, verbose=True):
        self.graph_ham = graph_hamiltonian
        self.num_vertices = self.graph_ham.shape[0]
        self.num_qubits = int(np.log2(self.num_vertices))
        self.qubits = [cirq.LineQubit(i)
            for i in range(self.num_qubits)]
```

```
        self.t = t
        self.verbose = verbose

    @staticmethod
    def diagonal_exponential(qubits, eigen_vals, t):
        circuit = cirq.Circuit()
        q1 = qubits[0]
        q2 = qubits[1]
        circuit.append(cirq.CZ(q1, q2) **
                (-eigen_vals[-1] * t / np.pi))
        circuit.append([cirq.X(q2), cirq.CZ(q1, q2) **
                (-eigen_vals[-2] * t / np.pi), cirq.X(q2)])
        circuit.append([cirq.X(q1), cirq.CZ(q1, q2) **
                (-eigen_vals[-3] * t / np.pi), cirq.X(q1)])
        circuit.append(
            [cirq.X(q1), cirq.X(q2), cirq.CZ(q1, q2) **
                (-eigen_vals[-4] * t / np.pi),
                  cirq.X(q1), cirq.X(q2)])
        return circuit
```

The unitary evolution circuit based on the Hamiltonian and time of evolution *t* is constructed in the unitary function shown here:

```
def unitary(self):
    eigen_vals, eigen_vecs = np.linalg.eigh(self.graph_ham)
    idx = eigen_vals.argsort()[::-1]
    eigen_vals = eigen_vals[idx]
    eigen_vecs = eigen_vecs[:, idx]
    if self.verbose:
        print(f"The Eigen values: {eigen_vals}")

    self.circuit = cirq.Circuit()
    self.circuit.append(cirq.H.on_each(self.qubits))
    self.circuit += self.diagonal_exponential(self.qubits,
    eigen_vals, self.t)
    self.circuit.append(cirq.H.on_each(self.qubits))
```

We simulate the random walk circuit using the function `simulate` and use the `final_state` functionality of Cirq to get the final state directly instead of a probability distribution over a different basis through measurement.

```python
def simulate(self):
    sim = cirq.Simulator()
    results = sim.simulate(self.circuit).final_state
    prob_dist = [np.abs(a) ** 2 for a in results]
    return prob_dist

def main(self):
    self.unitary()
    prob_dist = self.simulate()
    if self.verbose:
        print(f"The converged prob_dist: {prob dist}")
    return prob_dist

if __name__ == '__main__':
    graph_hamiltonian = np.ones((4, 4))
    time_to_simulate = 4
    steps = 80
    time_trace = []
    prob_dist_trace = []
    for t in np.linspace(0, time_to_simulate):
        gqrq = GraphQuantumRandomWalk(
                graph_hamiltonian=graph_hamiltonian, t=t)
        prob_dist = gqrq.main()
        time_trace.append(t)
        prob_dist_trace.append(prob_dist)
    prob_dist_trace = np.array(prob_dist_trace)
    plt.plot(time_trace, prob_dist_trace[:, 0])
    plt.show()
    rows, cols = np.where(graph_hamiltonian == 1)
    edges = zip(rows.tolist(), cols.tolist())
    gr = nx.Graph()
    gr.add_edges_from(edges)
```

```
nx.draw(gr,node_size=4)
plt.show()
```

-x- output -x-

The Eigen values: [4.00000000e+00 -1.23259516e-32 -3.42450962e-16 -9.89816667e-16]

The converged prob_dist: [0.2658776231786675, 0.24470737592319214, 0.2447074054083629, 0.2447074054083629]

The converged probability distribution shown previously is based on the Hamiltonian evolution for a time period of t=0.75. In general, the converged probability distribution depends on the time of simulation t, as we can see in Figure 7-8. Based on the time of evolution of the Hamiltonian, the probability of vertex 0 not only differs but oscillates in a periodic pattern. It starts off with probability 1 since we start with all probability mass assigned to state $|00\rangle$, which represents vertex 0, and then the probability reduces to the lowest value of about 0.25, which corresponds to the equal probability state. The oscillations are sinusoidal in nature.

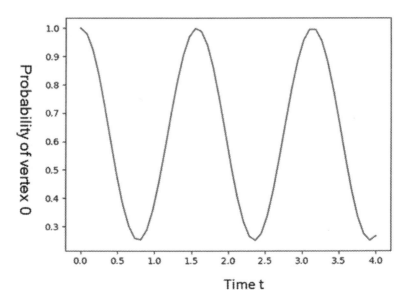

Figure 7-8. *Probability of vertex 0 for different times of the simulation*

The Hamiltonian H_g graph has the eigenvalues of $[4, 0, 0, 0]$, which makes the diagonal unitary operator $U_D(t)$ look like below:

$$\begin{bmatrix} e^{-i4t} & 0 & 0 & 0 \\ 0 & 1 & 0 & 0 \\ 0 & 0 & 1 & 0 \\ 0 & 0 & 0 & 1 \end{bmatrix} \tag{7-71}$$

The complex exponential e^{-i4t} causes the oscillatory behavior that we see in Figure 7-8.

Summary

With this we come to the end of this chapter and the book. The topics discussed in the book are advanced quantum optimization techniques that can change the way optimization is performed in different domains today. The good thing about these quantum optimization techniques is that they do not require a perfect quantum computer to execute. Since these optimization techniques are to some extent approximate approaches, they are perfect for noisy near-term quantum computers. Readers are advised to go through the topics in this chapter in great detail to extract the most from this interesting and exciting paradigm of quantum-based optimization. We wish you all the best for your upcoming endeavors.

Index

Printed in the United States
by Baker & Taylor Publisher Services